Applying Business Intelligence and Innovation to Entrepreneurship

Kannapat Kankaew
International College, Burapha University, Thailand

Parinya Nakpathom
International College, Burapha University, Thailand

Alhuda Chnitphattana
International College, Burapha University, Thailand

Krittipat Pitchayadejanant
International College, Burapha University, Thailand

Siwaporn Kunnapapdeelert
Faculty of Logistics and Transportation Management, Panyapiwat Institute of Management, Thailand

A volume in the Advances in Business Strategy and Competitive Advantage (ABSCA) Book Series

IGI Global
PUBLISHER of TIMELY KNOWLEDGE

Published in the United States of America by
IGI Global
Business Science Reference (an imprint of IGI Global)
701 E. Chocolate Avenue
Hershey PA, USA 17033
Tel: 717-533-8845
Fax: 717-533-8661
E-mail: cust@igi-global.com
Web site: http://www.igi-global.com

Library of Congress Cataloging-in-Publication Data

Names: Kannapat Kankaew, 1973- editor. | Nakpathom, Parinya, 1983- editor. | Chanitphattana, Alhuda, 1987- editor.
Title: Applying business intelligence and innovation to entrepreneurship / edited by Kannapat Kankaew, Parinya Nakpathom, Alhuda Chanitphattana, Krittipat Pitchayadejanant, Siwaporn Kunnapapdeelert.
Description: Hershey, PA : Business Science Reference, [2024] | Includes bibliographical references and index. | Summary: "This edited book aims to address various types of entrepreneurship and its adoption of business intelligence in small and medium enterprises"-- Provided by publisher.
Identifiers: LCCN 2023054120 (print) | LCCN 2023054121 (ebook) | ISBN 9798369318461 (hardcover) | ISBN 9798369318478 (ebook)
Subjects: LCSH: Entrepreneurship. | New business enterprises--Management. | Business intelligence. | Technological innovations--Economic aspects.
Classification: LCC HB615 .A725 2024 (print) | LCC HB615 (ebook) | DDC 658.4/21--dc23/eng/20240119
LC record available at https://lccn.loc.gov/2023054120
LC ebook record available at https://lccn.loc.gov/2023054121

This book is published in the IGI Global book series Advances in Business Strategy and Competitive Advantage (ABSCA) (ISSN: 2327-3429; eISSN: 2327-3437)

British Cataloguing in Publication Data
A Cataloguing in Publication record for this book is available from the British Library.

All work contributed to this book is new, previously-unpublished material.
The views expressed in this book are those of the authors, but not necessarily of the publisher.

For electronic access to this publication, please contact: eresources@igi-global.com.

Advances in Business Strategy and Competitive Advantage (ABSCA) Book Series

ISSN:2327-3429
EISSN:2327-3437

Editor-in-Chief: Patricia Ordóñez de Pablos, Universidad de Oviedo, Spain

MISSION

Business entities are constantly seeking new ways through which to gain advantage over their competitors and strengthen their position within the business environment. With competition at an all-time high due to technological advancements allowing for competition on a global scale, firms continue to seek new ways through which to improve and strengthen their business processes, procedures, and profitability.

The **Advances in Business Strategy and Competitive Advantage (ABSCA) Book Series** is a timely series responding to the high demand for state-of-the-art research on how business strategies are created, implemented and re-designed to meet the demands of globalized competitive markets. With a focus on local and global challenges, business opportunities and the needs of society, the **ABSCA** encourages scientific discourse on doing business and managing information technologies for the creation of sustainable competitive advantage.

COVERAGE

- Core Competencies
- Strategic Management
- Customer-Orientation Strategy
- Value Chain
- Outsourcing
- Tacit Knowledge
- Co-operative Strategies
- Entrepreneurship & Innovation
- Value Creation
- Globalization

IGI Global is currently accepting manuscripts for publication within this series. To submit a proposal for a volume in this series, please contact our Acquisition Editors at Acquisitions@igi-global.com or visit: http://www.igi-global.com/publish/.

The Advances in Business Strategy and Competitive Advantage (ABSCA) Book Series (ISSN 2327-3429) is published by IGI Global, 701 E. Chocolate Avenue, Hershey, PA 17033-1240, USA, www.igi-global.com. This series is composed of titles available for purchase individually; each title is edited to be contextually exclusive from any other title within the series. For pricing and ordering information please visit http://www.igi-global.com/book-series/advances-business-strategy-competitive-advantage/73672. Postmaster: Send all address changes to above address.

Titles in this Series

For a list of additional titles in this series, please visit:
www.igi-global.com/book-series/advances-business-strategy-competitive-advantage/73672

Convergence of Digitalization, Innovation, and Sustainable Development in Business
Alper Erturk (Australian University, Kuwait) Stephen Edward Colbran (Central Queensland University, Australia) Erman Coşkun (Izmir Bakircay University, Turkey) Faidon Theofanidis (Australian University, Kuwait) and Oualid Abidi (Australian University, Kuwait)
Business Science Reference • copyright 2024 • 303pp • H/C (ISBN: 9798369307984) • US $275.00 (our price)

Green Economy and Renewable Energy Transitions for Sustainable Development
Rui Alexandre Castanho (WSB University, Poland)
Engineering Science Reference • copyright 2024 • 314pp • H/C (ISBN: 9798369312971) • US $275.00 (our price)

Trends, Challenges, and Practices in Contemporary Strategic Management
Filiz Mızrak (Beykoz University, Turkey)
Business Science Reference • copyright 2024 • 355pp • H/C (ISBN: 9798369311554) • US $275.00 (our price)

Fostering Global Entrepreneurship Through Business Model Innovation
Varun Gupta (Multidisciplinary Research Centre for Innovations in SMEs, Gisma University of Applied Sciences, Potsdam, Germany & Department of Economics and Business Administration, Universidad de Alcalá, Alcalá de Henares (Madrid), Spain)
Business Science Reference • copyright 2024 • 293pp • H/C (ISBN: 9781668469750) • US $275.00 (our price)

Sustainable Consumption Experience and Business Models in the Modern World
Maria Amélia Machado Carvalho (Business School, Polytechnic Institute of Porto, Portugal) and Maria Antónia Rodrigues (CEOS, Business School, Polytechnic Institute of Porto, Portugal)
Business Science Reference • copyright 2024 • 257pp • H/C (ISBN: 9781668492772) • US $240.00 (our price)

For an entire list of titles in this series, please visit:
www.igi-global.com/book-series/advances-business-strategy-competitive-advantage/73672

IGI Global
PUBLISHER of TIMELY KNOWLEDGE

701 East Chocolate Avenue, Hershey, PA 17033, USA
Tel: 717-533-8845 x100 • Fax: 717-533-8661
E-Mail: cust@igi-global.com • www.igi-global.com

Table of Contents

Preface xv

Chapter 1
The Systematic Literature Review on Business Intelligence Towards Entrepreneurial Orientation of Ventures 1
Jinumoni Nazir, Sikkim University, India
Pradip Kumar Das, Sikkim University, India

Chapter 2
Role of Technology Business Incubator in Enhancing Entrepreneurship Ecosystem 21
Satya Ranjan Acharya, Entrepreneurship Development Institute of India, India
Yamini Chandra, Entrepreneurship Development Institute of India, India

Chapter 3
Blockchain and Entrepreneurship 35
Kande Archana, Malla Reddy College of Engineering, India
Aarti Gloth, Malla Reddy College of Engineering, India

Chapter 4
Introduction to Operation and Supply Chain Management for Entrepreneurship 52
Ali Said Jaboob, Dhofar University, Oman
Ali Mohsin Ba Awain, University of Technology and Applied Science, Oman
Khairul Anuar Mohd Ali, National University of Malaysia, Malaysia
Al Montaser Mohammed, Zarqa University, Jordan

Chapter 5
Neuromarketing as a Digital Marketing Strategy to Unravel the Evolution of Marketing Communication 81
Kavindu Millagala, Australian Management School, Sri Lanka
Nandana Gunasinghe, Rajarata University of Sri Lanka, Sri Lanka

Chapter 6
Fintech Startups and Cryptocurrency in Business: Revolutionizing Entrepreneurship 106
Muhammad Usman Tariq, Abu Dhabi University, UAE & University of Glasgow, Glasgow, UK

Chapter 7
Requirements of Adopting SMEs for Business Intelligence Systems: A Field Study in the Industrial Zone of Setif in Algeria 125
Hichem Mezhoud, Mila University Center, Algeria

Chapter 8
Design Thinking and Creativity in Entrepreneurial Innovation 155
Mustafa Kayyali, HE Higher Education Ranking, Syria

Chapter 9
Business Intelligence and Innovation Moderating Roles on Entrepreneurship and Management Using Champiopreneurship Approach 171
Harry Orugba Ovharhe, University of Port Harcourt, Nigeria

Chapter 10
Impact of Board of Directors Composition, Activity, and Compensation on the ESG Performance in an International Context 224
Tijani Amara, Higher Institute of Business Administration, University of Gafsa, Tunisia
Ali Ahmadi, Higher Institute of Business Administration, University of Gafsa, Tunisia

Chapter 11
Sustainability in Transformational and Transactional Leadership: Turkish Textile Industry Example 241
Korhan Arun, Namık Kemal Üniversitesi, Turkey

Chapter 12
A Study on the Interaction Between Civil Business Groups and the State From the Perspective of Public Sphere Theory: A Comparison Between the Shangha 258
Wei Yao, Nanjing University, China
Yuhong Li, Nanjing University, China
Tingxuan Liu, Nanjing University, China

Chapter 13
Going Back to Basics as an Innovative Way Forward on Muslim Health Tourism: Keep Sharia in the Loop 277
Aniesa Samira Bafadhal, University of Brawijaya, Indonesia

Compilation of References 297

About the Contributors 338

Index 343

Detailed Table of Contents

Preface... xv

Chapter 1
The Systematic Literature Review on Business Intelligence Towards Entrepreneurial Orientation of Ventures...1
Jinumoni Nazir, Sikkim University, India
Pradip Kumar Das, Sikkim University, India

Business intelligence has been a recent information tool which was introduced in the entrepreneurship world. The present study is an extensive systematic literature review based on PRISMA framework which aims to explore the influence of business intelligence (BI) on the entrepreneurial orientation (EO) among the ventures. Four journal databases have been used, namely Emerald, JStor, ScienceDirect, and EBSCOhost to gather the articles for the study. "Business intelligence" and "Entrepreneurial orientation" were the keywords used to identify studies from the journal databases. 23 articles were finalised for the study after going through the identification, screening and included process which comes under the PRISMA (preferred reporting items for systematic reviews and meta-analyses) framework. It has been found that very little research has been done in this field. So, this systematic literature review will give an insight into the possible gaps that can be covered by the upcoming researchers in this field.

Chapter 2
Role of Technology Business Incubator in Enhancing Entrepreneurship Ecosystem 21
Satya Ranjan Acharya, Entrepreneurship Development Institute of India, India
Yamini Chandra, Entrepreneurship Development Institute of India, India

This chapter examines the role of technology business incubators (TBIs) in improving the effectiveness, viability, and overall development of startups. The chapter attempts to establish a connection between the support offered by these TBIs and its effects on the overall operational effectiveness of these startups by referring to various available relevant literature. Further, the chapter investigates the assistance offered by these TBIs as well as the challenges encountered throughout the process from the ideation and commercialization of funded ideas. Through the empirical analysis of Gujarat's entrepreneurial ecosystem, a comprehensive framework is given that can be used to improve the existing support system.

Chapter 3
Blockchain and Entrepreneurship 35
Kande Archana, Malla Reddy College of Engineering, India
Aarti Gloth, Malla Reddy College of Engineering, India

Blockchain technology has emerged as a disruptive force with the potential to reshape entrepreneurship and business ventures across various industries. Its decentralized, immutable ledger system offers a foundation for innovative solutions, fostering transparency, security, and efficiency. Entrepreneurs are harnessing blockchain for a myriad of applications, from supply chain management to tokenized assets and decentralized finance (DeFi). This chapter delves into the symbiotic relationship between blockchain and entrepreneurship, exploring the transformative role of blockchain in startups, raising capital through initial coin offerings (ICOs), and streamlining processes through smart contracts. As this decentralized ledger technology continues to evolve, entrepreneurs face not only opportunities for innovation but also regulatory and scalability challenges. A comprehensive understanding of blockchain's impact on entrepreneurship is crucial for navigating this evolving landscape, fostering new business models, and realizing the full potential of blockchain technology.

Chapter 4
Introduction to Operation and Supply Chain Management for Entrepreneurship52
Ali Said Jaboob, Dhofar University, Oman
Ali Mohsin Ba Awain, University of Technology and Applied Science, Oman
Khairul Anuar Mohd Ali, National University of Malaysia, Malaysia
Al Montaser Mohammed, Zarqa University, Jordan

This chapter explores the main objectives of supply chain management and operations management, highlighting their importance for the success and endurance of entrepreneurial ventures. It delves into how good management of these areas may increase competitiveness, achieve efficiency and cost-effectiveness, and guarantee customer satisfaction. The importance of operations and supply chain management in fostering business growth and sustainability is emphasized. Addedly, the chapter highlights upcoming trends and changing problems, pushing entrepreneurs to adopt best practices and methods to manage their supply chains and operations for long-term success.

Chapter 5
Neuromarketing as a Digital Marketing Strategy to Unravel the Evolution of Marketing Communication 81
Kavindu Millagala, Australian Management School, Sri Lanka
Nandana Gunasinghe, Rajarata University of Sri Lanka, Sri Lanka

This chapter examines the pivotal role of neuromarketing as a digital marketing strategy in deciphering the dynamic evolution of marketing communication. Rooted in neuroscience and psychology, neuromarketing employs advanced neuroscientific tools to unveil subconscious consumer responses. In the context of the digital revolution, this chapter elucidates how neuromarketing seamlessly integrates with evolving marketing communication channels, emphasizing personalization and emotional engagement. The authors explore the significance of personalized content in cultivating consumer trust and loyalty and discuss the emergence of neuroanalytics as a metric for evaluating campaign success in the digital sphere. Ethical considerations surrounding the responsible use of neurodata are addressed, highlighting the need for industry guidelines. This chapter posits neuromarketing as a transformative force, guiding businesses toward a nuanced understanding of consumer behaviour in the ever-changing landscape of digital marketing.

Chapter 6
Fintech Startups and Cryptocurrency in Business: Revolutionizing Entrepreneurship 106
Muhammad Usman Tariq, Abu Dhabi University, UAE & University of Glasgow, Glasgow, UK

This book chapter explains the significant influence of cryptocurrencies and fintech startups on business models and entrepreneurship by examining their revolutionary junction. The chapter thoroughly examines fintech's birth and development, charting its disruptive path inside the conventional financial services industry. It simultaneously explores the history of cryptocurrencies, revealing the blockchain's technical foundations and growing popularity in the corporate community. The story highlights the explosive rise of fintech companies and identifies its driving forces, including changes in consumer preferences, legislative changes, and technology breakthroughs. The chapter's main focus is how companies embrace cryptocurrencies, use them for transactions, hold ICOs to raise money, and add them to investment portfolios. The chapter also discusses technological difficulties and regulatory issues when merging fintech and cryptocurrency solutions.

Chapter 7
Requirements of Adopting SMEs for Business Intelligence Systems: A Field Study in the Industrial Zone of Setif in Algeria...125
Hichem Mezhoud, Mila University Center, Algeria

In this chapter, the authors will discuss the requirements for small and medium-sized enterprises (SMEs) to adopt business intelligence systems and make them more competitive. Currently, communication technologies are evolving rapidly and continuously. Companies are adopting modern methods and tools to ensure their survival and gain a sustainable competitive advantage. This necessitates keeping pace with developments that affect the business sector, including the emergence of business intelligence systems, which are among the latest and most important cost management tools. These systems involve shaping big data, creating mechanisms for collecting it accurately and efficiently, analyzing it, and innovating methods to process its understanding. The resulting information is used to make various decisions within the company. This chapter will address and analyze various technical, human, and organizational requirements for SMEs located in the industrial region of Setif, Algeria, to adopt business intelligence systems.

Chapter 8
Design Thinking and Creativity in Entrepreneurial Innovation.........................155
Mustafa Kayyali, HE Higher Education Ranking, Syria

This study explores the pivotal role of design thinking and creativity in the realm of entrepreneurial innovation. The need for innovative ways to problem-solving and idea production is becoming more and more obvious as the entrepreneurial landscape changes. Iterative and human-centered design thinking provides entrepreneurs with a special framework for navigating the challenges of innovation. This study explores the interplay between design thinking and creativity, illuminating how these ideas merge to promote entrepreneurial success. Through a comprehensive analysis of case studies and empirical evidence, this study demonstrates the multifaceted impact of design thinking and creativity on fostering innovation in entrepreneurial ventures. The findings underscore the significance of cultivating a creative mindset and embracing design thinking principles as catalysts for entrepreneurial innovation in today's dynamic business environment.

Chapter 9
Business Intelligence and Innovation Moderating Roles on Entrepreneurship and Management Using Champiopreneurship Approach 171
Harry Orugba Ovharhe, University of Port Harcourt, Nigeria

The study explored business intelligence and innovation moderating roles on entrepreneurship and management using champiopreneurship approach. The dimensions of business intelligence capture were competitive intelligence (CI) and decision support system (DSS). The innovation was focused on selected simplex innovation (product, process, service, technology, among others) and complex innovation (sustainable, transformational and systematic). The study orchestrates champiopreneurship approach as entrepreneurs with championship characteristics and management acumen on entrepreneurial opportunities. This poses that entrepreneurship is a viable concept for enterprise to achieve their vision, mission, dreams, and entrepreneurial journey. In conclusion, the synchronization of entrepreneurship and management boosts the tendency of prospective and potential entrepreneurs to be equipped with spirit of champiopreneurship by the intensive application of business intelligence and innovation.

Chapter 10
Impact of Board of Directors Composition, Activity, and Compensation on the ESG Performance in an International Context..224
Tijani Amara, Higher Institute of Business Administration, University of Gafsa, Tunisia
Ali Ahmadi, Higher Institute of Business Administration, University of Gafsa, Tunisia

A growing body of research suggests that the Board of Directors Composition, Activity, and Compensation can influence its environmental, social, and governance (ESG). This chapter seeks to fill this gap in the literature by testing the impact of board size, board meetings, women on the board, executive compensation, and ESG controversies on ESG performance. Using one of the largest datasets to date, consisting of an unbalanced panel dataset consisting of 31040 firm-year observations from 5500 listed firms, covering a period of 16 years (2002–2017) from 60 countries around the world, these findings are fivefold. First, these results suggest that board size is positively associated with ESG performance. Second, the authors show that the number of meeting of the board per year is positively related to the environmental, social and governance score. Third, the main empirical evidence shows that the relationship between women on the board of directors and a firm's ESG performance is a strongly significant. Fourth, these results reveal that executive compensation has a positive effect only for some geographic areas. Fifth, there is a negative link between ESG performance and ESG controversies.

Chapter 11
Sustainability in Transformational and Transactional Leadership: Turkish Textile Industry Example...241
Korhan Arun, Namık Kemal Üniversitesi, Turkey

The relationship between leadership and sustainability in organizations is a topic of significant interest, focusing on the impact of transformational and transactional leadership styles on organizational sustainability. This study emphasized the importance of transformational and transactional leadership in driving sustainable practices and outcomes, addressing the gap between leadership styles and sustainability. Path analysis results show that transformational and transactional leadership styles significantly influence sustainability. However, interestingly, transformational leadership decreases sustainability expenditures, and both leadership styles increase nitrogen emissions. The relationship between transformational leadership and negative outcomes for sustainability needs to be directly addressed in the available literature. In the textile industry in developing countries, both transformational and transactional leadership and environmental sustainability have negative correlations, and transformational leaders may decrease environmental expenditures.

Chapter 12
A Study on the Interaction Between Civil Business Groups and the State From the Perspective of Public Sphere Theory: A Comparison Between the Shangha....................258
Wei Yao, Nanjing University, China
Yuhong Li, Nanjing University, China
Tingxuan Liu, Nanjing University, China

This chapter attempts to use public sphere theory as a starting point to compare the behavior of the British government in protecting the interests of British business in China in the 19th century with the Chinese government's neglect of the interests of Chinese business in the Philippines. This chapter uses the Shanghai Branch of the China Association and Philippine Chinese Charitable Association Inc. as representatives of private business groups in the UK and China. For the UK, due to the public sphere of competition with the central government within the UK, private business groups must consult with relevant private business groups when implementing any economic foreign policy. This process promotes consensus between the British government and society and promotes the British government's determination to maintain British business in China. However, for China, due to the absence of a public sphere where the central government interacts with society, even though Chinese private business groups have huge interests overseas, the state and society have always been unable to form a positive interaction. At the same time, this situation also results in Chinese businesses in the Philippines having to rely on their abilities to maintain their local interests.

Chapter 13
Going Back to Basics as an Innovative Way Forward on Muslim Health Tourism: Keep Sharia in the Loop....................277
Aniesa Samira Bafadhal, University of Brawijaya, Indonesia

The fast growth of health tourism has been attributed to creating a health and prevention boom era expected to usher in new economic power. Offering a different approach derived from the Sharia, Muslim health tourism poses a proximity between religion, tourism, and health. Amid the urgency to understand Muslim tourists as a potential market with such unique characteristics and specific needs, it is unfortunate that no model describes the decision-making behaviour when selecting a Muslim-friendly health destination. As a result, the author suggests a Muslim health tourist behaviour model. This study also highlighted Sharia salons and spas as one of the forms of Muslim health tourism business. It's becoming increasingly clear that for the Muslim health tourism business to truly understand its market, going back to basics is the most innovative approach.

Compilation of References 297

About the Contributors 338

Index 343

Preface

In the dynamic landscape of today's global economy, the integration of technology, business intelligence, and innovation has become pivotal for entrepreneurs seeking to navigate and thrive in the ever-evolving business environment. As the world witnesses a digital revolution, marked by the widespread application of artificial intelligence and the continuous emergence of smart technologies, entrepreneurs find themselves at the forefront of transformative change.

This edited reference book, *Applying Business Intelligence and Innovation to Entrepreneurship*, is a collaborative effort by Kannapat Kankaew, Parinya Nakpathom, Alhuda Chnitphattana, Krittipat Pitchayadejanant, and Siwaporn Kunnapapdeelert, along with various authors from around the world. It is designed to provide insights into the intricate interplay between technology, business intelligence, and innovation in entrepreneurship across diverse sectors.

In this era of the innovation economy, where technological advancements propel commerce forward, entrepreneurs play a vital role in shaping and redefining industries. From agricultural products to fast-moving consumer goods, from the hospitality industry to cultural and indigenous products, entrepreneurship is a catalyst for creativity and circular economies within communities and societies.

This book delves into the multifaceted realm of entrepreneurial business management, emphasizing the symbiotic relationship between technology and business intelligence. It explores how entrepreneurs can leverage digitalization for sustainability, innovation, and a competitive edge in various sectors. Notably, the book addresses the challenges faced by entrepreneurs in today's dynamic business environment and provides valuable insights into successful business strategies.

Our aim is to cater to a diverse audience, including academicians, researchers, undergraduate/postgraduate/doctoral students, and professionals in both private and public enterprises. The content covers a spectrum of topics, ranging from traditional entrepreneurship and management to cutting-edge areas like Fintech startups, cryptocurrency in business, community startups, and the integration of local wisdom into innovative practices.

The recommended topics span the breadth of entrepreneurship, including the adoption of business intelligence by small and medium enterprises, innovation in social enterprise management, the dynamics of the hospitality and tourism industry, and the influence of digital marketing and marketing communication. Additionally, the book explores emerging trends such as delivery services, operation and supply chain management, data science for business, blockchain in entrepreneurship, technology management, and sustainable innovation.

In this book, the chapters unfold a comprehensive exploration of the dynamic interplay between technology, business intelligence, and innovation in the entrepreneurial landscape. From a systematic literature review on the influence of business intelligence on entrepreneurial orientation to an in-depth analysis of the role of technology business incubators in startup development, each chapter offers valuable insights and practical perspectives. The disruptive force of blockchain technology, the pivotal role of supply chain and operations management, the transformative impact of Neuromarketing in the digital era, and the revolutionary influence of cryptocurrencies and fintech startups are among the diverse topics covered. Additionally, the chapters delve into the adoption of business intelligence by small and medium-sized enterprises, the significance of design thinking and creativity in entrepreneurial innovation, and the exploration of environmental, social, and governance performance in corporate boards. With a wide-ranging scope, this collection is a valuable resource for academicians, researchers, students, and professionals seeking a nuanced understanding of the ever-evolving landscape of entrepreneurship in the digital age.

Chapter 1 conducts an extensive systematic literature review, employing the PRISMA framework, to delve into the influence of business intelligence (BI) on entrepreneurial orientation (EO) within ventures. By analyzing articles from notable databases, the study uncovers a scarcity of research in this domain, emphasizing the need for further exploration. With "Business intelligence" and "Entrepreneurial orientation" as keywords, 23 articles are scrutinized, providing a foundation to identify gaps for future researchers in the dynamic intersection of BI and entrepreneurship.

Focusing on the role of technology business incubators (TBIs), Chapter 2 explores their impact on startup effectiveness and overall development. Through a comprehensive literature review and empirical analysis of Gujarat's entrepreneurial ecosystem, the chapter establishes a framework connecting TBI support to operational effectiveness. It offers insights into the challenges faced by startups from ideation to commercialization, presenting a valuable resource for entrepreneurs and policymakers aiming to enhance the existing support systems.

Investigating the disruptive force of blockchain technology, Chapter 3 explores its potential to reshape entrepreneurship across various industries. From supply chain management to decentralized finance, the paper examines the symbiotic relationship between blockchain and entrepreneurship. It sheds light on opportunities for innovation, challenges, and the transformative role of blockchain in startups, emphasizing the need for entrepreneurs to navigate the evolving landscape strategically.

Chapter 4 delves into the critical objectives of supply chain and operations management, underscoring their significance for entrepreneurial ventures' success and sustainability. Exploring how effective management in these areas enhances competitiveness and customer satisfaction, the chapter also addresses emerging trends. Entrepreneurs are guided toward adopting best practices in supply chain and operations management for long-term success in today's dynamic business environment.

Examining Neuromarketing as a digital marketing strategy, Chapter 5 explores its role in evolving marketing communication. Rooted in neuroscience, it reveals how Neuromarketing integrates with digital channels, emphasizing personalization and emotional engagement. The chapter highlights the significance of personalized content, ethical considerations, and the transformative impact of Neuromarketing in decoding consumer behavior in the digital marketing landscape.

Chapter 6 traces the revolutionary impact of cryptocurrencies and fintech startups on business models and entrepreneurship. Exploring their development and disruptive influence on the financial services industry, the chapter investigates how companies embrace cryptocurrencies, conduct ICOs, and integrate them into investment portfolios. It also addresses technological challenges and regulatory issues, providing insights into the dynamic merger of fintech and cryptocurrency solutions.

Focused on small and medium-sized enterprises (SMEs), Chapter 7 addresses the requirements for adopting business intelligence systems. Emphasizing the evolving communication technologies and the importance of business intelligence for sustainable competitive advantage, the chapter analyzes technical, human, and organizational requirements for SMEs in the industrial region of Setif, Algeria.

Exploring the nexus of design thinking and creativity in entrepreneurial innovation, Chapter 8 highlights their significance in problem-solving and idea generation. Through case studies and empirical evidence, it demonstrates how these concepts foster innovation in entrepreneurial ventures. The chapter emphasizes the need for a creative mindset and the application of design thinking principles in navigating the challenges of innovation in the contemporary business environment.

Chapter 9 employs a champiopreneurship approach to explore the influence of business intelligence and innovation on entrepreneurship and management. Focusing on competitive intelligence and decision support systems, it orchestrates champiopreneurship as a concept aligning entrepreneurship and management for prospective entrepreneurs. The study underscores the synchronization of entrepreneurship and management through the intensive application of business intelligence and innovation.

Using one of the largest datasets to date, Chapter 10 investigates the impact of board characteristics on ESG (Environmental, Social, and Governance) performance. Findings reveal relationships between board size, meeting frequency, women on the board, executive compensation, and ESG performance, offering valuable insights for businesses worldwide. The chapter emphasizes the importance of diverse and responsible board practices in enhancing ESG performance.

Addressing the relationship between leadership styles and sustainability, Chapter 11 explores the impact of transformational and transactional leadership on organizational sustainability. The study employs path analysis to reveal the influence of leadership styles on sustainability outcomes, shedding light on the complexities of leadership in promoting sustainable practices. It highlights the need for a nuanced understanding of leadership's role in fostering sustainability.

Drawing on Public Sphere theory, Chapter 12 compares the behavior of the British government in protecting British business in China with the Chinese government's approach to Chinese business in the Philippines in the 19th century. Using private business groups as representatives, the chapter highlights the role of public sphere interaction in shaping economic foreign policies and promoting government-business consensus.

Investigating the growth of health tourism, particularly Muslim health tourism, Chapter 13 proposes a Muslim Health Tourist Behavior Model. The study explores decision-making behaviors when selecting Muslim-friendly health destinations and identifies Sharia salons and spas as forms of Muslim health tourism businesses. The chapter emphasizes the need for a comprehensive understanding of the unique characteristics and needs of Muslim health tourists.

We believe that this edited reference book serves as a valuable resource, providing a comprehensive understanding of the evolving entrepreneurial landscape. The contributors bring a wealth of knowledge and expertise, making this book a practical guide for those navigating the intersection of business, technology, and innovation.

We extend our gratitude to the contributors for their insightful contributions, and we hope that this book inspires and informs the next generation of entrepreneurs and business leaders.

Editors,

Kannapat Kankaew
International College, Burapha University, Thailand

Parinya Nakpathom
International College, Burapha University, Thailand

Alhuda Chnitphattana
International College, Burapha University, Thailand

Krittipat Pitchayadejanant
International College, Burapha University, Thailand

Siwaporn Kunnapapdeelert
Faculty of Logistics and Transportation Management, Panyapiwat Institute of Management, Thailand

Chapter 1
The Systematic Literature Review on Business Intelligence Towards Entrepreneurial Orientation of Ventures

Jinumoni Nazir
https://orcid.org/0000-0002-9098-938X
Sikkim University, India

Pradip Kumar Das
Sikkim University, India

ABSTRACT

Business intelligence has been a recent information tool which was introduced in the entrepreneurship world. The present study is an extensive systematic literature review based on PRISMA framework which aims to explore the influence of business intelligence (BI) on the entrepreneurial orientation (EO) among the ventures. Four journal databases have been used, namely Emerald, JStor, ScienceDirect, and EBSCOhost to gather the articles for the study. "Business intelligence" and "Entrepreneurial orientation" were the keywords used to identify studies from the journal databases. 23 articles were finalised for the study after going through the identification, screening and included process which comes under the PRISMA (preferred reporting items for systematic reviews and meta-analyses) framework. It has been found that very little research has been done in this field. So, this systematic literature review will give an insight into the possible gaps that can be covered by the upcoming researchers in this field.

DOI: 10.4018/979-8-3693-1846-1.ch001

INTRODUCTION

Globally, there is an enormous boom of information. Prior to the communication age, which is commonly defined as 20–30 years ago, the rate of information growth was arithmetical. Information is growing in geometric series these days (Sen et al., 2016). It has been a few decades since people began to live and work online much more frequently (Corvello et al., 2022). With the advent of digitization, business executives are encouraged to use a huge amount of data to align their operations and generate innovative products to cater to their customers (Saleem et al., 2020). A new venture's creation and the development of its launch are impacted by enabling technologies, such as artificial intelligence and big data (Oukil, 2011). Businesses have to work hard to get the data they need to make better decisions in a highly competitive, dynamic, and unstable market. Due to the availability of more data via electronic channels for communication, processing, and acquisition, business intelligence (BI) has gained popularity. This data may serve as the foundation for intelligence techniques (Caseiro & Coelho, 2018). Strategic orientations of global market organisations are linked to knowledge management, and big data is an area that is closely tied to business intelligence (Cadogan, 2012). The era of big data that businesses are in has an impact on how they process and use conventional intelligence e.g., collection, utilisation (Gnizy, 2019). It is possible to achieve a 4–6% increase in productivity in business processes using big data usage (Müller et al., 2018). A business's chances of succeeding in its industry's digital competition increase with its level of entrepreneurship. This is due to the fact that entrepreneurs are more receptive to new technologies and quick to adapt to shifting trends (Ismail, 2023). Gathering and evaluating data are two steps in the creation of intelligence. Information regarding market trends must be gathered by the entire organisation; the marketing department is not the only one responsible for these efforts. Investment and entrepreneurship are finding new opportunities in several domains thanks to big data (Sedkaoui, 2020). The use of big data techniques, such as Hadoop and MapReduce, to gain insight from large amounts of data (H. Chen et al., 2012). In order to find new prospects, entrepreneurial orientation (EO) promotes exploration activities and places a strong emphasis on knowledge discovery (H. Chen & Hsu, 2013). Many organisational traits have been proposed by academics to help us comprehend the place of entrepreneurial orientation in the nomological network that surrounds managers' use of information systems and their capacity for sensing (Roberts et al., 2016).

On the other hand, small enterprises are finding it easier to obtain market intelligence resources thanks to government support and technology-assisted delivery. Small companies might benefit from online personalised portals. Features more user-friendly and adaptable dashboards that offer segmentations, real-time transactional data, and customer profiles (Carson et al., 2020). Over the past several decades, one of the most important changes in international commerce has been the use of digital technologies, platforms, and infrastructures made possible by the Internet (Gnizy, 2019). Top-performing organisations use sophisticated information and analytics techniques five times more frequently than low-performing organisations, according a global study of 3000 company managers, executives, and analysts from a range of industries and regions (Lavalle et al., 2011).

The business environment is ever-changing due to advancements in technology, industry trends, and economic fluctuations. As BI technologies and approaches advance, it becomes more crucial than ever to comprehend how they affect entrepreneurial orientation. Start-ups or ventures have started adopting artificial intelligence for smooth functioning of their businesses. Now a days, it has become easy to store huge data on the cloud and make it easily accessible to both the employees and the managers. However, it can only be helpful if the entrepreneurs or the business person have an adequate knowledge to use it. So, even though BI tools have been introduced in the business world, its influence needs to be known that up to what extend BI technology has been helpful in the entrepreneurial world. Therefore, by this systematic literature review we can explore the influence of BI on the EO of the ventures.

THE CONNECTION BETWEEN BUSINESS INTELLIGENCE (BI) AND ENTREPRENEURIAL ORIENTATION (EO)

Since entrepreneurial orientation and business intelligence are relatively new topics in the academic arena, there aren't many empirical studies that demonstrate their direct correlation. A study (Caseiro & Coelho, 2018) explored among various firms located in different European countries and stated that how business intelligence (BI), entrepreneurial orientation (EO), and startup competitiveness are related to one another. It does this by looking at how EO influences BI's impact on startup competitiveness as well as how BI directly influences it. Because business intelligence entails using information to make better decisions, which can affect a firm's entrepreneurial orientation, the study predicts a favourable association between EO and BI. The competitiveness of a business, which is impacted by EO, might benefit from BI techniques and attributes. It is recommended that practitioners increase the knowledge of how business intelligence (BI) affects organisational elements and think about including BI methods into startup training and information sessions. As a result, the indirect correlation between these variables can be shown because no more research has been conducted on the direct relationship between EO and BI, only other features or sub-themes like big data analysis, business analysis, big data usage etc. With the help of BI, entrepreneurs can make educated decisions by receiving fast and accurate information. As a result, it becomes possible to recognise and seize fresh chances in a proactive (one of the dimensions of EO) manner. BI also helps them make wise decisions and develop their strategic skills. Business intelligence fosters an innovative and adaptable culture that improves entrepreneurial orientation. Successful use of BI by entrepreneurs may provide them a competitive edge and help them better manage the ever-changing business environment.

RESEARCH METHODOLGY

Through a "PRISMA 2020" systematic review of existing literature, this study aims to identify how business intelligence can be influencing entrepreneurial orientation among the ventures that need to be addressed for future research agendas.

Identification

In order to identify the resources, the first stage entails filtering out journals from the various databases, such as Science Direct, Emerald Insight, Ebscohost, and JStor, since they are some of the main chosen databases for evaluation and financing in Indian social science research. Utilizing keywords such as "Business Intelligence" AND "Entrepreneurship Orientation" will allow to search the four database journals for the resource. This study includes only English-language research papers, review articles, early-cite publications, and peer-reviewed articles that were published between 2010 and 2023.

Screening

In order to find relevant articles, keywords are used to search for resources. The screening process led to the retrieval of 306 articles (59 from Science Direct, 235 from Emerald Insight, 4 from EBSCOhost, and 8 from JStor). A duplicate article was identified during the compilation process and removed. 37 articles were sorted after reading the abstracts and the titles, and 269 were discarded. There were 13 articles that had no full-text available, as well.

Included

The titles of the papers were screened before moving on to the abstracts as part of the selection process. Articles were chosen in the next phase according to the research question. Nevertheless, the research did not include any papers whose full texts

Table 1. Result of the database search protocol

Journal Database	Articles
Science Direct	59
Emerald	235
EBSCOhost	4
JStor	8
Total	**306**

Table 2. Criteria for Inclusion and Exclusion

	Criteria
Inclusion	Articles, early cite articles, research articles, peer reviewed articles, entrepreneurial orientation, business intelligence, big data analytics, market intelligence, entrepreneurship, business.
Exclusion	Full text not available, Thesis, Books.

were not accessible. To decide if the publications in this round should be a part of our research, we carefully reviewed each one. The study of our research topics did not include any articles that did not include a process or result examination. After reviewing the whole text of the study, 23 articles were included in response to the research question.

RESULT AND DISCUSSION

Based on the PRISMA framework of 2020 this study followed an approach to review published works related to business intelligence and entrepreneurial orientation. The aim was to locate, assess and analyse research contributions, on a research topic. While the primary objective of a PRISMA based review is to evaluate treatment effects these types of studies can also have objectives. The chronological order of articles by year of publication demonstrates the steadily rising level of scholarly interest in the discipline, with 2019 and 2022 being the most active years.

The graph based on the year wise publication has been depicted by the trending line that only a few papers have been published from 2010 to 2023 out of which in the years 2019 and 2022 has the highest (5 papers) publications. This is a very new topic and thus more exploration is required.

Asia (Iran, Israel, India, Bangladesh, China, and Taiwan) is by far the most prolific continent to far (about 57% of the contributions) in terms of the studies conducted,

Figure 1. Identification of studies through various journal database

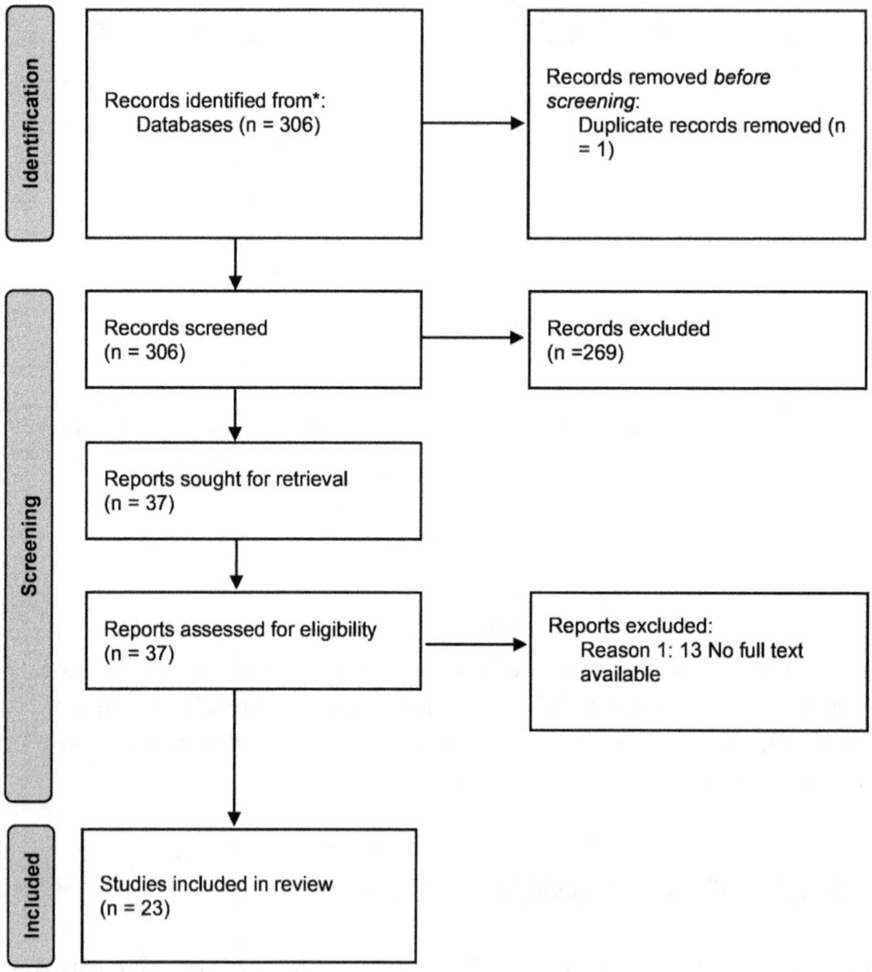

Table 3. Year wise number of researches done

Year of publication	No. of researches done
2013	1
2016	2
2018	2
2019	5
2020	4
2022	5
2023	4

Figure 2. Year wise number of researches done

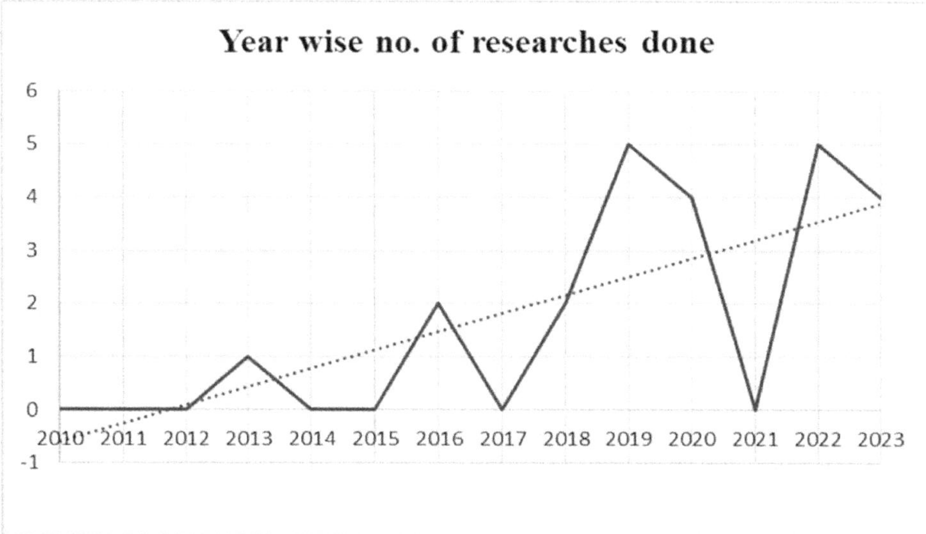

according to the distribution by nation followed by Europe (Italy and other countries) which is 22% of the contribution whereas South America (Brazil), North America (U.S.A.) and Africa (Tanzania) contributes 7% of the studies.

Next comes papers published per journals out of which only Journal of Enterprise Information Management (3 articles published) and Management Decision (2 articles published) has the most journals published based on this topic.

Table 4. Country wise number of researches done

Countries	No. of Researches Done
European Countries	3
China	2
Iran	2
Taiwan	1
USA	1
Tanzania	1
Brazil	1
India	1
Israel	1
Bangladesh	1

Figure 3. Country wise number of researches done

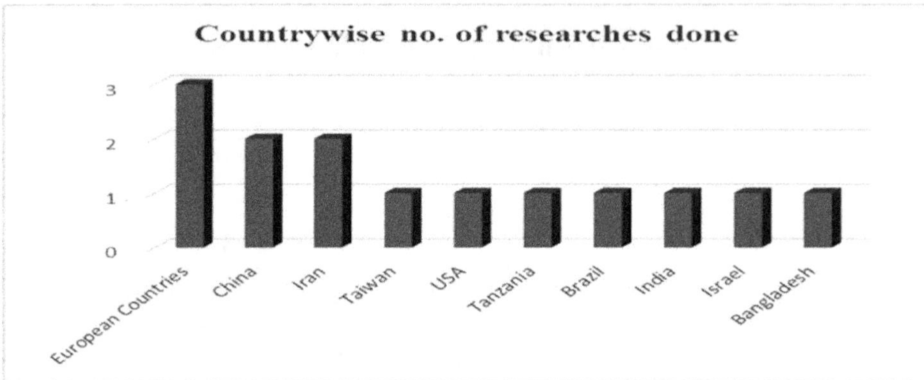

Table 5. Continent wise researches done

Continents	Researches done
Asia	8
Europe	3
North America	1
South America	1
Africa	1

Figure 4. Continent wise researches done

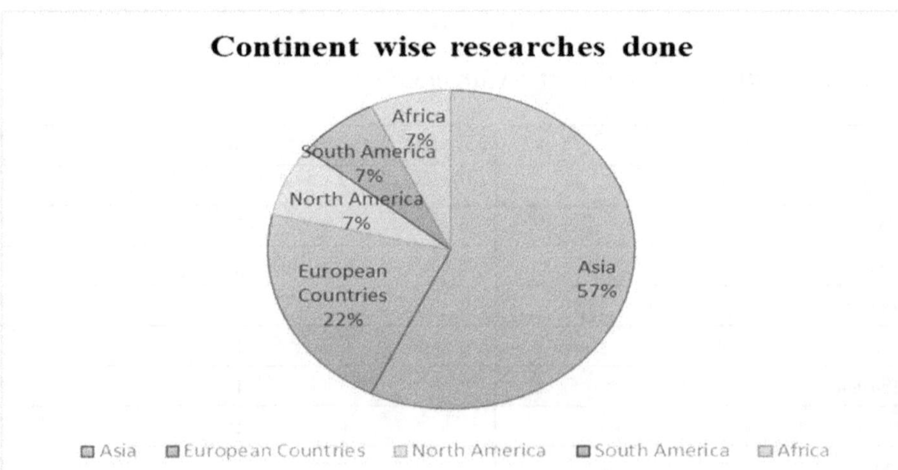

Figure 5. Journal wise number of papers published

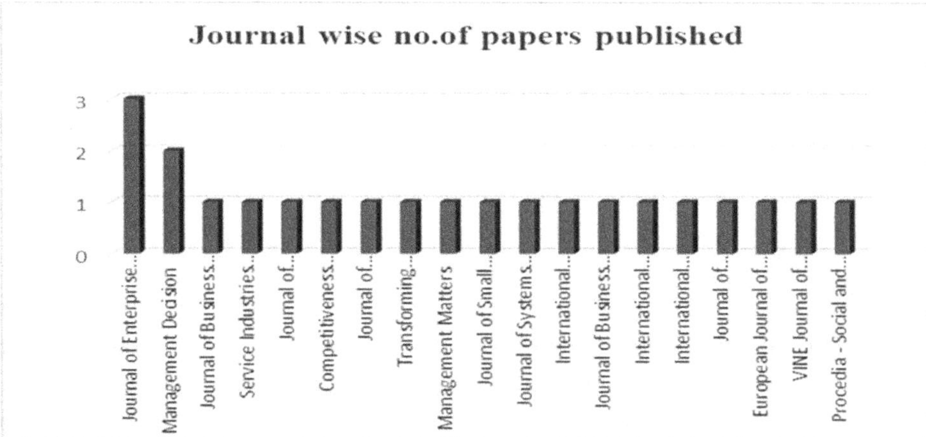

Table 6. Types of paper

Paper types	No. of researches done
Review paper	7
Quantitative	11
Qualitative	2
Mixed	2
Conceptual	1

Furthermore, 48% of the papers are quantitative followed by 30% review (systematic literature review, bibliometric analysis, meta-analysis) papers, 9% qualitative paper and mixed papers and rest is conceptual paper.

The term "business intelligence" is quite extensive. Covers a range of approaches, processes and technological resources that are used to gather, store and analyse data in order to support decision making (Wanda & Stian, 2015). The field of intelligence research provides an opportunity to explore advancements in collecting and analysing data, managing information making decisions and enhancing capabilities. Intelligence focuses on extracting value from data, information and the dynamic nature of organizations (López-Robles et al., 2019). Business Intelligence (BI) is a valuable tool that has to be created and utilised for information collecting, analysis, and distribution to enable improved decision-making (Caseiro & Coelho, 2018). To provide information and insights, for decision making strategic intelligence combines various types of intelligence such as business intelligence, competitive intelligence and knowledge management. Intelligence, in its entirety, analytical and practical intelligence significantly influences entrepreneurship by affecting numerous aspects of the process. This includes recognizing opportunities making decisions and employing thinking (Ahmadi et al., 2020). A study demonstrates how the interaction between digital technology and entrepreneurs' everyday activities shapes the nature of their business. The qualities and dynamics of the surrounding environment influence how various digital tools are used, and their use is interrelated. The digital revolution in entrepreneurship is not the product of deliberate design, but rather an evolutionary, practice-based phenomena. The results have important ramifications for software development companies that cater to entrepreneurs, universities that are interested in entrepreneurial education, and entrepreneurs who want to comprehend the dynamics of their working practices (Corvello et al., 2022). One way to find various strategic levers for encouraging innovation and taking advantage of technology opportunities is through the strategic integration of data-driven orientation, skills upgrading, and innovation development (Visvizi et al., 2022).

On the other hand, the methods, procedures, and choices used throughout the decision-making process that result in a new market entrance are referred to as entrepreneurial orientation (EO) (Lumpkin & Dess, 1996; Covin & Miller, 2014). EO is crucial to a firm's entrepreneurial process, which is in identifying opportunities, innovation processes, and opportunity exploitation. It is an effective way to handle competitive risks and minimise competitive pressures (Y. C. Chen et al., 2012). Proactiveness, inventiveness, and risk-taking comprise the three components that make up entrepreneurial orientation as a combined construct (Covin & Miller, 2014). The concept of entrepreneurial orientation centres on an organization's procedures, leadership perspectives, and enterprising actions, encompassing the generation of novel ideas via digital transformation. Businesses may increase the speed and accuracy of business intelligence operations by digitising data collecting and analysis processes and minimising manual labour. Therefore, it is concluded in a study that digitization improves business intelligence via streamlining procedures related to data collecting, analysis, and decision-making; it also boosts productivity and gives researchers access to insightful information from a variety of sources (Ismail, 2023). When it comes to leveraging information systems (IS) to identify chances for innovation, EO which entails actions that bring about change in the company or market is a crucial component. With autonomy, managers may think through more possibilities and alternatives, which improves their capacity to spot chances when utilising IS. Using IS to identify possibilities also requires creativity and taking calculated risks. Decision support systems (DSS) may give managers the information and understanding they need to spot possible areas for innovation. Examples of DSS include business intelligence tools and analytics (Roberts et al., 2016). In a recent study (Caseiro & Coelho, 2018) conducted among various startups located in different European countries, it has been stated that BI and EO significantly influence each other. BI has the potential to augment the aspects of entrepreneurial orientation and facilitate the adoption of risk-taking, innovation, and proactivity by entrepreneurs.

One of the study (López-Robles et al., 2019) topics that has the most potential for growth in the upcoming years is business intelligence. The study offers a conceptual analysis of the definitions of intelligence that are currently available in the literature, quantifies bibliometric performance indicators, identifies key researchers and research topics, and uses SciMAT, a bibliometric analysis programme, to assess the field's evolution. BI is strongly connected to other theme areas including Big Data, text mining, queries, data warehouses, and business intelligence systems. It appears that the demand to use and analyse vast volumes of data is rising, which might lead to this potential rise. It is crucial to stress that business intelligence, in its broadest sense, is solely concerned with the creation and application of information technology, not with specifics pertaining to business organisation. Modern business intelligence solutions can capture and analyse almost any kind of data. BI has been a rising star in the information systems industry, and it is presently experiencing a new boost within the Big Data Analytics movement (Wanda & Stian, 2015). A revolutionary new way to store intelligence and analyse it is being made possible by big data. Big data-related entrepreneurship entails the founding of new businesses and the application of novel ideas while utilising data analytics to spur success and innovation (Sedkaoui, 2020). However, the distribution of market intelligence (another component of BI, it particularly relates to gathering and evaluating data about the market and client demands.) promotes acceptable decision making, incorporates creative entrepreneurial orientation into already-existing technology or expertise, and lessens the negative effects of overly proactive behaviour by reducing the number of poor judgements made (H. Chen & Hsu, 2013). Exposure of small businesses to market intelligence fosters the development of marketing competencies that maximise adaptability and client response. Market intelligence supplements the experience-based informal market knowledge of small businesses, guiding the intuition of owners and managers and boosting their confidence in creative ideas (Carson et al., 2020).

Furthermore, in a study (Sen et al., 2016), it has been stated that big data has great promise and potential for SMEs. Through the development of real-time solutions to problems in every industry, big data may foster alliances in SMEs. Utilising openness for decision-making can help achieve this. SMEs are chosen in this particular situation for two primary reasons: Because of their general economic situation, SMEs can react to modest changes more quickly and flexibly than bigger companies; and adapt to changes in an efficient manner. SMEs may get more precise and thorough performance data on anything from product inventories to sick days as they generate and maintain more transactional data digitally. This allows them to uncover variability and improve performance. Big data enables considerably more accurate and ever-narrower client segmentation customised goods and services. SMEs tend to be more quickly adaptable, have fewer legacy problems, and have more flexible IT infrastructure. Big Data may help SMEs focus on innovation, increase efficiency, and launch new ventures. That means that some of the main obstacles can be removed. It is anticipated that SMEs would be able to assess the usage and potential of big data by concentrating on the growth prospects it presents. Big Data can be used by SMEs for a variety of purposes, including market segmentation, demand forecasting, process optimisation, predictive inventory planning, predictive maintenance, and in-depth data analysis to identify correlations, risks, and opportunities. SMEs may be able to view the broad picture as a result of the extensive usage of big data. The systematic view is based on the detailed identification, which will provide important concepts via the broad picture. Also, a study shows how crucial business function (information systems) strategy is to enabling overall business strategy-making for bringing forth innovations within the company (Yoshikuni & Dwivedi, 2023).

According to another study's authors (Oesterreich et al., 2022), future theory development should be guided by their increased grasp of the mechanisms resulting in big data analytics (BDA)-induced economic value. Prioritising the sociotechnical aspect of BDA is important for managers and decision-makers starting new BDA initiatives. The significance of social and technological elements in generating economic value from BDA is investigated in this research using a meta-analysis of 107 individual studies.

A bibliometric study (Rialti et al., 2019) has revealed that organisational performance and decision-making processes are greatly impacted by big data and BDA systems. Managers can utilise the forecasts generated by BDA systems regarding future trends to decide on sales, revenues, and production needs. Real-time consumer analytics from BDA enable managers to respond quickly to changing customer preferences. Managers can be better equipped to make decisions that improve organisational efficiency in the production and supply chain by using insights from BDA. BDA systems may provide managers with information about sales, manufacturing, and supply, allowing them to react quickly to changes and make wise choices. Also, enhancing the quality of information and facilitating its efficient exchange across supply chain networks makes an enterprise more capable of quickly and effectively responding to interruptions (Hyun et al., 2023). For example a study (Nayak et al., 2019) noted that wearable technology relies heavily on big data and big data analytics since these technologies may provide commercial value for the healthcare sector and extract value from vast amounts of information.

In accordance with the aspects of the idea of business intelligence use, a study (Gnizy, 2019) based on Israeli firms implements Big Data (BD) utilisation widely. Using pertinent components from previous research, it evaluates international market orientation (IMO), international entrepreneurial orientation (IEO), and international learning orientation (ILO). BD is essential to improving IEO (International Entrepreneurial Orientation) in businesses; yet, the sources included do not specifically address the link between BD and IEO. Using BD increases a company's ability to compete, willingness to take chances, and desire for innovative leadership—all of which are indicators of their IEO. Businesses may use BD to support their decisions and actions by analysing data, which is in line with the entrepreneurial spirit of looking for and seizing global market possibilities. Businesses may use BD to get and evaluate market intelligence, spot new trends, and make data-driven decisions—all crucial elements of an entrepreneurial orientation in a global setting. In order to differentiate BD apart from typical datasets, a paper (Ciampi et al., 2020) outlines the characteristics of BD, such as size, diversity, velocity, variability, value, authenticity, and visualisation. Crucial resources, including human skills, data-driven organisational learning, and integration methodologies, storage, processing, and other physical and intangible resources, are needed for the successful application of BD analytics capabilities (BDAC).

Also, a study (Ciasullo et al., 2022) aims to explore the connections between organisational resilience and big data analytics (BDA) skills in 192 European big data SMEs. Improving small and medium companies' (SMEs) ability to withstand adversity and pivotal moments is the goal of this article. It is suggested that practitioners improve their responsiveness in times of crisis by identifying the micro foundations of SMEs' resilience-building capabilities. For small and medium-sized businesses (SMEs), radical innovation results from the effective integration of big data usage (BDU) in business operations, which aligns company strategy and boosts operational efficiency. Radical innovation and the creation of cutting-edge goods that satisfy consumer demands are the results of BDU's assistance in helping SMEs match their business strategy with organisational objectives (Wang et al., 2023).

Moreover, in another study conducted among 192 Bangladesh companies identified that a firm's performance and agility are greatly impacted by its ability to use business analytics (an extension of business intelligence) skills to enhance resources like information quality and inventive capability. The link between performance, agility, and business analytics (BA) capabilities is moderated by industry dynamism. The objective of using data to inform business decisions and boost performance is one that both BI and BA strive to achieve. It is evident that BA goes beyond the technical elements of data characteristics and emphasises how organisational resources must change in order for an organisation to become data-driven (Khan et al., 2022).

Therefore, a study (Zeng & Khan, 2019) looks at how EO and resource orchestration work together to create value in emerging economies using big data. It implies that in order to improve performance by combining and coordinating resources from big data, enterprises in emerging economies must use EO to generate value. In order to comprehend value creation techniques using big data in emerging economies, it blends EO and resource orchestration theory. It emphasises how crucial asset orchestration and resource coordination are to extracting value from big data. The results highlight the necessity for businesses in emerging economies to organise resources and take advantage of entrepreneurial attitude in order to generate value using big data. It implies that businesses may control the extent of testing by using data insights, progressively expanding their concepts to reduce risk.

CONCLUSION

The absence of knowledge about universal criteria that make systematic reviews reproducible and sufficiently scientifically shown is often evident. The PRISMA framework provides a recognised, peer-reviewed method based on a best-practice checklist. 23 articles are extensively reviewed by the authors out of 306 articles. Only 8 studies (which makes 57% of the total) are done in Asian countries (which is highest among all the continents). It is relatively new in the literature of business and management to discuss entrepreneurial orientation and business intelligence and thus only a few articles have been shortlisted in this study. Also, year wise the rate of article publication is slow according to the trending line.

In the information systems sector, BI is a developing area that focuses on developing and using information technologies. It has been observed that not much study has been done on the influence of BI on EO. Although related studies have been identified based on this topic like big data analytics, strategic intelligence, business analytics, market intelligence and their impact on entrepreneurship or small business enterprise or any business. These are either the components of BI or are related to it directly or indirectly. The use of BI tools for entrepreneurial activities can enhance an organizations competitiveness which can have impacts, on the nations position, in the market. BI has a major impact on entrepreneurship via thinking, decision-making, and influencing possibilities. Universities, software development firms, and entrepreneurs are all impacted by the practice-based, evolutionary digital revolution in entrepreneurship. Innovation development, skills upgrading, and data-driven orientation may be strategically integrated to foster innovation and take advantage of technological opportunities. By expediting the processes of data gathering, analysis, and decision-making, digitization enhances business intelligence. EO is taking calculated risks and being creative in order to effect change within the firm or industry. BI and EO have a big impact on each other, which encourages entrepreneurs to take risks, be creative, and be proactive. One part of BI is market intelligence, which encourages decision-making, integrates an entrepreneurial orientation, and minimises bad decisions. Exposure to market intelligence facilitates the development of marketing capabilities, improves flexibility, and increases customer responsiveness for small enterprises. It enhances trust in original ideas and adds to unofficial market knowledge. The Big Data Analytics (BDA) movement is gaining traction and offers a novel approach to data analysis and archiving. Prioritising the sociotechnical element of BDA, future theory development should concentrate on comprehending the mechanisms arising from BDA-induced economic value.

However, improving International Entrepreneurial Orientation (IEO) in organisations requires the use of Big Data (BD). Innovative leadership, risk-taking, and competitiveness are all improved by BD. Data-driven decision making, market intelligence, and decision making are all supported by it. Size, diversity, rapidity, variability, value, authenticity, and visualisation are some of BD's traits. Human skills, data-driven organisational learning, and resources including processing, storage, and processing are necessary for successful application. For SMEs, big data has enormous promise since it can create partnerships and offer quick fixes for issues across a range of sectors. SMEs are able to enhance performance and adapt effectively because of their ability to respond swiftly and adaptably to changes in the economy. Moreover, precise consumer segmentation and personalised products and services may be made possible by big data. Focusing on growth possibilities can help SMEs evaluate the use and potential of big data. The applications of this technology include detailed data analysis, process optimisation, demand forecasting, market segmentation, and predictive inventory planning.

Therefore, research on this area can assist firms remain up to date with the newest developments in BI technologies and comprehend how developing technologies may be used to achieve entrepreneurial success as they continue to improve.

CONTRIBUTION OF THE STUDY

This study aims to provide insights, into the impact of BI methods and tools towards the entrepreneurial activities in the ventures. By understanding this, organizations can make informed choices ultimately leading to improved outcomes. Understanding the connection, between BI and EO can potentially boost an entrepreneur's abilities, willingness to take risks, innovative capacities and overall entrepreneurial mindset. Businesses that effectively utilize BI for pursuits can experience improvements, in productivity, sustainability and competitiveness. As a result, this study will contribute to growth and the creation of employment opportunities. BI can also assist companies in optimizing resource allocation through the use of real time data and analytics. Exploring this field of research will also help to gain insights, into the impact of BI on resource utilization and discover strategies for improved efficiency and effectiveness, in resource management. Using BI for activities can help organizations enhance their competitiveness. This in turn can have impacts, on the nations position, in the market. BI can also help detect and reduce risks related to entrepreneurial endeavours. So, this study may give business owners advice on how to utilise BI for risk management, resulting in more robust and sustainable enterprises along with the larger consequences for global economic growth and competitiveness, given the opportunity for BI-driven entrepreneurial activity to contribute to economic development.

The relationship, between innovation and EO is quite strong. This study describes the effects of BI and provide insights into how BI technologies contribute to fostering innovation generating ideas and developing products and services that benefit society as a whole. The findings from this research can be helpful for policymakers, business support groups and incubators in creating an environment that effectively integrates BI. This could potentially create an atmosphere for small businesses. The knowledge gained from research may also have an impact on programs by shaping the development of curricula that equip aspiring entrepreneurs and students, with the skills and knowledge to effectively utilize BI in their endeavours. Although not much research has been made on the influence of business intelligence on entrepreneurial orientation so this systematic literature review will give us an insight view of the possible gaps that can be covered by the upcoming researchers in this field.

LIMITATIONS

In comparison to more established fields, these emerging fields may not have garnered as much attention from researchers as they should have. Only four databases have been used for this study, upcoming researches can other databases as well for their future studies. The 23 papers show that, in contrast to the allied themes of BI, relatively few of the studies have examined the direct influence of BI on EO. Articles published between 2010-2023 have only been reviewed. Time constraint is another limitation of this study.

FUTURE DIRECTIONS

A research approach that combines insights from business, information systems, and entrepreneurship may be necessary at the intersection of business intelligence and entrepreneurial orientation. Therefore, developing collaborative platforms that facilitate data sharing and analysis between researchers and industry professionals. It has been observed from the 23 articles that only a very few articles have considered the direct impact of BI on EO instead more emphasise has been given on the related themes of BI (like BDA, market intelligence, business analytics etc.) so it can be suggested that studies purely based on BI and EO can be conducted for more in-depth knowledge. This area has not been explored much so this can be a good opportunity for the upcoming researchers and scholars to uncover more of it. In order to develop practical insights and provide guidance for businesses, policymakers, educators, and researchers, there is a need for more research into the influence of BI on EO. Business sustainability and success are increasingly dependent on data, and it can be used to shape the future of entrepreneurship. Businesses may optimise their BI system installation by knowing how BI affects EO. This involves customising BI tools to address the particular requirements and difficulties that entrepreneurship presents.

REFERENCES

Ahmadi, M., Baei, F., Hosseini-Amiri, S.-M., Moarefi, A., Suifan, T. S., & Sweis, R. (2020). Proposing a model of manager's strategic intelligence, organization development, and entrepreneurial behavior in organizations. *Journal of Management Development, 39*(4), 559–579. doi:10.1108/JMD-11-2018-0317

Cadogan, J. W. (2012). International marketing, strategic orientations and business success: Reflections on the path ahead. *International Marketing Review, 29*(4), 340–348. doi:10.1108/02651331211242656

Carson, G., O'Connor, C., & Simmons, G. (2020). The crucial role of market intelligence in the development of small business marketing capabilities. *Journal of Small Business and Enterprise Development, 27*(5), 797–816. doi:10.1108/JSBED-12-2019-0394

Caseiro, N., & Coelho, A. (2018). Business intelligence and competitiveness: The mediating role of entrepreneurial orientation. *Competitiveness Review, 28*(2), 213–226. doi:10.1108/CR-09-2016-0054

Chen, H., Chiang, R. H. L., & Storey, V. C. (2012). Business intelligence and analytics: From big data to big impact. *Management Information Systems Quarterly, 36*(4), 1165–1188. doi:10.2307/41703503

Chen, H., & Hsu, C.-H. (2013). Entrepreneurial orientation and firm performance in non-profit service organizations: Contingent effect of market orientation. *Service Industries Journal, 33*(5), 445–466. https://search.ebscohost.com/login.aspx?direct=true&db=crh&AN=86994939&site=ehost-live. doi:10.1080/02642069.2011.622372

Chen, Y. C., Li, P. C., & Evans, K. R. (2012). Effects of interaction and entrepreneurial orientation on organizational performance: Insights into market driven and market driving. *Industrial Marketing Management, 41*(6), 1019–1034. doi:10.1016/j.indmarman.2012.01.017

Ciampi, F., Marzi, G., Demi, S., & Faraoni, M. (2020). The big data-business strategy interconnection: A grand challenge for knowledge management. A review and future perspectives. *Journal of Knowledge Management, 24*(5), 1157–1176. doi:10.1108/JKM-02-2020-0156

Ciasullo, M. V., Montera, R., & Douglas, A. (2022). Building SMEs' resilience in times of uncertainty: the role of big data analytics capability and co-innovation. *Transforming Government: People. Transforming Government, 16*(2), 203–217. doi:10.1108/TG-07-2021-0120

Corvello, V., De Carolis, M., Verteramo, S., & Steiber, A. (2022). The digital transformation of entrepreneurial work. *International Journal of Entrepreneurial Behaviour & Research, 28*(5), 1167–1183. doi:10.1108/IJEBR-01-2021-0067

Covin, J. G., & Miller, D. (2014). International Entrepreneurial Orientation: Conceptual Considerations, Research Themes, Measurement Issues, and Future Research Directions. *Entrepreneurship Theory and Practice, 38*(1), 11–44. doi:10.1111/etap.12027

Gnizy, I. (2019). Big data and its strategic path to value in international firms. *International Marketing Review, 36*(3), 318–341. doi:10.1108/IMR-09-2018-0249

Hyun, Y., Park, J., Kamioka, T., & Chang, Y. (2023). Organizational agility enabled by big data analytics: Information systems capabilities view. *Journal of Enterprise Information Management, 36*(4), 1032–1055. doi:10.1108/JEIM-03-2022-0077

Ismail, I. J. (2023). I have to apply this strategy! Understanding the mediating effect of digitalization on strategic orientations and sustainable competitive advantage among small enterprises in Tanzania. *Management Matters, 20*(1), 53–73. doi:10.1108/MANM-01-2022-0019

Khan, A., Talukder, M. S., Islam, Q. T., & Islam, A. K. M. N. (2022). The impact of business analytics capabilities on innovation, information quality, agility and firm performance: the moderating role of industry dynamism. *VINE Journal of Information and Knowledge Management Systems.* doi:10.1108/VJIKMS-01-2022-0027

Lavalle, S., Lesser, E., Shockley, R., Hopkins, M. S., & Kruschwitz, N. (2011). Big Data, Analytics and the Path From Insights to Value. *MIT Sloan Management Review, 52*(2), 21–31.

López-Robles, J. R., Otegi-Olaso, J. R., Porto Gómez, I., & Cobo, M. J. (2019). 30 years of intelligence models in management and business: A bibliometric review. *International Journal of Information Management*, *48*, 22–38. doi:10.1016/j.ijinfomgt.2019.01.013

Lumpkin, G. T., & Dess, G. G. (1996). Clarifying the Entrepreneurial Orientation Construct and Linking It to Performance. *Academy of Management Review, 21*(1), 135–172.

Müller, O., Fay, M., & vom Brocke, J. (2018). The Effect of Big Data and Analytics on Firm Performance: An Econometric Analysis Considering Industry Characteristics. *Journal of Management Information Systems*, *35*(2), 488–509. doi:10.1080/07421222.2018.1451955

Nayak, B., Bhattacharyya, S. S., & Krishnamoorthy, B. (2019). Integrating wearable technology products and big data analytics in business strategy. *Journal of Systems and Information Technology*, *21*(2), 255–275. doi:10.1108/JSIT-08-2018-0109

Oesterreich, T. D., Anton, E., Teuteberg, F., & Dwivedi, Y. K. (2022). The role of the social and technical factors in creating business value from big data analytics: A meta-analysis. *Journal of Business Research*, *153*, 128–149. doi:10.1016/j.jbusres.2022.08.028

Oukil, M.-S. (2011). A development perspective of technology-based entrepreneurship in the Middle East and North Africa. *Annals of Innovation & Entrepreneurship*, *2*(1), 6000. doi:10.3402/aie.v2i1.7986

Rialti, R., Marzi, G., Ciappei, C., & Busso, D. (2019). Big data and dynamic capabilities: A bibliometric analysis and systematic literature review. *Management Decision*, *57*(8), 2052–2068. doi:10.1108/MD-07-2018-0821

Roberts, N., Campbell, D. E., & Vijayasarathy, L. R. (2016). Using Information Systems to Sense Opportunities for Innovation: Integrating Postadoptive Use Behaviors with the Dynamic Managerial Capability Perspective. *Journal of Management Information Systems*, *33*(1), 45–69. https://search.ebscohost.com/login.aspx?direct=true&db=crh&AN=116238037&site=ehost-live. doi:10.1080/07421222.2016.1172452

Saleem, H., Li, Y., Ali, Z., Ayyoub, M., Wang, Y., & Mehreen, A. (2020). Big data use and its outcomes in supply chain context: The roles of information sharing and technological innovation. *Journal of Enterprise Information Management*, *34*(4), 1121–1143. doi:10.1108/JEIM-03-2020-0119

Sedkaoui, S. (2020). How data analytics is changing entrepreneurial opportunities? *International Journal of Innovation Science*, *10*(2), 274–294. doi:10.1108/IJIS-09-2017-0092

Sen, D., Ozturk, M., & Vayvay, O. (2016). An Overview of Big Data for Growth in SMEs. *Procedia: Social and Behavioral Sciences*, *235*, 159–167. doi:10.1016/j.sbspro.2016.11.011

Visvizi, A., Troisi, O., Grimaldi, M., & Loia, F. (2022). Think human, act digital: Activating data-driven orientation in innovative start-ups. *European Journal of Innovation Management*, *25*(6), 452–478. doi:10.1108/EJIM-04-2021-0206

Wanda, P., & Stian, S. (2015). The Secret of my Success: An exploratory study of Business Intelligence management in the Norwegian Industry. *Procedia Computer Science, 64*(1877), 240–247. doi:10.1016/j.procs.2015.08.486

Wang, Y., Ali, Z., Mehreen, A., & Hussain, K. (2023). The trickle-down effect of big data use to predict organization innovation: The roles of business strategy alignment and information sharing. *Journal of Enterprise Information Management*, *36*(1), 323–346. doi:10.1108/JEIM-10-2021-0439

Yoshikuni, A. C., & Dwivedi, R. (2023). The role of enterprise information systems strategies enabled strategy-making on organizational innovativeness: A resource orchestration perspective. *Journal of Enterprise Information Management*, *36*(1), 172–196. doi:10.1108/JEIM-10-2021-0442

Zeng, J., & Khan, Z. (2019). Value creation through big data in emerging economies. *Management Decision*, *57*(8), 1818–1838. doi:10.1108/MD-05-2018-0572

Chapter 2
Role of Technology Business Incubator in Enhancing Entrepreneurship Ecosystem

Satya Ranjan Acharya
Entrepreneurship Development Institute of India, India

Yamini Chandra
https://orcid.org/0000-0002-7860-9559
Entrepreneurship Development Institute of India, India

ABSTRACT

This chapter examines the role of technology business incubators (TBIs) in improving the effectiveness, viability, and overall development of startups. The chapter attempts to establish a connection between the support offered by these TBIs and its effects on the overall operational effectiveness of these startups by referring to various available relevant literature. Further, the chapter investigates the assistance offered by these TBIs as well as the challenges encountered throughout the process from the ideation and commercialization of funded ideas. Through the empirical analysis of Gujarat's entrepreneurial ecosystem, a comprehensive framework is given that can be used to improve the existing support system.

INTRODUCTION

The term entrepreneurship ecosystem refers to a complex network of highly interrelated activities. There is a paucity of knowledge on how ecosystems interact and contribute to the growth of interconnected components that support entrepreneurship. The

DOI: 10.4018/979-8-3693-1846-1.ch002

interconnectedness of its constituent parts, which reinforce and maintain one another, is often referred to as an ecosystem. Examining these interactions is crucial to fully comprehend how the environment influences the development and expansion of new employment in the residential environment (Acs et al., 2012; Ács et al., 2014, 2016; Alvedalen & Boschma, 2017). These components are knitted together in a way to empowers the entrepreneur. Van De Ven, (1993) states that several components interconnectedly contribute to the development of the ecosystem, some of which primarily relate to the role entrepreneurs play.

Certain characteristics of the entrepreneurial ecosystem make it an attractive setting for a variety of supporting activities. These include the promotion of present and future knowledge, the intense attention of investment firms, institutions for skill improvement and training, governance, access to legal and financial resources, and the desire to invent and create. Recent studies, particularly theoretical contributions, provide a useful framework for identifying qualities essential to the success of a startup environment. Van De Ven, (1993) is one of the prominent researchers who has extensively worked with business enterprises and advocates that industrial infrastructure can help to produce an enabling environment that contributes to the entrepreneurial ecosystem. This infrastructure consists of functional arrangements for technology management and implementation., the provision of basic scientific information services, the estimation of the amount of financing, skilled labor, research facilities, and marketing and logistics support that are readily available. The university, the government, the professionals, support services, capital services, and the talent team are all cited as important elements of the business environment (Cohen, 2006; Neck et al., 2004).

DEFINING ENTREPRENEURIAL ENVIRONMENT AND ENTREPRENEURSHIP ECOSYSTEM

The entrepreneurial environment, as defined by Spigel, (2017), consists of eleven traits that give entrepreneurs security, encouragement, and access to resources. Aspects include supporting culture, entrepreneurial history, investor talent, networks, advisers, and successful businesses, as well as academics, virtual infrastructure, and market support (Spigel, 2017; Spigel & Harrison, 2018). Researchers have put forth various frameworks for explaining the role of the entrepreneurial journey which should be a combination of different elements including affirmative culture, streamlined policies and leadership, access to exclusive funding, fair utilization of labor, user-friendly product markets, and a variety of institutional and infrastructure support (Isenberg, 2014). Further, the interaction of stakeholders in the physical environment as well as access to a variety of intangible resources, such as skill set, services, and capital, interconnected in cutting-edge settings further contribute to the ecosystem (Feld, 2012).

In one of its investigations, Oxford Global Innovation Consultancy recommends a simple method for identifying ecosystem gaps. The business ecosystem consists mostly of academic and research institutions, government agencies, business and industrial groups, and other non-profit organizations. A framework for ecosystem support based on the Babson Entrepreneurship Ecosystem Project seeks to develop world-class entrepreneurs (Isenberg, 2010) Babson Business Entrepreneurship focuses on six key areas that are essential for creating a strong business case at the national level, including a corporate governance culture characterized by social trends and success stories, a financial infrastructure that is accessible to entrepreneurs, and a high level of staff due to the quality of the educational systems used and the character of the staff. Each modern business environment is as distinct as the environment we are in because hundreds of ecosystems interact in complicated and polarising ways (Isenberg, 2011).

Because the stakeholders in these areas view entrepreneurs and startups as distinct entities with a variety of skills and resources and the capacity to function in social and commercial contexts, the approach to the entrepreneurship ecosystem is unique to industrial districts, suburbs, and regions with high concentrations of tech clusters. Recent publications on the business environment. Feld, (2012), Isenberg, (2011), and Spigel (2017), have suggested effective company success and its impact on technological entrepreneurship without clearly articulating and demonstrating the origins and impacts of these effects.

GUJARAT ENTREPRENEURIAL ECOSYSTEM

Gujarat is one of those ecosystems where the state government has pledged to an enormous number of startups right from the seed stage by providing support with early-stage grants. Through student startup interventions at several technology and non-technology universities, Gujarat made systematic efforts at its pre-incubation layer. Gujarat's ecosystem has been significantly shaped by ecosystem actors from the non-government sector, particularly from the perspectives of mentoring, early investment, and incubation. In the most recent Gujarat Budget, more than 200 crores were distributed to several departments of the Government of Gujarat to stimulate entrepreneurship. The state government has launched several programs to direct these financial resources. Some of these prominent programs are, (a) a scheme for availing assistance to startups/ innovations under Gujarat Industrial Policy (2015), which emphasizes recognizing Nodal Institutions (NIs) in the state for extending startup support, (b) the Student Startup and Innovation Policy, governed by Gujarat

Knowledge Society, Directorate of Technical Education, and (c) Electronics & IT/ ITeS Start-up Policy for the state of Gujarat (2016-21) governed by Department of Science & Technology (DST), Govt. of Gujarat (GoG).

Along with initiatives and support from the government, various corporate institutions, trade associations, and academia have come together for the same. It is very interesting to note that many states have scaled up institutional mechanisms based on the Gujarat ecosystem's lessons learned. Pre-incubation and university startup ideas in Kerala, Andhra Pradesh, and across the nation through AICTE have drawn a lot of inspiration from Gujarat-driven academic projects. While the Gujarat startup ecosystem is envisioning modern mechanisms and institutions to cater to knowledge-driven startup needs as well, it has already acted quite early in the 1980s by institutionalizing its processes through entities like the Centre for Entrepreneurship Development (CED), Industrial Extension Bureau (iNDEXTb), and others.

If we look at Figure 1, the Ahmedabad district has the most DST-approved TBIs which comes to 21, 8 of which are supported by both commercial and public educational institutions. These TBIs also oversee NI, and it should be emphasized that 28 of the 33 NI they oversee—which are recognized under the Gujarat Industrial Policy-2015's startup program—were established in academic institutions. The research, project, and incubation activities taking place across Gujarat's academic institutions and universities are the foundation of the supply side of the technology and innovation value chain of the Gujarat ecosystem. The State's incubation support structure can be broadly mapped by Tables 1 and 2.

Table 1. Gujarat state's incubation support by government schemes or department

SN	Schemes and (or) Department	No. of Incubation Centres
1	Startup Scheme, Industries Commissionerate, GoG	33
2	Student Startup & Innovation Policy, Directorate of Technical Education, GoG - University Incubators	19
3	Department of Electronics and Information Technology (DEIty) by Ministry of Electronics and Information Technology (MEITy)	2
4	Ministry of Human Resource Development (MHRD)	4
5	Department of Biotechnology	2
6	Ministry of Micro, Small, and Medium Enterprises (MSME)	6
7	Science and Technology Parks	4
8	Atal Incubation Centres	4
9	Science and Technology Entrepreneurship Parks, DST, GoI	2

Source: Author

Table 2. additional institutional setups in the Gujarat state

Additional Institutional Setups	Numbers
Fab Labs	33
IP Facilitation Centres	4
Pre-Incubation Facilities	57
Regional Innovation Centres	4

Source: Author

Figure 1. Gujarat entrepreneurial ecosystem – district-wise distribution of institutional setups and incubators
(Source: Author)

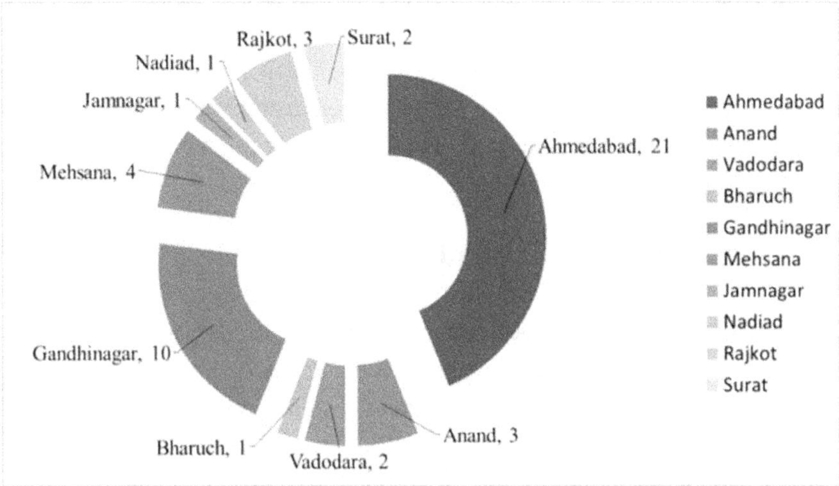

TECHNOLOGY BUSINESS INCUBATORS (TBIS) IN ENHANCING ENTREPRENEURIAL ECOSYSTEMS

For many years, science, technology, and innovation have advanced together. The entrepreneurial input and the surrounding support structure, which includes institutional setup, have a significant impact on the creation of new technology-based inventions. The development of mobility indicators between innovators and other organizations, across sectors that produce and use research, and inside businesses is necessary. The market incentives that drive technology endeavors like research and development by businesses and result in a competitive advantage have been recommended to be mapped. Such work also produces knowledge spillover, which boosts overall economic growth and increases economic competitiveness.

It essentially illustrates the precise function that technology entrepreneurs play by developing new concepts, obtaining patents, and entering markets.

Technology Business Incubators (TBIs) support the early stage and development of startups by offering various technological, managerial, and other administrative support. National Business Incubation Association (NBIA), has identified main goal of an incubator is to create profitable, self-sustaining businesses. The goal of the incubator is to help aspiring business owners get off the ground. A business consultant can help bridge the gap that exists in many areas from mentoring to funding support. By offering entrepreneurs fundamental training, the chance to launch a firm, and in certain circumstances, the chance to interact with other potential future investors in the company, incubator programs fill the gap (Burns & Jim, 1996).

TBIs aim to use technology, resources, and first-hand experience to foster entrepreneurial talent, speed up the growth of the art industry, and ultimately speed up the selling of technology (Hackett & Dilts, 2004a, 2004b). They collaborate closely with colleges, research facilities, and technological parks. Technology business incubators are an endeavor to offer a supportive environment for technology-based businesses, new product and service development for the technology sector, and new market delivery.

Technology Business Incubation: Gujarat

Gujarat is making significant investments in creating a solid ecosystem for fostering innovation and startups to promote job growth and drive economic expansion. As per the information from GoG, the state has an ambitious goal to build about 200,000 square meters of incubator space, construct about 100 incubators, and support at least 2,000 companies over the next few years. To date, Gujarat has given 175 businesses financial support totaling INR 220 million (IJSD 3 million) during the last two years. By 2021, the government had assisted 2,000 startups. 26 firms in the state are being sponsored by High-Net-Worth Individuals in addition to the 175 startups with government funding. The government has distributed institutional incubation support through several programs and projects that come under different departments (see Figure 2).

A typical model of incubation support in Gujarat state relates to helping startups in the form of mentoring, counsel, and resources. One of these is a very well-known event called a "Demo-Day," which aims to draw the startup investor community's attention to cutting-edge startup ideas by hosting a series of investment pitches from innovators to investors. TBIs typically provide physical places for shared resources and other incubation events in addition to offering dedicated office space or co-working space to startups (and sometimes even encouraging companies to locate

Figure 2. Showing government initiatives and schemes to support startups
(Source: Author)

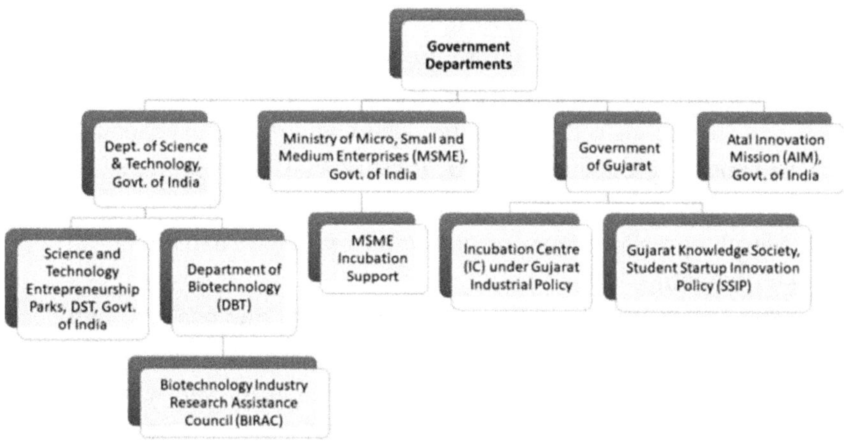

their own dedicated space). Business incubators frequently provide businesses with exclusive office and development space for a predetermined amount of time.

While having a discussion with TBI heads from the state, it was observed that business incubators get involved from the very beginning of a startup's development, from ideation to the stage where revenue is generated, and they can even go as far as the later growth stage. However, because this is the time at which most businesses normally benefit from outside assistance, most incubators tend to concentrate on relatively early-stage entrepreneurs. Incubated startups are often admitted in batches offering 1-3 batches every year during the incubator and accelerator's usual incubation procedure. While some are more generalist, some incubators concentrate on a particular industry, market, technology, stage, or other thrust areas. The majority attempt to conduct a screening and application process before incubation.

TBI's Role in Enhancing Operational Performance and Sustainability in Startups

Operational Performance

When it comes to assessing the performance of the startups, several elements (or factors) are highlighted which can be considered. The higher levels of technological exploration are predicted to slow down the outsourcing of research and development (R&D) activities and make it more expensive for new enterprises to achieve since doing so has a substantial influence and can contribute to long-term uncertainty and knowledge. It is anticipated to result from lower levels of outsourcing technologies when choosing sales and marketing initiatives that focus on technology-related goods and services (Koza et al., 1998; Koza & Lewin, 1998; Lavie & Rosenkopf, 2006). Marketing-related activities are frequently left out and unreliable (such as product performance information and expected benefits), leaving outsourcing to at least sales and marketing activities for products and services that contain high levels of technical knowledge and uncertainty. Because market outsourcing and sales are frequently less susceptible to the degree of exploration activity, we anticipate that improved levels of technical exploration activity will have a major negative impact on R&D outsourcing.

The performance measurement tool concept – "startup cockpit" introduced by Ripsas, Shaper, and Toger, (2018) focused on indicators such as customer service, financial vision, and procedure. These three indicators are relevant while investigating startup efficiency. Further indicators such as economic survival and profitability are believed to be assessed while evaluating financial forecasts. Liquidity, burn rate, margin analysis, and return on investment are further sub-layers of performance evaluation. From investors' perspective, client acquisition expenses, customer lifetime value, and learning curve can be other indicators.

As a startup expands, making decisions need more information. It is therefore frequently stated that startups should specialize in fields that are thought to be of utmost relevance to spend time and resources effectively and efficiently. Startups are therefore expected to perform better in areas that management deems more crucial and less significant.

Sustainability

Now when it comes to assessing the sustainability aspect of the startups, researchers have suggested evaluating the implementation phases. Building, measuring, and learning were the initial three stages as stated by Eric Ries, (2016). Successful startups complete the business iteration loop model in the early stages until training and insights from client feedback offer sufficient proof that the business model is successful and pertinent (Ries, 2016; Ries & Euchner, 2013; Ripsas et al., 2018a, 2018b; Ripsas & Hentschel, 2017)

Croll and Yoskovitz (2017),identified five basic categories that can be investigated when assessing the sustainability of startups, these include adherence, empathy, average customer experiences, vitality of product/service, and income generated. Empathy is the stage at which the needs of actual customers that cannot be satisfied are recognized. The most important aspect is when a startup learns how to address its demands and retain clients. Customers will promote a product or service to others if they are happy with the response. This is frequently the initial phase of a startup's existence. The startups are currently growing larger. After all, all startups must begin generating revenue (profit category). Startups are currently focusing on the concept of a resilient and long-lasting company model.

Analysing Sustainable Business Operations (SBO), which combines business management and sustainable business management, is yet another method of evaluating the sustainability of startups. SBO specifically examines how elements such as opportunities, environmental conditions, and economic progress are taken care of (Belz & Binder, 2017).SBO specifically evaluates social responsibility, economic performance, and environmental protection (Kuckertz & Wagner, 2010) and further accepts a public responsibility that involves environmental and social entrepreneurs since it provides continual care.

SCIENCE, TECHNOLOGY, INNOVATION, AND ENTREPRENEURSHIP POLICY FRAMEWORKS

The activities of its stakeholders are directed by specific policy support in order to create an environment that can promote innovations. The push toward technology-driven activities has been the focus of worldwide science, technology, and innovation policy in the previous two decades due to the rise in the number of technology entrepreneurs. The bulk of policy tools attempts to lower regulatory barriers to entrepreneurship due to the high risk involved and the longer gestation period in the technology-driven entrepreneurial process. It entails aiding in the form of improved access to money, information, and training while fostering an entrepreneurial culture. The support systems and fresh stakeholders that are available to technology-driven entrepreneurs have changed the entrepreneurial environment. The regional economies have been more significantly impacted by technological entrepreneurship Global Startup Ecosystem Report (2023). Due to this, regional economic strategies have been altered to incorporate entrepreneurial activities.

Adding the entrepreneurial economy model to the current science, technology, and innovation policies will cause volatility. Innovation is required in the setting of competitive dynamics in place of assurance and customization is required in place of expertise. The science, technology, and innovation policies, up until recently, were centered on the work being done in the specialist fields. However, as the economy shifts toward unpredictability, the entrepreneurial stakeholders must adapt and customize in order to master the art of flexibility (Nicotra et al., 2018; Romano et al., 2014). Interventions in policy must be adjusted with the necessary indicators.

It is also important to focus on specific initiatives that can support technology entrepreneurs by developing a structure of hand-holding support throughout various phases of venture growth over an extended period. In order to do this, relevant indicators' measurement techniques and their capacity to chart progress must be changed. The regional policy connects investment in knowledge, human capital, and infrastructure with the trajectory of technological growth.

CONCLUSION

Despite the evolution of natural entrepreneurs, data shows that incubators have improved and increased their function as training, communication, and advisory hubs for business owners in all sectors of expertise rather than as traditional business centers with offices. Incubators have prioritized raising the success rate of innovation by supporting entrepreneurs in overcoming their youth and young challenges, in addition to the diversity of perspectives and evolution of the models and services supplied (Dettwiler et al., 2006; Mireftekhari, 2017; Schwartz, 2013). Monitoring new technological developments has a significant impact and may help support long-term knowledge and uncertainties expected as a result of lower levels of outsourcing technologies when choosing sales and marketing, where increased levels of technology exploration are expected to slow the pace of outsourcing research and development activities and increase the cost of entry for new firms (Koza et al., 1998; Koza & Lewin, 1998; Lavie & Rosenkopf, 2005, 2006b, 2006a).

Figure 3. Showing the areas of importance for science, technology, innovation, and entrepreneurship policies
(Source: Author)

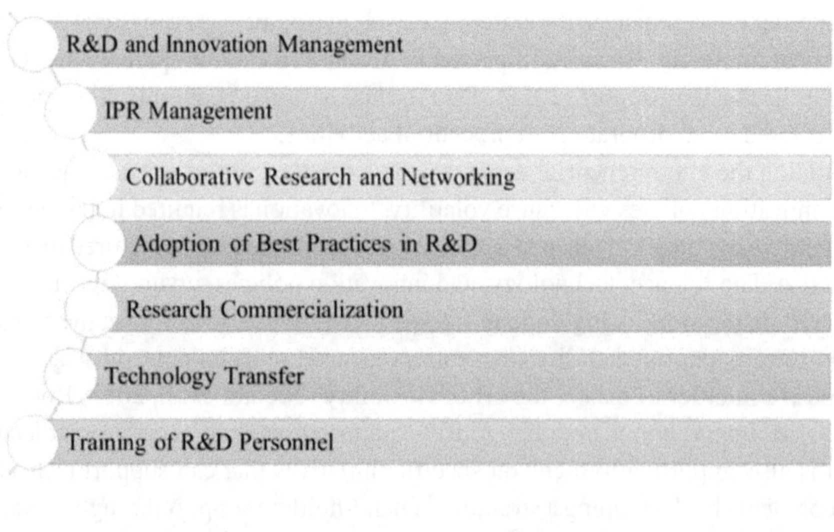

National Science, Technology, Innovation, and Entrepreneurship policies and strategies are thought to be essential for maximizing the benefits of new and emerging technologies. The following represents areas of vivid importance in policy implementation at the national level and further can be taken for future research (see Figure 3). Entrepreneurship reflects the entrepreneur's work with participation, creativity, and risk when assessing sustainability and performance efficiency. This chapter is an overview of various literature when assessing the operational performance and sustainability of startups. Further, we have also highlighted the science, technology, innovation, and entrepreneurship policies in enhancing the performance of technology-based applications from the support of technology business incubators. We have taken a reference from Gujarat, India as an ecosystem of strategic change in the field. the following chapter will be useful for scholars in the field and will be useful when assessing various players in the startup ecosystem.

REFERENCES

Acs, Z. J., Autio, E., & Szerb, L. (2012). National Systems of Entrepreneurship: Measurement Issues and Policy Implications. SSRN *Electronic Journal*. doi:10.2139/ssrn.2008160

Ács, Z. J., Autio, E., & Szerb, L. (2014). National Systems of Entrepreneurship: Measurement issues and policy implications. *Research Policy*, *43*(3), 476–494. Advance online publication. doi:10.1016/j.respol.2013.08.016

Ács, Z. J., Autio, E., & Szerb, L. (2016). National Systems of Entrepreneurship: Measurement issues and policy implications. In Global Entrepreneurship, Institutions and Incentives. doi:10.4337/9781784718053.00040

Alvedalen, J., & Boschma, R. (2017). A critical review of entrepreneurial ecosystems research: Towards a future research agenda. *European Planning Studies*, *25*(6), 887–903. doi:10.1080/09654313.2017.1299694

Belz, F. M., & Binder, J. K. (2017). Sustainable Entrepreneurship: A Convergent Process Model. *Business Strategy and the Environment*, *26*(1), 1–17. doi:10.1002/bse.1887

Burns, P., & Jim, D. (1996). Small business and entrepreneurship (Eds). Macmillan.

Cohen, B. (2006). Sustainable valley entrepreneurial ecosystems. *Business Strategy and the Environment*, *15*(1), 1–14. doi:10.1002/bse.428

Croll, A., & Yoskovitz, B. (2017). Lean Analytics: use data to build a better startup faster. O'Reilly, 53(9).

Dettwiler, P., Lindelöf, P., & Löfsten, H. (2006). Business environment and property management issues: A study of growth firms in Sweden. *Journal of Corporate Real Estate*, *8*(3), 120–133. Advance online publication. doi:10.1108/14630010610711748

Feld, B. (2012). Startup Communities: Building an Entrepreneurial Ecosystem in Your City. In Municipal World.

Global Startup Ecosystem Report 2023. (n.d.). *Startup Genome*. https://startupgenome.com/report/gser2023

Hackett, S. M., & Dilts, D. M. (2004a). A real options-driven theory of business incubation. *The Journal of Technology Transfer*, *29*(1), 41–54. doi:10.1023/B:JOTT.0000011180.19370.36

Hackett, S. M., & Dilts, D. M. (2004b). A Systematic Review of Business Incubation Research. *The Journal of Technology Transfer*, *29*(1), 55–82. doi:10.1023/B:JOTT.0000011181.11952.0f

Isenberg, D. (2010). *How to Start an Entrepreneurial Revolution*. HBR. www.hbr.org

Isenberg, D. (2011). *The Entrepreneurship Ecosystem Strategy as a New Paradigm for Economic Policy: Principles for Cultivating Entrepreneurship*. Institute of International and European Affairs.

Isenberg, D. (2014). What an Entrepreneurship Ecosystem Actually Is. *Harvard Business Review*.

Koza, M. P., & Lewin, A. Y. (1998). The Co-evolution of Strategic Alliances. *Organization Science*, *9*(3), 255–264. Advance online publication. doi:10.1287/orsc.9.3.255

Koza, M. P., Lewin, A. Y., Science, S. O., Issue, S., Partnerships, M., Koza, M. P., & Lewin, A. Y. (1998). The Co-Evolution of Strategic Alliances Linked references are available on JSTOR for this article : The Co-evolution of Strategic Alliances. *Organization Science*, *9*(3), 255–264. doi:10.1287/orsc.9.3.255

Kuckertz, A., & Wagner, M. (2010). The influence of sustainability orientation on entrepreneurial intentions - Investigating the role of business experience. *Journal of Business Venturing*, *25*(5), 524–539. Advance online publication. doi:10.1016/j.jbusvent.2009.09.001

Lavie, D., & Rosenkopf, L. (2005). Balancing exploration and exploitation in alliance formation: A multidimensional perspective. *Academy of Management 2005 Annual Meeting: A New Vision of Management in the 21st Century, AOM 2005*. IEEE. 10.5465/ambpp.2005.18778391

Lavie, D., & Rosenkopf, L. (2006a). Balancing exploration and exploitation in alliance formation. *Academy of Management Journal*, *49*(4), 797–818. doi:10.5465/amj.2006.22083085

Lavie, D., & Rosenkopf, L. (2006b). BALANCING EXPLORATION AND EXPLOITATION IN ALLIANCE FORMATION University of Texas at Austin. *Academy of Management Journal*, *49*(4). doi:10.5465/amj.2006.22083085

Mireftekhari, S. (2017). *Business incubator, a solution for startup's challenges. A qualitative look at business incubator's support for startups to overcome the liability of newness and smallness*. DUO. https://www.duo.uio.no/handle/10852/57517

Neck, H. M., Meyer, G. D., Cohen, B., & Corbett, A. C. (2004). An Entrepreneurial System View of New Venture Creation. In Journal of Small Business Management (Vol. 42, Issue 2). doi:10.1111/j.1540-627X.2004.00105.x

Nicotra, M., Romano, M., Del Giudice, M., & Schillaci, C. E. (2018). The causal relation between entrepreneurial ecosystem and productive entrepreneurship: A measurement framework. *The Journal of Technology Transfer*, *43*(3), 640–673. doi:10.1007/s10961-017-9628-2

Oxford Global Innovation Consultancy. (n.d.). *Oxentia*. Oxford's Global Innovation Consultancy. https://www.oxentia.com/

Ries, E. (2016). *The Lean Startup by Eric Ries*. The Starta.

Ries, E., & Euchner, J. (2013). Conversations: What Large Companies Can Learn from Start-ups: An Interview with Eric Ries. *Research Technology Management*, *56*(4), 12–16. doi:10.5437/08956308X5604003

Ripsas, S., & Hentschel, B. (2017). Vom Businessplan zum Startup-Cockpit. In Crowd Entrepreneurship. Springer. doi:10.1007/978-3-658-17031-8_4

Ripsas, S., Schaper, B., & Tröger, S. (2018a). A Startup Cockpit for the Proof-of-Concept. In Handbuch Entrepreneurship. Springer. doi:10.1007/978-3-658-04994-2_21

Ripsas, S., Schaper, B., & Tröger, S. (2018b). A Startup Cockpit for the Proof-of-Concept. In Handbuch Entrepreneurship. Springer. doi:10.1007/978-3-658-05263-8_21-2

Romano, A., Passiante, G., Del Vecchio, P., & Secundo, G. (2014). The innovation ecosystem as booster for the innovative entrepreneurship in the smart specialisation strategy. *International Journal of Knowledge-Based Development*, *5*(3), 271–288. doi:10.1504/IJKBD.2014.065315

Schwartz, M. (2013). A control group study of incubators' impact to promote firm survival. *The Journal of Technology Transfer*, *38*(3), 302–331. doi:10.1007/s10961-012-9254-y

Spigel, B. (2017). The Relational Organization of Entrepreneurial Ecosystems. *Entrepreneurship Theory and Practice*, *41*(1), 49–72. Advance online publication. doi:10.1111/etap.12167

Spigel, B., & Harrison, R. (2018). Toward a process theory of entrepreneurial ecosystems. *Strategic Entrepreneurship Journal*, *12*(1), 151–168. doi:10.1002/sej.1268

Van De Ven, H. (1993). The development of an infrastructure for entrepreneurship. *Journal of Business Venturing*, *8*(3), 211–230. doi:10.1016/0883-9026(93)90028-4

Chapter 3
Blockchain and Entrepreneurship

Kande Archana
Malla Reddy College of Engineering, India

Aarti Gloth
Malla Reddy College of Engineering, India

ABSTRACT

Blockchain technology has emerged as a disruptive force with the potential to reshape entrepreneurship and business ventures across various industries. Its decentralized, immutable ledger system offers a foundation for innovative solutions, fostering transparency, security, and efficiency. Entrepreneurs are harnessing blockchain for a myriad of applications, from supply chain management to tokenized assets and decentralized finance (DeFi). This chapter delves into the symbiotic relationship between blockchain and entrepreneurship, exploring the transformative role of blockchain in startups, raising capital through initial coin offerings (ICOs), and streamlining processes through smart contracts. As this decentralized ledger technology continues to evolve, entrepreneurs face not only opportunities for innovation but also regulatory and scalability challenges. A comprehensive understanding of blockchain's impact on entrepreneurship is crucial for navigating this evolving landscape, fostering new business models, and realizing the full potential of blockchain technology.

DOI: 10.4018/979-8-3693-1846-1.ch003

INTRODUCTION

In the realm of entrepreneurship, the fusion of blockchain technology has given rise to a landscape of unprecedented opportunities and innovations. This introductory exploration will focus on the profound impact of blockchain on entrepreneurship, with a specific emphasis on its diverse applications that are reshaping the entrepreneurial landscape. Before delving into its applications, let's establish a fundamental understanding of blockchain. At its core, blockchain is a decentralized and tamper-resistant digital ledger that records transactions across a distributed network of computers. Unlike traditional centralized systems, blockchain operates on a trustless network, where transactions are verified by consensus, enhancing security and transparency.

Blockchain's inception can be traced back to the release of Bitcoin in 2009, credited to an entity or individual known as Satoshi Nakamoto. Bitcoin was the pioneering application of blockchain technology, introducing the concept of a decentralized digital currency. However, blockchain's potential extends well beyond cryptocurrencies, impacting a wide array of industries and entrepreneurial endeavors. Blockchain technology has catalyzed a wave of transformation in entrepreneurship through various applications:

1. Cryptocurrency Ventures: Cryptocurrencies like Bitcoin and Ethereum have enabled entrepreneurs to create new digital currencies and decentralized financial platforms, revolutionizing how we store and transfer value.
2. Initial Coin Offerings (ICOs): Entrepreneurs can raise capital through ICOs, allowing for the democratization of investment opportunities for projects and startups.
3. Smart Contracts: These self-executing contracts, written in code, automate business processes, reducing the need for intermediaries and enhancing trust in transactions.
4. Supply Chain Management: Blockchain offers end-to-end transparency and traceability in supply chains, reducing fraud, ensuring product quality, and fostering consumer trust.
5. Identity Verification: Blockchain-based digital identities are transforming industries like finance, healthcare, and e-commerce by providing secure, verifiable identification.
6. Intellectual Property Protection: Entrepreneurs can timestamp and protect intellectual property rights using blockchain, reducing the risk of copyright infringement.
7. Global Market Access: Blockchain's decentralized nature facilitates entry into the global market, eliminating geographical barriers for entrepreneurs.

While the potential of blockchain applications in entrepreneurship is vast, entrepreneurs must navigate challenges and risks. These include regulatory complexities, scalability issues, interoperability concerns, and the need to adapt to an evolving technology landscape.

The future of blockchain entrepreneurship is a canvas of promise. Entrepreneurs are at the forefront of innovation, continually finding new ways to apply blockchain solutions across various industries, pushing the boundaries of what's achievable. Success in this dynamic landscape depends on adaptability, a forward-thinking mindset, and a willingness to seize emerging opportunities.

The integration of blockchain technology and entrepreneurship is a powerful force driving change in traditional business models. It offers the potential to disrupt industries, empower individuals, and stimulate global economic transformation. In the upcoming segments of this series, we will dive deeper into specific applications of blockchain in entrepreneurship, explore real-world examples, and analyze the regulatory considerations shaping this dynamic intersection. Join us on this exciting journey into the world of blockchain and its applications in entrepreneurship.

LITERATURE SURVEY

A literature survey on the intersection of blockchain and entrepreneurship reveals a rich and dynamic landscape, brimming with research, insights, and diverse perspectives. This survey aims to provide an overview of key themes and seminal works in this field, illustrating the depth and breadth of knowledge that has been amassed. While this list is not exhaustive, it offers a representative sample of notable contributions to the understanding of blockchain's impact on entrepreneurship.

"Blockchain and Smart Contracts for Supply Chain Management: A Literature Review" (2021) by Mohammad T. Uddin, Emmanouil Stiakakis, Sanjiban Sekhor Nath This review paper provides insights into the applications of blockchain and smart contracts in supply chain management, shedding light on their impact on entrepreneurship. It discusses the challenges and opportunities associated with blockchain adoption in supply chain processes.

"Blockchain Entrepreneurship: Decentralized and Distributed Autonomous Organizations" (2019) by John M. Kline and Phillip L. Swint This research paper explores the emergence of decentralized and distributed autonomous organizations (DAOs) enabled by blockchain technology. It discusses the entrepreneurial implications of these new organizational structures and the challenges they pose for traditional businesses. "The Impact of Blockchain Technology on Business: A Systematic Review" (2018) by Simon Oberthür, Carsten H. Gellings, and Anette Mikes This systematic review examines the impact of blockchain technology on various business aspects. It provides insights into the opportunities and challenges that entrepreneurs may encounter when integrating blockchain into their operations. “Blockchain for the Internet of Things: A Systematic Literature Review” (2018) by Monica Ribeiro, João Marco Cunha, and Akebo Yamakami This literature review explores the integration of blockchain and the Internet of Things (IoT) and its relevance to entrepreneurship. It delves into the potential applications of blockchain in IoT-based entrepreneurial ventures. “Smart Contracts in Healthcare: The Prisma Project Approach” (2017) by Maurizio Veca, Francesco Napolitano, and Angelo P. Giordano Focusing on smart contracts, this paper discusses their role in healthcare and the potential for entrepreneurial ventures in this sector. It offers insights into how blockchain technology can disrupt the healthcare industry, creating entrepreneurial opportunities. “The Potential and Challenges of Blockchain in Entrepreneurship” (2017) by Carlos Agostinho, Sergio Lopes, and Bruno Oliveira This research paper assesses the potential and challenges of blockchain technology in entrepreneurship. It delves into the benefits of blockchain adoption, including enhanced transparency and security, while also addressing scalability and regulatory issues. “Blockchain for the Internet of Things: A Systematic Literature Review” (2017) by Luca Valcarenghi, Riccardo Rovatti, and Gianluca M. Cornetta This systematic literature review explores the integration of blockchain technology with the Internet of Things (IoT). It discusses the potential applications of blockchain in IoT-driven entrepreneurial initiatives. “Decentralized Applications: Harnessing Bitcoin’s Blockchain Technology” (2016) by Siraj Raval and Maksim Balashev. This paper provides insights into decentralized applications (DApps) and their connection to blockchain technology. It discusses how DApps can offer entrepreneurial opportunities in a decentralized, trustless ecosystem. “Blockchain: A Brief Primer and Its Entrepreneurial Potential in Financial Services” (2016) by Richard T. Harrison and Jongmin Lee. Focusing on the financial services sector, this paper offers a primer on blockchain technology and explores its entrepreneurial potential in the context of FinTech, digital payments, and financial innovation. “Blockchain Technology in the Chemical Industry: Machine-to-Machine Electricity Market” (2014) by Isaac Arthur, Stephanie Hurder, and Britanny Arthur. “Bitcoin: A Peer-to-Peer Electronic Cash System” (2008) by Satoshi Nakamoto. The foundational whitepaper introducing Bitcoin and its underlying blockchain technology. “Bitcoin: An Innovative Alternative Digital Currency” (2011) by Iwa Salami

An exploration of the entrepreneurial potential of Bitcoin and cryptocurrencies. “The Blockchain: A New Framework for Robotic Process Automation” (2016) by Nick White Discusses the potential of blockchain in automating business processes and its implications for entrepreneurship. “Blockchain Technology as Disruptive Innovation” (2017) by Matheus F. C. A. Martins and Luis G. G. M. Meirelles. Explores the disruptive potential of blockchain technology and its implications for entrepreneurs. "Understanding Bitcoin: Cryptography, Engineering, and Economics" (2018) by Pedro Franco. An interdisciplinary approach to understanding Bitcoin's technology, economics, and entrepreneurial significance. "Initial Coin Offerings: Financing growth with cryptocurrency token sales" (2018) by Sabrina T. Howell, Marina Niessner, and David Yermack. Explores ICOs and their role in entrepreneurial fundraising. "Smart Contracts: Bridging the Gap Between Expectation and Reality" (2019) by Li Ming Wong and Daniel Reijsbergen . Discusses the implications of smart contracts in blockchain technology and entrepreneurship. "Blockchain Technology and Its Applications" (2019) by Bhavesh Borisaniya et al. Explores blockchain technology applications across various industries, including entrepreneurship. "Blockchain Business Models" (2020) by Karim Lakhani, Marco Lansiti, and Karim R. Lakhani. Analyzes different business models that blockchain technology enables and their implications for entrepreneurship. "Entrepreneurship and the Blockchain: A New Paradigm for The Social Sciences" (2021) by Jason Potts and Chris Berg. Explores the broad implications of blockchain technology for entrepreneurship and the social sciences.

THE EVOLUTION OF BLOCKCHAIN

The evolution of blockchain technology can be categorized into three main phases, often referred to as Blockchain 1.0, 2.0, and 3.0. These phases represent distinct stages in the development of blockchain systems, each marked by unique characteristics, use cases, and innovations.

Blockchain 1.0: Digital Currency (2008 - Early 2010s): Blockchain 1.0 is synonymous with the creation of Bitcoin and the emergence of the first blockchain-based cryptocurrency. Key features of this phase include:

- Bitcoin's Birth: The release of the Bitcoin whitepaper by Satoshi Nakamoto in 2008 marked the beginning of blockchain technology. Bitcoin, as a digital currency, was designed to facilitate peer-to-peer transactions without the need for intermediaries.
- Mining and Consensus: Blockchain 1.0 introduced the concept of proof-of-work (PoW) consensus mechanisms, which played a crucial role in validating and securing transactions. Miners would use their computing power to solve complex mathematical puzzles in exchange for newly created Bitcoins and transaction fees.
- Digital Currency Dominance: During this period, the primary use case of blockchain was as a digital currency, focusing on peer-to-peer payments and financial transactions.

Blockchain 2.0: Smart Contracts and Decentralized Applications (Mid-2010s - Late 2010s): Blockchain 2.0 represented a significant leap beyond digital currency, introducing the concept of smart contracts and expanding the capabilities of blockchain technology:

- Ethereum and Smart Contracts: Ethereum, launched in 2015 by Vitalik Buterin, was a groundbreaking development. It allowed developers to create decentralized applications (DApps) with self-executing smart contracts, which are code-based agreements that automatically execute when predefined conditions are met.
- Interoperability: The emergence of blockchain platforms like Ethereum led to the development of a wide range of DApps and tokens. Interoperability between different blockchains became a focus, as projects aimed to address issues of scalability and compatibility.
- Initial Coin Offerings (ICOs): Blockchain 2.0 also saw the rise of ICOs, a novel fundraising method that enabled startups to raise capital by issuing tokens on blockchain platforms. This innovation democratized access to investment opportunities.

Figure 1. The evolution of blockchain

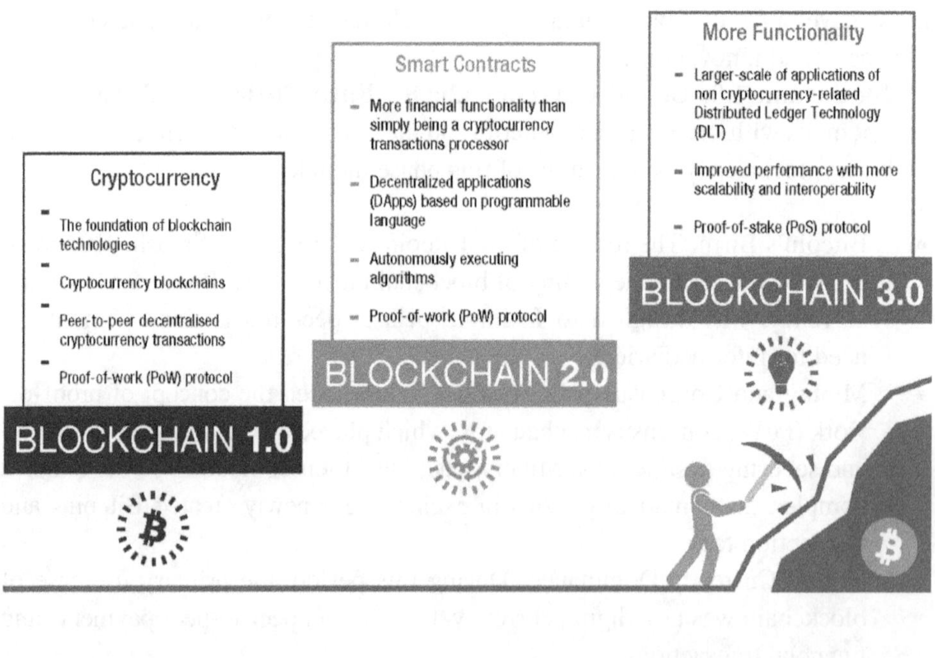

Blockchain 3.0: Scalability, Interoperability, and Real-World Applications (Late 2010s - Present): Blockchain 3.0 represents the current phase of blockchain technology, characterized by efforts to address scalability, interoperability, and real-world applications:

- Scalability Solutions: To overcome the limitations of early blockchains, various scalability solutions, such as sharding and Layer 2 solutions (e.g., Lightning Network for Bitcoin), are being developed to increase transaction throughput and reduce fees.
- Interoperability Standards: Interoperability is a key focus in Blockchain 3.0. Projects like Polkadot and Cosmos aim to connect multiple blockchains, enabling the seamless transfer of assets and data between different networks.
- Real-World Use Cases: Blockchain technology is increasingly being applied to real-world problems beyond finance. Industries like supply chain management, healthcare, identity verification, and voting systems are exploring blockchain's potential for transparency, security, and efficiency.
- Proof-of-Stake (PoS): Many projects are transitioning from PoW to PoS consensus mechanisms to reduce energy consumption and improve scalability.
- DeFi, NFTs, and Web3: The rise of Decentralized Finance (DeFi) platforms and Non-Fungible Tokens (NFTs) is indicative of the diversification of use cases in Blockchain 3.0, focusing on decentralized financial services and unique digital assets.

Blockchain technology has evolved significantly over the years, with each phase building upon the innovations of the previous one. While the journey of blockchain is ongoing, the potential for transformative applications and further advancements in technology remains promising.

How Does Works Blockchain Technology on Entrepreneurship

Blockchain technology plays a fundamental role in facilitating transactions through networks in the realm of entrepreneurship. Here's how it works:

- **Decentralized Ledger:**

Blockchain is a decentralized and distributed ledger technology. It consists of a network of computers (nodes) that maintain an identical copy of the ledger. When a transaction occurs, it is added to a block, which is then linked to the previous block, creating a chronological chain of transactions.

Figure 2. Works on blockchain technology on entrepreneurship

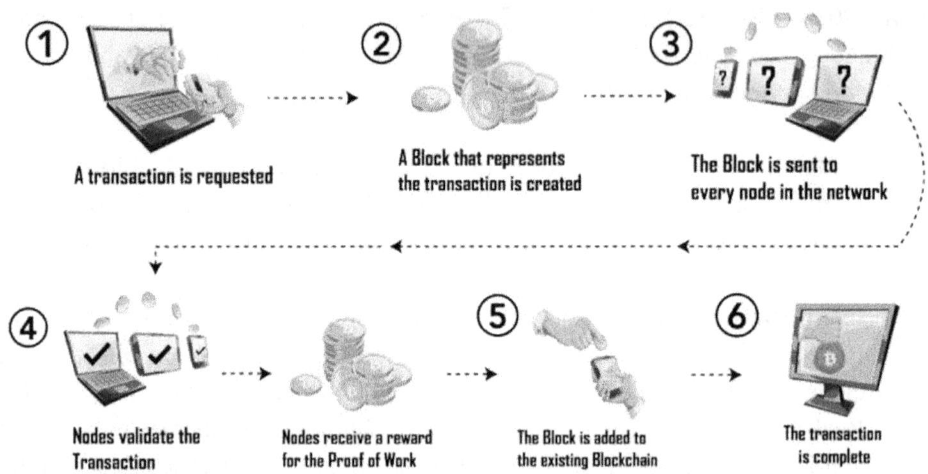

- **Transaction Initiation:**

An entrepreneur initiates a transaction by creating a digital record of it. This record can represent various types of transactions, including financial payments, the transfer of digital assets, the creation of a smart contract, or the logging of supply chain data.

- **Digital Signatures:**

Transactions on the blockchain are secured using digital signatures. The entrepreneur signs the transaction with their private key to prove ownership and authorization. The recipient, in turn, can verify the transaction's authenticity using the entrepreneur's public key.

- **Validation and Consensus:**

Once a transaction is initiated, it is broadcast to the network of nodes. These nodes collectively validate the transaction to ensure it follows the rules and adheres to the consensus mechanism (e.g., proof-of-work or proof-of-stake). Consensus mechanisms vary depending on the blockchain platform.

- **Mining (Proof of Work):**

In a proof-of-work (PoW) blockchain, miners compete to solve complex mathematical puzzles. The first miner to solve the puzzle gets the right to add the new block of transactions to the blockchain. This process is resource-intensive and requires significant computational power.

- **Block Confirmation:**

Once the block containing the transaction is confirmed by the network, it is added to the blockchain. The transaction is now considered finalized, and the data is recorded in an immutable and transparent manner.

- **Immutable Records:**

Blockchain's immutability means that once a transaction is recorded on the blockchain, it cannot be altered or deleted. This feature ensures the integrity of transaction records, reducing the risk of fraud and disputes.

- **Transaction Finality:**

The transaction is considered final when it is added to the blockchain. This finality is one of the key benefits of blockchain technology, as it reduces the need for trust in a centralized authority to verify transactions.

- **Blockchain Networks:**

Different blockchain networks may have varying transaction processing speeds, costs, and consensus mechanisms. Public blockchains, like Bitcoin and Ethereum, are open to anyone and can handle a global volume of transactions. Private or consortium blockchains may have faster transaction speeds and controlled access for specific participants.

- **Smart Contracts:**

In addition to simple transactions, entrepreneurs can also deploy smart contracts on certain blockchain platforms. Smart contracts are self-executing programs that automatically perform actions based on predefined conditions. These can streamline complex business processes and reduce the need for intermediaries.

- **Global Transactions:**

Blockchain technology allows for cross-border transactions without the need for currency conversion or traditional intermediaries. This can be particularly advantageous for global entrepreneurship, facilitating international trade and cooperation.

In summary, blockchain technology provides a decentralized, transparent, and secure environment for conducting and recording transactions in entrepreneurship. It eliminates the reliance on centralized intermediaries, reduces the risk of fraud, and opens up new possibilities for innovative business models, automation through smart contracts, and efficient global transactions.

OVERVIEW ON RESEARCH DETAILS ON BLOCKCHAIN TECHNOLOGY AND ENTREPRENEURSHIP

Blockchain technology and entrepreneurship have become focal points of research, capturing the imagination of academics, business leaders, and policymakers. The interplay between these two domains has spurred an array of studies and investigations, shedding light on the opportunities, challenges, and implications for both fields. In this overview, we'll explore the current state of research in blockchain and entrepreneurship, highlighting key themes and findings.

One prominent area of research examines how entrepreneurs and startups are adopting blockchain technology to revolutionize traditional business models. Researchers have documented various use cases, such as supply chain management, digital identity verification, and intellectual property protection, to understand the impact on entrepreneurship. Studies on blockchain-based fundraising mechanisms, such as Initial Coin Offerings (ICOs) and Security Token Offerings (STOs), have analyzed the dynamics of these alternative financing options for startups. Researchers explore the factors influencing the success of ICOs and the challenges they pose in terms of regulation and investor protection.

Smart contracts, a cornerstone of blockchain technology, have been a subject of interest for researchers. They examine how these self-executing contracts can automate various aspects of business operations and enhance trust in entrepreneurial transactions. Research in this domain focuses on how blockchain can transform supply chain management. It assesses the impact of blockchain on reducing fraud, improving transparency, and enhancing consumer trust within supply chains. Case studies provide insights into the practical applications of blockchain in this area.

The evolving regulatory landscape concerning blockchain and cryptocurrency is a crucial research topic. Scholars delve into the challenges and opportunities presented by regulatory frameworks, aiming to provide recommendations for achieving a balance between innovation and compliance. Research investigates how blockchain's decentralized nature enables entrepreneurs to access global markets and scale their businesses across borders. This exploration touches on the challenges related to cross-border transactions and regulatory disparities.

The protection of intellectual property rights through blockchain is a subject of interest, particularly for entrepreneurs. Researchers examine how blockchain can help timestamp and safeguard intellectual property, reducing the risks of infringement. The security and privacy implications of blockchain technology are another key area of research. It involves exploring the vulnerabilities, threats, and privacy challenges associated with blockchain applications in entrepreneurship. Understanding the barriers to blockchain adoption in entrepreneurship is a central research theme. These studies investigate factors such as scalability issues, interoperability challenges, and the readiness of entrepreneurs to embrace this emerging technology.

Researchers analyze real-world case studies to provide insights into successful blockchain entrepreneurship ventures and their impact on various industries. These studies offer valuable lessons and best practices for aspiring entrepreneurs. Blockchain and entrepreneurship research often adopts an interdisciplinary approach, drawing from fields like economics, computer science, law, and sociology to provide a holistic understanding of the technology's impact on entrepreneurial endeavors. In line with the rapidly evolving nature of blockchain and entrepreneurship, research also anticipates future trends and innovations. Researchers attempt to forecast how emerging technologies like DeFi (Decentralized Finance) and NFTs (Non-Fungible Tokens) will shape the entrepreneurial landscape.

The current research landscape at the intersection of blockchain and entrepreneurship is rich and diverse. It encompasses a wide array of topics, from practical applications and regulatory challenges to the exploration of emerging trends and innovations. As the blockchain space continues to evolve, research in this domain will remain a vital source of knowledge, guiding entrepreneurs, policymakers, and academics in harnessing the full potential of this transformative technology.

RESEARCH ON BUSINESS AND ECONOMICS USING ENTREPRENEURSHIP

Entrepreneurship is a driving force in the world of business and economics, continuously shaping industries, creating jobs, and fostering innovation. Research in this field is multifaceted and dynamic, exploring various dimensions of entrepreneurial activities, from startup ventures to established enterprises. In this comprehensive overview, we will delve into the wide-ranging research on business and economics through the lens of entrepreneurship, examining key areas of investigation and their implications.

- **Entrepreneurial Ecosystems**

Understanding the ecosystems that foster entrepreneurship is a central theme in research. Studies explore how local, national, and global factors, including access to capital, supportive policies, educational institutions, and networking opportunities, influence the development of entrepreneurship.

- **Startups and Innovation**

Research often focuses on the dynamics of startups and their role in fostering innovation. Studies investigate how innovative business models, disruptive technologies, and creative problem-solving drive economic growth and competition.

- **Entrepreneurial Finance**

Examining the financial aspects of entrepreneurship is crucial. Research in this area delves into funding sources, investment strategies, and the impact of crowdfunding, venture capital, and angel investors on business development.

- **Small and Medium-sized Enterprises (SMEs)**

The contribution of SMEs to the economy is a prominent research topic. Studies analyze the challenges and opportunities faced by small and medium-sized enterprises, including their role in job creation, economic resilience, and international expansion.

- **Social and Sustainable Entrepreneurship**

Researchers investigate how entrepreneurship can be a force for social and environmental good. Studies delve into the growing field of social entrepreneurship, emphasizing the creation of businesses with a positive impact on society and the planet.

- **Entrepreneurial Education**

The role of education in nurturing entrepreneurial skills and mindsets is a key area of research. Studies assess the effectiveness of entrepreneurship education programs and their impact on the success of entrepreneurs.

- **Women and Minority Entrepreneurship**

Research explores the experiences and challenges faced by women and minority entrepreneurs. It aims to understand the factors that influence their success and identify ways to promote diversity and inclusion in entrepreneurship.

- **International Entrepreneurship**

Cross-border entrepreneurship is an evolving field of study. Research investigates the motivations and challenges of international expansion, including market entry strategies, cultural considerations, and the role of technology in globalization.

- **Technology and Digital Entrepreneurship**

The digital transformation has brought technology-driven entrepreneurship to the forefront. Research examines the impact of digitalization on business models, e-commerce, and emerging trends in areas such as blockchain, artificial intelligence, and e-health.

- **Entrepreneurship Policy and Regulation**

The regulatory environment plays a critical role in entrepreneurship. Research evaluates the effectiveness of policies and regulations in supporting or hindering entrepreneurial activities, with a focus on areas like taxation, intellectual property, and business registration.

- **Family Business and Succession**

Research explores the unique challenges and opportunities associated with family-owned businesses. Studies investigate succession planning, governance structures, and the long-term sustainability of these enterprises.

- **Failure and Resilience**

Failure is an inherent part of entrepreneurship, and research acknowledges its role in the learning process. Studies examine the factors contributing to business failure and the strategies entrepreneurs employ to recover and thrive.

- **Entrepreneurial Networks and Collaboration**

Understanding the role of networks and collaboration in entrepreneurship is a growing field. Research explores how entrepreneurial ecosystems are shaped by networks, alliances, and partnerships.

- **Industry-specific Research**

Research in entrepreneurship extends to various industries, including healthcare, agriculture, fintech, and more. Studies investigate sector-specific challenges, opportunities, and innovations.

- **Impact Assessment**

Evaluating the impact of entrepreneurship on economic growth, job creation, and societal well-being is a central research theme. Researchers aim to quantify and understand the contributions of entrepreneurial activities to the broader economy.

Research in business and economics through the lens of entrepreneurship is a vibrant and ever-evolving field. It provides valuable insights into the mechanisms that drive economic growth, foster innovation, and shape our modern world. As the entrepreneurial landscape continues to transform, research remains an essential tool for policymakers, entrepreneurs, and scholars to navigate and harness the power of entrepreneurship in a rapidly changing global economy.

CONCLUSION

The intersection of blockchain technology and entrepreneurship has yielded transformative possibilities, redefining the landscape of business and innovation. In this culmination, we draw together the threads of our exploration, highlighting the key takeaways, and looking ahead to the future of this dynamic fusion. Blockchain empowers entrepreneurs by offering tools and platforms that challenge traditional business models. The elimination of intermediaries, cost reductions, and enhanced security and transparency create a fertile ground for innovation. Entrepreneurs can now disrupt industries, create new business models, and access global markets more easily than ever before. Blockchain-based fundraising methods, such as ICOs and STOs, democratize access to capital. Entrepreneurs can now raise funds globally without the need for traditional financial intermediaries. This presents both opportunities and challenges, as regulatory frameworks evolve to adapt to these novel approaches. Smart contracts, a hallmark of blockchain technology, automate processes, making business operations more efficient. These self-executing contracts reduce the need for human intervention, enhancing trust in agreements and transactions. They have the potential to revolutionize supply chain management, legal processes, and more. Blockchain's transparency and traceability make it a game-changer for supply chain management. Entrepreneurs can reduce fraud, ensure product quality, and build consumer trust by leveraging blockchain to track goods from production to delivery. This transparency also allows for ethical and sustainable sourcing. The establishment of secure digital identities on the blockchain is a breakthrough with far-reaching implications. Entrepreneurs are leveraging this technology to create trusted identity verification systems, improving security and streamlining processes in industries like finance, healthcare, and e-commerce. Entrepreneurs can use blockchain to protect intellectual property rights through timestamping and secure verification. This reduces the risk of copyright infringement and opens new avenues for content creators and innovators to safeguard their creations.

Blockchain's decentralized nature opens doors to global market expansion. Entrepreneurs can reach customers and partners worldwide, breaking down geographical barriers. This global reach can lead to increased opportunities and higher revenue potential. The regulatory environment for blockchain and cryptocurrencies is still evolving. Entrepreneurs face regulatory uncertainties and compliance challenges. Policymakers and industry stakeholders are working together to strike a balance between innovation and consumer protection, with regulations varying significantly across regions. Blockchain technology faces challenges in terms of interoperability and scalability. Entrepreneurs and developers need to address these issues to ensure that blockchain solutions can seamlessly integrate with existing systems and handle large transaction volumes.

The success of blockchain entrepreneurship relies on visionary leaders who can navigate the complex regulatory landscape, adapt to evolving technology, and identify untapped opportunities. Entrepreneurial spirit and innovation are the driving forces behind blockchain's continued evolution. The future of blockchain entrepreneurship holds promise. Emerging trends like Decentralized Finance (DeFi) and Non-Fungible Tokens (NFTs) are reshaping the landscape. Entrepreneurs will continue to pioneer new applications of blockchain technology, from cross-border payments and remittances to real-time data sharing and more. Collaboration within the blockchain ecosystem is essential for its growth. Entrepreneurs, developers, regulators, and consumers must work together to shape a secure and innovative environment that benefits society as a whole.

In conclusion, the fusion of blockchain technology and entrepreneurship is a dynamic and transformative force, reshaping industries, breaking down barriers, and challenging the status quo. It has the potential to drive economic growth, foster innovation, and empower individuals on a global scale. As this intersection continues to evolve, staying informed, adaptable, and proactive will be key to success for entrepreneurs in the blockchain space.

REFERENCES

Alcaraz, C., Zeadally, S., & Chakraborty, S. (2018). Fog computing for the internet of things. *Survey (London, England).*

Aste, T., Tasca, P., & Di Matteo, T. (2017). *Blockchain technologies: The foreseeable impact on society and industry*. IEEE.

Beck, R., & Müller-Bloch, C. (2017). *Blockchain as radical innovation: A framework for engaging with distributed ledgers*. Research Gate.

Eyal, I., Sirer, E. G. (2018). *Majority is not enough: Bitcoin mining is vulnerable*. ACM.

Howell, S. T., Niessner, M., & Yermack, D. (2018). *Initial Coin Offerings: Financing growth with cryptocurrency token sales*. NBER.

Kamilaris, A., Fonts, A., & Prenafeta-Boldú, F. X. (2019). *The Rise of Blockchain Technology in Agriculture and Food Supply Chains*. Science Direct.

Li, J., & Fan, K. (2017). *A survey on the security of blockchain systems*. Research Gate.

Martinez, S., Stöcker, C., & Ward, C. (2017). *From bitcoin to the internet of value*. Audencia.

Mougayar, W. (2016). *The Business Blockchain: Promise*. Practice, and Application of the Next Internet Technology.

Nakamoto, S. (2008). *Bitcoin: A Peer-to-Peer Electronic Cash System*. USSC.

Potts, J., & Berg, C. (2021). *Entrepreneurship and the Blockchain: A New Paradigm for The Social Sciences*. Science Direct.

Rana, M. E., & Khan, M. A. (2017). *The Impact and Potential of Blockchain on Entrepreneurship*. Research Gtae.

Raval, S. (2016). *Decentralized Applications: Harnessing Bitcoin's Blockchain Technology*. Research Gate.

Swan, M. (2015). *Blockchain: blueprint for a new economy*. Research Gate.

Tama, B. A., Yao, L., Raissi, H., & Babar, S. A. (2018). *The Rise of Blockchain Technology in Agriculture and Food Supply Chains*. Research Gate.

Tapscott, D., & Tapscott, A. (2016). *Blockchain Revolution: How the Technology Behind Bitcoin Is Changing Money*. Business, and the World.

Voshmgir, S. (2019). *Token Economy: How Blockchain and Smart Contracts Are Changing the Economic Landscape.*

Yli-Huumo, J., Ko, D., Choi, S., Park, S., & Smolander, K. (2016). Where Is Current Research on Blockchain Technology?—. *Systematic Reviews.*

Zheng, Z., Xie, S., Dai, H. N., Chen, X., & Wang, H. (2017). *An overview of blockchain technology: Architecture, consensus, and future trends.*

Chapter 4
Introduction to Operation and Supply Chain Management for Entrepreneurship

Ali Said Jaboob
https://orcid.org/0000-0003-1233-4211
Dhofar University, Oman

Ali Mohsin Ba Awain
https://orcid.org/0000-0002-5969-337X
University of Technology and Applied Science, Oman

Khairul Anuar Mohd Ali
https://orcid.org/0000-0001-6631-7463
National University of Malaysia, Malaysia

Al Montaser Mohammed
Zarqa University, Jordan

ABSTRACT

This chapter explores the main objectives of supply chain management and operations management, highlighting their importance for the success and endurance of entrepreneurial ventures. It delves into how good management of these areas may increase competitiveness, achieve efficiency and cost-effectiveness, and guarantee customer satisfaction. The importance of operations and supply chain management in fostering business growth and sustainability is emphasized. Addedly, the chapter highlights upcoming trends and changing problems, pushing entrepreneurs to adopt best practices and methods to manage their supply chains and operations for long-term success.

DOI: 10.4018/979-8-3693-1846-1.ch004

INTRODUCTION

In this era, entrepreneurship is the blood of any financial system globally. The novel ideas that are implemented in new companies maintain society and provide wide scopes for a promising future. Without duty and sustainability, however, this future could be bleak, and destiny generations won't revel in the same development. Therefore, a new era of marketers has risen which can be pushed by using earnings, like any entrepreneur, but have an actual hobby closer to sustainability. Those types of marketers are found in all industries, but inside the shipping and supply chain quarter, they add an instantaneous and widespread impact. Given the effect of transport in nowadays world, it is very crucial to research how entrepreneurs began to convert this quarter.

In addition, the world is now developing rapidly, in particular in commercial enterprise and enterprise. This affects the exclusivity competition of the business or present commercial enterprise. Many experiments are achieved to provide various perceptions (Zhao and Zhu 2014). The principal trouble in enterprise or business today is the way to create great thoughts and boom. This purpose can be accomplished if the commercial enterprise or enterprise uses the right manufacturing strategies (Zhao and Zhu 2014). Consistent with Gungor and Gupta (1999), the manufacturing process is the technique of changing (remodeling) a product or product (output) into every other product (release) of better price or added value. Business management performs a crucial position within the business enterprise's manufacturing manner, and the paintings created through commercial enterprise control may be very crucial for the sustainable development of the corporation (Heizer and Render, 2015).

From an operations control angle, various scholars' studies and exercise a fruitful technique that leads not best to new insights but also results in tangible blessings for companies. As such, scholars have embarked on the journey to have a look at operations management on the interface to other disciplines (Linderman and Chandrasekaran, 2010), which include human aid control (e.g., Cook et al., 2002), marketing (e.g., Ho and Tang, 2009), or finance (e.g., Kumar and Turnbull, 2008), and As such, scholars have embarked on the journey to have a look at operations management on the interface to other disciplines (Linderman and Chandrasekaran, 2010), which include human aid control (e.g., Cook et al., 2002), marketing (e.g., Ho and Tang, 2009), or finance (e.g., Kumar and Turnbull, 2008), and the intersection of operations management and entrepreneurship (Kickul et al., 2011). Similarly, research on entrepreneurship has grown notably during the last many years, and inquiries on the intersection between "operations control and supply chain" and entrepreneurship are fantastically scarce. Contributing to the knowledge the chapter takes a good step toward illustrating the role of operation and supply chain management in the entrepreneurship field such as understanding operation and supply chain management:

navigating the entrepreneurial landscape, key concepts in operation and supply chain management, definition, scope, and importance of entrepreneurship, significance of entrepreneurship, key objectives and goals of entrepreneurial, the role of operation and supply chain management in entrepreneurship the role of operation and supply chain management in entrepreneurship, the entrepreneurial perspective in operation and supply chain management, and the chapter catcher the limitation part of operation and supply chain management for entrepreneurship.

UNDERSTANDING OPERATION AND SUPPLY CHAIN MANAGEMENT: NAVIGATING THE ENTREPRENEURIAL LANDSCAPE

In the world of entrepreneurship, the delicate balance between Operation and Supply Chain Management (OSCM) is crucial for achieving long-term success. As entrepreneurs endeavor to establish their presence in markets it becomes essential to have a comprehension of how operations and supply chains operate. In this examination, we will embark on a voyage to uncover the complexities of OSCM shedding light on its significance, within the entrepreneurial landscape.

Defining Operation and Supply Chain Management

Operations management involves the art and science of overseeing processes that transform inputs, into products or services (Russell and Taylor 2019). This encompasses a range of activities, including planning, production managing inventory ensuring quality control, and optimizing processes. In a context efficient, operations play a role in delivering high-quality products or services promptly which contributes to customer satisfaction and loyalty (Traynor et al., 2022). In addition to operations management supply chain management plays a role in coordinating the flow of materials, information, and resources from the stages of production to the ultimate delivery to customers. Supply chains are networks that connect suppliers, manufacturers, distributors, and retailers (Russell and Taylor 2019). It requires coordination for operation. A managed supply chain is an advantage, for entrepreneurs as it enables cost-effectiveness and responsiveness to market demands.

The Symbiosis of Operations and Supply Chain Management

The relationship between operations and supply chain is vital for the success of any business venture. When operations are executed flawlessly it helps streamline production processes reduce waste and optimize resource utilization. Similarly, an integrated and flexible supply chain ensures access to raw materials and efficient distribution of finished products (Mohammed and Biswas 2018).

Let's imagine a scenario where an entrepreneur wants to introduce a product to the market. The success of this venture relies not only on the product features but also on the smooth coordination of operations and supply chain elements (Krämer and Engell 2018). From sourcing materials to manufacturing, packaging, and distribution each step must be done carefully. Executed to ensure that the end consumer receives the product in excellent condition at the right time and, at a competitive price.

Significance of OSCM in Entrepreneurship

In the world of entrepreneurship, where being quick and adaptable is crucial, operations and supply chain management (OSCM) plays a role, in multiple ways. Firstly, it acts as a tool to control costs by helping entrepreneurs identify inefficiencies in their operations and streamline processes thus reducing expenses. Secondly, effective OSCM contributes to improving the quality of products or services which's essential for customer satisfaction and loyalty – both critical factors for long-term business success (Seyedghorban et al., 2022). Furthermore, OSCM is closely connected to innovation (Shibin et al., 2022). To stay ahead in markets entrepreneurs must constantly strive to enhance and innovate their operations and supply chains (Shibin et al., 2022). This may involve embracing technologies exploring sourcing strategies or implementing sustainable practices. An entrepreneur's ability to adapt and innovate within the realm of OSCM can be a differentiating factor, in an evolving business landscape.

Operational Strategies: A Deeper Dive

Understanding how to effectively manage business processes is crucial, for entrepreneurs seeking to optimize their operations. This requires an approach to designing, implementing, and controlling the steps that convert inputs into outputs (Roberts et al., 2018). Operational strategies encompass a range of decisions from selecting the location for facilities and planning capacity to efficiently managing the workforce and embracing relevant technologies. Efficiency serves as a pillar of strategy. Entrepreneurs must strive to eliminate waste reduce production costs and boost productivity (Saidi et al., 2022). This can involve implementing practices that focus on minimizing activities that don't add value or adopting Six Sigma methodologies for process improvement and defect reduction. Moreover, flexibility plays a role, in strategy. Entrepreneurs need to be able to adapt to changing market conditions evolving customer preferences and unexpected disruptions. By building an operation that's both flexible and responsive businesses can successfully navigate uncertainties. Seize emerging opportunities (Saidi et al., 2022).

Navigating the Supply Chain Landscape

The supply chain operates like a dance with a series of interconnected steps that ultimately deliver products or services to the end consumer. In the context of entrepreneurship, it is crucial to understand and optimize the supply chain (Fernie and Sparks 2018). Effective supply chain management includes components such, as procurement, manufacturing, logistics, and distribution (Mentzer et al., 2008). Procurement lays the groundwork for the supply chain by sourcing materials or components. Entrepreneurs need to select suppliers wisely based on factors like quality, cost, and reliability (Hugos, 2018). Developing relationships with suppliers encourages collaboration. Can lead to mutual benefits. Manufacturing is at the core of the supply chain and involves transforming materials into finished goods. Entrepreneurs must find a balance between production efficiency, quality control, and scalability. Employing strategies like manufacturing principles, in-time inventory management, and technology integration helps optimize the manufacturing process (Nakamura et al., 2019). Logistics and distribution complete the cycle by moving goods from production facilities to consumers. Efficient logistics management minimizes lead times and reduces transportation costs. Ensures products arrive intact at their destination. Entrepreneurs can utilize technologies such as tracking systems and data analytics to enhance visibility and control, over their supply chain (Hossain et al., 2020).

The Technological Thread in OSCM

In today's business world technology plays a role, in shaping the field of supply chain management (OSCM). The incorporation of technologies not only improves efficiency but also fosters innovation and competitiveness. Entrepreneurs who embrace these advancements in their supply chain strategies gain a strategic advantage in an increasingly digital era (Proença et al., 2022). Automation is at the forefront of integrating technology into operations. Entrepreneurs can utilize robotics and artificial intelligence to automate tasks resulting in improved accuracy and efficiency (Ng KK et al., 2021). Whether implementing robotic process automation for back-office functions or deploying manufacturing on the shop floor automation helps streamline processes while allowing human resources to focus on activities that add value. In the realm of supply chain management technologies like blockchain and the Internet of Things (IoT) are revolutionizing practices. Blockchain ensures transparency and traceability within the supply chain by creating a record of transactions (H Hu et al., 2023). IoT devices provide real-time data on the location and condition of goods during transit facilitating decision-making and responsiveness to disruptions (Li C.Z et al., 2018). Data analytics serves as another tool, for entrepreneurs engaged in OSCM. By harnessing the amount of data generated throughout the supply chain and operational processes, entrepreneurs can extract insights (Richey et al., 2023). Predictive analytics for example enable forecasting demand optimizing inventory levels and mitigating disruptions (Tan CL et al., 2023).

Challenges and Opportunities in OSCM for Entrepreneurs

While there are advantages, to operating in the field of Operations and Supply Chain Management (OSCM) entrepreneurs face challenges along the way. These challenges include disruptions in the supply chain unpredictable changes in demand and evolving market dynamics (Castillo, 2018). Additionally, with global supply chains becoming increasingly complex entrepreneurs must have an understanding of factors, regulatory shifts, and environmental considerations. However, these challenges also present opportunities for innovation. Entrepreneurs who can proactively tackle these obstacles and take advantage of emerging trends can gain an edge (Elkington and Hartigan 2008). For instance, incorporating sustainability practices into the supply chain is not only a choice but also a strategic move since environmentally conscious consumers are driving market preferences. The emergence of e-commerce and the digitalization of business operations open up avenues for exploration (Elkington and Hartigan, 2008). The rise of platforms has reshaped traditional supply chain dynamics through, consumer models. Entrepreneurs can leverage these changes to build responsive supply chains that meet evolving consumer expectations (Shcherbakov and Silkina 2021).

KEY CONCEPTS IN OPERATION AND SUPPLY CHAIN MANAGEMENT

As entrepreneurs embark on the journey of mastering Operation and Supply Chain Management (OSCM), they come across a range of concepts that lay the foundation for effective business processes (Rushton et al, 2022). In this section, we will explore the core principles that define OSCM providing insights into each concept and its strategic implications, for entrepreneurial ventures.

Designing and Planning the Supply Chain

When entrepreneurs embark on setting up their infrastructure, they start by designing and planning their supply chain. This involves mapping out the network of supplier's production facilities and distribution centers. These decisions have an impact on costs. How well the business can respond to market changes. Planning also involves anticipating demand aligning resources and optimizing the flow of goods and information. A thought-out supply chain design helps entrepreneurs navigate uncertainties, adapt to market dynamics, and seize growth opportunities (Dolgui et al., 2018).

Forecasting Customer Demand

Demand forecasting acts as an entrepreneurial crystal ball that provides insights into customer needs. Entrepreneurs analyze data, market trends, and external factors to accurately predict demand (Kim et al., 2017). This allows them to align production and distribution with anticipated market requirements while avoiding inventory or stockouts. In industries with short product lifecycles agile demand forecasting is crucial for staying on trends and maintaining an edge (Jayender and Kundu 2021). Having a nuanced understanding of demand forecasting empowers entrepreneurs to optimize resource allocation enhance customer satisfaction and proactively respond to market shifts (Jayender and Kundu 2021).

Embracing Lean Principles for Waste Reduction

Inspired by the philosophy of improvement (known as Lean Principles) entrepreneurs strive for operational excellence, in their businesses (Zhou, 2016). Through examination of processes and the elimination of value-adding activities entrepreneurs can reduce waste and improve efficiency. The principles of methodology go beyond the shop floor permeating throughout the entire organizational culture to foster a mindset of continuous improvement. Waste reduction not only helps trim costs but also makes businesses more adaptable. Entrepreneurs who practice principles are well prepared to respond to changing market demands enhance product quality and cultivate a culture of innovation. Therefore, Lean Principles are not merely tools, for efficiency but strategic assets that position entrepreneurs for long-term success in markets (Kudrekodlu Venkatesh & Venkatesan, 2022).

Logistics and Distribution

Efficient logistics and distribution play a role in supply chains by ensuring products reach consumers promptly and in condition (Rushton et al, 2022). Entrepreneurs excel at optimizing the flow of goods through expertise in transportation, warehousing, and order fulfillment (Sarkar et al., 2022). Key considerations include placing distribution centers selecting transportation modes and integrating technology solutions effectively. In today's era dominated by e-commerce last mile delivery capabilities and real-time tracking become factors for success (Klein and Popp 2022). Entrepreneurs who demonstrate excellence in logistics and distribution gain an advantage by meeting customer expectations for reliable deliveries. That is not about moving products; it is about creating an end-to-end experience that enhances customer satisfaction and fosters brand loyalty.

Collaboration and Partnerships

Collaboration and partnerships play a role, in today's interconnected world of supply chains (Al-Omoush et al., 2023). For entrepreneurs, it's not just about engagements with suppliers, manufacturers, and distributors. It's about building relationships by aligning goals sharing information and tackling challenges together (Hussain et al., 2023). These collaborative partnerships boost the resilience of supply chains enabling responses to disruptions and fostering innovation. Entrepreneurs understand that their success is tied to the success of their partners (Hussain et al., 2023). Through collaboration they can access markets share risks and leverage expertise to navigate the complexities of the global marketplace. By operating as isolated individual entrepreneurs position themselves as contributors to an interconnected ecosystem (MacDonald et al., 2018).

Technology and Innovation

The infusion of technology and innovation into OSCM (Operations and Supply Chain Management) is a journey for entrepreneurs. Technology acts as a catalyst that enhances visibility and control throughout the supply chain (Edsand, 2017). Advanced analytics and artificial intelligence provide insights that guide decision-making and predict trends. Blockchain technology ensures transparency and traceability, in industries that prioritize sourcing practices. Internet of Things (IoT) devices offer real-time data that optimizes inventory management and logistics operations. Innovation goes beyond technology itself; it also encompasses processes and business models (H Hu et al., 2023).

Entrepreneurs who embrace advancements not only improve their operational efficiency but also establish themselves as industry pioneers. The field of Operations and Supply Chain Management (OSCM) becomes a platform, for problem-solving, where innovation's not just a competitive advantage but a powerful catalyst that propels businesses toward future success (Caiado et al., 2023).

DEFINITION, SCOPE, AND IMPORTANCE OF ENTREPRENEURSHIP

Definition of Entrepreneurship

Starting and running a firm from scratch is at the heart of what entrepreneurs do. Finding a profitable business model requires figuring out what customers want, coming up with novel ways to meet those wants, and sticking with the process until the end. This procedure usually calls for a healthy dose of bravery, ingenuity, and the capacity to adjust to shifting market conditions (Diandra and Azmy 2020).

Scope of Entrepreneurship

Entrepreneurship covers a broad and ever-changing terrain, which is reflective of the fluidity of business and innovation. At its heart, it is the process of ideation through which business owners come up with, evaluate, and ultimately implement new business concepts (Jacobs and Chase 2018). This creative phase is vital as it creates the framework for what the firm will become. The next crucial step is to build a business model, in which the business's operations, income streams, and value creation for consumers and stakeholders are mapped out. This framework is the road map that brought from idea to execution (Nandan, 2013). Conducting research into potential customers is also essential for any entrepreneur. It entails learning about the market, finding your ideal clientele, and checking out the competition (Sharma, 2021). This research is crucial for establishing the viability of the business concept and developing effective expansion plans. Market research is an integral part of financial planning. Entrepreneurs need to create in-depth financial plans that detail everything from the sources of capital to the expected revenue and expenses. Effective financial management is crucial for the viability and growth of the company (Blundel et al., 2017). The entrepreneurial vision becomes a reality through the implementation of the company plan. This phase calls for precise planning, clear communication, and methodical execution of strategies. To achieve success, entrepreneurs need to master the challenges of running a firm every day (Mohanty, 2005).

Operations and supply chain management play a crucial role in the implementation phase. Entrepreneurs have the responsibility of ensuring the timely and accurate delivery of their products or services while keeping expenses to a minimum without sacrificing quality (Kumar, 2008). Logistics, stock control, vendor relations, and customer support are all part of this. In today's fast-paced business climate, the capacity to adapt and respond to supply chain difficulties is crucial (Korpysa et al., 2020). Human resource management expertise is also crucial for entrepreneurs. Successful businesses require leaders who can build and motivate teams, create positive work environments, and keep employees happy and productive (Hora and Dutta 2013). Business owners need to be aware of how technological developments affect their strategies, processes, and potential customer bases. Legal considerations also represent an integral aspect of the entrepreneurial scope (Rao C.H., 1971). Corporate governance, compliance, intellectual property rights, and employment law are just a few of the many areas of law that entrepreneurs must understand to run a successful business (Fosso Wamba et al., 2022). Mainly, entrepreneurship is multifaceted and calls for knowledge and abilities from many fields. It calls for a unique set of skills, including imagination, planning, skill, and flexibility. The job of the entrepreneur, facing new obstacles and taking advantage of possibilities in a dynamic global market, is always shifting as the business world develops.

Importance of Entrepreneurship

1 **Economic Growth**: Entrepreneurs stimulate economic growth by creating jobs, introducing innovations, and boosting productivity. They play a critical role in generating new wealth and advancing economic development (Jengeta et al., 2021).
2 **Innovation and Technological Advancement**: Entrepreneurs often lead the way in technological advancements and innovation. They bring new products and services to the market, fostering a culture of innovation (Jacobs and Chase 2018).
3 **Social Change**: Through their ventures, entrepreneurs can address societal challenges and contribute to social change. They often drive progress in areas like sustainability, healthcare, and education (Jacobs and Chase 2018).
4 **Personal Fulfillment**: Entrepreneurship provides individuals with the opportunity to pursue their passions, achieve personal growth, and realize their creative potential (Bosma, 2013).
5 **Global Impact**: Entrepreneurs can have a global impact by creating solutions that transcend borders. This is especially relevant in the age of globalization and digital connectivity (Perrini and Vurro 2006).

SIGNIFICANCE OF ENTREPRENEURSHIP

The value of entrepreneurs is not limited to starting new companies. Entrepreneurship is a key factor in the expansion of the economy, the creation of new products, and the general progress of society (Blinova, 2022). Here, we'll take a close look at some of its most salient features:

Economic Growth and Job Creation: Entrepreneurs are vital for economic growth and job creation. When people start enterprises, they not only employ people directly but also stimulate the growth of related sectors. Small and medium-sized firms (SMEs), which comprise the bulk of entrepreneurial initiatives, are often the principal producers of new jobs in an economy (Perrini and Vurro 2006).

Innovation and Technological Advancement: Entrepreneurs are frequently the first to introduce groundbreaking new technologies. They push innovation in technology forward by constantly looking for better ways to do things and fresh approaches to old issues. This quest results in the creation of cutting-edge products and services that advance numerous industries, such as medicine, computing, and green power (Janjić and Rađenović 2019).

Competition and Market Dynamism: Market rivalry is boosted by entrepreneurial efforts. They provide a threat to established businesses and industries, which typically results in better goods, services, and support for consumers. Consumers may benefit from more options and more activity in the market as a result of increased competition (Sarkar et al., 2001).

Economic Flexibility and Resilience: The entrepreneurial spirit gives the economy more adaptability and stability. New businesses are better able to respond quickly to market shifts and structural shifts by testing out new markets and adjusting their business strategies (Thurik, 2009).

Social Change and Community Development: The drive to make a difference in the world is a driving force for many businesses. Entrepreneurship with a social mission seeks to improve society in areas such as health, education, and the environment. This approach can lead to considerable improvements in quality of life and community cohesion (Sarkar et al., 2001).

Global Impact and Connectivity: As a result of globalization, today's business owners may make an international difference. They connect markets, stimulate international trade, and contribute to global innovation networks, making the globe more integrated (Fayolle, 2007).

Personal Fulfillment and Skill Development: People can follow their visions and find success by starting their businesses. Entrepreneurship is great for developing skills like critical thinking, innovation, leadership, and perseverance (Fayolle, 2007).

Figure 1. Significance of entrepreneurship

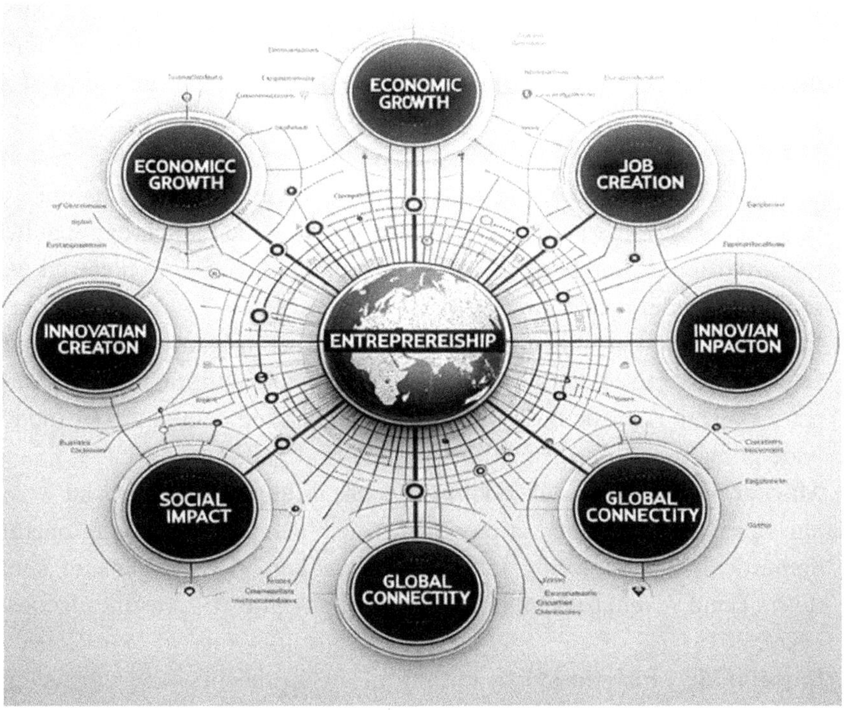

Wealth Creation and Distribution

Entrepreneurs help generate wealth, which, if distributed fairly, can improve living standards for everybody. When businesses are successful, they pay taxes that help the government provide essential services to citizens (Kutzhanova et al., 2009).

Here's a figure 1 that sums up the value of becoming an entrepreneur in graphical form. There are different-sized bars representing various factors, such as "Economic Growth," "Job Creation," "Innovation," "Social Impact," and "Global Connectivity," among others. The chart's color-coding technique, alongside its clear labels and legend, makes it particularly user-friendly.

Key Objectives and Goals of Entrepreneurial

The many different things that entrepreneurial endeavors want to accomplish can be seen in the wide variety of their primary objectives and ambitions. Some of the most important ones are listed below:

- **Innovation**: One of the principal objectives of entrepreneurship is to bring innovative products, services, or processes to the market. Entrepreneurs aim to fill gaps in the market by offering novel solutions that meet unaddressed needs or improve upon existing offerings (Hsuan Mikkola and Skjøtt-Larsen 2004).
- **Value Creation**: Entrepreneurs strive to create value for customers, stakeholders, and society at large. This involves not just economic value in terms of revenue and profit but also social value, which can manifest in improved living standards, access to essential services, or enhanced quality of life (Belvedere and Grando 2017).
- **Economic Growth and Job Creation**: A fundamental goal of entrepreneurship is to contribute to economic growth by creating jobs and stimulating economic activity. This is particularly important in emerging economies or industries undergoing rapid transformation (Mangla et al., 2019).
- **Market Expansion and Global Reach**: Many entrepreneurial ventures aim to expand their market presence, which can include scaling operations domestically or exploring international markets. This expansion helps in diversifying revenue streams and achieving a global footprint (Jacobs and Chase 2018).
- **Sustainable Practices**: Increasingly, entrepreneurs are focusing on sustainability as a core objective. This involves adopting environmentally friendly practices, ensuring ethical supply chains, and contributing to the sustainable development of communities (Mor R.S et al., 2022).
- **Personal and Professional Development**: For many entrepreneurs, a key goal is personal growth and the development of professional skills. Entrepreneurship often involves continuous learning, adaptability, and the honing of leadership and management skills (Jacobs and Chase 2018).
- **Financial Independence and Wealth Creation**: Achieving financial independence and creating wealth for themselves and their stakeholders is a common objective among entrepreneurs. This financial success can also enable further investments in new ventures or social causes (Schönsleben, 2022).
- **Social Impact and Community Engagement**: Social entrepreneurship, in particular, focuses on creating a positive impact on societal issues. Goals can include addressing poverty, education, healthcare, or environmental challenges, and engaging with and supporting local communities (Mentzer et al., 2008).
- **Industry Leadership and Influence**: Many entrepreneurs aspire to be leaders in their industry, influencing trends, setting standards, and being at the forefront of technological and market developments (Grant et al., 2017).

- **Building a Brand and Reputation**: Establishing a strong, reputable brand is often a key goal. This involves building customer trust, establishing a market presence, and being recognized as a reputable and reliable entity in the industry (Grant et al., 2017).

The Pivotal Role of Operation and Supply Chain Management in Entrepreneurship

In the world of entrepreneurship, the success and long-term viability of a venture often depend on the interplay, between Operation and Supply Chain Management (OSCM). The relationship between operations and a managed supply chain is crucial for entrepreneurial endeavors, shaping how businesses navigate dynamic and unpredictable markets.

Boosting Efficiency and Cost Control: At its core entrepreneurs strive to maximize efficiency in transforming inputs into products or services. OSCM provides tools to streamline processes minimize waste and optimize resource utilization. Efficient operations do not help control costs. It also enhances the overall agility of the business enabling entrepreneurs to promptly respond to market fluctuations while staying competitive (Serale et al., 2018).

Cultivating Customer Satisfaction and Loyalty: Operations and supply chains play a role in delivering products or services that meet or exceed customer expectations. A designed supply chain ensures the availability of materials and timely delivery of finished goods contributing to customer satisfaction. In entrepreneurship where building a customer base is paramount OSCM plays a role in creating positive customer experiences and fostering brand loyalty (Khadka & Maharjan 2017).

Navigating Market Dynamics through Adaptability: Entrepreneurial ventures operate in changing markets where adaptability is key, to survival. OSCM provides a framework that helps entrepreneurs build operations and supply chains (Gölgeci et al, 2019). It allows them to adjust production levels respond effectively to changes, in demand, and navigate disruptions with confidence ensuring their businesses can adapt and thrive in times.

Making the Most of Resources: Entrepreneurs understand the importance of cost effectiveness especially when resources are limited. OSCM enables entrepreneurs to optimize resource allocation reduce costs and improve the financial health of their businesses. By managing resources, entrepreneurs can make capital investments that drive growth (Barrena-Martínez et al., 2019).

Managing Risks and Building Resilience: The entrepreneurial journey is filled with risks like supply chain disruptions and market fluctuations. OSCM equips entrepreneurs with tools to identify, assess, and mitigate these risks effectively. Building supply chains diversifying suppliers and having contingency plans in place are aspects of OSCM that ensure businesses can overcome unforeseen challenges and come out stronger (Koczberski et al., 2018).

Embracing Innovation and Technology: In this era of advancement, OSCM provides an opportunity for innovation. Entrepreneurs can leverage technologies like intelligence (AI) Internet of Things (IoT). Blockchain to improve visibility, across their supply chains automate processes efficiently, and create more responsive systems. Innovation in Operations and Supply Chain Management (OSCM) not only boosts efficiency but also positions entrepreneurs as forward-thinking leaders in their respective industries (Byun et al., 2018).

Decision Making and Long-Term Planning: OSCM goes beyond day-to-day operations, it involves decision-making and long-term planning (Poncelet et al., 2020). Entrepreneurs need to take into account aspects like designing the supply chain forecasting demand and integrating technology to create a roadmap for success. Strategic OSCM ensures that the operational intricacies align with business goals making sure that every part of the supply chain contributes to the success of the venture.

Friendly and Ethical Practices: Given the importance of ethical considerations in today's business practices, OSCM provides a framework for responsible entrepreneurship. Entrepreneurs can implement eco initiatives ensure sourcing practices and contribute to social responsibility through their supply chain operations. This not only aligns with consumer values but also future-proofs businesses in an increasingly conscious marketplace.

To put it simply, Operations and Supply Chain Management are not just functions in entrepreneurship; they play a role that influences every aspect of a business (Kim, 2020).

Entrepreneurs who understand the complexities of OSCM do not set themselves up for success, in their operations. Also, establish a foundation for long-term growth resilience in the face of obstacles and the capacity to drive innovation within their respective industries. As businesses navigate the evolving landscape of entrepreneurship OSCM serves as a guiding force that shapes the path, toward prosperity and lasting achievements.

The Entrepreneurial Perspective in Operation and Supply Chain Management

The entrepreneurial perspective in operations and supply chain management is pivotal for the success of any business, particularly in how it aligns with broader strategic objectives. This perspective involves several key areas:

Entrepreneurial Objectives in a Company and Supply Chain: Entrepreneurs work on synchronizing their companies' aims with their day-to-day activities and their supply chains. By combining these processes, they can make sure that the supply chain not only helps to achieve the other goals but, actually helps the practitioners to do them better (Prostean et al., 2020).

Resolving Conflicting Entrepreneurial Objectives: Entrepreneurial goals and business reality don't always line up. For instance, supply chain scalability or budgetary limits could prevent rapid market expansion from happening. These tensions can only be resolved by striking a balance between the entrepreneur's ambition and the practical constraints (Diandra and Azmy 2020).

Customer Order Penetration Point (OPP) and Coordination with Product and Process Design: Supply chain management relies heavily on the OPP. In the context of the supply chain, this term designates the stage at which products are tailored to individual buyers. Meeting consumer needs while keeping operations efficient requires close collaboration between product designers, process designers, and the OPP (Jacobs and Chase 2018).

Target Area Flexibility: Adapting quickly to shifts in the market necessitates spending money on the kinds of supporting organizations, processes, and technologies that make that possible. One of the keys to business success is the ability to quickly respond to changes in demand and supply (Nandan, 2013).

Enabling Technologies Toward Personalized Production: Artificial intelligence (AI), the Internet of Things (IoT), and advanced analytics have all contributed to the development of more tailored and effective manufacturing methods. Business owners can obtain an edge in the market by using these innovations to focus on customers and their needs (Sharma, 2021).

CONCLUSION

Entrepreneurship is typified by a relentless pursuit to uncover and capitalize on fresh opportunities while solving challenging challenges; it is the very embodiment of invention and the desire for transformative change. The scope of this ever-evolving industry goes far beyond traditional measures of economic success such as job growth and GDP contributions. Its real value lies in its ability to inspire creative thinking, close communication barriers around the world, and speed up development in many fields. Entrepreneurs are not just innovators who establish new businesses but also disrupt established industries and practices.

In conclusion, the intricate relationship between entrepreneurship and operations and supply chain management (OSCM) is fundamental to the success and innovation of modern business. An understanding of OSCM is vital, encompassing key concepts like efficient supply chain design and planning, accurate demand forecasting, implementation of lean principles for waste reduction, and effective logistics and distribution strategies. These elements, alongside fostering collaboration and partnerships and leveraging technology and innovation, are crucial for operational excellence and competitive edge. Some of the most important ideas in business today come from the fields of Operations and Supply Chain Management (OSCM). Some examples are using lean concepts to cut down on waste and boost output, improving the accuracy of demand forecasts, and designing more efficient supply networks. Strong relationships and collaborations need to be fostered, and novel logistics and distribution tactics must be implemented. Together, these ideas guarantee that OSCM will continue to develop and grow as an essential part of today's businesses. Supply Chain Design and Planning involves strategically structuring a supply chain to optimize efficiency and responsiveness. This process includes decisions on sourcing, manufacturing locations, logistics, and inventory management, aimed at balancing cost-effectiveness with customer satisfaction and agility in responding to market changes. future customer demand using historical data, market trends, and statistical models. This critical function enables businesses to make informed decisions about production, inventory management, and resource allocation, ensuring they meet customer needs efficiently while minimizing excess inventory and costs. Lean Principles and Waste Reduction focus on streamlining operations by eliminating non-value-adding activities, thereby enhancing efficiency and productivity. This approach emphasizes continuous improvement, waste minimization in processes, and optimizing resource utilization, leading to cost savings and improved customer value. Logistics and Distribution in supply chain management involve the coordinated planning and execution of transporting goods from suppliers to customers. This process encompasses warehousing, inventory management, transportation, and order fulfillment, all aimed at ensuring timely and cost-effective delivery of products to meet customer demands. Stakeholders. Collaboration and Partnerships in supply chain management are about building and maintaining effective relationships with suppliers, distributors, and other stakeholders. This collaborative approach enhances communication, aligns goals, and fosters mutual benefits, leading to improved efficiency, innovation, and resilience in the supply chain.

The Entrepreneurial Perspective in Operation and Supply Chain Management emphasizes innovation, flexibility, and strategic agility in managing supply chains. Entrepreneurs approach these aspects with a mindset geared towards identifying and leveraging new opportunities, optimizing resources, and adapting quickly to market changes. This perspective often involves innovative solutions and technologies to streamline operations and create competitive advantages. Top of Form in the realm of entrepreneurship, the definition, scope, and importance are far-reaching, extending beyond business creation to include market innovation, economic growth, and societal impact. The significance of entrepreneurship is highlighted by its role in job creation, technological advancements, and global connectivity. Entrepreneurs set diverse objectives and goals, from value creation and market expansion to personal growth and societal impact. The role of OSCM in entrepreneurship is pivotal, providing the backbone for efficient and sustainable business operations. Finally, the entrepreneurial perspective in OSCM underscores the need for agility, strategic planning, and adaptability, integrating entrepreneurial enthusiasm with systematic operational management. This blend of entrepreneurship with OSCM is essential for the development of resilient, impactful, and forward-thinking business ventures, contributing significantly to broader economic and social progress.

Entrepreneurial aspirations might range from the superficial to the profound. They incorporate the aspiration to produce not just monetary, but also social and environmental value. In their pursuit of growth, many entrepreneurs look beyond traditional barriers like geography and culture to find new opportunities. Entrepreneurship relies heavily on a wide range of skills, including leadership, resilience, and strategic thinking, all of which may be developed through personal growth. In addition, pursuing entrepreneurial endeavors frequently results in substantial societal consequences, tackling crucial concerns like sustainability, education, and health care. Nimbleness and long-term thinking mark supply chain operations that take an entrepreneurial tack. Entrepreneurs in today's dynamic and ever-changing business climate need to be experts at resource management, trend forecasting, and rapid adaptation. This calls for originality in operational processes and supply chain management, in addition to a solid grasp of market dynamics. To maximize productivity, cut expenses, and delight patrons, this method is essential. To sum up, due to its multidimensional nature, entrepreneurship calls for an all-encompassing strategy that strikes a balance between creative and realistic business tactics. The importance of entrepreneurs is growing as the world becomes more complex and interconnected. They are the motors that propel forward into a future that is sustainable, inclusive, and prosperous in all ways imaginable.

Implications of Operation and Supply Chain Management for Entrepreneurship: A Comprehensive Analysis

Operation and Supply Chain Management (OSCM) plays a role, in entrepreneurship going beyond the complexities of a business. The impact of OSCM extends across the landscape influencing factors such as competitiveness, adaptability, and sustainability. In this analysis, we explore the implications of OSCM for entrepreneurship examining how strategic management of operations and supply chains shapes the success and trajectory of ventures.

Gaining Competitive Advantage and Market Differentiation: The foundation of success lies in achieving an advantage and setting oneself apart in the market. Effective OSCM emerges as a source of such an advantage (Tönnissen & Teuteberg, 2020).

Businesses that strategically design and optimize their supply chains gain an edge. A managed supply chain ensures operations, timely deliveries, and cost efficiency setting businesses apart from others in the market. This competitive advantage goes beyond cost reduction; it also involves creating an agile structure that can quickly adapt to changing market conditions. This phenomenon aligns with resource-based views and dynamic capabilities theory. The resource-based view suggests that competitive advantage stems from valuable resources possessed by firms. Efficient OSCM then becomes a resource that's not easily replicable, by competitors. Dynamic capabilities theory emphasizes a company's capacity to effectively integrate, develop, and adapt both external competencies to navigate rapidly changing environments. Within this context, operational supply chain management (OSCM) serves as a capability that empowers entrepreneurs to continuously adapt and innovate thereby contributing to the attainment of competitive advantage (Tönnissen & Teuteberg 2020).

Enhancing Operational Efficiency and Cost Reduction: For ventures aiming to optimize resource utilization and minimize costs, operational efficiency stands as a metric. OSCM plays a role, in enhancing efficiency by streamlining processes reducing waste, and optimizing resource allocation. The implications extend beyond cost savings; they encompass the establishment of an agile operational framework that bolsters overall adaptability for the business. From a perspective, the relationship between OSCM and operational efficiency aligns with principles derived from systems theory and efficiency theories. Systems theory asserts that organizations operate as systems with interconnected components that rely on one another for functioning. By implementing OSCM practices entrepreneurs effectively optimize the system by ensuring each component works harmoniously together. Efficiency theories emphasize the significance of minimizing resource wastage while maximizing output. Through the integration of OSCM practices, entrepreneurs adhere to these principles of efficiency ensuring optimal resource utilization (Inman & Green 2018).

Prioritizing Customer Satisfaction and Fostering Loyalty: Within the ecosystem prioritizing customer satisfaction is crucial, for establishing a customer base. OSCM plays a role, in ensuring that products are available and delivered on time and consistently of quality. The impact of OSCM on customer satisfaction aligns with the Service Profit Chain theory, which suggests that satisfied customers result in increased loyalty, repeat business, and positive word of mouth. Efficient OSCM contributes to a seamless supply chain enhancing customer experiences and fostering brand loyalty (Mahmoud et al., 2018). This relationship is emphasized by the principles of customer relationship management (CRM) and service quality theories. CRM highlights the significance of managing and nurturing long-term customer relationships for profitability. When designed with a customer approach OSCM aligns with CRM principles to ensure that the entire supply chain is focused on meeting and surpassing customer expectations. Furthermore, service quality theories emphasize that consistent delivery of high-quality service leads to customer satisfaction and retention. Within the context of OSCM service quality extends beyond the product to encompass the supply chain process.

Mitigating Risks and Building Resilience: Entrepreneurial ventures inherently face risks including supply chain disruptions and market uncertainties. OSCM serves as a tool, for identifying assessing, and mitigating these risks. The impact of Operations and Supply Chain Management (OSCM), on risk management is in line with the principles of resilience theory and risk management frameworks. Resilience theory emphasizes a system's ability to absorb shocks adapt and reorganize to maintain functionality. Effective OSCM practices contribute to resilience by enabling responses to disruptions ensuring continuity and minimizing risks. From a perspective risk management framework like the COSO Enterprise Risk Management framework provides an approach to identify and mitigate risks. Efficient OSCM aligns with these frameworks offering entrepreneurs a way to evaluate and address supply chain risks. This not only protects businesses from disruptions but also contributes to long-term sustainability.

Innovation and Adaptability: Innovation and adaptability are also implications of OSCM for ventures operating in dynamic markets. OSCM becomes a catalyst for improvement allowing businesses to adapt to emerging trends seize opportunities and stay ahead in an ever-changing marketplace (Kim & Marcouiller 2018). The scientific foundation of this relationship lies in innovation theories and organizational learning principles. Innovation theories suggest that businesses must continuously innovate to remain competitive. When viewed as a capability OSCM aligns with this idea by fostering an environment of ongoing improvement. Organizational learning theories highlight the importance of adaptability and knowledge acquisition, for success. OSCM, as a way to learn from market feedback and adapt operations aligns with these principles ensuring that businesses adapt to changing environments.

Expanding Globally and Reaching Markets; Entrepreneurial ventures aiming for expansion face challenges regarding logistics, customs, and distribution (Moshood et al., 2021). The impact of OSCM on reaching global markets aligns with business theories and strategies for market entry. International business theories emphasize the importance of adaptability and responsiveness to markets. Efficient OSCM practices equip entrepreneurs with the tools needed to navigate these challenges and ensure that supply chains are tailored to the demands of markets. Market entry strategies such as exporting, licensing, and strategic alliances are influenced by the efficiency of supply chain operations. From a perspective, the connection between OSCM and global expansion is in line with transaction cost economics which suggests that the choice of market entry mode is influenced by transaction efficiency. Effective OSCM reduces transaction costs associated with operations making international expansion more viable for ventures.

Sustainable and Ethical Practices; In an era where sustainability and ethical considerations are fundamental, in business practices, the implications of OSCM extend into responsibility. Entrepreneurs who embrace ethical practices in their supply chains not meet the expectations of socially conscious consumers but also foster long-term trust and reputation, for their brands. The connection between these practices and corporate social responsibility (CSR) theories as ethical supply chain management frameworks is supported by scientific research (Mani et al., 2020). CSR theories emphasize the significance of businesses contributing to societal well-being beyond profit making (Brin & Nehme 2019). By implementing practices in operations and supply chain management that consider social impacts entrepreneurs position themselves as responsible corporate citizens. Ethical supply chain management frameworks, such as the UN Global Compact offer guidance to businesses in ensuring practices throughout their supply chains. Entrepreneurs who incorporate these frameworks into their strategies contribute to ethical entrepreneurship.

Data-Driven Decision-Making: Furthermore, the implications of operations and supply chain management extend to data-driven decision-making for entrepreneurs. By leveraging advancements and utilizing data analytics within their supply chains entrepreneurs gain insights. This scientific relationship aligns, with the principles of data-driven decision-making, which emphasize using data and analytics to inform choices. From a perspective integrating data analytics into operations and supply chain management resonates with business intelligence principles and decision support systems. Business intelligence utilizes data analysis tools to provide insights, for decision making whereas decision support systems (Nikiforova et al., 2022).

REFERENCES

Al-Omoush, K. S., de Lucas, A., & del Val, M. T. (2023). The role of e-supply chain collaboration in collaborative innovation and value-co creation. *Journal of Business Research, 158*, 113647. doi:10.1016/j.jbusres.2023.113647

Barrena-Martínez, J., López-Fernández, M., & Romero-Fernández, P. M. (2019). Towards a configuration of socially responsible human resource management policies and practices: Findings from an academic consensus. *International Journal of Human Resource Management, 30*(17), 2544–2580. doi:10.1080/09585192.2017.1332669

Belvedere, V. and Grando, A., (2017). *Sustainable operations and supply chain management*. John Wiley & Sons.

Blinova, E., Ponomarenko, T., & Knysh, V. (2022). Analyzing the Concept of Corporate Sustainability in the Context of Sustainable Business Development in the Mining Sector with Elements of Circular Economy. *Sustainability (Basel)*, *14*(13), 8163. doi:10.3390/su14138163

Blundel, R., Lockett, N., & Wang, C. (2017). Exploring entrepreneurship. *Sage (Atlanta, Ga.)*.

Bosma, N., 2013. The Global Entrepreneurship Monitor (GEM) and its impact on entrepreneurship research. *Foundations and Trends® in Entrepreneurship, 9*(2), pp.143-248.

Brin, P. V., & Nehme, M. N. (2019). *Corporate social responsibility: analysis of theories and models.*

Byun, J., Sung, T. E., & Park, H. W. (2018). Technological innovation strategy: How do technology life cycles change by technological area. *Technology Analysis and Strategic Management*, *30*(1), 98–112. doi:10.1080/09537325.2017.1297397

Caiado, R. G. G., Scavarda, L. F., Azevedo, B. D., de Mattos Nascimento, D. L., & Quelhas, O. L. G. (2022). Challenges and benefits of sustainable industry 4.0 for operations and supply chain management—A framework headed toward the 2030 agenda. *Sustainability (Basel)*, *14*(2), 830. doi:10.3390/su14020830

Castillo, V. E. (2018). *An Inquiry into Supply Chain Strategy Implications of the Sharing Economy for Last Mile Logistics.*

Cook, L. S., Bowen, D. E., Chase, R. B., Dasu, S., Stewart, D. M., & Tansik, D. A. (2002). Human issues in service design. *Journal of Operations Management*, *20*(2), 159–174. doi:10.1016/S0272-6963(01)00094-8

Diandra, D., & Azmy, A. (2020). Understanding definition of entrepreneurship. International Journal of Management. *Accounting and Economics*, *7*(5), 235–241.

Dolgui, A., Ivanov, D., & Sokolov, B. (2018). Ripple effect in the supply chain: An analysis and recent literature. *International Journal of Production Research*, *56*(1-2), 414–430. doi:10.1080/00207543.2017.1387680

Edsand, H. E. (2017). Identifying barriers to wind energy diffusion in Colombia: A function analysis of the technological innovation system and the wider context. *Technology in Society*, *49*, 1–15. doi:10.1016/j.techsoc.2017.01.002

Elkington, J., & Hartigan, P. (2008). *The power of unreasonable people: How social entrepreneurs create markets that change the world.* Harvard Business Press.

Fayolle, A. (2007). *Entrepreneurship and new value creation: the dynamic of the entrepreneurial process*. Cambridge university press. doi:10.1017/CBO9780511488689

Fernie, J., & Sparks, L. (Eds.). (2018). Logistics and retail management: emerging issues and new challenges in the retail supply chain. Kogan page publishers.

Fosso Wamba, S., Queiroz, M. M., Guthrie, C., & Braganza, A. (2022). Industry experiences of artificial intelligence (AI): Benefits and challenges in operations and supply chain management. *Production Planning and Control*, *33*(16), 1493–1497. doi:10.1080/09537287.2021.1882695

Gölgeci, I., Assadinia, S., Kuivalainen, O., & Larimo, J. (2019). Emerging-market firms' dynamic capabilities and international performance: The moderating role of institutional development and distance. *International Business Review*, *28*(6), 101593. doi:10.1016/j.ibusrev.2019.101593

Grant, D.B., Wong, C.Y. & Trautrims, A. (2017). *Sustainable logistics and supply chain management: principles and practices for sustainable operations and management*. Kogan Page Publishers.

Gungor, A., & Gupta, S. M. (1999). Issues in environmentally conscious manufacturing and product recovery: A survey. *Computers & Industrial Engineering*, *36*(4), 811–853. doi:10.1016/S0360-8352(99)00167-9

Ho, T. H., & Tang, C. S. (2009). Introduction to the special issue on marketing and operations management interfaces and coordination. *Production and Operations Management*, *18*(4), 363–364. doi:10.1111/j.1937-5956.2009.01037.x

Hora, M., & Dutta, D. K. (2013). Entrepreneurial firms and downstream alliance partnerships: Impact of portfolio depth and scope on technology innovation and commercialization success. *Production and Operations Management*, *22*(6), 1389–1400. doi:10.1111/j.1937-5956.2012.01410.x

Hossain, N. U. I., El Amrani, S., Jaradat, R., Marufuzzaman, M., Buchanan, R., Rinaudo, C., & Hamilton, M. (2020). Modeling and assessing interdependencies between critical infrastructures using Bayesian network: A case study of inland waterway port and surrounding supply chain network. *Reliability Engineering & System Safety*, *198*, 106898. doi:10.1016/j.ress.2020.106898

Hsuan Mikkola, J., & Skjøtt-Larsen, T. (2004). Supply-chain integration: Implications for mass customization, modularization and postponement strategies. *Production Planning and Control*, *15*(4), 352–361. doi:10.1080/0953728042000238845

Hu, H., Xu, J., Liu, M., & Lim, M. K. (2023). Vaccine supply chain management: An intelligent system utilizing blockchain, IoT and machine learning. *Journal of Business Research, 156*, 113480. doi:10.1016/j.jbusres.2022.113480 PMID:36506475

Hugos, M. H. (2018). Essentials of supply chain management. John Wiley & Sons.

Hussain, G., Nazir, M. S., Rashid, M. A., & Sattar, M. A. (2023). From supply chain resilience to supply chain disruption orientation: The moderating role of supply chain complexity. *Journal of Enterprise Information Management, 36*(1), 70–90. doi:10.1108/JEIM-12-2020-0558

Inman, R. A., & Green, K. W. (2018). Lean and green combine to impact environmental and operational performance. *International Journal of Production Research, 56*(14), 4802–4818. doi:10.1080/00207543.2018.1447705

Jacobs, F.R. & Chase, R.B. (2018). *Operations and supply chain management.* McGraw-Hill.

Janjić, I., & Rađenović, T. (2019). The importance of managing innovation in modern enterprises. *Ekonomika (Nis), 65*(3), 45–54. doi:10.5937/ekonomika1903045J

Jayender, P., & Kundu, G. K. (2021). Intelligent ERP for SCM agility and graph theory technique for adaptation in automotive industry in India. *International Journal of System Assurance Engineering and Management*, 1-22.

Jengeta, M., & Phiri, M. A. (2021). Graduate perceptions on the scope of university entrepreneurship education in a turbulent economy: Case of CUT Zimbabwe. *Journal of African Education, 2*(2), 67. doi:10.31920/2633-2930/2021/v2n2a3

Khadka, K., & Maharjan, S. (2017). *Customer satisfaction and customer loyalty: Case trivsel städtjänster (trivsel siivouspalvelut).*

Kickul, J. R., Griffiths, M. D., Jayaram, J., & Wagner, S. M. (2011). Operations management, entrepreneurship, and value creation: Emerging opportunities in a cross-disciplinary context. *Journal of Operations Management, 29*(1-2), 78–85. doi:10.1016/j.jom.2010.12.004

Kim, H., & Marcouiller, D. W. (2018). Mitigating flood risk and enhancing community resilience to natural disasters: Plan quality matters. *Environmental Hazards, 17*(5), 397–417. doi:10.1080/17477891.2017.1407743

Kim, M. Y. (2020). Ethical behavior in the context of green credit card services: The role of individuals' regulatory focus. *International Journal of Advanced Culture Technology, 8*(1), 107–112.

Kim, T. Y., Dekker, R., & Heij, C. (2017). Spare part demand forecasting for consumer goods using installed base information. *Computers & Industrial Engineering*, *103*, 201–215. doi:10.1016/j.cie.2016.11.014

Klein, P., & Popp, B. (2022). Last-Mile Delivery Methods in E-Commerce: Does Perceived Sustainability Matter for Consumer Acceptance and Usage? *Sustainability (Basel)*, *14*(24), 16437. doi:10.3390/su142416437

Koczberski, G., Curry, G. N., Bue, V., Germis, E., Nake, S., & Tilden, G. M. (2018). Diffusing risk and building resilience through innovation: Reciprocal exchange relationships, livelihood vulnerability and food security amongst smallholder farmers in Papua New Guinea. *Human Ecology: an Interdisciplinary Journal*, *46*(6), 801–814. doi:10.1007/s10745-018-0032-9

Korpysa, J., Halicki, M., & Lopatka, A. (2020). Entrepreneurial management of project supply chain–a model approach. *Problems and Perspectives in Management*, *18*(3), 211–223. doi:10.21511/ppm.18(3).2020.18

Krämer, S., & Engell, S. (2018). *Resource efficiency of processing plants: monitoring and improvement*. John Wiley & Sons.

Kudrekodlu Venkatesh, P., & Venkatesan, V. (2022). Lean readiness factors for construction organizations. [IJEMS]. *Indian Journal of Engineering and Materials Sciences*, *28*(6), 608–619.

Kumar, P., & Turnbull, S. M. (2008). Optimal patenting and licensing of financial innovations. *Management Science*, *54*(12), 2012–2023. doi:10.1287/mnsc.1080.0898

Kumar, S. A. (2008). *Entrepreneurship development*. New Age International.

Kutzhanova, N., Lyons, T. S., & Lichtenstein, G. A. (2009). Skill-based development of entrepreneurs and the role of personal and peer group coaching in enterprise development. *Economic Development Quarterly*, *23*(3), 193–210. doi:10.1177/0891242409336547

Li, C. Z., Xue, F., Li, X., Hong, J., & Shen, G. Q. (2018). An Internet of Things-enabled BIM platform for on-site assembly services in prefabricated construction. *Automation in Construction*, *89*, 146–161. doi:10.1016/j.autcon.2018.01.001

Linderman, K., & Chandrasekaran, A. (2010). The scholarly exchange of knowledge in operations management. *Journal of Operations Management*, *28*(4), 357–366. doi:10.1016/j.jom.2009.11.012

MacDonald, A., Clarke, A., Huang, L., Roseland, M., & Seitanidi, M. M. (2018). Multi-stakeholder partnerships (SDG# 17) as a means of achieving sustainable communities and cities (SDG# 11). Handbook of sustainability science and research, 193-209.Springer.

Mahmoud, M. A., Hinson, R. E., & Adika, M. K. (2018). The effect of trust, commitment, and conflict handling on customer retention: The mediating role of customer satisfaction. *Journal of Relationship Marketing*, *17*(4), 257–276. doi:10.1080/15332667.2018.1440146

Mangla, S. K., Luthra, S., Jakhar, S. K., Kumar, A., & Rana, N. P. (Eds.). (2019). *Sustainable Procurement in Supply Chain Operations*. CRC Press. doi:10.1201/9780429466328

Mani, V., Jabbour, C. J. C., & Mani, K. T. (2020). Supply chain social sustainability in small and medium manufacturing enterprises and firms' performance: Empirical evidence from an emerging Asian economy. *International Journal of Production Economics*, *227*, 107656. doi:10.1016/j.ijpe.2020.107656

Mentzer, J. T., Stank, T. P., & Esper, T. L. (2008). Supply chain management and its relationship to logistics, marketing, production, and operations management. *Journal of Business Logistics*, *29*(1), 31–46. doi:10.1002/j.2158-1592.2008.tb00067.x

Mentzer, J. T., Stank, T. P., & Esper, T. L. (2008). Supply chain management and its relationship to logistics, marketing, production, and operations management. *Journal of Business Logistics*, *29*(1), 31–46. doi:10.1002/j.2158-1592.2008.tb00067.x

Mohammed, F., Biswas, W. K., Yao, H., & Tadé, M. (2018). Sustainability assessment of symbiotic processes for the reuse of phosphogypsum. *Journal of Cleaner Production*, *188*, 497–507. doi:10.1016/j.jclepro.2018.03.309

Mohanty, S. K. (2005). *Fundamentals of entrepreneurship*. PHI Learning Pvt. Ltd.

Mor, R.S., Kamble, S.S. & Sangwan, K.S. (2022). *Operations and Supply Chain Management in the Food Industry*. Springer Singapore.

Moshood, T. D., Nawanir, G., Mahmud, F., Mohamad, F., Ahmad, M. H., & Abdul Ghani, A. (2021). Expanding policy for biodegradable plastic products and market dynamics of bio-based plastics: Challenges and opportunities. *Sustainability (Basel)*, *13*(11), 6170. doi:10.3390/su13116170

Nakamura, M., Pendlebury, D., Schnell, J., & Szomszor, M. (2019). Navigating the structure of research on sustainable development goals. *Policy*, *11*, 12.

Nandan, H. (2013). *Fundamentals of entrepreneurship*. PHI Learning Pvt. Ltd.

Ng, K. K., Chen, C. H., Lee, C. K., Jiao, J. R., & Yang, Z. X. (2021). A systematic literature review on intelligent automation: Aligning concepts from theory, practice, and future perspectives. *Advanced Engineering Informatics*, *47*, 101246. doi:10.1016/j.aei.2021.101246

Nikiforova, A., Daskevics, A., & Azeroual, O. (2022). NoSQL security: can my data-driven decision-making be affected from outside? *arXiv preprint arXiv:2206.11787.*

Perrini, F., & Vurro, C. (2006). Social entrepreneurship: Innovation and social change across theory and practice. In *Social entrepreneurship* (pp. 57–85). Palgrave Macmillan UK. doi:10.1057/9780230625655_5

Poncelet, K., Delarue, E., & D'haeseleer, W. (2020). Unit commitment constraints in long-term planning models: Relevance, pitfalls and the role of assumptions on flexibility. *Applied Energy*, *258*, 113843. doi:10.1016/j.apenergy.2019.113843

Proença, A. P., Gaspar, P. D., & Lima, T. M. (2022). Lean Optimization Techniques for Improvement of Production Flows and Logistics Management: The Case Study of a Fruits Distribution Center. *Processes (Basel, Switzerland)*, *10*(7), 1384. doi:10.3390/pr10071384

Prostean, G., Villahoz, J. J. L., Brancu, L., & Bakacsi, G. (2020). *Innovation in Sustainable Management and Entrepreneurship*. Springer International Publishing. doi:10.1007/978-3-030-44711-3

Rao, C. H. (1971). Uncertainty, entrepreneurship, and sharecropping in India. *Journal of Political Economy*, *79*(3), 578–595. doi:10.1086/259769

Richey, R. G. Jr, Chowdhury, S., Davis-Sramek, B., Giannakis, M., & Dwivedi, Y. K. (2023). Artificial intelligence in logistics and supply chain management: A primer and roadmap for research. *Journal of Business Logistics*, *44*(4), 532–549. doi:10.1111/jbl.12364

Roberts, A. P., Stanton, N. A., & Fay, D. T. (2018). Go Deeper, Go Deeper: Understanding submarine command and control during the completion of dived tracking operations. *Applied Ergonomics*, *69*, 162–175. doi:10.1016/j.apergo.2018.02.003 PMID:29477324

Rushton, A., Croucher, P., & Baker, P. (2022). *The handbook of logistics and distribution management: Understanding the supply chain*. Kogan Page Publishers.

Russell, R. S., & Taylor, B. W. (2019). *Operations and supply chain management*. John Wiley & Sons.

Sarkar, B., Takeyeva, D., Guchhait, R., & Sarkar, M. (2022). Optimized radio-frequency identification system for different warehouse shapes. *Knowledge-Based Systems*, *258*, 109811. doi:10.1016/j.knosys.2022.109811

Sarkar, M. B., Echambadi, R. A. J., & Harrison, J. S. (2001). Alliance entrepreneurship and firm market performance. *Strategic Management Journal*, *22*(6-7), 701–711. doi:10.1002/smj.179

Sarkar, M. B., Echambadi, R. A. J., & Harrison, J. S. (2001). Alliance entrepreneurship and firm market performance. *Strategic Management Journal*, *22*(6-7), 701–711. doi:10.1002/smj.179

Schönsleben, P. (2022). Logistics, operations, and supply chain management. In *Handbook Integral Logistics Management: Operations and Supply Chain Management Within and Across Companies* (pp. 7–70). Springer Berlin Heidelberg.

Serale, G., Fiorentini, M., Capozzoli, A., Bernardini, D., & Bemporad, A. (2018). Model predictive control (MPC) for enhancing building and HVAC system energy efficiency: Problem formulation, applications and opportunities. *Energies*, *11*(3), 631. doi:10.3390/en11030631

Seyedghorban, Z., Samson, D., & Swink, M. (2022). Quo vadis OSCM? An analysis of past and future trends in operations and supply chain management research. *Decision Sciences*, *53*(3), 429–451. doi:10.1111/deci.12519

Sharma, S. (2021). *Entrepreneurship development*. PHI Learning Pvt. Ltd.

Shcherbakov, V., & Silkina, G. (2021). Supply chain management open innovation: Virtual integration in the network logistics system. *Journal of Open Innovation*, *7*(1), 54. doi:10.3390/joitmc7010054

Shibin, K. T., Dubey, R., & Hazen, B. T. (2022). Partial least squares in supply chain management: An example study on sustainable supply chain management practices. Handbook of research methods for supply chain management, 221-243. Springer.

Tan, C. L., Tei, Z., Yeo, S. F., Lai, K. H., Kumar, A., & Chung, L. (2023). Nexus among blockchain visibility, supply chain integration and supply chain performance in the digital transformation era. *Industrial Management & Data Systems*, *123*(1), 229–252. doi:10.1108/IMDS-12-2021-0784

Thurik, A.R. (2009). Entreprenomics: entrepreneurship, economic growth and policy. *Entrepreneurship, growth and public policy, 10*(6), 219-249.

Tönnissen, S., & Teuteberg, F. (2020). Analysing the impact of blockchain-technology for operations and supply chain management: An explanatory model drawn from multiple case studies. *International Journal of Information Management*, *52*, 101953. doi:10.1016/j.ijinfomgt.2019.05.009

Traynor, M., Bernard, S., Moreo, A., & O'Neill, S. (2022). Investigating the emergence of third-party online food delivery in the US restaurant industry: A grounded theory approach. *International Journal of Hospitality Management*, *107*, 103299. doi:10.1016/j.ijhm.2022.103299

Van Goor, A. R., van Amstel, W. P., & van Amstel, M. P. (2019). *European distribution and supply chain logistics*. Routledge.

Zhao, Y., & Zhu, Q. (2014). Evaluation on crowdsourcing research: Current status and future direction. *Information Systems Frontiers*, *16*(3), 417–434. doi:10.1007/s10796-012-9350-4

Zhou, B. (2016). Lean principles, practices, and impacts: A study on small and medium-sized enterprises (SMEs). *Annals of Operations Research*, *241*(1-2), 457–474. doi:10.1007/s10479-012-1177-3

Chapter 5
Neuromarketing as a Digital Marketing Strategy to Unravel the Evolution of Marketing Communication

Kavindu Millagala
https://orcid.org/0000-0002-2274-7434
Australian Management School, Sri Lanka

Nandana Gunasinghe
Rajarata University of Sri Lanka, Sri Lanka

ABSTRACT

This chapter examines the pivotal role of neuromarketing as a digital marketing strategy in deciphering the dynamic evolution of marketing communication. Rooted in neuroscience and psychology, neuromarketing employs advanced neuroscientific tools to unveil subconscious consumer responses. In the context of the digital revolution, this chapter elucidates how neuromarketing seamlessly integrates with evolving marketing communication channels, emphasizing personalization and emotional engagement. The authors explore the significance of personalized content in cultivating consumer trust and loyalty and discuss the emergence of neuroanalytics as a metric for evaluating campaign success in the digital sphere. Ethical considerations surrounding the responsible use of neurodata are addressed, highlighting the need for industry guidelines. This chapter posits neuromarketing as a transformative force, guiding businesses toward a nuanced understanding of consumer behaviour in the ever-changing landscape of digital marketing.

DOI: 10.4018/979-8-3693-1846-1.ch005

INTRODUCTION

In an era dominated by rapid technological advancements and shifting consumer behaviours, the field of marketing undergoes continuous transformation. As traditional marketing strategies grapple with the challenges posed by the digital age, an innovative approach emerges at the intersection of neuroscience and marketing—Neuromarketing. This chapter delves into the profound implications of incorporating Neuromarketing as a digital marketing strategy, offering insights into its capacity to unravel the intricate layers of marketing communication evolution.

The term Neuromarketing, coined by Ale Smidt's in 2002 (Smidt's, 2002), represents a change in basic assumptions in how businesses comprehend and engage with their target audience. Grounded in the principles of neuroscience and psychology, Neuromarketing employs sophisticated tools such as electroencephalography (EEG), functional magnetic resonance imaging (fMRI), and eye-tracking to decipher the subconscious responses of consumers to marketing stimuli (Lee et al., 2007; Plassmann et al., 2012). By peering into the neural processes underlying consumer decision-making, Neuromarketing transcends traditional market research methodologies, offering a deeper understanding of the emotional and cognitive factors that influence purchasing behavior.

The evolution of marketing communication in the digital age necessitates a revaluation of conventional strategies. Digital channels, encompassing social media, online advertising, and influencer marketing, have become integral components of the modern marketing toolkit. Within this context, Neuromarketing assumes significance as it seamlessly aligns with the intricacies of digital communication. This chapter explores how Neuromarketing, as a digital marketing strategy, augments the effectiveness of campaigns in the online landscape.

Personalization stands as a cornerstone of contemporary marketing, and Neuromarketing provides a unique lens through which to achieve it. The analysis of neurodata enables marketers to tailor content based on individual preferences, creating a more personalized and resonant consumer experience (Hubert & Kenning, 2008). This chapter discusses the role of personalization in enhancing consumer engagement and building enduring connections between brands and their audience.

As businesses navigate the digital frontier, measuring the success of marketing campaigns requires a more nuanced approach. Traditional metrics often fall short in capturing the emotional and subconscious impact of digital initiatives. Enter neuroanalytics—a set of tools and methodologies derived from Neuromarketing principles. Neuroanalytics offers a more comprehensive understanding of campaign effectiveness by measuring emotional engagement, brand recall, and other nuanced indicators (Ohme et al., 2010). The incorporation of neuroanalytics into digital marketing evaluation is explored, providing marketers with a richer set of data for informed decision-making.

However, the adoption of Neuromarketing is not without its ethical considerations. The responsible use of neurodata, privacy concerns, and the need for transparent practices emerge as critical issues. This chapter addresses these ethical dimensions, emphasizing the importance of establishing industry guidelines to ensure the ethical application of Neuromarketing techniques.

BACKGROUND

The evolution of marketing communication has been a dynamic journey, shaped by societal changes, technological advancements, and shifts in consumer behavior. Traditional marketing approaches, once the bedrock of brand promotion, now find themselves grappling with the transformative forces of the digital age. As businesses navigate this complex landscape, Neuromarketing emerges as a promising paradigm, offering a deeper understanding of consumer cognition and emotional responses to marketing stimuli.

The roots of Neuromarketing trace back to the early 2000s when Ale Smidt's coined the term, signifying a convergence of neuroscience, psychology, and marketing (Smidt's, 2002). Drawing inspiration from the field of neuroeconomics, which explores the neural underpinnings of economic decision-making, Neuromarketing pioneers the application of neuroscientific tools to decipher the intricate dance between the consumer's brain and marketing messages (Lee et al., 2007). This interdisciplinary approach positions Neuromarketing as a revolutionary force in understanding consumer behavior.

Digitalization has ushered in a new era of marketing communication, necessitating a revaluation of strategies. The rise of social media, online advertising, and influencer marketing has transformed the way brands connect with their audience. In this context, Neuromarketing serves as a bridge between the traditional and the digital, offering insights into how the human brain responds to the rapidly evolving landscape of online communication.

One key aspect of this evolution is the growing emphasis on personalization in marketing. Consumers, inundated with a deluge of information, seek personalized experiences that resonate with their individual preferences and needs (Hubert & Kenning, 2008). Neuromarketing, with its ability to decode neurodata, provides marketers with the tools to tailor content and messages, creating a more personalized and engaging consumer journey.

The digital realm, however, poses challenges in assessing the effectiveness of marketing campaigns. Traditional metrics often fall short in capturing the nuanced impact of digital initiatives. Enter neuroanalytics—a branch of Neuromarketing that employs neuroscientific principles to evaluate the success of marketing strategies (Ohme et al., 2010). By measuring emotional engagement, attention, and memory recall, neuroanalytics offers a more comprehensive understanding of the complex interplay between consumer psychology and digital marketing.

Nevertheless, the integration of Neuromarketing into digital strategies is not without ethical considerations. The collection and use of neurodata raise questions about privacy, consent, and the responsible application of this technology (Plassmann et al., 2012). As businesses embrace Neuromarketing, ethical guidelines and industry standards become imperative to ensure the transparent and ethical utilization of neuroscientific tools.

WHAT IS NEUROMARKETING?

Neuromarketing, at its core, represents a multidisciplinary field that converges insights from neuroscience, psychology, and marketing to comprehend the intricacies of consumer decision-making and behavior. At the inception of this innovative discipline, Ale Smidt's (2002) coined the term, marking a significant departure from traditional market research methodologies. Neuromarketing harnesses advanced neuroscientific tools, including electroencephalography (EEG), functional magnetic resonance imaging (fMRI), and eye-tracking, to delve into the neural underpinnings of consumer responses to marketing stimuli (Lee et al., 2007; Plassmann et al., 2012).

By adopting these neuroscientific methods, Neuromarketing transcends the limitations of conventional market research. EEG, for instance, enables the measurement of electrical brain activity, offering real-time insights into cognitive processes related to attention, engagement, and emotional responses (Lee et al., 2007). fMRI provides a glimpse into the brain's functional areas, aiding in the identification of neural correlates associated with preferences and decision-making (Plassmann et al., 2012). Eye-tracking, another integral tool, records eye movements, uncovering visual attention patterns and aiding in the optimization of visual elements in marketing materials.

The foundation of Neuromarketing rests on the premise that consumer decisions are often influenced by subconscious processes and emotions (Lee et al., 2007). Traditional market research techniques, reliant on self-reported data, may fall short in capturing these underlying factors. Neuromarketing, by directly accessing neural responses, provides a more accurate and comprehensive understanding of consumer behavior.

Neuromarketing's application extends across various domains, including product design, advertising, and brand management. The discipline facilitates the identification of stimuli that evoke positive emotional responses, enabling marketers to tailor campaigns that resonate with consumers on a deeper, emotional level (Plassmann et al., 2012). The emphasis on emotions is rooted in the recognition that emotional engagement often precedes and influences rational decision-making. Neuromarketing operates on the premise that the brain's intricate processes shape consumer preferences and choices. By leveraging neuroscience and psychological insights, this discipline serves as a powerful tool for marketers seeking to decode the complexities of consumer decision-making in an ever-evolving marketplace.

Demystifying Neuromarketing Techniques

The integration of neuroscientific tools into marketing research has revolutionized our understanding of consumer behavior. Functional Magnetic Resonance Imaging (fMRI), a non-invasive imaging technique, provides real-time insights into brain activity by measuring blood flow changes (Lee et al., 2007). Electroencephalography (EEG) captures electrical activity on the scalp, offering a high-temporal resolution view of cognitive processes (Plassmann et al., 2012). Eye-tracking technology records eye movements, enabling the analysis of visual attention and engagement (Holmqvist et al., 2011). These technologies collectively offer marketers unprecedented access to the subconscious responses of consumers.

FMRI as Unveiling Real-Time Neural Responses

Functional Magnetic Resonance Imaging (fMRI) stands as a pivotal tool in Neuromarketing, offering real-time insights into the neural responses of consumers during exposure to marketing stimuli. Rooted in the principles of neuroscience, fMRI provides a non-invasive means of peering into the human brain, allowing researchers to decipher the intricacies of emotional and cognitive processes that influence consumer decision-making (Lee et al., 2007). The application of fMRI in marketing research has enabled a profound understanding of how individuals respond to various elements such as advertisements, product packaging, and brand logos.

The essence of fMRI lies in its ability to map changes in blood flow within the brain, providing a spatial representation of neural activity associated with specific stimuli. As individuals engage with marketing content, fMRI captures the activation of distinct brain regions, revealing the emotional and cognitive responses evoked by visual and auditory stimuli (Lee et al., 2007). This real-time mapping of neural responses offers marketers unprecedented insights into the subconscious reactions of consumers.

Research by Lee and colleagues (2007) exemplifies the power of fMRI in unravelling real-time neural responses to marketing content. The study demonstrated that exposure to brand logos led to activation in the ventral part of the brain associated with reward processing. This finding underscores the link between visual stimuli, emotional responses, and the brain's reward system, shedding light on the neurobiological basis of brand affinity and loyalty. Such insights derived from fMRI studies inform marketers about the neurological underpinnings of consumer preferences and contribute to the strategic crafting of visually impactful brand elements.

Moreover, fMRI allows for the exploration of emotional engagement throughout the consumer journey. By analysing brain activity at various stages, from initial exposure to post-purchase experiences, marketers gain a holistic view of consumer responses. This temporal dimension of fMRI data provides valuable information about the longevity of emotional impact, enabling brands to tailor their strategies for enduring consumer connections (Plassmann et al., 2012).

The integration of fMRI into Neuromarketing practices facilitates a nuanced approach to campaign optimization. Marketers can identify the specific elements within advertisements or product displays that trigger emotional responses, guiding the refinement of content for maximum impact. For instance, Plassmann and colleagues (2012) utilized fMRI to study the neural correlates of consumer responses to wine tasting. The findings highlighted the role of price information in modulating the neural experience of taste, highlighting how fMRI can uncover the intricate interplay between sensory perception and external cues.

fMRI emerges as a powerful ally in the Neuromarketing arsenal, providing real-time insights into the neural responses of consumers. By unveiling the neurobiological underpinnings of emotional and cognitive processes, fMRI enables marketers to craft more resonant and impactful campaigns. The marriage of neuroscience and marketing, facilitated by fMRI, transforms our understanding of consumer behavior and empowers businesses to navigate the intricacies of the modern marketplace.

EEG to Capturing Cognitive Dynamics

Electroencephalography (EEG) emerges as a pivotal neuroscientific tool within Neuromarketing, offering a high-temporal resolution view of cognitive dynamics during consumer engagement with marketing stimuli. Rooted in neuroscience principles, EEG provides a non-invasive means of recording electrical activity on the scalp, allowing researchers to delve into the rapid fluctuations associated with cognitive processes (Plassmann et al., 2012). The temporal precision of EEG enables the exploration of the dynamic nature of cognitive responses as consumers interact with marketing content.

EEG's application in marketing research extends beyond traditional approaches, offering insights into attention, emotional engagement, and memory encoding. The real-time nature of EEG captures the immediacy of cognitive responses, allowing for the identification of critical moments in the consumer journey. Research by Plassmann and colleagues (2012) exemplifies EEG's utility in uncovering the temporal dynamics of consumer responses. The study revealed distinct EEG patterns associated with the evaluation of consumer choices, shedding light on the cognitive mechanisms underlying decision-making processes.

Furthermore, EEG aids in the examination of attentional mechanisms during marketing exposure. By tracking neural oscillations associated with attention, researchers can discern the ebb and flow of cognitive resources directed towards specific elements within advertisements or product displays. This granular understanding of attentional dynamics informs marketers about the saliency of visual and auditory cues, guiding the optimization of content for maximum impact (Lee et al., 2007).

The versatility of EEG is exemplified in its ability to assess emotional engagement throughout the consumer journey. The identification of specific EEG signatures associated with emotional responses allows marketers to gauge the intensity and duration of emotional experiences. For instance, during video ad viewing, EEG can reveal the moments of heightened emotional engagement, guiding the strategic placement of emotionally impactful content within the narrative (Ohme et al., 2010).

Moreover, EEG's portability facilitates research in real-world settings, enabling marketers to study consumer responses in naturalistic environments. This ecological validity enhances the applicability of EEG findings to real marketing scenarios, offering insights that align with authentic consumer experiences. Such field studies empower marketers to tailor strategies that resonate with consumers in diverse contexts, fostering a deeper understanding of the cognitive dynamics in play during actual purchase decisions (Ohme et al., 2010).

EEG serves as an invaluable tool within the Neuromarketing toolkit, capturing the cognitive dynamics of consumer responses in real-time. By offering insights into attention, emotional engagement, and memory encoding, EEG enables marketers to optimize content and design for maximum impact. The integration of EEG into Neuromarketing practices represents a change in basic assumptions in understanding the temporal nuances of consumer behavior, contributing to the creation of more nuanced and effective marketing strategies.

Eye-Tracking as the Decoding Visual Attention

Eye-tracking technology stands as a powerful instrument in Neuromarketing, offering a nuanced understanding of visual attention patterns during consumer engagement with marketing stimuli. This methodology, rooted in neuroscience and psychology, records eye movements, fixations, and gaze duration, providing valuable insights into how individuals allocate attention to specific elements within advertisements, websites, and product displays (Holmqvist et al., 2011). The application of eye-tracking in marketing research unveils the intricate interplay between visual stimuli and consumer attention, guiding marketers in optimizing the visual elements of their campaigns.

The essence of eye-tracking lies in its ability to decode the visual hierarchy perceived by individuals. By analysing the sequence and duration of fixations, researchers gain a comprehensive understanding of which elements capture attention and how attention shifts across the visual field (Holmqvist et al., 2011). This information is instrumental in guiding the placement of key elements, such as call-to-action buttons or brand logos, to ensure optimal visibility and engagement.

Research in Neuromarketing has utilized eye-tracking to explore the impact of visual stimuli on consumer behavior. For instance, studies have demonstrated that certain design elements, such as the use of contrasting colours or bold fonts, can attract more visual attention (Holmqvist et al., 2011). By leveraging eye-tracking data, marketers can refine visual content to align with the visual preferences of the target audience, enhancing the effectiveness of their campaigns.

Eye-tracking technology is particularly valuable in assessing the effectiveness of digital platforms, where visual engagement plays a pivotal role. In the context of website design, eye-tracking reveals the visual journey of users, from the initial landing page to subsequent interactions. This dynamic understanding of visual attention allows marketers to optimize website layouts, ensuring that crucial information and CTAs are strategically positioned for maximum visibility (Holmqvist et al., 2011).

Moreover, eye-tracking offers insights into the user experience of online advertisements. By tracking gaze patterns during ad viewing, researchers can identify which elements attract the most attention and whether there are distractions that divert focus from the main message. This granular understanding of visual attention guides the creation of visually compelling advertisements that capture and retain audience engagement (Holmqvist et al., 2011).

In addition to optimizing static visual elements, eye-tracking is instrumental in understanding the dynamics of video content consumption. By tracking gaze patterns during video ads, researchers can identify key moments of visual engagement and potential points of disengagement. This knowledge informs the strategic placement of crucial information or emotional cues within the video narrative, contributing to the creation of more impactful and emotionally resonant content.

Eye-tracking technology plays a pivotal role in Neuromarketing by decoding visual attention patterns during consumer interactions with marketing stimuli. By revealing the visual hierarchy perceived by individuals, eye-tracking guides the optimization of visual content, from website design to video advertising. The integration of eye-tracking into Neuromarketing practices empowers marketers with a visual roadmap of consumer attention, fostering the creation of more engaging and effective marketing campaigns.

Unlocking the Emotional Drivers

Visual Stimuli

The significance of visual stimuli, particularly imagery, emerges as a driving force in shaping consumer perceptions and responses. Informed by principles of neuroscience and psychology, the exploration of visual stimuli involves a deep understanding of how elements such as colour, composition, and design activate specific brain regions associated with emotion and memory (Plassmann et al., 2012). The application of visual stimuli in marketing not only captures attention but also wields the power to evoke emotions and influence decision-making processes.

Colour, as a fundamental aspect of visual stimuli, has been extensively studied in Neuromarketing. Neuroscientific research reveals that assorted colours evoke distinct emotional responses, tapping into the neural pathways associated with feelings and perceptions (Plassmann et al., 2012). For instance, warm colours like red and orange may elicit emotions of excitement or urgency, while cool colours like blue and green may evoke calmness or trust. Marketers harness this knowledge to strategically select colours that align with the emotional tone they wish to convey in their branding or advertising materials.

Beyond colour, the composition of visual stimuli plays a crucial role in capturing and maintaining attention. Eye-tracking studies demonstrate that certain compositional elements, such as focal points and visual hierarchy, guide the viewer's gaze and influence the perceived importance of different elements within an image (Holmqvist et al., 2011). Understanding these compositional dynamics empowers marketers to strategically design visuals that lead the viewer's attention toward key brand messages or product features.

Design elements within visual stimuli contribute to the overall aesthetic appeal and emotional impact. The arrangement of images, graphics, and text elements can evoke specific emotions and enhance the memorability of a brand or product. Neuroimaging studies using fMRI reveal that aesthetically pleasing designs activate reward centres in the brain, underscoring the neural basis of the aesthetic experience (Plassmann et al., 2012). By incorporating visually appealing design elements, marketers can create a positive and memorable impression that extends beyond conscious awareness.

Furthermore, the role of visual stimuli extends to brand logos and product packaging, both of which are pivotal in shaping consumer perceptions. Neuroscientific research employing fMRI illustrates that exposure to familiar brand logos activates brain regions associated with positive emotions and reward processing (Lee et al., 2007). This finding emphasizes the power of visual stimuli in establishing and reinforcing brand associations. Similarly, product packaging design influences consumer expectations and can evoke emotional responses that impact purchase decisions (Plassmann et al., 2012).

The dynamic nature of visual stimuli is particularly pronounced in the context of digital marketing. In the era of social media and online content consumption, the strategic use of visually compelling images is instrumental in capturing user attention and fostering engagement. Research suggests that the brain processes visual information faster than text, making visual stimuli a potent tool for communicating brand messages quickly and effectively (Plassmann et al., 2012).

Language and Storytelling

In the realm of Neuromarketing, the strategic use of language and storytelling emerges as a potent means of crafting neurologically impactful narratives that resonate with consumers. Rooted in neuroscience principles, the understanding of how language influences brain activity enables marketers to tailor messages that evoke specific emotional and cognitive responses (Lee et al., 2007). The power of language extends beyond mere communication; it serves as a gateway to the emotional centres of the brain, influencing perceptions, attitudes, and consumer behavior.

Neuroscientific research reveals that specific words and narrative structures elicit distinct patterns of brain activity associated with emotion and cognition. Language, when aligned with neurologically informed principles, becomes a tool for tapping into the emotional brain regions and creating a more profound impact on the audience (Lee et al., 2007). The choice of words, tone, and narrative structure all contribute to the emotional resonance of a message.

In the context of Neuromarketing, storytelling emerges as a compelling vehicle for delivering brand messages. Narratives, when crafted effectively, engage multiple brain regions, including those responsible for processing emotions and forming memories (Plassmann et al., 2012). The neurobiological basis of storytelling lies in its ability to stimulate the release of neurochemicals like oxytocin, fostering a sense of connection and empathy between the storyteller and the audience (Plassmann et al., 2012). This neurochemical response contributes to the creation of lasting and positive brand associations.

Moreover, the structure of a narrative can significantly impacts its neurological impact. Research indicates that stories following a classic narrative arc, with a beginning, middle, and end, trigger heightened neural activity and enhance the encoding of information into memory (Plassmann et al., 2012). Marketers can leverage this insight to structure brand narratives that captivate attention, evoke emotions, and are more likely to be retained in the consumer's memory.

The neuroscientific perspective also sheds light on the importance of coherence and congruence in language. Inconsistent or incongruent messaging may lead to cognitive dissonance, triggering negative emotional responses (Lee et al., 2007). Therefore, the alignment of language with brand values, imagery, and overall messaging is crucial for maintaining a positive and coherent consumer experience.

Language in Neuromarketing extends to the realm of persuasion, where specific linguistic elements can influence decision-making processes. Framing, for example, involves presenting information in a way that emphasizes gains or losses, impacting the perceived value of a product or message (Lee et al., 2007). By understanding the neural processes associated with framing, marketers can strategically craft messages that resonate with the motivational and decision-making centres of the brain.

Furthermore, language plays a pivotal role in creating a sense of urgency and motivation. Neurologically informed copywriting involves choosing words and phrases that tap into the brain's reward system and elicit a desire for immediate action (Hubert & Kenning, 2008). This approach aligns with the science of persuasion, where the strategic use of language becomes a catalyst for influencing decisions and shaping consumer behavior.

Measuring the Unconscious

In the landscape of Neuromarketing, the pursuit of understanding consumer behavior goes beyond traditional self-report data, delving into the realms of the unconscious mind. The limitations of self-report methods, reliant on conscious reflection and articulation of thoughts, necessitate alternative approaches that tap into the implicit and automatic processes guiding decision-making (Hubert & Kenning, 2008). Neuromarketing, with its foundation in neuroscience principles, leverages advanced techniques to measure the unconscious, providing insights unattainable through conventional research methods.

One such approach involves the use of neuroimaging techniques like fMRI and EEG to directly observe brain activity associated with consumer responses (Lee et al., 2007; Plassmann et al., 2012). These technologies offer a window into the neural processes that underlie decision-making, emotion, and memory formation. By bypassing conscious self-reporting, neuromarketers gain access to implicit reactions and preferences, unveiling insights that consumers may not be consciously aware of or able to express.

The application of eye-tracking technology is another avenue for measuring unconscious responses, particularly in the realm of visual attention (Holmqvist et al., 2011). Eye movements and gaze patterns provide valuable information about which elements of a visual stimulus capture attention, guiding marketers in optimizing designs and layouts. Eye-tracking data offers a direct measure of visual engagement, bypassing the need for consumers to verbally articulate their visual preferences or focus areas.

Implicit reaction time measures, rooted in psychological research, constitute an additional method for gauging unconscious responses (Hubert & Kenning, 2008). The speed at which individuals respond to stimuli, such as images or words, reflects the automaticity of their reactions. Faster reaction times indicate stronger associations or preferences, offering a glimpse into the implicit attitudes and preferences that may not be fully accessible through explicit self-report measures.

Furthermore, facial expression analysis provides a non-verbal avenue for understanding emotional responses. Technologies capable of detecting and interpreting facial expressions enable the measurement of emotional states in real-time (Plassmann et al., 2012). Unconscious emotional reactions, often fleeting and subtle, can be captured through facial expressions, offering a more direct and immediate insight into the emotional impact of marketing stimuli.

Implicit association tests (IATs) represent a well-established method in psychology for measuring implicit attitudes and biases (Greenwald et al., 1998). In the context of Neuromarketing, IATs can be adapted to explore implicit associations with brands, products, or marketing messages. By examining the speed with which participants associate stimuli with positive or negative attributes, marketers gain insights into the unconscious associations that influence consumer perceptions.

Neuromarketing techniques, in measuring the unconscious, hold the potential to uncover discrepancies between stated preferences and actual responses. Studies have shown instances where self-report data and neuroimaging results diverge, emphasizing the importance of tapping into unconscious processes to obtain a more comprehensive understanding of consumer behavior (Hubert & Kenning, 2008). This nuanced approach challenges traditional research paradigms and allows for a richer exploration of the factors shaping consumer decision-making.

Neuromarketing in Action to Transforming Digital Strategies

Optimizing Websites and User Experiences

Neuromarketing transcends theoretical realms and finds practical application in the digital landscape, particularly in optimizing websites and user experiences. By leveraging neuroscientific insights, marketers can enhance website design, navigation, and call-to-action (CTA) placement, influencing user behavior. A study by Lindstrom (2008) demonstrated that subtle changes in website design, informed by neuromarketing principles, can significantly impact user engagement and conversion rates.

Enhancing User Engagement Through Visual Hierarchy

In the digital landscape, optimizing user engagement is a paramount goal, and Neuromarketing offers invaluable insights into achieving this objective through the strategic implementation of visual hierarchy. Visual hierarchy involves the deliberate arrangement of elements on a webpage to guide users' attention and create an intuitive flow of information (Holmqvist et al., 2011). Drawing upon principles of neuroscience, particularly eye-tracking studies, Neuromarketing informs the design process by identifying how users naturally navigate visual stimuli. The integration of these insights into visual hierarchy enhances user engagement by ensuring a seamless and purposeful user experience.

Eye-tracking research, as highlighted by Holmqvist and colleagues (2011), elucidates the patterns of visual attention and fixation durations, guiding the placement of critical elements like call-to-action (CTA) buttons or key information on a webpage. By aligning visual hierarchy with these natural eye movement patterns, marketers can capture and maintain user attention more effectively. Furthermore, understanding the principles of visual hierarchy allows for the strategic emphasis of high-priority content, ensuring that users are guided through a logical and compelling journey on the website.

The application of Neuromarketing in optimizing visual hierarchy extends to considerations of colour, contrast, and font choices. Neuroscientific insights demonstrate that certain colour combinations and contrasts attract more attention, influencing user perception and enhancing the saliency of specific elements (Plassmann et al., 2012). Additionally, font choices, guided by neuromarketing principles, can impact the emotional response of users, contributing to a more engaging and memorable user experience. The harmonious integration of these design elements within the framework of visual hierarchy elevates the overall usability of a website, fostering increased engagement and satisfaction among users.

Neuromarketing and Persuasive Design Elements

The amalgamation of Neuromarketing principles with persuasive design elements represents a transformative approach to shaping user behavior and enhancing digital experiences. Rooted in the understanding of neural responses to design elements, Neuromarketing guides the strategic incorporation of persuasive techniques that influence user decisions and actions. Hubert and Kenning (2008) emphasize the importance of consumer neuroscience in shaping persuasive design, highlighting how insights into the brain's reward system and decision-making processes can inform the creation of compelling and influential digital interfaces.

One fundamental aspect of persuasive design influenced by Neuromarketing is the strategic use of visuals and imagery. Neuroscientific research, particularly utilizing fMRI, reveals that visually appealing design activates reward centres in the brain, contributing to a positive emotional response (Plassmann et al., 2012). By aligning design elements with the brain's natural inclination towards aesthetically pleasing visuals, marketers can create persuasive and engaging digital interfaces that captivate users and foster positive brand associations.

The implementation of persuasive design also involves leveraging the science of scarcity and urgency, principles deeply rooted in consumer neuroscience. Hubert and Kenning (2008) discuss how scarcity, the perception of limited availability, triggers neural responses associated with increased desirability. Integrating this principle into digital interfaces, such as limited time offers or exclusive deals, capitalizes on the brain's response to scarcity, motivating users to take prompt and decisive actions. Through the application of Neuromarketing, persuasive design elements can be strategically embedded in websites and applications to influence user decision-making, fostering a sense of urgency, and driving desired behaviours.

Moreover, the concept of social proof, deeply ingrained in persuasive design, finds validation through Neuromarketing insights into the brain's reliance on social validation and conformity (Plassmann et al., 2012). Incorporating elements like customer testimonials, reviews, or social media endorsements into digital interfaces aligns with the brain's natural inclination to trust and follow the actions of others. This integration of social proof not only establishes credibility but also fosters a sense of community, influencing user perceptions and behaviours in a manner that transcends conscious awareness.

The convergence of Neuromarketing principles with the strategic implementation of visual hierarchy and persuasive design elements represents a change in basic assumptions in digital marketing strategies. By understanding and leveraging neural responses to visual stimuli and persuasive techniques, marketers can create digital interfaces that not only capture attention but also guide user behavior in alignment with business objectives. This symbiotic relationship between Neuromarketing and design elements is poised to reshape the digital landscape, offering a more nuanced and effective approach to enhancing user engagement and driving desired outcomes.

Crafting Compelling Video Ads

Understanding Brain Activity During Video Ad Viewing

Neuromarketing endeavours to unravel the intricacies of consumer responses to video advertisements by delving into the realm of brain activity. The utilization of neuroimaging techniques such as functional Magnetic Resonance Imaging (fMRI) allows marketers to gain real-time insights into the neural processes engaged during video ad consumption. Research by Lee and colleagues (2007) highlights how fMRI unveils the specific brain regions activated by visual and auditory stimuli, offering a window into the emotional and cognitive responses of viewers. This methodological approach enables the identification of key moments in the video narrative that trigger heightened neural activity, thus providing a roadmap for optimizing video content.

The power of fMRI lies in its ability to map changes in blood flow within the brain, resulting in a spatial representation of neural activation patterns. As individuals engage with video ads, fMRI captures the dynamic interplay of brain regions associated with emotion, memory, and reward processing (Lee et al., 2007). By decoding these neural responses, marketers gain valuable insights into the effectiveness of different elements within the video, ranging from visual aesthetics to narrative structures. This neuroscientific understanding guides the refinement of video content for maximum impact, ensuring that the brain responds in a manner conducive to positive brand associations and heightened emotional engagement.

Furthermore, the temporal dimension of fMRI data allows for a nuanced exploration of the enduring impact of video content on the brain. Studies employing fMRI have demonstrated that certain video elements create sustained neural responses, extending beyond the duration of the ad itself (Plassmann et al., 2012). This insight into the persistence of emotional and cognitive engagement informs marketers about the lasting impact of video ads, enabling them to craft content that resonates with viewers long after the initial exposure.

The integration of fMRI into the study of brain activity during video ad viewing not only enhances the understanding of consumer responses but also provides a quantitative measure of the effectiveness of marketing strategies. By correlating neural activation patterns with key performance indicators, marketers can objectively assess the impact of video content on brand perception and consumer behavior. This data-driven approach aligns with the core principles of Neuromarketing, leveraging neuroscientific insights to inform strategic decision-making in the creation and optimization of video advertising.

Emotional Engagement Through Storytelling Techniques

Neuromarketing recognizes the profound impact of storytelling techniques on emotional engagement, unravelling the intricate interplay between narrative structures and the human brain. The application of neuroscience principles to storytelling goes beyond conventional self-report methods, tapping into the subconscious reactions and neural responses of individuals. Plassmann and colleagues (2012) highlight the neurobiological basis of storytelling, emphasizing its ability to stimulate the release of neurochemicals such as oxytocin, fostering a sense of connection and empathy between the storyteller and the audience. This neurochemical response forms the foundation for emotional engagement, a critical component in crafting resonant and memorable brand narratives.

The neuroscientific exploration of storytelling involves examining brain regions associated with emotion, memory, and social cognition. Functional Magnetic Resonance Imaging (fMRI) studies reveal that storytelling activates areas such as the amygdala and hippocampus, which play pivotal roles in emotional processing and memory formation (Plassmann et al., 2012). By understanding the neural underpinnings of storytelling, marketers can tailor narratives that align with the brain's natural mechanisms, creating narratives that are not only emotionally impactful but also more likely to be retained in the long-term memory of the audience.

Moreover, the structure of a narrative significantly influences its neurobiological impact. Research underscores the potency of stories following a classic narrative arc, characterized by a beginning, middle, and end. Plassmann and colleagues (2012) reveal that this structure triggers heightened neural activity and enhances the encoding of information into memory. Marketers leveraging Neuromarketing principles in storytelling can strategically structure brand narratives to captivate attention, evoke emotions, and ensure that key brand messages are more effectively embedded in the audience's memory.

The integration of storytelling techniques in Neuromarketing also extends to considerations of visual and auditory elements within the narrative. Eye-tracking studies provide insights into the patterns of visual attention during storytelling, guiding the placement of visuals that complement and enhance the narrative flow (Holmqvist et al., 2011). Additionally, understanding how auditory elements, such as voice tone and pacing, impact neural responses allow marketers to optimize storytelling for maximum emotional resonance. The understanding of brain activity during video ad viewing and the strategic application of storytelling techniques represents pivotal aspects of Neuromarketing. By leveraging neuroimaging techniques and insights into narrative structures, marketers can optimize video content to elicit specific neural responses and enhance emotional engagement. This neuroscientific approach not only provides a deeper understanding of consumer behaviour but also paves the way for the creation of more impactful and memorable brand narratives.

The Power of Social Media Storytelling

Neuromarketing and Tailored Content for Platforms

Neuromarketing intersects with the dynamic landscape of digital platforms, offering a nuanced understanding of consumer behavior that guides the creation of tailored content. The diverse nature of online platforms, from social media to e-commerce websites, necessitates an adaptive approach informed by neuroscientific insights. Research by Lee and colleagues (2007) emphasizes the importance of aligning content with the unique features and user experiences of each platform, acknowledging the distinct neural responses associated with different digital environments.

Tailoring content for platforms involves a strategic integration of visual and textual elements that resonate with the specific preferences and attention patterns of users. Eye-tracking studies, as outlined by Holmqvist and colleagues (2011), contribute to this understanding by revealing how users visually engage with content on various platforms. Marketers, armed with insights into visual attention and gaze patterns, can optimize the placement of key elements such as product images, calls-to-action, or social sharing buttons, ensuring optimal visibility and engagement.

The integration of Neuromarketing principles into tailored content extends to considerations of colour psychology, design aesthetics, and user interface elements. Neuroscientific research demonstrates that colour choices evoke distinct emotional responses (Plassmann et al., 2012). By aligning colour palettes with the emotional tone desired for the brand or message, marketers can create visually appealing and emotionally resonant content. Furthermore, the principles of visual hierarchy, as informed by eye-tracking studies, guide the arrangement of design elements to enhance user experience and facilitate a seamless journey through the platform.

Understanding the neurobiological responses to tailored content on digital platforms also involves recognizing the influence of social and interactive elements. The brain's reliance on social validation and the pleasure derived from social interactions, as highlighted by Plassmann and colleagues (2012), underscores the significance of incorporating social components into content. Strategies such as user-generated content, interactive features, and social sharing functionalities leverage the brain's social cognition mechanisms, fostering a sense of community and engagement among users.

Additionally, the temporal dynamics of platform usage play a crucial role in content tailoring. The brevity of user attention spans on certain platforms, such as social media, necessitates concise and impactful messaging. Neuromarketing insights, particularly from fMRI studies, inform the creation of content that captures attention rapidly and sustains engagement throughout brief interactions (Lee et al., 2007). This adaptation to the temporal constraints of digital platforms aligns with the principles of Neuromarketing, optimizing content for the brain's rapid processing of information in digital environments.

Curating Emotionally Resonant Content

In the realm of Neuromarketing, the curation of emotionally resonant content emerges as a strategic imperative, capitalizing on neuroscientific insights into the neural mechanisms underlying emotional processing. Plassmann and colleagues (2012) underscore the neurobiological basis of emotional engagement, emphasizing the role of specific brain regions such as the amygdala and prefrontal cortex. The application of these insights to content curation involves tailoring messaging, imagery, and storytelling techniques to evoke desired emotional responses that align with brand objectives.

Understanding the neural correlates of emotions enables marketers to craft content that triggers positive emotional experiences. Neuroimaging techniques, such as fMRI, offer a window into the brain's emotional processing centres during exposure to diverse types of content (Plassmann et al., 2012). This neuroscientific lens allows for the identification of content elements, be it visual aesthetics, language choice, or narrative structures, that resonate most strongly with the emotional centres of the brain. By curating content that elicits positive emotional responses, marketers can forge stronger emotional connections with their audience.

The integration of Neuromarketing principles into content curation also involves an appreciation of individual differences in emotional responses. Lee and colleagues (2007) highlight the variability in neural activation patterns across individuals, emphasizing the importance of personalized approaches. The advent of machine learning and data analytics facilitates the segmentation of audiences based on neurologically informed emotional responses, enabling marketers to tailor content to specific demographics or psychographics. Personalization, rooted in understanding individual variations in emotional processing, fosters a more intimate and resonant connection between brands and consumers.

Moreover, the neuroscientific exploration of storytelling techniques contributes to emotionally resonant content curation. Plassmann and colleagues (2012) reveal the neurobiological basis of storytelling, emphasizing its ability to stimulate the release of oxytocin and foster a sense of connection. Marketers leveraging storytelling in content creation can strategically structure narratives that align with the brain's natural mechanisms, creating emotionally resonant experiences that go beyond mere information dissemination. The incorporation of storytelling into content curation offers a narrative framework that not only captivates attention but also leaves an impression in the memory of the audience.

The constructive collaboration between Neuromarketing and tailored content for digital platforms, coupled with the strategic curation of emotionally resonant content, represents a change in basic assumptions in contemporary marketing strategies. By integrating neuroscientific insights into platform-specific content creation and leveraging the neural basis of emotional engagement, marketers can forge deeper connections with their audience, enhance brand perceptions, and drive desired consumer behaviours.

The Science of Persuasion to Language and Copywriting

Neuromarketing Guiding Word Choice and Framing

The strategic use of language in Neuromarketing extends beyond mere communication, delving into the neuroscientific principles that underlie the impact of word choice and framing on consumer behavior. Lee and colleagues (2007) emphasize the role of language in influencing brain activity and shaping neural responses, underscoring the importance of selecting words that resonate with the emotional and cognitive centres of the brain. The neurobiological basis of language processing allows marketers to guide consumer perceptions and decisions through a nuanced understanding of how specific words elicit distinct neural responses.

Neuromarketing insights into word choice involve an exploration of the emotional valence associated with different terms. Neuroscientific research reveals that positive and negative words trigger divergent patterns of neural activation, influencing the emotional tone of the message (Lee et al., 2007). By aligning word choices with the desired emotional response, marketers can craft messaging that elicits positive associations and engages the brain's reward system. This neurologically informed approach to word choice extends to considerations of tone, style, and cultural nuances, ensuring that the language used resonates authentically with the target audience.

Framing, a persuasive technique deeply rooted in Neuromarketing, involves presenting information in a way that emphasizes gains or losses to influence decision-making processes (Lee et al., 2007). The brain's susceptibility to framing effects is evident in neuroimaging studies that illustrate how different framings activate distinct neural circuits associated with reward and risk processing. Marketers leveraging framing techniques can strategically position their products or messages to trigger positive associations and mitigate perceived risks, aligning with the brain's inherent valuation processes.

Moreover, the neuroscientific exploration of language extends to the realm of brand messaging. Neuroimaging techniques, such as fMRI, enable researchers to investigate the neural responses to brand names and slogans, providing insights into the emotional and cognitive associations elicited by specific linguistic elements (Lee et al., 2007). By understanding the neurobiological basis of brand language, marketers can tailor their messaging to evoke desired brand perceptions and enhance the overall effectiveness of communication strategies.

The integration of Neuromarketing principles into word choice and framing strategies not only optimizes the effectiveness of marketing messages but also addresses the cognitive biases and heuristics that influence decision-making. The alignment of language with the brain's natural processing tendencies contributes to a more seamless and persuasive communication process, fostering a deeper connection between brands and consumers.

Creating Urgency and Motivation Through Neurologically Informed Copy

Neuromarketing unfolds its potential in the strategic creation of urgency and motivation through neurologically informed copywriting. The understanding of how the brain processes information related to time, reward, and motivation informs the crafting of compelling messages that prompt immediate action. Hubert and Kenning (2008) emphasize the significance of urgency in consumer decision-making, highlighting the brain's sensitivity to time-sensitive cues and the role of the limbic system in processing motivational information.

Neurologically informed copywriting involves the strategic use of language and framing to convey a sense of urgency and scarcity. The brain's response to time-related cues, as observed in fMRI studies, illustrates the heightened neural activity associated with perceived urgency (Hubert & Kenning, 2008). By incorporating time-sensitive language and framing messages within a temporal context, marketers can tap into the brain's motivational centres, prompting a desire for immediate action. This neuroscientific approach aligns with the psychology of scarcity, where the perception of limited availability triggers neural responses associated with increased desirability and motivation.

The concept of neurologically informed urgency extends to considerations of visual elements within marketing communication. Eye-tracking studies provide insights into the patterns of visual attention during the consumption of visual stimuli, guiding the placement of urgent messaging and call-to-action buttons (Holmqvist et al., 2011). Strategic visual cues complement neurologically informed copy, creating a cohesive and impactful message that captures attention and motivates users to act promptly.

Furthermore, the brain's response to reward-related stimuli plays a pivotal role in motivating consumer behavior. Neuroscientific insights into the neural processes associated with reward anticipation inform the creation of copy that emphasizes the immediate benefits or gains associated with taking a specific action (Hubert & Kenning, 2008). By aligning messaging with the brain's reward system, marketers can enhance the perceived value of products or services, fostering a sense of motivation and driving desired behaviours.

The integration of Neuromarketing principles into copywriting strategies for urgency and motivation also considers individual differences in cognitive processing. Lee and colleagues (2007) discuss the variability in neural activation patterns across individuals, emphasizing the importance of personalized approaches. By tailoring urgency-driven messaging to specific audience segments based on neurologically informed insights, marketers can optimize the effectiveness of their copywriting strategies for motivation and prompt action.

The Future of Marketing Communication as a Brain-Powered Landscape

As we gaze into the future of marketing communication, a transformative shift unfolds—a landscape increasingly powered by insights derived from the intricacies of the human brain. The advent of Neuromarketing has redefined the contours of consumer understanding, transcended traditional methodologies and ushered in an era where neuroscience principles guide the strategic orchestration of marketing strategies. This brain-powered landscape not only challenges conventional approaches but also heralds a new frontier characterized by a profound understanding of the neural mechanisms that underlie decision-making, emotion, and perception.

In this brain-powered future, the integration of advanced neuroimaging technologies, such as functional Magnetic Resonance Imaging (fMRI) and Electroencephalography (EEG), becomes more pervasive. The real-time insights offered by these technologies unlock the ability to observe neural responses during consumer interactions with marketing stimuli, providing a granular understanding of how the brain engages with content and experiences. Researchers and marketers alike leverage fMRI to map neural activation patterns associated with emotions and cognitive processes, while EEG captures the dynamic cognitive dynamics as individuals navigate the digital landscape (Lee et al., 2007; Plassmann et al., 2012). This neuroscientific lens enables a deeper comprehension of consumer responses, guiding the tailoring of marketing communication to resonate with the brain's innate processes.

The future of marketing communication is also characterized by a heightened emphasis on individualized and personalized strategies, attuned to the neurodiversity of consumers. The recognition that neural responses vary across individuals underscores the importance of tailored approaches that consider the unique cognitive and emotional profiles of diverse audience segments (Lee et al., 2007). Machine learning algorithms and data analytics, informed by neurologically driven insights, pave the way for hyper-personalization, ensuring that marketing messages resonate at a level that transcends generic appeals.

Moreover, the continued evolution of virtual and augmented reality (VR and AR) technologies contributes to the immersive and experiential dimension of marketing communication. As consumers engage with VR and AR experiences, their neural responses are intricately woven into the fabric of the marketing narrative. The fusion of neuroscience with these technologies offers unprecedented opportunities to create immersive brand experiences that directly impact the brain's sensory and emotional centres, forging lasting and memorable connections with the audience (Holmqvist et al., 2011).

The emergence of a brain-powered landscape in marketing communication also necessitates a revaluation of ethical considerations. As the ability to decode neural responses to marketing stimuli advances, questions of consumer privacy, consent, and the responsible use of neuroscientific insights come to the forefront. Ethical frameworks must evolve alongside technological advancements to ensure that neurodata is handled with sensitivity and respect for individual autonomy, fostering trust between consumers and marketers (Hubert & Kenning, 2008).

Furthermore, the future of marketing communication embraces the fusion of creativity and neuroscience, giving rise to a new breed of marketing professionals—neuro-creatives. These individuals adeptly navigate both the artistic realms of storytelling and design and the scientific landscapes of neural responses and behavioural economics. The constructive collaboration of creativity and neuroscience yields campaigns that not only captivate the imagination but also strategically tap into the brain's cognitive and emotional circuitry, amplifying the impact of marketing messages (Plassmann et al., 2012). The future of marketing communication unfolds as a brain-powered landscape, where the integration of neuroscience principles reshapes strategies, technologies, and ethical considerations. The profound insights derived from the human brain illuminate a path toward more empathetic, personalized, and immersive marketing experiences. As the realms of neuroscience and marketing converge, this symbiotic relationship promises to redefine the very essence of consumer-brand interactions, unlocking a new era of strategic communication that resonates with the intricate workings of the mind.

CONCLUSION

Neuromarketing as a digital marketing strategy unravelling the evolution of marketing communication, the convergence of neuroscience and marketing has emerged as a powerful paradigm. The journey traversed through the chapters has delved into the neuroscientific foundations of consumer behavior, the application of advanced technologies in marketing research, and the strategic implementation of neuromarketing across various digital domains. As we conclude this discourse, it becomes evident that Neuromarketing offers a transformative lens through which marketers can decipher the intricate workings of the human brain to inform and optimize their strategies.

The integration of neuroimaging techniques such as fMRI, EEG, and eye-tracking has allowed marketers to peer into the neural responses evoked by marketing stimuli. This neuroscientific gaze, coupled with an understanding of the emotional drivers and cognitive dynamics, has empowered marketers to tailor their approaches in unprecedented ways. By decoding real-time neural responses, businesses can craft more resonant messaging, optimize user experiences, and forge deeper emotional connections with their audience.

The elucidation of the power of visual stimuli, language, and storytelling techniques has unveiled the subtle art of persuasion, providing marketers with a nuanced toolkit to influence consumer decisions. Neuromarketing not only guides the selection of imagery and language but also informs the strategic placement of content to capture attention and sustain engagement. The science of persuasion, rooted in the principles of neuroscience, underscores the capacity to influence decisions at a neurobiological level.

As we peer into the future of marketing communication, the brain-powered landscape emerges as a frontier characterized by hyper-personalization, immersive technologies, and the delicate interplay between creativity and neuroscience. The neuro-creative professional, adept at blending the artistic with the scientific, becomes a linchpin in this evolving landscape. However, this vision of the future also beckons a careful consideration of ethical dimensions, as the handling of neurodata necessitates a delicate balance between innovation and consumer privacy.

It is essential to underscore that Neuromarketing does not merely represent a set of techniques but a profound shift in the understanding of consumers as individuals with unique neurocognitive profiles. The integration of neuroscience principles into digital marketing strategies signifies a departure from one-size-fits-all approaches, offering a more empathetic and personalized communication model. As marketing communication continues to evolve, the symbiotic relationship between neuroscience and marketing promises a future where brands connect with consumers at a level that resonates with the very essence of human cognition and emotion.

REFERENCES

Ariely, D., & Berns, G. S. (2010). Neuromarketing: The hope and hype of neuroimaging in business. *Nature Reviews. Neuroscience*, *11*(4), 284–292. doi:10.1038/nrn2795 PMID:20197790

Damasio, A. R. (1994). Descartes' error and the future of human life. *Scientific American*, *271*(4), 144. doi:10.1038/scientificamerican1094-144 PMID:7939563

Falk, E. B., Berkman, E. T., & Lieberman, M. D. (2012). From neural responses to population behavior: Neural focus group predicts population-level media effects. *Psychological Science*, *23*(5), 439–445. doi:10.1177/0956797611434964 PMID:22510393

Häusser, J. A., & Förderer, S. (2019). Consumer neuroscience-based metrics predict recall, liking, and viewing duration in online advertising. *Frontiers in Neuroscience*, *13*, 225.

Holmqvist, K., Nyström, M., Andersson, R., Dewhurst, R., Jarodzka, H., & Van de Weijer, J. (2011). *Eye tracking: A comprehensive guide to methods and measures*. Oxford University Press.

Hsu, M., Yoon, C., Hajcak, G., & Berns, G. S. (2009). Monetary loss and the brain: An ERP study of the influence of task relevance and motivation. *Social Cognitive and Affective Neuroscience*, *4*(4), 321–329.

Hubert, M., & Kenning, P. (2008). A current overview of consumer neuroscience. *Journal of Consumer Behaviour*, *7*(4–5), 272–292. doi:10.1002/cb.251

Kenning, P., & Linzmajer, M. (2011). Consumer neuroscience: An overview of an emerging discipline with implications for consumer policy. *Journal of Consumer Policy*, *34*(3), 263–276.

Knutson, B., Rick, S., Wimmer, G. E., Prelec, D., & Loewenstein, G. (2007). Neural predictors of purchases. *Neuron*, *53*(1), 147–156. doi:10.1016/j.neuron.2006.11.010 PMID:17196537

Langleben, D. D., Loughead, J. W., Bilker, W. B., Ruparel, K., Childress, A. R., Busch, S. I., & Gur, R. C. (2009). Telling truth from lie in individual subjects with fast event-related fMRI. *Human Brain Mapping*, *30*(3), 745–757. PMID:16161128

Lee, N., Broderick, A. J., & Chamberlain, L. (2007). What is 'neuromarketing'? A discussion and agenda for future research. *International Journal of Psychophysiology*, *63*(2), 199–204. doi:10.1016/j.ijpsycho.2006.03.007 PMID:16769143

Lim, S. L., O'Doherty, J. P., & Rangel, A. (2011). The decision value computations in the vmPFC and striatum use a relative value code that is guided by visual attention. *The Journal of Neuroscience : The Official Journal of the Society for Neuroscience*, *31*(37), 13214–13223. doi:10.1523/JNEUROSCI.1246-11.2011 PMID:21917804

McCabe, D. P., Roediger, H. L. III, McDaniel, M. A., Balota, D. A., & Hambrick, D. Z. (2010). The relationship between working memory capacity and executive functioning: Evidence for a common executive attention construct. *Neuropsychology*, *24*(2), 222–243. doi:10.1037/a0017619 PMID:20230116

Ohme, R., Reykowska, D., Wiener, D., & Choromanska, A. (2009). Application of frontal EEG asymmetry to advertising research. *Journal of Economic Psychology*, *30*(5), 856–867.

Plassmann, H., O'Doherty, J., & Rangel, A. (2007). Orbitofrontal cortex encodes willingness to pay in everyday economic transactions. *The Journal of Neuroscience : The Official Journal of the Society for Neuroscience*, *27*(37), 9984–9988. doi:10.1523/JNEUROSCI.2131-07.2007 PMID:17855612

Plassmann, H., Ramsøy, T. Z., & Milosavljevic, M. (2012). Branding the brain: A critical review and outlook. *Journal of Consumer Psychology*, *22*(1), 18–36. doi:10.1016/j.jcps.2011.11.010

Smith, D. V., Hayden, B. Y., Truong, T. K., Song, A. W., Platt, M. L., & Huettel, S. A. (2010). Distinct value signals in anterior and posterior ventromedial prefrontal cortex. *The Journal of Neuroscience : The Official Journal of the Society for Neuroscience*, *30*(7), 2490–2495. doi:10.1523/JNEUROSCI.3319-09.2010 PMID:20164333

Venkatraman, V., Dimoka, A., Pavlou, P. A., Vo, K., Hampton, W., Bollinger, B., Hershfield, H. E., Ishihara, M., & Winer, R. S. (2015). Predicting advertising success beyond traditional measures: New insights from neurophysiological methods and market response modeling. *JMR, Journal of Marketing Research*, *52*(4), 436–452. doi:10.1509/jmr.13.0593

Yoon, C., Gutchess, A. H., Feinberg, F., & Polk, T. A. (2006). A functional magnetic resonance imaging study of neural dissociations between brand and person judgments. *The Journal of Consumer Research*, *33*(1), 31–40. doi:10.1086/504132

Zak, P. J., & Knack, S. (2001). Trust and growth. *Economic Journal (London)*, *111*(470), 295–321. doi:10.1111/1468-0297.00609

Chapter 6
Fintech Startups and Cryptocurrency in Business:
Revolutionizing Entrepreneurship

Muhammad Usman Tariq
https://orcid.org/0000-0002-7605-3040
Abu Dhabi University, UAE & University of Glasgow, Glasgow, UK

ABSTRACT

This book chapter explains the significant influence of cryptocurrencies and fintech startups on business models and entrepreneurship by examining their revolutionary junction. The chapter thoroughly examines fintech's birth and development, charting its disruptive path inside the conventional financial services industry. It simultaneously explores the history of cryptocurrencies, revealing the blockchain's technical foundations and growing popularity in the corporate community. The story highlights the explosive rise of fintech companies and identifies its driving forces, including changes in consumer preferences, legislative changes, and technology breakthroughs. The chapter's main focus is how companies embrace cryptocurrencies, use them for transactions, hold ICOs to raise money, and add them to investment portfolios. The chapter also discusses technological difficulties and regulatory issues when merging fintech and cryptocurrency solutions.

DOI: 10.4018/979-8-3693-1846-1.ch006

OVERVIEW: FINTECH STARTUPS AND CRYPTOCURRENCY IN BUSINESS—REVOLUTIONIZING ENTREPRENEURSHIP

Fintech firms and cryptocurrencies are seeing a dramatic junction in the ever-evolving environment of the modern business ecosystem. This chapter aims to provide readers with a thorough knowledge of the significant influence of these creative forces on company models, investment strategies, and financial transactions. As we investigate this junction, it becomes clear that the mutually beneficial link between fintech and cryptocurrencies is more than just a fad. Rather, it is a revolutionary force influencing the course of global enterprise.

Fintech's Development and Emergence: Upending Conventional Financial Services

It is crucial first to examine the formation and expansion of the fintech sector to appreciate the significance of this convergence fully. Fintech, a combination of "financial technology," refers to using technology to improve and simplify financial services. This sector has changed quickly, using digital technological breakthroughs to upend established financial services (Smith, 2017). The chapter begins with examining how fintech companies, propelled by technology advancements, have questioned and transformed traditional financial conventions. We provide the foundation for comprehending fintech's crucial position in the modern corporate environment by outlining essential principles and charting the historical development of the industry.

Overview of Cryptocurrency: History, Blockchain Technology, and Increasing Acceptance in Business

Investigating the world of cryptocurrencies is essential as we embark on our journey. Since the launch of Bitcoin in 2009, cryptocurrencies have developed from a specialised idea to a central topic of conversation regarding the direction of finance (Narayanan et al., 2016). A review of blockchain technology, a decentralised, unchangeable ledger system, is part of an overview of cryptocurrencies. The chapter explains how cryptocurrencies are becoming increasingly accepted in the business sector, opening the door for novel financial practices because of their decentralised structure, cryptographic security, and transparency (Swan, 2015).

Fintech Startups' Rapid Growth: Technological Developments, Customer Demand, and Regulatory Shifts

After that, the story thoroughly examines the financial businesses' explosive expansion. The digital revolution has enabled these entrepreneurs to provide innovative financial services and solutions through technological developments (Arner et al., 2016). The elements contributing to their success are discussed, including the growing need for smooth and convenient financial experiences and the effect of legislative reforms that have made room for innovation (Zohar, 2015). The chapter sheds light on the ever-changing environment that financial firms operate in by examining particular examples and trends.

Businesses Using Cryptocurrencies: Investment Portfolios, ICOs, and Transactions

An important aspect of the research is how companies use cryptocurrency. A thorough analysis is conducted on using cryptocurrencies in transactions, their inclusion into investment portfolios, and their fundraising through Initial Coin Offerings (ICOs). The practical effects of Bitcoin adoption are highlighted in this part, providing insight into how companies use this innovative digital money to increase productivity, save expenses, and open up new funding sources (Catalini & Gans, 2016).

Impact on Entrepreneurship: Fintech Innovations Facilitate New Business Models

As the story progresses, it becomes more of a thorough examination of how fintech companies and cryptocurrencies affect entrepreneurship. Examining the fresh business models that resulted from fintech advancements is part of this. Demirgüç-Kunt et al. (2020) examine disruptive models such as peer-to-peer lending, crowdfunding, and decentralised finance (DeFi) that upend established financial intermediaries and give entrepreneurs more control. The conversation also covers how these technologies revolutionise several commercial domains, such as payments, remittances, and financial inclusion.

Real-world Examples: Fintech Operations' Effective Integration of Cryptocurrency

The chapter includes real-world case studies of profitable fintech startups and companies that have successfully incorporated cryptocurrencies into their operations to demonstrate how these ideas may be applied. These case studies, which cover a range of industries and geographical areas, provide a nuanced understanding of the many uses and results of integrating fintech and cryptocurrencies (Gai, 2018).

Integration Difficulties: Cybersecurity Risks, Technological Complexities, and Market Volatility

This life-changing adventure comes with difficulties, however. The challenges that companies have when incorporating fintech and cryptocurrency solutions are covered in this chapter. Cong et al. (2018) emphasise that strategic methods are necessary for effective integration due to the major difficulties of technological complexity, cybersecurity threats, and market volatility. This section highlights how crucial it is to fully comprehend and address these issues to utilise fintech and cryptocurrencies in corporate operations.

Regulatory Environment: Adherence to AML Guidelines, Financial Regulations, and Consumer Protection

Managing the regulatory environment is yet another important topic covered in this chapter. The regulatory issues that companies need to consider when implementing fintech and cryptocurrency solutions are the topic of discussion. These technologies' effective and long-lasting integration depends on following financial rules, adhering to anti-money laundering (AML) requirements, and guaranteeing consumer safety (Narayanan et al., 2016).

Looking Ahead: Fintech Startups' Future Course and the Use of Cryptocurrency in Business

After that, the story adopts a forward-looking stance, investigating the potential paths fintech businesses may follow and the changing significance of cryptocurrencies in the commercial world. Insights for entrepreneurs, investors, and policymakers to predict and adjust to the dynamic changes in the financial ecosystem are provided by the discussion of emerging trends, possible innovations, and the changing landscape of financial technology (Mishkin et al., 2016).

This chapter concludes with a summary of the profound influence that fintech companies and cryptocurrencies have had on redefining business and entrepreneurship. It emphasises how crucial these technologies are to fostering inclusion, efficiency, and innovation in the financial industry. The chapter is a call to action, emphasising that players must cooperate, innovate, and adapt strategically to you, fintech and cryptocurrencies in the business sector. This chapter provides a path for navigating the complex world of fintech businesses and cryptocurrency integration, helping to shape the future of entrepreneurship globally as we stand at the intersection of technical innovation and financial change.

INTRODUCTION TO FINTECH AND CRYPTOCURRENCY

The convergence of Bitcoin and financial technology (fintech) in the twenty-first century has changed the face of traditional financial services and drastically changed the nature of modern business. This introduction explores the origins and development of fintech, following its path of disruption as it questions established financial conventions.

Fintech's Development and Emergence: Upending Conventional Financial Services

The combination of technology and finance, or fintech, has become essential to developing financial services. Fintech firms have emerged due to the quick development of digital technology, which has changed how people and organisations interact with financial transactions (Arner et al., 2016). The story opens with a background review, followed by definitions of important terms and an explanation of the fintech industry's complex development.

Fintech has grown due to technological advancements in cloud computing, blockchain, artificial intelligence and machine learning (Smith, 2017). Fintech firms have challenged the old banking paradigm by developing creative solutions to consumers' growing need for seamless and user-friendly financial experiences (Demirgüç-Kunt et al., 2018). The chapter examines how important fintech is to democratise financial services, promoting financial inclusion, and fixing the financial industry's long-standing inefficiencies.

Fintech's disruptive influence spans the financial services industry, not just consumer-facing apps. Fintech is redefining traditional banking, democratising investment options, and streamlining financial procedures; examples include peer-to-peer lending platforms, robo-advisors, and mobile payment systems (Zohar, 2015). A detailed examination of particular use cases and success stories reveals fintech's wide range of uses and revolutionary potential in reshaping the financial industry.

The discourse encompasses the elements fueling the expansion of fintech enterprises, such as the emergence of financial products oriented towards consumers, evolving regulatory frameworks, and the incorporation of cutting-edge technology (Narayanan et al., 2016). Particularly, regulatory improvements have been crucial in creating a favourable climate for fintech innovation by allowing firms to move more quickly and nimbly through intricate regulatory environments (Catalini & Gans, 2016).

As the chapter comes to a close, we take a closer look at the disruptive power of fintech and consider how traditional financial services continue to change due to the rapid advancement of technology. The story lays the groundwork for an in-depth investigation of the mutually beneficial link between fintech and cryptocurrencies and their combined effects on the world economy.

THE GROWTH OF FINTECH STARTUPS AND ADOPTION OF CRYPTOCURRENCY

The explosive rise of fintech companies in the constantly changing financial sector is evidence of the revolutionary potential of technological innovation. This section examines the various causes that have contributed to the rapid growth of these companies, such as significant legal changes, growing customer demand, and technological developments.

Fintech Startups' Rapid Growth: Technological Developments

The rapid improvement of technology significantly impacts the growth trajectory of fintech businesses. These firms can now develop creative financial services and solutions because of the integration of cutting-edge technology like machine learning, big data analytics, and artificial intelligence (Arner et al., 2016). .. As we go deeper into the technology environment, the conversation moves through particular fintech apps, explaining how these businesses employ technology to improve user experiences, optimise workflows, and develop innovative financial solutions (Zavolokina et al., 2016).

This chapter looks at how technological agility helps create a competitive and dynamic financial sector. According to Demirgüç-Kunt et al. (2018), startups that effectively use technology advancements may react quickly to market needs, surpass established financial institutions in product creation, and profit from developing trends. Case studies from the real world highlight situations in which technological expertise has been a crucial differentiator, highlighting the mutually beneficial link between financial firms and technology breakthroughs.

Customer Demand as the Main Engine

Customer demand is one of the main drivers of fintech startup expansion. This section explores how customer expectations are changing in the digital era and highlights how people are choosing more convenient, individualised financial services (Gerrard & Cunningham, 2020). Fintech firms have positioned themselves as nimble disruptors capable of catering to the varied requirements of a tech-savvy customer base by matching their services with these evolving tastes.

Fintech businesses' success largely depends on their understanding of customer behaviour. By utilising data-driven insights and user-centric design concepts, these firms may customise their offerings to target certain issues in traditional financial services, giving them a competitive advantage (Lusardi & Mitchell, 2014). The story examines the tactics used by fintech businesses to increase financial literacy, foster customer trust, and produce seamless digital experiences that appeal to today's consumers.

Regulation Modifications: Handling a Changing Environment

The regulatory environment significantly shapes the trajectory of financial businesses. This section examines the potential and obstacles these companies have faced due to legislative reforms, which are frequently the result of an awareness of the need for innovation in the financial sector (Hodgson & Mei, 2019). Fintech-friendly legislation has arisen as governments adjust to the digital era, creating a climate favourable to innovation and development.

There are obstacles to overcome while negotiating the regulatory environment, however. The story explores the challenges fintech firms must overcome, such as licencing processes, compliance requirements, and balancing innovation and regulatory conformity carefully (Ahmed et al., 2020). Using examples from around the world, the report shows how regulatory regimes in various jurisdictions have facilitated or hindered the emergence of fintech businesses.

Conclusively, the section provides a comprehensive comprehension of the fast expansion of fintech companies by integrating technological expertise, customer behaviour, and regulatory subtleties. The story lays the groundwork for a detailed investigation of how fintech companies incorporate cryptocurrencies into their operations, spurring more innovation and changing the financial environment by examining how these elements interact.

Adoption of Cryptocurrencies by Businesses: Transactions, ICOs, and Investment Portfolios

A significant paradigm change in the financial environment is being marked by the incorporation of cryptocurrencies into the operations of businesses. This section examines the many ways in which companies have used cryptocurrencies. These include transactions, initial coin offerings (ICOs), and adding digital assets to investment portfolios.

Acceptance of Digital Currency in Transactions

According to Narayanan et al. (2016), cryptocurrencies, particularly Bitcoin, have become a feasible means of conducting financial transactions, upending preconceived ideas about money and payment methods. This section explores the advantages and disadvantages of using decentralised and cryptographic currencies in commercial transactions. It also explains the complexities involved in implementing cryptocurrencies.

The chapter examines how using bitcoins in transactions might help firms become more efficient and save money. Due to its immutability, blockchain technology enables safe and transparent financial transactions, lowering the danger of fraud and minimising the need for middlemen (Swan, 2015). Case studies from the real world show how companies from different industries have effectively incorporated cryptocurrencies into their payment systems, highlighting the useful consequences and results of this kind of adoption.

The use of cryptocurrency in transactions is easy, however. The story examines the difficulties of scalability, volatility, and the technological learning curve that companies wishing to enter the decentralised digital currency space must overcome (Catalini & Gans, 2016). Examples from the industry are used to provide insights that illuminate the tactics companies use to handle these difficulties successfully.

Using Initial Coin Offerings (ICOs) to Raise Money

The emergence of Initial Coin Offerings (ICOs) has brought about a new paradigm in fundraising, upending conventional approaches to obtaining finance. This section explores how companies use initial coin offerings (ICOs) to raise money by issuing and selling digital tokens. The story looks at the workings of initial coin offerings (ICOs), the legal issues surrounding these methods of generating money, and how they affect investors and companies.

In order to present effective examples of how companies have applied this cutting-edge fundraising technique, ICO case studies are examined. The benefits of initial coin offerings (ICOs) are explained in this section. These benefits include enhanced liquidity, access to a worldwide investor base, and the ability to democratise investment possibilities (Momtaz, 2017). It also critically examines the risks and difficulties of initial coin offerings (ICOs), such as market speculation, fraudulent activity, and regulatory ambiguity.

Mixture With Investment Portfolios

Businesses are adding more and more digital assets to their investing portfolios as cryptocurrencies gain traction. This section examines companies' strategic decisions when incorporating cryptocurrency into their investment plans. A thorough summary of this paradigm change is given by examining the advantages of diversification, risk management strategies, and the changing position of cryptocurrencies in institutional investing portfolios.

The chapter is based on observations from eminent asset management companies and financial institutions that have dabbled in Bitcoin investing. It examines how digital assets affect risk-adjusted returns, portfolio performance, and the larger ramifications for conventional investing paradigms (Foley et al., 2019). The regulatory environment around institutional Bitcoin investments is also covered in this section, highlighting the significance of risk reduction and compliance measures.

The section concludes by summarising the many aspects of companies implementing cryptocurrencies and providing a sophisticated analysis of their function in investments, fundraising, and transactions. The story explains how cryptocurrencies revolutionise conventional business practices by examining real-world uses and difficulties.

IMPACT ON ENTREPRENEURSHIP AND BUSINESS MODELS

There has been a paradigm change in the conventional business environment due to the mutually beneficial link between fintech advances and entrepreneurship. This section explores how fintech dramatically affects entrepreneurship, looking at how new business models are emerging and how it is changing important business features like payments, remittances, and financial inclusion.

Fintech Innovations' Impact on Entrepreneurship: New Business Models

The world of entrepreneurship has been completely transformed by fintech developments, which have given companies new tools and approaches to deal with the rapidly changing digital economy. The story opens by examining how fintech affects entrepreneurship and breaking down new company models that use technology breakthroughs. These revolutionary concepts, which question established financial intermediaries and democratised access to money, are best exemplified by peer-to-peer lending, crowdfunding, and decentralised finance (DeFi) (Demirgüç-Kunt et al., 2020).

The topic of discussion is how fintech has made it easier for business owners to enter the market by giving them access to finance sources other than traditional banking channels (Zavolokina et al., 2016). The story clarifies the practical ramifications and success stories of entrepreneurs who have used fintech technologies to disrupt and create within their respective industries by examining case studies and industry examples.

Additionally, the part looks at cooperative fintech ecosystems, with entrepreneurs frequently working with fintech startups to improve consumer engagement, operational efficiency, and overall business success (Arner et al., 2016). The article examines how fintech may support innovation and an entrepreneurial culture, emphasising the complex relationship between technology development and business ventures.

Transformative Effect on Business Aspects: Financial Inclusion, Remittances, and Payments

Fintech is changing company operations in fundamental ways that go beyond entrepreneurship. This story section explores how fintech innovations have transformed conventional methods, focusing on three crucial business dimensions: payments, remittances, and financial inclusion.

1. Compensation

Fintech has broadly impacted payments, including developing contactless payment methods, digital wallets, and blockchain-based transactions. This section examines the shift in payment methods from conventional to the digital environment enabled by fintech, including a thorough summary of the advantages, difficulties, and business ramifications (Narayanan et al., 2016). Global payment processors provide insights on how fintech solutions may be integrated to improve security, expedite transactions, and reinvent the payment experience for customers.

2. Transfers of funds

Fintech has drastically changed the remittance market by revolutionising cross-border money transfers for people and companies. The story examines how cutting-edge fintech platforms and blockchain technology might speed up, lower prices, and increase transparency in remittance procedures (Mansoori et al., 2018). Examples from the real world show how fintech-driven solutions have enabled companies to overcome the difficulties involved in transnational commercial dealings, enhancing global financial accessibility.

3. Inclusion of Finances

Fintech advances have accelerated the process of financial inclusion, which is a fundamental component of sustainable economic development. This section looks into how inclusive economic growth has been promoted by fintech by providing financial services to underrepresented communities (Demirgüç-Kunt et al., 2018). The story examines how blockchain-based solutions, digital payment systems, and mobile banking can help close the gap in financial inclusion. Case studies from various geographic areas highlight the useful ways that fintech is enabling financial accessibility and boosting businesses in underserved markets.

The section highlights the complex relationship between fintech and entrepreneurship throughout the investigation, showing how fintech's revolutionary influence on payments, remittances, and financial inclusion fosters an environment conducive to entrepreneurial endeavours. The story presents a thorough picture of how fintech is changing the face of entrepreneurship and rethinking conventional business models by fusing academic frameworks, empirical data, and real-world experiences.

CASE STUDIES OF SUCCESSFUL FINTECH AND CRYPTOCURRENCY VENTURES

A thorough examination of actual case studies illustrates the revolutionary effects of fintech and cryptocurrency integration. This section explores the achievements of trailblazing businesses, revealing the real-world uses, difficulties, and advantages of integrating fintech and cryptocurrencies into a variety of corporate activities.

Real-World Examples: Fintech Operations' Effective Integration of Cryptocurrency

The story starts by examining particular instances where fintech businesses have successfully incorporated cryptocurrencies into their business processes, demonstrating the complementary nature of these two creative forces. Case studies incorporate the insights of businesses like Coinbase, a prominent cryptocurrency exchange, and Ripple, a fintech enterprise that uses blockchain technology to facilitate international payments (Catalini & Gans, 2016; Narayanan et al., 2016).

The examination breaks into the tactics these businesses use to deal with cryptocurrency integration challenges. It investigates building user trust and guaranteeing a flawless user experience through user-friendly interfaces, security protocols, and regulatory compliance (Ahmed et al., 2020). Additionally, the part addresses how these connections affect the expansion and scalability of financial firms, offering insightful information about real-world issues and lessons discovered.

A Comprehensive View: Case Studies Across Different Industries and Locations

In order to provide a thorough grasp of the many uses and results of fintech and cryptocurrency integration, the investigation includes case studies from various industries and geographical locations. Case studies include a variety of industries, including digital banking, peer-to-peer lending, and decentralised finance (DeFi), demonstrating the flexibility and adaptation of these technologies in many contexts (Arner et al., 2016; Foley et al., 2019).

The story explores successful mergers in North America, Europe, Asia, and Africa by presenting a mosaic of case studies. Successful initiatives in the fields of peer-to-peer lending (Zopa), digital banking (Revolut), and decentralised finance (Compound) are a few examples. The section methodically assesses the regulatory environments and contextual details that influenced these businesses' success in the relevant industries and regions (Zavolokina et al., 2016).

Additionally, the thorough analysis explores how these connections affect financial inclusion, examining instances in which fintech and cryptocurrencies have been essential in helping underprivileged groups receive financial services (Demirgüç-Kunt et al., 2018). In addition to highlighting the revolutionary potential of these technologies in tackling global financial concerns, the debate clarifies the consequences for equitable economic growth.

This section assesses the benefits, drawbacks, and wider ramifications of fintech and cryptocurrency endeavours. Theoretical frameworks and empirical data support the analysis. The story provides a roadmap for organisations navigating their integration journeys while showcasing the versatility of these technologies by presenting a wide range of instances.

CHALLENGES AND REGULATORY CONSIDERATIONS

The combination of Bitcoin and financial firms creates a dynamic environment full of obstacles and complex regulations. The integration challenges—such as technological complexity, cybersecurity threats, and market volatility—are thoroughly examined in this section. At the same time, it looks at the complex regulatory environment, stressing the need to adhere to financial laws, anti-money laundering (AML) guidelines, and consumer protection.

Integration Challenges: Technological Complexities, Cybersecurity Risks, Market Volatility

1. **Technology Difficulties:** Fintech and cryptocurrency integration brings complex technology obstacles. The underlying technology of cryptocurrencies, blockchain, has its complications. Significant barriers to seamless integration include scalability concerns, consensus processes, and interoperability challenges (Catalini & Gans, 2016). Fintech firms need to address these intricacies to guarantee the stability and expandability of their platforms.

Furthermore, because blockchain technology is dynamic, it requires constant modification. Keeping up with technology improvements is a difficulty brought on by the quick speed of innovation and is essential for maintaining security and competitiveness in the ever-changing fintech ecosystem (Arner et al., 2016).

2. **Cybersecurity Risks:** Using cryptocurrencies in fintech projects increases the likelihood of cybersecurity issues. The danger landscape grows as financial transactions become more digitally transacted. Exchanges, wallets, and cryptocurrency transactions are vulnerable to fraud, hacking, and unauthorised access (Foley et al., 2019). The necessity of strong cybersecurity measures is examined in this part, with a focus on the importance of encryption, secure key management, and constant monitoring as elements of an all-encompassing cybersecurity strategy (Narayanan et al., 2016).

Case studies of cybersecurity breaches in the financial and cryptocurrency sectors show the possible consequences of insufficient cybersecurity procedures. The story illustrates how to protect user assets and preserve ecosystem trust, successful integration necessitates technology fortification and a proactive cybersecurity posture.

3. **Market Volatility:** Fintech firms face a significant obstacle due to the intrinsic volatility of cryptocurrency markets. The value of cryptocurrencies can fluctuate dramatically, affecting user confidence and the viability of the platforms that use them financially (Swan, 2015). This section explores the methods fintech companies use to lessen the impact of market volatility, including real-time analytics, risk management procedures, and creative financial products to insure against market fluctuations (Foley et al., 2019).

The Chapter also looks at the tightrope fintech companies have to walk when exposing consumers to the possible rewards of cryptocurrency investing while minimising the hazards involved. Successful entrepreneurs and industry professionals share their insights on how a nuanced response to market volatility is essential for long-term growth and consumer confidence.

Regulatory Landscape: Compliance with Financial Regulations, AML Standards, Consumer Protection

1. Compliance with Financial Regulations: Financial services are governed by a complicated regulatory framework that fintech businesses must traverse. This part examines the difficulties in adhering to financial rules, such as licencing requirements and Know Your Customer (KYC) guidelines (Arner et al., 2016). The story emphasises how crucial it is to comprehend and work within national, regional, and global regulatory frameworks to guarantee legal compliance and the long-term viability of fintech initiatives.

Compliance-centric technology, strategic relationships, and proactive interaction with regulatory authorities are key factors in surmounting regulatory difficulties, as demonstrated by case studies of FinTech businesses that have found success. The story underscores how financial rules are dynamic and stresses how fintech companies must adapt quickly to these developments.

2. AML requirements: A vital component of the fintech and cryptocurrency integration regulatory environment is enforcing strict Anti-Money Laundering (AML) requirements. The difficulties in putting into practice effective AML measures—such as transaction monitoring, reporting suspicious behaviour, and customer due diligence—are examined in this section (Narayanan et al., 2016). The story explores the international efforts made to stop money laundering, highlighting how fintech companies uphold AML regulations to provide a safe and law-abiding financial sector.

Examples from the real world show how breaking AML regulations has resulted in reputational harm and legal consequences. The section highlights that to guarantee the integrity of their platforms, fintech firms must implement strong AML procedures, cooperate with regulatory agencies, and use cutting-edge technologies.

3. Consumer Protection: Ensuring consumer protection is crucial as fintech platforms are more and more of the entry point to financial services. The difficulties in protecting consumer interests are discussed in this paragraph. These difficulties include concerns about data privacy, openness, and redress procedures (Zavolokina et al., 2016). The story looks at fintech companies' obligations to secure customer data, create and disseminate clear terms of service, and offer channels for resolving disputes.

Case studies show how fintech companies have effectively incorporated customer-centric strategies to build loyalty and trust. The story highlights the mutually beneficial connection between consumer protection and the sustained prosperity of fintech endeavours, stressing the significance of adhering to regulations and implementing moral corporate conduct.

Finally, this section comprehensively analyses the regulatory issues and integration obstacles inherent in the fintech-cryptocurrency junction. Using theoretical frameworks, empirical data, and real-world examples, the story provides regulatory bodies, stakeholders, and fintech entrepreneurs with insightful information to help them navigate this dynamic and complicated environment.

CONCLUSION

To sum up, the convergence of fintech firms and cryptocurrencies has sparked a significant shift in business and entrepreneurship, redefining established ideas and changing the financial environment. The effect of these inventive forces has been thoroughly examined in this chapter, emphasising important topics that emphasise their combined influence on world economies.

Impact Summary: Fintech Startups and Digital Currency Changing the Meaning of Business and Entrepreneurship

Fintech companies and cryptocurrencies have a symbiotic relationship that has brought about unparalleled transformation in the modern era. Peer-to-peer lending and decentralised finance (DeFi) are two examples of how fintech developments have given entrepreneurs new tools and opportunities for financial inclusion. Simultaneously, adopting cryptocurrencies in commercial operations has transformed investment portfolios, transactions, and fundraising. Case studies from the real world have demonstrated the observable achievements of businesses that have successfully integrated these technologies, providing a window into the revolutionary potential of such integrations across many industries and geographical areas.

This chapter has examined the development of fintech companies, looking at how customer demand, legislative changes, and technology improvements drive their growth. Businesses' use of cryptocurrencies has been closely examined, revealing more about their functions in investments, transactions, and Initial Coin Offerings (ICOs). A detailed analysis of the revolutionary influence on entrepreneurship, company models, and important factors like payments and financial inclusion has been conducted.

Stressing the Need: Encouraging Creativity, Effectiveness, and Diversity in the Banking Industry

It is impossible to overestimate the role that fintech companies and cryptocurrencies have played in fostering inclusion, efficiency, and innovation in the financial industry. These technologies have removed traditional obstacles, democratising access to financial services and encouraging an entrepreneurial culture. Fintech advancements have allowed new company models to arise, which has given aspirant entrepreneurs access to capital and collaborative opportunities previously closed off. Due to its decentralised structure, cryptocurrency has improved security and transparency while redefining what it means to be trusted in financial transactions.

Furthermore, the wider financial ecosystem is affected in a transformational way in addition to specific firms. Integration of fintech and cryptocurrencies has improved payment processing, decreased remittance fees, and increased financial inclusion worldwide. The increased productivity and lower costs brought about by these breakthroughs impact the stability and growth of the economy.

Call to Action: To Maximise Potential Leverage, Maintain Innovation, Strategic Adaptation, and Cooperation

The chapter ends with a call to action for all parties involved in the financial and cryptocurrency space. Because these technologies are developing quickly, more innovation is needed to realise their full potential. Fintech companies need to be on the cutting edge of technology development, adjusting their approaches to take advantage of new possibilities and solve new problems.

For regulatory agencies as well as enterprises, strategic adaptability is essential. As technology advances, it is anticipated that the regulatory environment will change as well. Regulators have a tightrope to walk when it comes to encouraging innovation and maintaining financial stability, consumer safety, and AML compliance. For entrepreneurs to effectively navigate this complex ecosystem, they, in turn, must remain knowledgeable and work in tandem with authorities.

The issue of collaboration is crucial for the future. Technology developers, regulators, investors, and entrepreneurs must work together to create a sustainable and inclusive fintech and cryptocurrency future. Maximising the potential leverage of these disruptive technologies requires cross-industry cooperation, information exchange, and a dedication to ethical practices.

The chapter highlights the long-lasting influence of fintech companies and cryptocurrencies in transforming business and entrepreneurship. They are positioned to be key players in the financial sector going forward due to their capacity to spur innovation, improve efficiency, and advance inclusion. For fintech and cryptocurrency to fulfil their potential and help consumers, businesses, and the world economy, we must all remain committed to continuous innovation, strategic adaptation, and cooperative efforts.

REFERENCES

Ahmed, R., Ahmed, M., Ahmad, N., & Abidin, S. Z. (2020). Fintech: A Review on its Evolution, Adoption, Challenges, and Future. *Journal of Theoretical and Applied Information Technology*, *98*(1), 83–96.

Aldrich, H. (1999). Organizations evolving. *Sage (Atlanta, Ga.)*.

Amalia, F. (2016). The fintech book: The financial technology handbook for investors, entrepreneurs and visionaries. *Journal of Indonesian Economy and Business: JIEB.*, *31*(3), 345. doi:10.22146/jieb.23554

Arner, D. W., Barberis, J., & Buckley, R. P. (2016). The Evolution of Fintech: A New Post-Crisis Paradigm? *Georgetown Journal of International Law*, *47*(4), 1271–1320.

Barbu, C. M., Florea, D. L., Dabija, D. C., & Barbu, M. C. R. (2021). Customer experience in fintech. *Journal of Theoretical and Applied Electronic Commerce Research*, *16*(5), 1415–1433. doi:10.3390/jtaer16050080

Blakstad, S., & Allen, R. (2018). FinTech revolution. Cham, Switzerland: Springer.

Cao, S., Nie, L., Sun, H., Sun, W., & Taghizadeh-Hesary, F. (2021). Digital finance, green technological innovation and energy-environmental performance: Evidence from China's regional economies. *Journal of Cleaner Production*, *327*, 129458. doi:10.1016/j.jclepro.2021.129458

Catalini, C., & Gans, J. S. (2016). *Some Simple Economics of the Blockchain*. (NBER Working Paper No. 22952). NBER.

Chishti, S., & Barberis, J. (2016). *The Fintech book: The financial technology handbook for investors, entrepreneurs and visionaries*. John Wiley & Sons. doi:10.1002/9781119218906

Demirgüç-Kunt, A., Klapper, L., & Randall, D. (2020). Digital Financial Inclusion: Lessons from International Experience. *The World Bank Research Observer*, *35*(1), 65–100.

Demirgüç-Kunt, A., Klapper, L., Singer, D., Ansar, S., & Hess, J. (2018). *The Global Findex Database 2017: Measuring Financial Inclusion and the Fintech Revolution*. [World Bank Policy Research Working Paper, 8440]. World Bank.

Feng, S., Zhang, R., & Li, G. (2022). Environmental decentralization, digital finance and green technology innovation. *Structural Change and Economic Dynamics, 61*, 70–83. doi:10.1016/j.strueco.2022.02.008

Foley, S., Karlsen, J. R., & Putniņš, T. J. (2019). Sex, Drugs, and Bitcoin: How Much Illegal Activity Is Financed Through Cryptocurrencies? *Review of Financial Studies, 32*(5), 1798–1853. doi:10.1093/rfs/hhz015

Gomber, P., Kauffman, R. J., Parker, C., & Weber, B. W. (2018). On the fintech revolution: Interpreting the forces of innovation, disruption, and transformation in financial services. *Journal of Management Information Systems, 35*(1), 220–265. doi:10.1080/07421222.2018.1440766

Hanelt, A., Bohnsack, R., Marz, D., & Antunes Marante, C. (2021). A systematic review of the literature on digital transformation: Insights and implications for strategy and organizational change. *Journal of Management Studies, 58*(5), 1159–1197. doi:10.1111/joms.12639

Hughes, L., Dwivedi, Y. K., Misra, S. K., Rana, N. P., Raghavan, V., & Akella, V. (2019). Blockchain research, practice and policy: Applications, benefits, limitations, emerging research themes and research agenda. *International Journal of Information Management, 49*, 114–129. doi:10.1016/j.ijinfomgt.2019.02.005

Li, K., Kim, D. J., Lang, K. R., Kauffman, R. J., & Naldi, M. (2020). How should we understand the digital economy in Asia? Critical assessment and research agenda. *Electronic Commerce Research and Applications, 44*, 101004. doi:10.1016/j.elerap.2020.101004 PMID:32922241

Lin, B., & Ma, R. (2022). How does digital finance influence green technology innovation in China? Evidence from the financing constraints perspective. *Journal of Environmental Management, 320*, 115833. doi:10.1016/j.jenvman.2022.115833 PMID:35940011

Mansoori, P., Mohapatra, S., & Srinivasan, T. (2018). *The Future of Cross-Border Payments: An Introduction to Central Bank Digital Currencies*. International Monetary Fund.

Momtaz, P. (2017). *Initial Coin Offerings: Financing growth with cryptocurrency token sales*. Deloitte University Press.

Murinde, V., Rizopoulos, E., & Zachariadis, M. (2022). The impact of the FinTech revolution on the future of banking: Opportunities and risks. *International Review of Financial Analysis, 81*, 102103. doi:10.1016/j.irfa.2022.102103

Narayanan, A., Bonneau, J., Felten, E., Miller, A., & Goldfeder, S. (2016). *Bitcoin and Cryptocurrency Technologies: A Comprehensive Introduction*. Princeton University Press.

Palmié, M., Wincent, J., Parida, V., & Caglar, U. (2020). The evolution of the financial technology ecosystem: An introduction and agenda for future research on disruptive innovations in ecosystems. *Technological Forecasting and Social Change*, *151*, 119779. doi:10.1016/j.techfore.2019.119779

Panagariya, A. (2022). Digital revolution, financial infrastructure and entrepreneurship: The case of India. *Asia and the Global Economy*, *2*(2), 100027. doi:10.1016/j.aglobe.2022.100027

Schilirò, D. (2021). Fintech in Dubai: Development and Ecosystem. *International Business Research*, *14*(11), 61–70. doi:10.5539/ibr.v14n11p61

Suryono, R. R., Budi, I., & Purwandari, B. (2020). Challenges and trends of financial technology (Fintech): A systematic literature review. *Information (Basel)*, *11*(12), 590. doi:10.3390/info11120590

Swan, M. (2015). *Blockchain: Blueprint for a New Economy*. O'Reilly Media.

Wilkins, C. (2016). *Fintech and the financial ecosystem: evolution or revolution?* Remarks to Payments Canada.

Zavolokina, L., Dolata, M., Schwabe, G., & Kude, T. (2016). Fintech – The Impact on Consumers and Regulatory Responses. *In Proceedings of the 24th European Conference on Information Systems (ECIS)*. IEEE.

Chapter 7
Requirements of Adopting SMEs for Business Intelligence Systems:
A Field Study in the Industrial Zone of Setif in Algeria

Hichem Mezhoud
https://orcid.org/0000-0001-7237-5563
Mila University Center, Algeria

ABSTRACT

In this chapter, the authors will discuss the requirements for small and medium-sized enterprises (SMEs) to adopt business intelligence systems and make them more competitive. Currently, communication technologies are evolving rapidly and continuously. Companies are adopting modern methods and tools to ensure their survival and gain a sustainable competitive advantage. This necessitates keeping pace with developments that affect the business sector, including the emergence of business intelligence systems, which are among the latest and most important cost management tools. These systems involve shaping big data, creating mechanisms for collecting it accurately and efficiently, analyzing it, and innovating methods to process its understanding. The resulting information is used to make various decisions within the company. This chapter will address and analyze various technical, human, and organizational requirements for SMEs located in the industrial region of Setif, Algeria, to adopt business intelligence systems.

DOI: 10.4018/979-8-3693-1846-1.ch007

INTRODUCTION

As it is known, small and medium-sized industrial enterprises play a prominent developmental role for any national economy. They effectively contribute to positive impacts on various economic, social, and technological variables. This can be achieved through their continuous contribution to creating innovative utility value, maximizing the Gross Domestic Product (GDP), promoting the country's external exports, and positively influencing its trade balance. In addition to providing both permanent and temporary employment opportunities, they contribute to the development of technology patterns within the country, thereby reducing technological dependence on foreign entities and establishing national sovereignty in this field. However, there are many other positives that cannot be fully discussed here. In line with this, many researchers currently observe a significant increase in the adoption of Business Intelligence (BI) systems by economic institutions. Therefore, it transforms the traditional form of the enterprise's working environment into a more complex and digitally distinctive form. Products supported by the analysis of big data shift from their personalized form to a collective one. Despite their limited resources and capabilities, small and medium-sized industrial enterprises need to adapt more and more to the changing nature of consumer pathways. They also require the adoption of business intelligence and analytics in the midst of the digital economy era (Kotler, 2017, pp. 10, 11, 13, 14).

Currently, technologies are evolving continuously and rapidly, and industrial enterprises are adopting modern methods and tools to ensure sustainability and gain a competitive edge. This necessity arises from the need to keep up with developments affecting the business sector, such as the emergence of Business Intelligence systems, which are considered as the latest and most important cost management tools (Blocher, Stout, & Cokins, 2010). These systems are based on shaping big data, establishing mechanisms for accurate and efficient data collection, analyzing it, and innovating methods to process and understand it. Evidently, the information derived from this process is then used to make various decisions within the industrial enterprise. BI is one of the most crucial mechanisms currently relied upon to control and reduce product costs, enhance production quality to meet market demands, and achieve the desired consumer surplus. Additionally, it facilitates timely responses to customer needs, known as the strategic triangle which represents: cost, quality, and timeliness (Poluha, 2016, pp. 22, 23). Many researchers believe that BI systems are the optimal and most effective solution to meet the needs of modern industrial enterprises. Reports from global companies such as "Australian Computer", "Oracle", "Gartner Group", and "Teradata" emphasize the paramount importance of information in overcoming various obstacles faced by economic institutions. By adopting and applying BI principles, enterprise management can simplify decision-making processes, improve customer relationship management, and remain highly alert to changes in its working environment (Olszak, 2020, p. 35). BI can provide an upward value for the enterprise when it is used in the right way by individuals. Cindi Howson sees that there is a positive correlation between the efficint use of business intelligence and the performance of the enterprise, since reaching data does not necessarily lead to efficiency and good results, but dealing, understanding, and using it in the right way is the key criterion. (Howson, Successful Business Intelligence: unlock the value of BI and big data, 2014, pp. 5, 6)

This chapter will attempt to study the nature of Business Intelligence (BI) systems that are compatible with small and medium-sized industrial enterprises, considering the distinctive characteristics of this type of institution compared to large enterprises. It will identify and analyze the various organizational, technical, and human requirements necessary for the successful adoption of BI systems by these enterprises, making it an effective tool for creating value, improving performance, and making the right decisions.

CHAPTER BACKGROUND

Field experiments have shown that small and medium-sized industrial enterprises tend to use various technologies encompassed within BI, seeking to acquire a level of flexibility towards market requirements and to respond to continuous changes in their external business environment. The use of these technologies enables them to have organizational capabilities that lead to a constant sensing of available opportunities and threats. Consequently, they have begun to support the idea of acquiring and exploiting data and information assets (internal and external) as factors that effectively contribute to creating and strengthening competitive advantages in a sustainable manner. (Rao-Graham, McNaughton, & Mansingh, 2020, p. XIII) As is known, small and medium-sized industrial enterprises possess a nature characterized by agility and mobility, primarily resulting from the simplicity of their organizational structure due to their small size. This makes it easier for them to adopt process-centered organization, which is more adaptable to external environmental conditions over time. Additionally, small and medium-sized industrial enterprises mostly adopt one of three types of manufacturing systems: the job shop, the flow shop, and the Cellular shop. These manufacturing systems endow them with many characteristics associated with the strategic triangle: low cost, high quality, and timeliness. For example, the job shop, due to its technical characteristics and structural composition, enables small and medium-sized industrial enterprises to easily and quickly modify and change the type, number, and characteristics of their products, thus giving them an extremely organizational agility and the ability to adjust their competitive positioning in a short period of time. These are features entirely lacking in large enterprises.

The nature of BI systems in small and medium-sized industrial enterprises differs significantly from that in large enterprises. Rao, Mansingh, and McNaughton argue that in the recent past, most researchers and specialists had a misconception that BI was only suitable for large resource-intensive enterprises. However, this has completely changed at present, as small and medium-sized industrial enterprises possess inherent organizational agility, which can only be enhanced by successfully adopting BI. (Rao-Graham, McNaughton, & Mansingh, 2020, p. XIII) This constitutes a considerable research gap, necessitating deeper theoretical and field research into the requirements for the successful adoption of BI by small and medium-sized industrial enterprises, taking into account their distinctive characteristics. That is, the need for methodical specification and detailing of the requirements for the successful adoption of BI, primarily associated with the requirements for establishing an operational BI system, the technical integration requirements of the BI system with operational processes, in addition to the level of maturity of information and communication technology (ICT) practices and the technical requirements for establishing a BI system. Also, the human requirements related to the training and qualification of individuals responsible for establishing and operating BI.

ORGANIZATION OF THE CHAPTER

This chapter is designed coherently from general to specific. It starts by sestion 1.4 entitled Basic Concepts of Business Intelligence in industrial smal and meduim sized enterprises, The section tackles characteristics and reasons of the emergence of BI systems, in addition to its historical and chronological development for its foundation, with aspecific emphasize on the concept of Business intelligence that suits the nature of industrial small and medium industrial enterprise. In section 1.5, we delve into explaining the benefits and advantages for industrial smal and meduim sized enterprise when adopting BI systems. Section 1.6 analyses the structural framework of Business Intelligence systems by explaining the different technical and managerial parts which interacts in it. Section 1.7 discusses different challanges which confront industrial smal and meduim sized enterprises when adopting BI systems. Section 1.8, discusses the necessary requirements for adopting industrial small and meduim sized enterprises to BI systems and it is divided into 6 sub-titles. Subtitles 1.8.1 and 1.8.2 and 1.8.3 explain the successful requirements of bI systems, 1.8.4 explains the methodology which determines its main aim and procesdures of analysis. Meanwhile, 1.8.5 demonstrates the analysis of the main findings and subtitle 1.8.6 disscusses the main findings. While subtitle 1.9 deals in detail with the conclusion.

BASIC CONCEPTS OF BUSINESS INTELLIGENCE IN INDUSTRIAL SMAL AND MEDUIM SIZED ENTERPRISES

The current business environment is characterized by its complexity and instability. To achieve a quick response to consumer demands, economic institutions face the inevitability of using information technology and various decision support systems. This necessitates acquiring technological communication tools and methods to gather a variety of data from different sources, analyze it, and transform it into new and useful knowledge for decision-making processes. Business Intelligence (BI) systems play a crucial role in this regard, serving as a set of practices, methods, tools, and applications that assist enterprise management in collecting, integrating, analyzing, and presenting data in an understandable and usable format, enhancing overall performance and decision-making (Olszak, 2020, p. 35). Therefore, BI includes practices and tools such as data warehousing, data mining, and reporting and querying tools contribute to informed decision-making (Deepmala, Anurag, Amizan, & S.B, 2023, pp. 32, 33). Therefore, Lila Rao-Graham, Maurice McNaughton, and GunjanMansingh argue that a business intelligence system provides small and medium-sized industrial enterprises with high organizational flexibility, in addition to their inherent organizational flexibility, derived from their small size. These enterprises completely lack the formal and bureaucratic organizational structures that largely constrain large enterprises. (Rao-Graham, McNaughton, & Mansingh, 2020, p. 4)

Conditions and Reasons for the Emergence of Business Intelligence in Industrial Small and Medium Sized Enterprises

The deep economic and technological transformations that have occurred in the industrial business environment since the early 21st century have significantly reshaped internal production activities. Globalization, technological advancements, and changes in communication, data storage, and information management have shifted industrial enterprises from traditional hierarchical models to horizontal structures focused on process-oriented organization. This shift is part of the reengineering philosophy introduced by James Chenpey and Michael Hammer, emphasizing process-centric organizations. In response to external pressures, businesses must adapt rapidly by engaging in continuous development and innovation activities, necessitating strategic, tactical, and operational decisions to maintain flexibility (Skyrius, 2021, p. 7).

Currently, businesses rely heavily on data and information, leading to informational chaos and noise due to the increasing volume and flow of data. The inconsistency and incompleteness of data used by decision-makers create uncertainty and reliance on diverse assumptions. To address this, successful companies establish specialized organizational units focusing on data collection and analysis, leading to the development of BI and Business Analytics (BA) fields. As a results, these fields concentrate on extracting useful data and information through the innovation of specialized software (Olszak, 2020, p. 3).

As a result of disruptive digital technologies, including the emergence of cloud computing, mobile computing, big data analytics, advances in machine learning and artificial intelligence, and increased reliance on social media, small and medium-sized industrial enterprises are compelled to rely on Information Technology and Communication (ITC) to adapt to current environmental conditions. There is a widespread belief among many researchers that information and communication technology plays a pivotal role in helping small and medium-sized industrial enterprises improve their operational performance and enhance their competitiveness. (Rao-Graham, McNaughton, & Mansingh, 2020, pp. 9, 10, 11)

Historical Evolution of Business Intelligence

The term Business Intelligence was coined by the Gartner Group in the mid-1990s, but its historical roots trace back to Management Information Systems (MIS) in the 1970s and Executive Information Systems (EIS) in the 1980s. These systems improved computerized management support, with MIS offering static two-dimensional reports, and EIS introducing dynamic multidimensional reports and trend analysis. In the 1990s, BI emerged, providing executives with all the information they needed (Sharda, Delen, & Turban, 2018, p. 16). Celina Olszak identifies three generations of BI systems: BI 1.0, BI 2.0, and BI 3.0. BI 1.0, which emerged in the 1970s and 1980s, and was closely tied to MIS, EIS, and Decision Support Systems (DSS). BI 2.0, which emerged from 1990 to 2005, had witnessed a continuous development in advanced data warehouses, OLAP techniques, and data extraction methods. It enabled enterprises to highlight their work online, aligning with market requirements. The latest generation, BI 3.0, introduced proactive solutions available to a large number of individuals within the enterprise, which was integrated with enterprise operations and offering cloud-based BI services (Olszak, 2020, pp. 42, 43).

The adoption of decision-making computing in enterprises began in the 1970s, experiencing five key stages to the present day.

Figure 1. The successive stages of computing adoption and the emergence of business intelligence and analytics
Source: *(Sharda, Delen, & Turban, 2018, p. 13)*

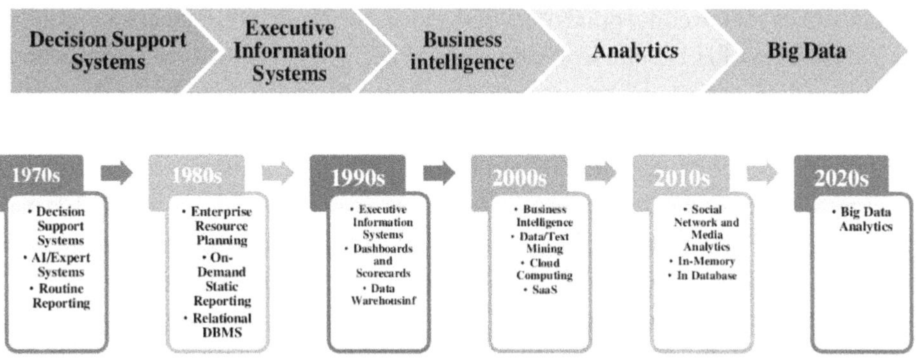

As shown in figure (1), we can say that Business Intelligence (BI) systems have emerged and evolved through five chronological stages since the early seventies of the twentieth century, with the emergence of Decision Support Systems. The seventies were characterized by relying on Management Information Systems (MIS) in decision-making. This involved preparing reports concerning various operational, organizational, and strategic variables over past time periods. The executive management relied on these reports for making future decisions. Additionally, Operations Research and Expert Systems techniques were used to solve complex problems faced by enterprise management. The second stage extended through the eighties and witnessed significant changes in how enterprise management obtained data related to its activities and fields. Traditional systems used to capture data from various units, such as marketing, accounting, and manufacturing, were integrated into a unified system at the enterprise level, known as Enterprise Resource Planning (ERP). During this stage, Relational Database Management Systems (RDBMS) were also introduced to improve data capture, storage, and computerized access. In the nineties, due to the need for more diverse reports for top management, Executive Information Systems (EISs) and Decision Support Systems (DSSs) were introduced. These systems were specifically designed for executive managers to meet their decision-making needs. They included visual information dashboards with performance metrics and essential indicators, relying on data warehouses to facilitate and expedite decision-making (Sharda, Delen, & Turban, 2018, pp. 13, 14, 15).

Definition Of Business Intelligence in Industrial Small and Medium Sized Enterprises

In our search for the conceptual roots of the term Business Intelligence, we found the first definition of H.P Luhn in 1958 where he defined it as the ability to understand the interrelationships among presented facts and how they lead to directing work towards desired goals. In the business field, Business Intelligence is an automatic system created and developed to disseminate information across various departments and parts of the organizational structure (Grossmann & Rinderle-ma, 2015, p. 1). Laura Zapata-Cantú, Teresa Treviño, and Flor Morton see Business Intelligence as referring to a wide range of methodologies, processes, infrastructures, architectures, and technologies that work together to provide solutions for managers to make sound and quick decisions. Eventually, it relies on the real-time analysis and aggregation of data, transforming it into useful information (Zapata-Cantu, Trevino, & Morton, 2020, p. 15). It is also know as a comprehensive concept for data structuring, analysis tools and software which is embedded in a specific way to enable entrprise managers for intractional reach of data and information simoultanously. Therefore, decision maker can have crystal clear visions for a sane administrative decision (Sharda, Delen, & Turban, 2018, p. 16). Business Intelligence comprises different activities, analysis means, works, and the necessary techniques to transform data into useful information, which in turn becoms knowledge. Thus, this knowledge is used in the enterprise to find plans which lead eventually to the adoption of operational and managerial procedures economic profits. (Loshin, 2013, p. 7)

Accordingly, Business Intelligence is a large structure of computerized media devices, means, technologies, computer software, and infrastructures. These elements are integrated according to a specific configuration, aligning with the activities and operations of the organization and its managerial levels and adopted organizational structure. The main purpose is to obtain vast data, in various forms and from different sources, both internal and external to the enterprise environment, associated with its field of activity. This data is then organized, analyzed, processed, and transformed into useful information in the management process and the making of correct decisions, thus creating knowledge. The following sequential stages are followed:

- Data collection and integration from various available sources, relying on ETL, data warehouses, and databases.
- Data analysis, organization, information production, and the preparation of various reports related to the enterprise's activities and operations. This relies on OLAP, query languages, and ad hoc analyses.
- Knowledge acquisition through data exploration, utilizing various data mining techniques.

- Making the right decisions based on the previous stages, ultimately achieving organizational success. (Olszak, 2020, p. 41)

As it is known, the large enterprise differs significantly from the small and medium-sized enterprise in terms of its organizational structure, financial and human resources, expertise levels, and production and technological capabilities. Consequently, the factors influencing the definition and adoption of Business Intelligence (BI) systems in SMEs differ radically from those in large enterprises. Therefore, it is crucial to establish a specific conceptual framework for BI, accurately encompassing the key factors driving the definition and adoption of BI in SMEs.

In Algeria, an industrial SME is defined as an economic entity with a workforce ranging from 01 to 250 employees and an annual turnover not exceeding four (04) billion Algerian dinars or a total annual turnover of one (01) billion dinars, meeting the conditions of independence, and engaging in productive activities by transforming raw materials and supplies into semi-finished or finished products. (People's Democratic Republic of Algeria, 2017, p. 5) According to this definition, the characteristics of industrial SMEs in Algeria do not differ globally due to the convergence of classification criteria, including the number of employees, annual turnover, and conditions of independence. Unlike large enterprises, which largely rely on extensive capital, technological resources, and human capital, SMEs are quite the opposite. Their owners, managers, and employees typically possess low levels of awareness and training in effectively utilizing information and communication technology (ICT), which is a fundamental pillar in defining and adopting BI systems and activating their role in value creation and overall performance improvement. Additionally, their ability to finance IT and BI projects is limited due to financial constraints.

Another key factor in defining BI systems suitable for industrial SMEs is the low levels of organizational and human knowledge, which determine their ability to collect, integrate, analyze, and organize necessary data and information. Furthermore, their capacity to design and manage operational processes horizontally and correctly integrate them with BI systems to effectively improve value creation is crucial.

Figure (2) illustrates the different factors associated with the conceptual aspect of BI systems, aligned with the nature and characteristics of SMEs.

The definition of BI as a large structure consisting of devices, tools, techniques, computer programs, and the infrastructure of computer-mediated communication is determined by specific maturity levels in the practices of managing SMEs for ICT. These practices are the cornerstone for the efficient integration and operation of these technical elements. Moreover, the technical skills of individuals responsible for ICT and BI systems design and operation are also crucial in defining BI for SMEs. This ensures the acquisition, analysis, and transformation of various data sources

Figure 2. Business Intelligence System in smal and meduim sized enterprises

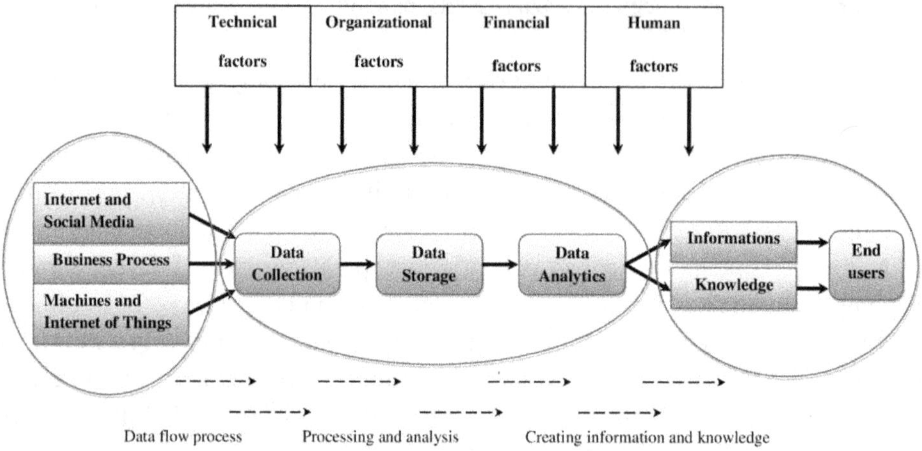

into relevant information tailored to the nature of the enterprise. Additionally, a fundamental factor in defining BI for SMEs is the necessary integration between BI system components and operational processes, activities, and organizational structure. This integration creates operational business intelligence, disseminating all pertinent data and information across the organizational structure according to their levels of importance.

BENEFITS AND POSITIVES OF BUSINESS INTELLIGENCE FOR INDUSTRIAL SMAL AND MEDUIM SIZED ENTERPRISE

The term Business Intelligence indicates the combination of data, information, technologies, and tools used for multidimensional data collection and analysis to improve decision-making processes. Business Intelligence systems primarily aim to achieve many benefits for industrial smal and meduim sized enterprise management, especially when employed correctly. The benefits can be summarized as follows:

- Providing necessary information and knowledge within the enterprise, contributing to improved decision-making, performance, and operational efficiency.
- Offering a wide range of essential information in management operations when needed, providing flexibility to external environmental changes and quick responsiveness to customers. (Grossmann & Rinderle-ma, 2015, p. 2)

- Enhancing the quality of the enterprise's experience related to making various decisions.
- Providing the ability to predict scenarios of different variables associated with decision-making industries.
- Discovering new knowledge, enabling the enterprise to build its competitive capabilities and enter new markets.
- Creating opportunities to gain new customers.
- Introducing new changes to the enterprise, enabling the possibility of innovating new products and services.
- Improving the relationship with suppliers, customers, and stakeholders.
- Providing opportunities to improve adopted strategies and, consequently, achieving a competitive advantage.
- Improving the enterprise's performance by enhancing its operations and reducing various associated risks. (Olszak, 2020, pp. 38, 39)

BUSINESS INTELLIGENCE ARCHITECTURE

Figure (3) demonstrates the overall engineering of the Business Intelligence system in the enterprise. It shows the flow of data from its various sources to the delivery of useful information to the end-user. The Technical Staff is responsible for building the data warehouse and performing access, manipulation, and results. Another

Figure 3. The overall business intelligence architecture
Source: *(Sharda, Delen, & Turban, 2018, p. 17)*

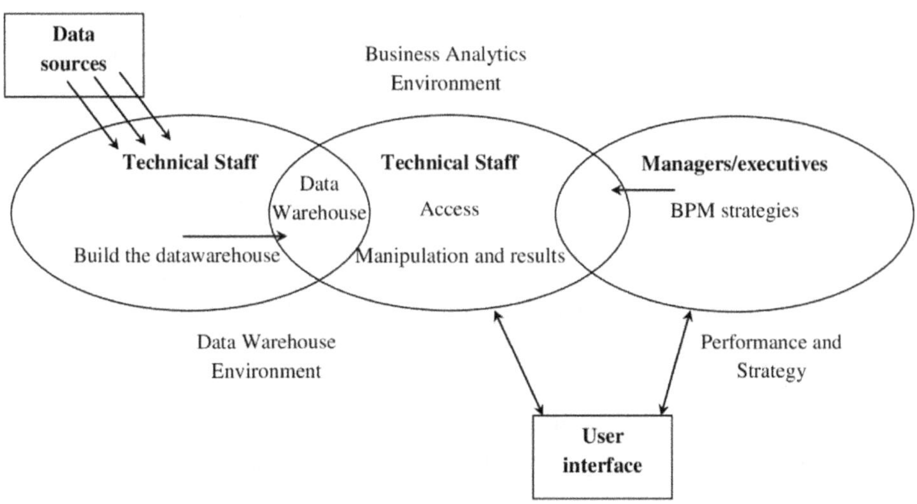

technical team is in charge of business analytics, sharing the obtained information and necessary data with managers, executive managers, and other individuals through the user interface. Managers and executive managers manage Business Performance Management (BPM) by monitoring and analyzing actual performance.

CHALLENGES OF BUSINESS INTELLIGENCE SUCCESS

Over the past two decades, the success of adopting economic enterprises in general, and small and medium-sized industrial enterprises in particular, faces many challenges related to the ambiguity that characterizes business intelligence systems in the ability to enhance the performance of various operational processes and other administrative aspects. The most important challenges are highlighted within the following points:

- The urgent need for enterprise managers to deal with business intelligence as more than just a provider of reports related to the operational activities of the enterprise.
- The necessity to adapt the components and parts of Information and Communication Technology (ICT) with business intelligence systems, so that the latter can operate more efficiently and effectively.
- The absence of a clear strategy and sound plans to integrate business intelligence systems with the operations of the enterprise, especially operational processes is affected by the sudden changes in the external environment. (Williams, 2016, p. 161)
- The lack of sufficient maturity of Information and Communication Technology (ICT) assets available in the enterprise, which does not allow them to adopt business intelligence systems in a way that supports business processes. This challenge necessitates improving the management and governance processes of information and communication technology.
- The lack of a precise and logical understanding by the management of the enterprise of how to deploy information and communication technology and business intelligence systems in the value creation process. (Gendron, 2013, pp. 5, 6)
- The limited financial capabilities that characterize small and medium-sized industrial enterprises, which may hinder their ability to allocate appropriate budgets to meet investment requirements in the field of business intelligence.
- The low maturity level of Information and Communication Technology (ICT) systems in small and medium-sized industrial enterprises poses a significant challenge to these enterprises in adopting business intelligence.

- The success of adopting business intelligence requires the availability of high-level human skills and organizational capabilities in the control of data collection, analysis, storage, extraction, and integration according to organizational requirements. These capabilities may be lacking in small and medium-sized industrial enterprises due to their limited resources.
- The weakness of available and acquired knowledge levels within small and medium-sized industrial enterprises due to their lack of experience in knowledge management. This adds a kind of challenge to the success of adopting business intelligence, considering that the latter is one of the most important sources of shaping knowledge.

REQUIREMENTS FOR SMALL AND MEDIUM-SIZED INDUSTRIAL ENTERPRISES TO ADOPT BUSINESS INTELLIGENCE SYSTEMS

Most managers and business leaders have specific and precise management and operational goals, along with constrained performance rates that must be achieved within programmed periods. Therefore, attempting to convince them of the idea of investing in business intelligence systems is fundamentally related to the real benefit that these systems will provide in various areas. This includes increasing revenue, reducing costs, improving profitability, enhancing customer relationships, increasing supply chain flexibility, improving productivity rates, enhancing customer services, and improving competitive positioning.(Williams, 2016, pp. 162, 163) The adoption of a business intelligence system is, thus, associated with a set of adoption requirements that must be met to ensure the desired benefit. These requirements ultimately lead to integrating business intelligence with the strategy, plans, and business practices of small and medium-sized industrial enterprises. More specifically, business intelligence systems and various Information and Communication Technologies (ICT) should play an innovative role by integrating them into all business processes of the enterprise to improve performance, rather than merely managing the costs of these technological systems and considering them as tracking only business operations. (Gendron, 2013, pp. 6, 7)

Many researchers believe that the success factors of adopting business intelligence systems are not limited to technological factors alone. Numerous other factors are of great importance. For example, Presthus believes that business intelligence is a socio-technical system where technical aspects are equal to human aspects. Yoon, Ghosh, and Jeong also emphasize the crucial importance of human aspects in adopting business intelligence systems, as they ensure positive social impact by creating a suitable learning environment. Researchers such as Yeon, Coronios, and

Popovic highlight the critical role of organizational and managerial requirements in the success of adopting business intelligence.(Skyrius, 2021, p. 213)

Celina Olszak suggests that analyzing and discussing the concept of business intelligence should be done from two fundamental perspectives: the technical perspective and the managerial perspective. The technical view, being the older of the two, considers business intelligence as an integrated set of tools, technologies, and software used to collect heterogeneous data from various sources, integrating, analyzing, and sharing it. The managerial view focuses on the crucial importance of information and knowledge as strategic resources for enterprise management. Data analysis not only allows for faster decision-making but also contributes to discovering valuable opportunities for future business success and sustaining profit achievement. (Olszak, 2020, pp. 38, 39) Sharda, Delen, and Turban argue that before adopting and designing a business intelligence system for the enterprise, top management should consider it as a tool that will fundamentally change the entire management approach. The reasons for investing in business intelligence should align with the enterprise's strategy. It should be considered a means to improve the efficiency and effectiveness of operations and activities. Planning for adoption is essential, involving the identification of organizational skills available to achieve business intelligence goals and a pre-assessment of the prevailing organizational culture's willingness to undergo appropriate changes. Integration between the business intelligence system and the enterprise's adopted information technology systems is also essential. (Sharda, Delen, & Turban, 2018, p. 20)

In fact, most executive managers link their decisions to allocate a budget for investing in business intelligence to the economic return expected over a specific time period following the adoption process. This economic return is strongly related to business processes that will improve their performance, known implicitly as Business Intelligence Opportunities (BIOs). BIOs are systematic approaches to identify optimal ways to use business intelligence to increase revenue, reduce costs, or both. These economic justifications depend on the business processes practiced and provide the economic basis for how a business intelligence system can create value for the enterprise. For example, the total investment amount, the time required to reach the break-even point, the nature and amount of risk associated with this investment, and the most critical factor, the factors and requirements for success and the extent to which the enterprise's management can fulfill them. (Williams, 2016, pp. 69, 70)

In the past, simultaneous with the emergence and initial use of business intelligence, it was believed that the top management's support for the idea of the enterprise adopting business intelligence systems was almost the only condition for the success of this initiative. However, successive radical transformations in the working environment of enterprises have imposed the inevitability of adopting a more integrated approach in this regard. Attention is paid to all branching and interconnected aspects of the idea of adopting business intelligence systems, known as Business Intelligence Opportunities. The distinctive features of small and medium-sized industrial enterprises compared to larger ones also give a special character to the idea of adoption. Therefore, an analytical framework will be adopted in this regard, dividing adoption requirements into three main groups: technological requirements, organizational requirements, and human requirements. Each aspect complements the other two, ultimately integrating business intelligence into the structure of small and medium-sized industrial enterprises to ensure maximum benefit, making this economic entity a stakeholder in what is currently known as the strategic triangle: cost, quality, and timeliness.

Organizational Requirements for Adopting Business Intelligence

According to the literature of management science and as per the thinker Peter Drucker, organization is considered the second stage of practice within the framework of any managerial process, following planning. Organizing is, therefore, an activity that involves designing the organizational structure, in addition to achieving coordination and harmony among its various parts and separate administrative units. This is to make the organization fully adaptable to the continuous changes occurring in its environment, providing it with organizational agility. Consequently, organizational requirements refer to the compatibility, harmony, and coordination that must be achieved between business intelligence as a system and the organizational structure of the entire institution. This ensures the smooth flow and proper distribution of data and information. Managers and executives must real, useful, detailed, and timely information concerning all practiced activities and external environmental conditions to achieve high performance and organizational efficiency. Thus, the operational business intelligence system is integrated with the overall operational system of the organization. (Howson, Successful Business Intelligence: Secrets to making BI a killer app, 2008, p. 23) Among the prominent reasons leading to the emergence of these organizational requirements are the modern organizational structures adopted by industrial enterprises, known as flat structures, horizontal structures, or structures centered around operations. Additionally, the new distribution of decision-making authority, by enabling individuals responsible for business operations to make various decisions, played a crucial role. (Olszak, 2020, p. 3) The urgent transformations in the work environment, the emergence of the digital economy, and competition based on quality and innovative competition played a decisive role in the need for enterprises to achieve high levels of internal coordination. Business intelligence systems can play a crucial role in this regard. For example, some of the organizational requirements that a business intelligence system should meet include:

- Identifying business decisions to be supported by business intelligence.
- Identifying business processes to be improved using the data and information provided by the business intelligence system.
- Assessing the economic impact resulting from the potential improvements in business operations.
- Determining the level and extent of change required in the organization's operations and its employees.
- Providing an accurate description of the information needed by the management of the organization. (Williams, 2016, pp. 70, 71)

During field visits to many small and medium-sized industrial enterprises in the industrial area of Setif, Algeria, extensive interviews were conducted with 32 managers and executives (CIO, CFO, COO, and CEO). Over a period of two months, 14 detailed questions were asked about activities that could be significantly improved using business intelligence systems. These questions were selected based on their connection to the enterprise's strategy, as well as their contribution to creating benefit. The interviews led to the following results:

- Using business intelligence contributes to predicting sales trends and discovering new markets.
- Relying on business intelligence leads to significant improvements in the distribution process to stores.
- Using business intelligence facilitates the measurement and improvement of customer satisfaction.
- Business intelligence can be used to achieve substantial improvements in supply chain management.
- Using business intelligence helps improve productivity across the enterprise.
- Business intelligence contributes to eliminating non-value-added activities.
- Business intelligence can be used to improve indirect cost allocation on products.
- Business intelligence can be used to improve inventory management.
- Business intelligence can be used to improve coordination between different functional departments.
- Business intelligence can be used to maintain a high level of competitive awareness.

Based on the results of these interviews, various organizational requirements that ensure the successful adoption of business intelligence can be categorized into two main groups:

- Requirements associated with establishing an operational business intelligence system, which focuses on providing data from internal activities.
- Requirements associated with management and control, aiming to provide comprehensive coordination between the parts of the organizational structure and achieve organizational effectiveness.

Organizational Requirements Associated With Establishing an Operational Business Intelligence System

When adopting a business intelligence system, it will necessarily include all operational activities and processes and all managerial levels of the organization, including suppliers, customers, and public data for citizens outside the organizational structure but in continuous relation with it. (Howson, Successful Business Intelligence: unlock the value of BI and big data, 2014, p. 4) In line with this approach, the operational system of the organization consists of a set of internal activities and processes that transform available resources into products and services directed to the market. At each step of these processes, users enter a set of data into the operating systems, which are then captured and used in the business intelligence system. Operational systems, also known as transaction processing systems or source systems and also referred to as Enterprise Resource Planning (ERP) systems, are the main source of quantitative data related to the organization. Various activities are practiced, involving the input of a considerable amount of data into these systems, covering many areas, such as:

- **Manufacturing system:** Entering a specific product production order into the manufacturing system, recording the quantity and quality of raw materials used, etc.
- **Sales system:** Entering customer purchase orders, along with all details.
- **Supply Chain System:** Executing orders once the product is available and entering shipping details.
- **Accounting system:** Recording all cash and financial transactions, such as customer invoices, etc. (Howson, Successful Business Intelligence: Secrets to making BI a killer app, 2008, p. 22)

Figure 4. Operational business intelligence
Source: *(Howson, Successful Business Intelligence: Secrets to making BI a killer app, 2008, p. 22)*

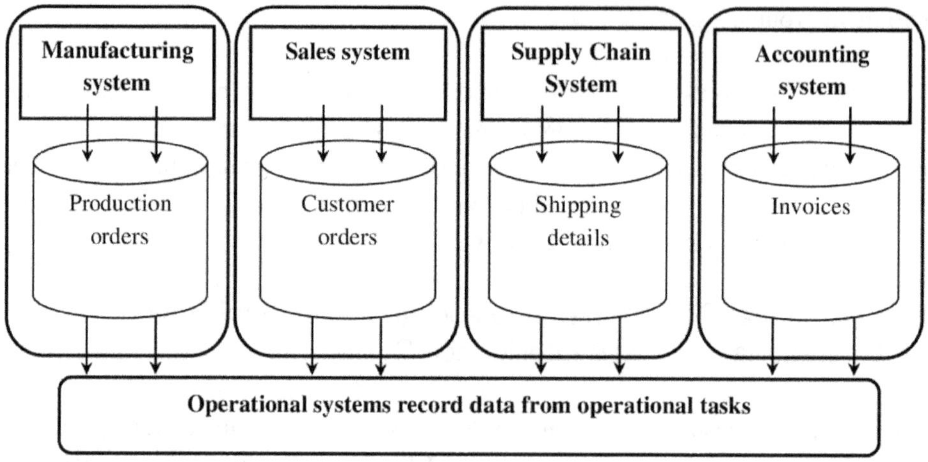

These operational systems form the primary and confirmed source of quantitative data related to the enterprise. At each step of the operational process, a considerable volume of data is inputted, covering various areas.

As shown in Figure (4), Operational Business Intelligence (OBI) relies on real operational systems (where production activities are performed) to obtain data. This data is derived from the following subsystems: Enterprise Resource Planning (ERP), Supply Chain Management (SCM), Customer Relationship Management (CRM), and Accounting systems. Additionally, it incorporates data from other internal sources such as distributors providing information on sales and inventory, clickstream data from websites displaying the most viewed products, and data on e-commerce shopping carts. Subsequently, this data is extracted, transformed, and loaded (ETL) into the data warehouse. (Howson, Successful Business Intelligence: Secrets to making BI a killer app, 2008, p. 24) The team responsible for the Business Intelligence system considers its integration with the operational system as the link that ensures the continuous creation of data related to internal activities of the organization. This contributes to the horizontal and vertical flow of data and information across different parts of the organizational structure.

Therefore, due to the simplicity of the organizational structure and the operational systems of small and medium-sized industrial enterprises, increasing operational flexibility becomes an achievable advantage, provided that there is a greater reliance on modern technological platforms. These platforms are used to digitize their operational infrastructure and processes. (Rao-Graham, McNaughton, & Mansingh, 2020, p. 3) This simplification leads to the achievement of the following:

- Providing real-time operational-level data for the enterprise, contributing to instant feedback for all practiced activities and reducing the time and errors associated with work performance.
- Eliminating non-value-added operational activities, thus reducing associated costs.
- Completely eliminating the possibility of distorting important information transferred from one department to another, linked to production characteristics. This provides significant opportunities to improve product quality and potentially reduce costs.
- Making the enterprise more responsive to market requirements.

The set of organizational requirements associated with management, control, and coordination

As an inevitable result of the radical changes that have affected the working environment of organizations, mentioned at the beginning of this chapter, organizational structures have shifted from hierarchical functional structures, which rely on precise work division, detailed specialization, and vertical organization of tasks as fundamental principles, to horizontal structures. These structures are centered around processes as their primary mode of operation. One of the main reasons for this transformation is an attempt to create greater value for consumers. Initially, organizations tried to improve the quality of their products and achieve faster responsiveness to market demands. They built an administrative and organizational model for their activities, illustrated in Figure (5).

In reality, organizations adopted this structure in the form of a cross-functional process due to the problems and drawbacks experienced by functional organizational structures. These drawbacks included slow responsiveness to market requirements, low levels of product and service quality, and cost inflation. The organization's management attempted to improve internal coordination between multiple departmental and functional activities that contribute to the same process. For example, Figure (5) illustrates the innovation and product development process. Initially, individuals responsible for consumer and market studies identify consumer

Figure 5. Product innovation and value chain
Source: *(Bhimani, Horngren, Datar, & Rajan, 2015, p. 13)*

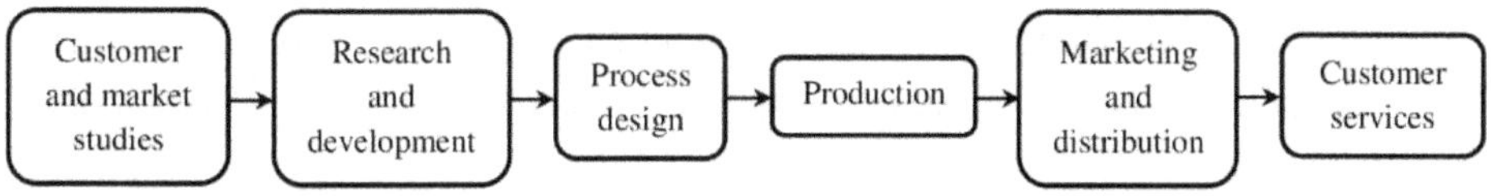

preferences, functional features performed by the developed product, and demand levels. This information is then passed on in a detailed report using the information system to another functional department, the Research and Development department. This department is responsible for arriving at desired product designs. The designs are then passed on to the production department, where those in charge design suitable production lines and initiate manufacturing processes. Afterward, sales and distribution operations, as well as general promotional campaigns, commence, followed by after-sales services. What actually occurred between these departments was the transfer of important data and information (in paper or electronically) crucial for decision-making regarding each step of the process as a whole. However, observations revealed limitations, delays, errors, and distortions in the transfer of this data and information, resulting from the incorrect transfer method. This often had a negative impact on production costs and quality.

During the 1990s, precisely in 1993, James Champy and Michael Hammer attempted to introduce the concept of Reengineering. They defined it as follows: Radical rethinking and radical redesign of the organizational structure of the enterprise and its operational processes to achieve significant improvements in performance and increase efficiency by reducing production costs, improving quality, satisfying consumers more, reducing response time to their desires, and enjoying greater flexibility towards external changes, as well as raising the level of coordination and integration for its activities and practices. (Hammer & Chempy, 1993, pp. 41-45)

The main goal behind reengineering is to transform the organizational structure of the enterprise from a functional to a process-centered organization, based on the belief that the latter is the most evolved form of organization and is more in line with external environmental conditions. This involves a radical departure from functions and departments, replacing them with a set of horizontal business processes formed by individuals with multiple functional specialties, namely:

- **Product Design and Workshop System Design Process:** This process includes all activities related to the development of new products. Due to the significant link between product design and the design of the workshop system, all these activities fall under one process, which is the process of designing new products and the workshop system.
- **Enterprise Resource Management Process:** This encompasses all activities related to obtaining capital resources, human resources, and managing the technology within the organization.
- **Product Supply Process:** This process includes a set of activities related to obtaining raw materials and various supplies used as inputs for the production system, culminating in the delivery of products and services to customers.

- **Customer Process:** The customer process includes another set of sub-processes that involve various activities, primarily focusing on selling and advertising the product. It involves gathering various market information and choosing the markets in which the organization will sell, as well as providing after-sales services.
- **Support Operations:** The organization carries out a set of support activities for its stakeholders both internally and externally. These activities mainly consist of legal operations associated with government entities, as well as providing various financial information and innovation support activities.

Proponents of reengineering believe that the horizontal organization of the enterprise's activities, according to operations rather than functions and departments, ensures the smooth and immediate flow of data and useful information for decision-making. This occurs among the responsible individuals for those operations and the individuals affiliated with them, considering they belong to diverse functional specialties and are granted high authority for decision-making. This ultimately guarantees solving cost, quality, and timeliness issues instantly and before they occur.

In line with this, Lila Rao-Graham, Maurice McNaughton, and Gunjan Mansingh believe that the adoption of Business Intelligence by small and medium-sized industrial enterprises makes them more flexible towards sudden changes in their external environment. This is achieved by providing the necessary coordination levels and ensuring a constant and immediate flow of data and information between the parts of their organizational structure. This is especially advantageous compared to larger enterprises due to the simplicity of their organizational structures. (Rao-Graham, McNaughton, & Mansingh, 2020, p. 4)

To illustrate the concept of organizational requirements related to management, control, and coordination, we refer to Figure (6), which outlines the activities constituting the process of product design and workshop system design.

In the beginning, we can observe that the process of designing a new product and the workshop system consists of three main activities. These are executed by three distinct and consecutive functional departments as follows:

- **Consumer and Market Study Department:** This department is responsible for uncovering consumer desires, meaning the precise identification of the functional characteristics of the product intended for development or innovation.
- **Research and Development Department:** This department, in turn, is responsible for its members reaching the design of the intended product.

Figure 6. product design and workshop system design process

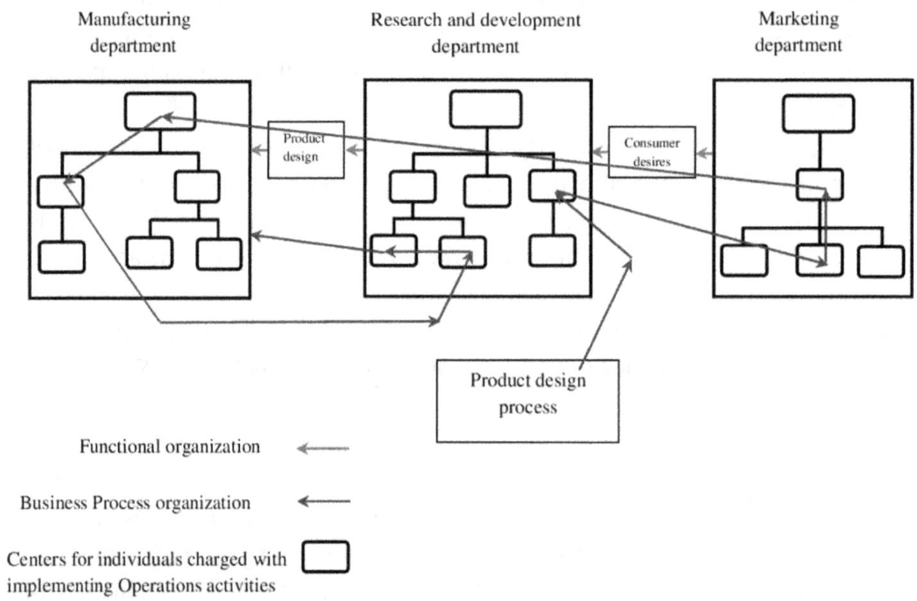

- **Manufacturing or Workshop Department:** The individuals in charge of this department design the appropriate production line for manufacturing the intended product in the required quantities.

What can be noticed regarding this process as a whole is the necessity for high-level coordination to ensure a smooth horizontal flow of data and information between all steps constituting multifunctional activities. This coordination has proven challenging to achieve within vertical organizational structures due to limited communication tools and mechanisms. Here precisely emerges the effective role of the Business Intelligence (BI) system in achieving the instantaneous and continuous transfer of data and information among individuals responsible for the process. Referring to Figure (5), we can see that the Business Intelligence system ensures the provision of crucial data and information to the team responsible for the process of designing new products. This team extends beyond the limits of a single function or department to include various functional departments. The process is virtually formed (while maintaining the type of adopted organization), including representatives from the marketing department, research and development department, and the production department. This helps reduce the risks resulting from handling work between departments and the possibility of distorting information related to product characteristics. The team responsible for the product design process receives instant information about all areas that will be affected by the product design, manufacturing, and marketing. This ensures the avoidance of such problems. Additionally, the natural characteristics of small and medium-sized industrial enterprises, associated with the simplicity of their organizational structure, contribute more to activating the organizational agility feature through the adoption of Information and Communication Technology (ICT) and Business Intelligence (BI). Therefore, organizational requirements related to management, control, and coordination impose the granting of full authority to all individuals constituting each process, ensuring the addition of value to production during the planning, execution, and control stages. This includes granting complete permissions for utilizing the data and information provided by the Business Intelligence system to guarantee its employment in decision-making processes and avoiding secondary problems resulting from the absence of crucial information instantly. These requirements are strongly connected to achieving organizational agility, which imposes a type of coordination and harmony in obtaining crucial data and information from inside and outside the organization. These pertain to the cost and quality of products and their distribution to a specific number of managers, executives, and individuals for their use in decision-making.

Technical Requirements for Adopting Business Intelligence

The technical requirements for Business Intelligence systems serve as their underlying infrastructure, enabling enterprise management to acquire, handle, manage, and use data and information in the areas of business analysis and decision-making. These requirements vary with Information Technology and Communication (ITC) assets but are closely integrated with them. The technical requirements for the successful adoption of Business Intelligence in small and medium-sized industrial enterprises differ from larger organizations. This is primarily due to the lower maturity level of Information Technology and Communication practices in small and medium-sized enterprises in general. This can be attributed to various factors such as limited resources, lower levels of expertise among individuals in the field of Information Technology and Communication, and a lack of a clear vision from management regarding the utilization of Information Technology and Communication in creating value.

Therefore, technical success requirements can be categorized into two main groups:

- Requirements associated with the maturity of Information Technology and Communication practices (ITC).
- Rechnical requirements specific to the Business Intelligence system itself.

The Set of Requirements Related to the Maturity of Information Technology and Communication Practices

Michael Gendron asserts that the success of an enterprise's adoption of Business Intelligence is strongly linked to the maturity of its practices in the field of Information Technology and Communication (ICT). This is evident through the ICT infrastructure, enabling the creation, aggregation, and transfer of data, and subsequently, its utilization in the realm of smart business solutions.(Gendron, 2013, pp. 4, 5) More precisely, enterprises generally have access to a vast and diverse array of ICT assets, enabling them to engage in electronic management practices. These technological assets are commonly used for general purposes and, in many cases, are functionally suitable for Business Intelligence purposes. (Williams, 2016, p. 189)

For the enterprise to maximize the benefits of ICT and BI, it is essential not only to use them to support internal operations but also to employ them in a well-organized manner that ultimately leads to value creation. To achieve this, the ICT infrastructure within the small and medium-sized industrial enterprise must encompass the following components:

- **Enterprise-wide components:** These components operate across all organizational departments but function as a unified system. Users interact with Information and Communication Technology (ICT) applications and enterprise systems, such as ERP, enterprise document management, enterprise content management, or knowledge management systems, through the front-end interface of each computer program. This interaction is consolidated at a central level known as the "Enterprise-wide component." It comprises a large set of servers, databases, computers, communication networks, front-end software, etc.
- **User Components:** This category includes all parts that users interact with directly and have direct daily control over. Individuals use these components to carry out their functional activities, such as computers, printers, scanners, and various software.
- **Service Components:** Represented by the network service used directly by individuals in the enterprise, consisting of network hardware and software. Managed and monitored by the Information and Communication Technology department, service components encompass various services such as printing, office communications, network storage service, internet protocol telephony, etc.
- **Network Components:** Comprising a set of networking and telecommunication equipment, including network devices, software, cables, media, routing hardware, network switching, and associated items.

These components are under the direct control of the Information and Communication Technology department but are utilized by individuals in the organization. Network components cover a wide range of services, such as printing, inter- and intra-office communications, network storage service, and internet protocol telephony, among others. There are various types of network services, including printing services, inter- and intra-office communications via fax or IP telephony, network-accessible storage, and other network-shared devices. (Gendron, 2013, pp. 22, 23)

Requirements Related to Business Intelligence System Components

Figure (7) illustrates the general aspects of a business intelligence system, depicts its technical aspects, the integration of its components, and explains the interactions that generate important and useful information for managers and other individuals in the organization.

Figure 7. Business intelligence system components
Source: *(Sharda, Delen, & Turban, 2018, p. 58)*

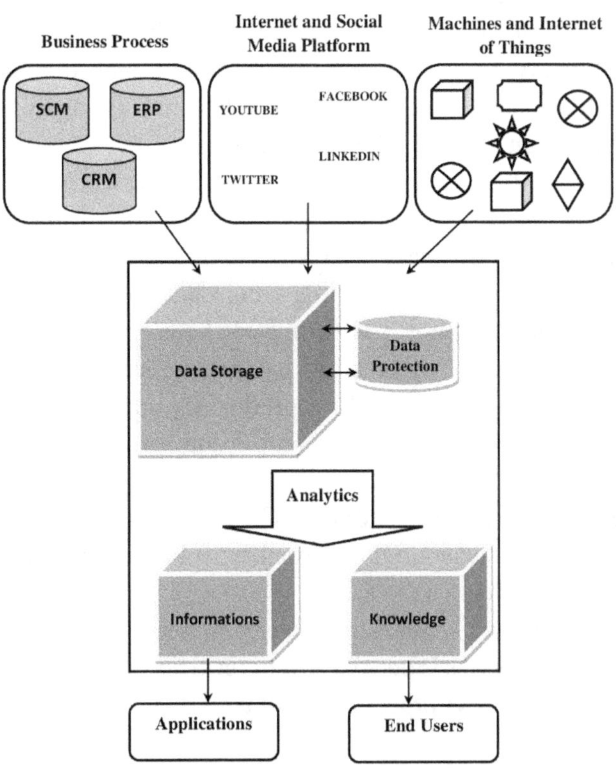

Figure (7) provides a detailed view of all technical aspects of the Business Intelligence system. These can be categorized into four groups:

- **Data Warehouse:** a technology through which data obtained from various sources is integrated.
- **Data Extraction and Transmission Tools:** primarily responsible for transferring data from various sources, including transactional systems and the internet, to the enterprise's data warehouse.
- **Data Analysis and Exploration Tools:** enables end-users to access and comprehensively analyze data, as well as extract insights.
- **Data Visualization:** encompasses a set of applications and tools responsible for presenting data and information transparently, facilitating access for end-users. (Olszak, 2020, pp. 45, 46)

Human Requirements for Adopting Business Intelligence

The human requirements for Business Intelligence encompass a diverse set of skills that should be possessed by business analysts, the individuals forming the technical team responsible for designing and operating the enterprise's Business Intelligence system. Small and medium-sized industrial enterprises often face limitations in having individuals with high-level technical skills due to their limited human resources. Additionally, Business Intelligence, business analysis, and data analysis are considered highly specialized and precise fields, making training individuals in these areas a significant challenge for management.

Bert Brijs identifies five types of skills that should be present in a business analyst:

- **Data Knowledge:** Business analysts should master linking data quality to master data management, starting from data profiling to analyzing data proportions. This requires in-depth knowledge of processes supporting applications responsible for creating, using, or modifying data.
- **Application Knowledge:** involves proficiency in working with Business Intelligence applications capturing real events and transactions within the organization, such as invoices, purchase and sales orders, etc. Familiarity with Customer Relationship Management (CRM), Enterprise Resource Planning (ERP), sales channels, and Online Analytical Processing (OLAP) is crucial as they are primary data sources.
- **Process Knowledge:** acquiring knowledge related to the nature of the organization's processes is one of the most critical skills for business analysts. Understanding business processes is vital as they are significant sources of data.

- **BI Skills:** encompasses skills to maximize enterprise value from using Business Intelligence. These skills are associated with integrating Business Intelligence components with the activities and processes practiced by the organization to contribute to maximizing the produced value.
- **Interpersonal Skills:** involves skills such as conducting interviews, gathering requirements, conducting workshops, brainstorming, and mediating between opposing factions. (Brijs, 2013, p. 343)

Research Methodology

Among 20 fieldwork visits to 20 small and meduim sized industrial enterprises located in the industrial zone of Setif district in algeria, we interviewed 32 managers, and executive managers(the chief information officer (CIO), chief financial officer (CFO), chief operating officer (COO), and the chief executive officer (CEO)over a period of two months, through we administered a questionnaire whixh contains two importatnt sections. The first section is about the interest of the administration of small and meduim sized enterprise towards the adoption of Business Intelligence Systems and it was administered to 20 enterprises. The second section of the questionnaire contains 14 questionnares and itwas administered to 11 enterprises. It was adiminsterd to the enterprises that has already adopted Business Intelligence Systems, and the managers were asked questions about the requirements of adopting Business Intelligence, and the activities which can be enhanced using BI Systems. These questions are selected on the basis of its correlation with enterprises strategy, in addition to its contribution to creating value. Henceforth, detaailed question were asked about practical application of BI systems which happened or could happen in the future at the level of the the enterprise.

Data View and Analysis

The first section of the questionnaire contained five questions administered to 20 small and meduim sized industrial enterprises, and it is related to how interested the adminstration of the enterprise is towards adopting BI system(question are set according to the technical basis of BI system). The results indicated that only 11 enterprises of the total number are interested in adopting BI systems, against 9 enterprises which show no interest at all. Based on the results obtained, we set 14 questions which correlates with the requirements of the responsibles for adopting BI in the enterprises. 85% of the 32 questioned managers indicated funding is not a difficult requirement for adopting BI and it does not determine its success.In addition, 90% see that designing the operation BI is considered as the basic elements for its success, as it works well when it is integrated with the enterprises activities and operational activities. However, 77% admit that offering complete freedom to executive individuals by benefiting from data and information provided by BI systems is one of the most successful requirements for its adoption. Meanwhile, 61% believe that relying on e-administration and ICT is key factor to adopt Business Intelligence systems, and 100 admit that the skillfullness of the technical team responsible for designing and operating business intelligence system determines to a large extent the success of adopting BI systems

Findings

It is clear that the requirements and success factors for adopting a business intelligence system are numerous and diverse, as a result of its connection to all parts of the organization. These are primarily organizational requirements, centered around the design of the operational business intelligence system, in addition to requirements related to management, control, and coordination. They are embodied in the method of integrating the business intelligence system into the organizational structure to ensure vertical and horizontal flow of data and information to enhance coordination levels. In addition to technical requirements, which are concentrated in a high level of maturity of information technology and communication within the enterprise. Moreover, a crucial requirement is the skills that individuals responsible for designing and operating the business intelligence system must possess.

CONCLUSION

This chapter dealt with the requirements of adopting Business Intelligence in small and medium-sized industrial enterprises. It tries to analyse the main reasons behind adopting Business Intelligence successfully, specifically in light of the characteristics of of such enterprises, like llimited resources, the simplicity of its organizational framework, and its limited market share. Business intelligence systems works with compiling large amount of data which is related to the field study of enterprise, after that the data is analuzed and tronsformed inuseful information. Thus, it guarantees that managers and excutive managers make correct operational decisions, and consequently it contributes in decreasing costs raising goods quality and achieve a quick response to market demands.

There are three sections of successful requirements which are: organizational requirements and it comprises both requirements which accompany operational business intelligence systems, and the requirements which are related to administration, control and coordination. The first section is very important, as is tries to integrate the enterprise's business intelligence in commercial operations by improving the flow of data and information both at the strategic and operational levels to ensure the creation of value. The second section comprises the technical requirements which is in turn divided into the requirements related to the growing interest in using ICT which is considered a basic element to oerationalize business intelligence. In addition to the technical requirements of business intelligence and it is divided into four main elements: Data warehouse, Data visualization Data extraction and transmission tools, Data analysis and exploration tools. The third section is concerned with human requirements as it deals with individuals and the skills they must have when adopting business intelligence which are namely, Data knowledge, Application knowledge, Process knowledge, BI skills, Interpersonal skills.

REFERENCES

Bhimani, A., Horngren, C., Datar, S., & Rajan, M. (2015). Management Cost Accounting (éd. Sixth edition). New Jersey, USA: Pearson.

Blocher, E., Stout, D., & Cokins, G. (2010). Cost Management (Vol. fifth edition). USA: McGraw-Hill.

Brijs, B. (2013). *Business analysis for business intelligence*. CRC Press.

Deepmala, S., Anurag, S., Amizan, O., & S.B, G. (2023). *Business intelligence and human resource management*. New York: Routledge.

Gendron, M. (2013). *Business Intelligence Applied: implementing an effective information and communications technology infrastructure*. John Wiley and sons Inc.

Grossmann, W., & Rinderle-ma, S. (2015). *Fundamentals of Business Intelligence*. Springer. doi:10.1007/978-3-662-46531-8

Hammer, M., & Chempy, J. (1993). le Reengineering. (M. le seac'h, Trad.) Paris, La France: Dunod.

Howson, C. (2008). Successful Business Intelligence: Secrets to making BI a killer app (éd. First Edition). USA, USA: McGraw-Hill.

Howson, C. (2014). Successful Business Intelligence: unlock the value of BI and big data (éd. Second Edition). USA, USA: McGraw-Hill.

Kotler, P. (2017). *Marketing 4.0: moving from traditional to digital*. John Wiley and sons Inc.

Loshin, D. (2013). Business Intelligence: the savvy manager's guide (Vol. Second Edition). Waltham, USA: Morgan Kaufmann.

Olszak, C. M. (2020). *Business intelligence and big data: drivers of organizational success*. CRC Press. doi:10.1201/9780429353505

Poluha, R. (2016). *The Quintessence of Supply Chain Management.* USA: Springer.

Rao-Graham, L., McNaughton, M., & Mansingh, G. (2020). *Business Intelligence fpr small and medium sized enterprises: an agile roadmap toward business sustainability*. CRC Press.

Sharda, R., Delen, D., & Turban, E. (2018). *Business intelligence analytics and data science: a managerial perspective*. Pearson.

Skyrius, R. (2021). *Business Intelligence*. Springer. doi:10.1007/978-3-030-67032-0

Williams, S. (2016). *Business Intelligence Strategy and Big Data Analytics: a general management perspective*. Morgan Kaufmann.

Zapata-Cantu, L., Trevino, T., & Morton, F. (2020). Using Customer Analytics to Succeed: the case of Mexican SMEs. In P. N. Melo & C. Machado (Eds.), *Business Intelligence and Analytics in small and medium entreprises* (pp. 13–24). CRC Press.

Chapter 8
Design Thinking and Creativity in Entrepreneurial Innovation

Mustafa Kayyali
https://orcid.org/0000-0003-3300-262X
HE Higher Education Ranking, Syria

ABSTRACT

This study explores the pivotal role of design thinking and creativity in the realm of entrepreneurial innovation. The need for innovative ways to problem-solving and idea production is becoming more and more obvious as the entrepreneurial landscape changes. Iterative and human-centered design thinking provides entrepreneurs with a special framework for navigating the challenges of innovation. This study explores the interplay between design thinking and creativity, illuminating how these ideas merge to promote entrepreneurial success. Through a comprehensive analysis of case studies and empirical evidence, this study demonstrates the multifaceted impact of design thinking and creativity on fostering innovation in entrepreneurial ventures. The findings underscore the significance of cultivating a creative mindset and embracing design thinking principles as catalysts for entrepreneurial innovation in today's dynamic business environment.

INTRODUCTION

Innovation has turned into nothing less than the lifeblood of entrepreneurship in today's vibrant and ever changing corporate environment (Kaplan, 2012). Creativity and the application of design thinking principles have become crucial components of entrepreneurship success. Businesses are at a crossroads where ongoing innovation is not just a choice but a need for existence as they contend with an ever-growing

DOI: 10.4018/979-8-3693-1846-1.ch008

sea of competition, the relentless march of disruptive technology, and the erratic fluctuations in customer tastes. This book chapter proposal, titled "Design Thinking and Creativity in Entrepreneurial Innovation," takes root within this complex web of opportunities and challenges. It is prepared to delve into the profound and crucial role that design thinking and creativity play in nourishing the rich ground of entrepreneurial innovation.

At its very core, entrepreneurship is a pursuit underpinned by innovation (Weerawardena, 2011). Entrepreneurs are the architects of change, visionaries who possess the extraordinary ability to discern opportunities hidden beneath the surface of the ordinary. They breathe life into novel products, services, or business models, offering them as gifts to the world. Yet, the journey to fruitful innovation is a path fraught with treacherous terrain, marked by challenges and uncertainties that can confound even the most brilliant minds (Hannon, 2013). To succeed in the quest for innovation, entrepreneurs must navigate this labyrinth with more than just the spark of brilliant ideas; they must possess a structured and methodical approach capable of transforming ideas into pragmatic solutions. This is where design thinking, a human-centered problem-solving methodology, unfurls its formidable wings and takes flight.

Entrepreneurs are the bold individuals who dare to dream large, disrupt markets, and influence the future. They are the ones who observe the world and consider what might be possible as well as what is. Entrepreneurship depends on innovation, which is what drives these dreamers to make their visions a reality (Elkington, 2008). Innovation is the driving force that distinguishes entrepreneurs, whether it's introducing a ground-breaking product, revolutionising a market, or founding a completely new sector. However, innovation is a complicated and comprehensive process that calls for a special combination of abilities, perspectives, and approaches. It is not a single endeavour. Design thinking and creativity come into play at this point, giving business owners a potent toolkit to deal with the difficulties and uncertainties of innovation.

Design thinking has changed from being solely related to the field of product design to becoming a dynamic and revolutionary method of problem-solving and innovation. Although it is not a novel idea, its use in entrepreneurship has acquired considerable momentum recently and changed how companies look at innovation. Design thinking is fundamentally an empathic, human-centered approach to problem-solving. It encourags business owners and their staff to fully immerse themselves in the lives of their clients in order to comprehend their needs, wants, and pain points. Entrepreneurs can find insights and possibilities that conventional analytical methodologies might miss by adopting the perspective of the end-user.

Design thinking is a flexible framework that can be tailored to the particular difficulties that each innovation project faces; it is not a one-size-fits-all approach.

Through brainstorming, prototype, testing, and iteration, it offers entrepreneurs a structured yet flexible process. With this iterative process, ideas may be improved based on input from the real world and different solutions can be explored (Carlgren, 2016). Entrepreneurial approaches to innovation have fundamentally changed as a result of design thinking. It exhorts business leaders to assume their clients' positions, view the world from their point of view, and go on empathetic journeys. Wide-ranging effects result from this change from an idea-centric to a user-centric approach.

In the past, business owners can begin with what they consider to be a wonderful idea, spend a lot of time and money creating it, and then learn that their intended audience doesn't find it compelling. This approach often leads to costly failures. In contrast, design thinking advocates for empathy as the starting point. It encourages entrepreneurs to deeply understand their customers' needs and pain points before generating ideas. This early investment in empathy significantly reduces the risk of developing solutions that miss the mark. Moreover, design thinking challenges individuals to put their preconceived views to the test, to let go of their fear of failing, and to see failure as an unavoidable crucible for learning and development. In the world of entrepreneurship, where uncertainty and risk are constant companions, this mindset shift is a game-changer. It empowers entrepreneurs to embrace failure not as a setback but as a valuable source of insights that can inform the next iteration of their innovation.

Design thinking also breathes new life into collaboration. It creates an atmosphere where interdisciplinary teams can combine their various skills and perspectives to tackle challenging problems with an unrestrained spirit of creativity (Liedtka, 2011). By bringing together individuals with diverse backgrounds, experiences, and expertise, design thinking fosters synergy and the cross-pollination of ideas. In a world where innovation often requires a holistic understanding of complex issues, interdisciplinary collaboration is a potent asset. It enables entrepreneurs to tackle multifaceted challenges by drawing from a rich pool of knowledge and approaches. Whether it's integrating technology, user experience design, psychology, or business strategy, design thinking encourages entrepreneurs to break down silos and leverage the collective intelligence of their teams.

In this mosaic of entrepreneurial exploration, our proposed book, "Applying Business Intelligence and Innovation to Entrepreneurship," emerges as a beacon of enlightenment. It stands poised to illuminate the corridors of entrepreneurial potential, shedding light on the myriad tools and strategies, with design thinking at the forefront, that can be harnessed to fuel the engines of entrepreneurial triumph. Within the pages of this chapter, we will embark on a profound journey, delving deep into the intricate and symbiotic relationship between design thinking and the entrepreneurial spirit. We will navigate the nuanced currents of their theoretical foundations, we will unearth the hidden gems of practical applications, and we will unveil the transformative power of real-world case studies. As we journey through these chapters, we invite all who share the entrepreneurial spirit, be they seasoned titans of industry or aspirants taking their first exhilarating steps, to join us on this odyssey of exploration and discovery. Together, we will unravel the intricate dance between design thinking and entrepreneurial innovation, unlocking the secrets that lie at the intersection of structured methodology and unbridled creativity. We beckon you to partake in this voyage, to be inspired by the stories of those who have charted similar courses, and to harness the boundless potential that design thinking affords. In the world of entrepreneurship, where possibilities are infinite and innovation is the lifeblood, this chapter serves as a guiding star, illuminating the path to a future where creativity and design thinking converge, forging a sustainable and enlightened route to success.

The fusion of design thinking and entrepreneurship is a disruptive force in the contemporary corporate environment. By putting the user at the centre of innovation and accepting failure as a stepping stone to success, it challenges conventional ideas about innovation. It redefines collaboration as a multidisciplinary activity that taps the pooled brainpower of several teams. We invite you to join us as we explore the many dimensions of design thinking and creativity in entrepreneurial innovation to fully realise the potential of this formidable strategy. Together, we can successfully traverse the difficulties of entrepreneurship with empathy, imagination, and a relentless pursuit of innovation, paving the way for long-term success in a world that is constantly changing.

THE THEORETICAL FOUNDATIONS OF DESIGN THINKING IN ENTREPRENEURIAL INNOVATION

The idea and practise of "design thinking," which has roots in many fields including industrial design, engineering, and architecture, has developed into a crucial strategy in the entrepreneurial world (Johansson-Sköldberg, 2013). Its rise to prominence is ascribed to its human-centric approach to problem-solving, which has a profound resonance with the opportunities and challenges faced by entrepreneurs in today's fast-paced business climate. In this thorough investigation, we will delve into the theoretical underpinnings of design thinking and how it fits with the entrepreneurial process, offering insights into how it enables businesspeople to innovate, create, and succeed. Design thinking is an all-encompassing strategy that draws influence from various fields of study. Its roots can be seen in the innovative and iterative methods used in industrial design, where the demands and experiences of users are crucial to the development of products. Additionally, it shares similarities with engineering and architectural problem-solving methodologies, which prioritize user-centric solutions. At its core, design thinking emphasizes empathy, problem definition, ideation, prototyping, and collaboration (Lor, 2017). These fundamental principles form the theoretical foundations that underpin its application in various domains, including entrepreneurship.

Empathy, the cornerstone of design thinking, revolves around deeply understanding the needs, desires, and pain points of end-users (Portnoy, 2019). This empathetic perspective closely aligns with the essence of entrepreneurship, where identifying unmet market needs is often the ignition for a venture's journey. Entrepreneurs who embrace design thinking immerse themselves in the world of their target audience. By adopting the perspective of their potential customers, they gain invaluable insights that can lead to the creation of innovative and compelling solutions. Understanding the user's experience becomes not just a goal but a driving force behind entrepreneurial endeavors. Through empathetic research methods, such as user interviews, observations, and surveys, entrepreneurs can uncover hidden pain points and unarticulated desires. Armed with this deep understanding, they are better equipped to develop products or services that genuinely resonate with their target market. This empathetic approach ensures that entrepreneurial ventures are built upon a foundation of user-centricity, increasing the likelihood of success in the competitive business landscape.

Entrepreneurship often presents challenges that are ambiguous and complex (Amit, 1993). Entrepreneurs must grapple with identifying the right problems to solve to drive innovation and growth. In this context, design thinking offers a structured framework for effective problem definition. Design thinking encourages entrepreneurs to articulate problem statements clearly and comprehensively (Ihugba, 2014). This process involves breaking down complex challenges into manageable components and exploring the root causes of issues. By defining problems with precision, entrepreneurs gain clarity and focus on the aspects of their venture that require attention. Effective problem definition is crucial for resource allocation, prioritization, and decision-making. It allows entrepreneurs to channel their creative energy and resources toward solving the most critical challenges. Moreover, it ensures that the entrepreneurial journey remains aligned with the needs and aspirations of the target audience, reducing the risk of developing solutions that miss the mark.

Ideation, the phase of generating ideas, is a pivotal aspect of design thinking that is highly relevant to entrepreneurship. Entrepreneurs thrive on innovation, and design thinking provides a structured approach to fostering creativity. In design thinking, ideation encourages entrepreneurs and their teams to generate a multitude of ideas without judgment. This approach promotes a culture of creativity where no idea is deemed too far-fetched or impractical. By suspending judgment, entrepreneurs open the door to unconventional and groundbreaking concepts. Techniques such as brainstorming, mind mapping, and idea sketching are integral to the ideation process. These methods encourage diverse thinking and collaboration among team members, leading to a rich pool of ideas. Entrepreneurs can explore a wide range of possibilities, allowing for the discovery of unique and innovative solutions. Ideation is not confined to the early stages of entrepreneurship; it permeates throughout the venture's lifecycle. It inspires entrepreneurs to continually seek fresh perspectives and explore novel approaches to address evolving challenges. By integrating ideation into their entrepreneurial mindset, innovators are better prepared to adapt to changing market dynamics and seize emerging opportunities.

Prototyping and testing are central components of design thinking (Liedtka, 2018), offering a structured approach to validating ideas and concepts. In the entrepreneurial context, these principles align seamlessly with the development of minimum viable products (MVPs) and the iterative process of innovation. Entrepreneurs often embark on their ventures with bold ideas and visions. However, translating these concepts into tangible products or services requires a systematic approach. Design thinking advocates for the creation of prototypes – scaled-down, functional representations of the envisioned solution – to gather user feedback and insights. Prototyping enables entrepreneurs to test their ideas in a real-world context, allowing them to identify strengths and weaknesses. This iterative approach ensures that entrepreneurs remain agile and responsive to evolving user needs and preferences. It also minimizes the risk associated with investing substantial resources in fully-fledged products or services that may not align with market demands. Testing is a continuous cycle of learning and improvement. Entrepreneurs collect feedback from users, refine their prototypes, and iterate on their solutions. This process of refinement and enhancement is the lifeblood of entrepreneurial innovation. It enables entrepreneurs to evolve their offerings in sync with market dynamics and emerging trends, increasing the likelihood of long-term success.

Design thinking places a strong emphasis on collaboration and interdisciplinary teamwork, which resonates profoundly with the entrepreneurial ecosystem (Taajamaa, 2013). Entrepreneurial ventures often require diverse skills, perspectives, and expertise to thrive and innovate. Entrepreneurs are rarely solo actors; they work with multifaceted teams comprising individuals with varied backgrounds, experiences, and skill sets. Design thinking methodologies enhance team dynamics and foster a culture of innovation within these entrepreneurial teams. One of the key benefits of design thinking is its ability to break down silos and encourage open communication. Cross-disciplinary teams collaborate seamlessly, drawing from their unique strengths and viewpoints to tackle complex problems. This interdisciplinary approach is particularly valuable in addressing multifaceted challenges that demand a holistic understanding of business, technology, user experience, and more. Furthermore, design thinking promotes a mindset of empathy and active listening within teams.

This empathetic approach not only strengthens interpersonal relationships but also enhances the quality of problem-solving. Team members become more attuned to each other's needs and perspectives, facilitating smoother collaboration and creative brainstorming sessions. Entrepreneurs who embrace design thinking in their ventures create an environment where every team member feels valued and empowered to contribute their insights and ideas. This inclusive approach often leads to innovative solutions that transcend the boundaries of traditional disciplines and push the envelope of what is possible in entrepreneurial endeavors.

In the dynamic landscape of entrepreneurship, design thinking emerges as a transformative force (Welsh, 2013), offering a structured and human-centric approach to innovation. Its theoretical foundations of empathy, problem definition, ideation, prototyping, and collaboration align seamlessly with the entrepreneurial process, empowering innovators to navigate the complexities of the business world with creativity and resilience. Entrepreneurs who incorporate design thinking into their ventures gain a competitive edge by deeply understanding their target audience, defining problems effectively, fostering creativity, and embracing an iterative approach to innovation. Moreover, they create a culture of collaboration that harnesses the collective intelligence of diverse teams, propelling their entrepreneurial endeavors to new heights of success. The combination of design thinking principles with the entrepreneurial spirit promises to be a driving force of innovation and a source of long-term success as the entrepreneurial landscape continues to change. Entrepreneurs that start on this revolutionary journey will be in a good position to navigate the constantly shifting business tides, access the limitless potential of human-centered problem-solving, and pave the way for an innovation-free future.

PRACTICAL APPLICATIONS OF DESIGN THINKING IN ENTREPRENEURSHIP

In the dynamic and ever-evolving realm of entrepreneurship, the practical applications of design thinking have become a transformative force (Batat, 2021). Having established the theoretical foundations of design thinking, we now embark on a journey into its tangible and impactful applications within the entrepreneurial context. This section will delve deep into how design thinking can be harnessed in the various stages of entrepreneurship, offering a roadmap for entrepreneurs to infuse innovation, empathy, and agility into their ventures. The journey of entrepreneurship often begins with an idea – a spark of inspiration that propels individuals into action.

However, nurturing that idea into a viable business requires more than mere inspiration; it demands a systematic approach to understanding the market, identifying customer needs, and refining the concept. Design thinking provides invaluable tools for entrepreneurs during these formative stages.

Empathy and Journey Mapping: At the heart of design thinking lies empathy – the ability to understand and connect with the experiences and needs of potential customers (Dam, 2021). Entrepreneurs can employ techniques like journey mapping to chart the customer's path, uncovering pain points and opportunities for improvement. This method allows entrepreneurs to view their venture through the lens of the customer, paving the way for user-centric innovation.

Empathy Interviews: Another powerful tool in the early stages of entrepreneurship is the empathy interview. These interviews involve direct conversations with potential customers, enabling entrepreneurs to delve deeper into their needs, preferences, and challenges. Through open-ended questions and active listening, entrepreneurs gain insights that inform their business strategies and product development.

Idea Generation: Design thinking encourages a free-flowing and creative approach to idea generation. Entrepreneurs are encouraged to brainstorm and explore a wide range of possibilities without judgment. This ideation phase fosters a culture of innovation, allowing entrepreneurs to identify unique value propositions and business opportunities.

Problem Refinement: Defining the problem is a crucial step in entrepreneurship. Design thinking provides a structured approach to problem definition, breaking down complex challenges into manageable components. Entrepreneurs can refine problem statements to ensure they are addressing the most critical issues and aligning their ventures with genuine market needs.

Once the entrepreneurial journey progresses beyond the ideation and market research phases, entrepreneurs transition into the critical stage of product and service development. Design thinking offers a structured framework to guide this process, ensuring that the final offering aligns with user needs and preferences.

Rapid Prototyping: Rapid prototyping is a cornerstone of design thinking and a game-changer for entrepreneurs. Entrepreneurs can create tangible representations of their product or service ideas quickly and inexpensively. These prototypes serve as functional models that allow for user testing and feedback. Through prototyping, entrepreneurs can validate their concepts, make necessary adjustments, and refine their offerings based on real-world insights.

Iterative Improvement: Entrepreneurial ventures often require flexibility and adaptability to succeed. Design thinking's iterative nature aligns perfectly with the need for agility in entrepreneurship. Entrepreneurs can continually iterate on their products or services, responding to market feedback and evolving user preferences. This iterative approach minimizes the risk of investing heavily in a solution that does not resonate with the target audience.

Effective Communication: Communicating the vision of a product or service is essential, both to internal teams and external stakeholders. Design thinking equips entrepreneurs with the tools to effectively convey their ideas (Elsbach, 2018). Visual aids, such as prototypes and storyboards, enable entrepreneurs to articulate their vision, garner support from investors, and inspire their teams to execute the vision with precision. In the turbulent waters of entrepreneurship, adaptability is often the key to survival and success. Entrepreneurs must be prepared to pivot their business models or strategies in response to changing market dynamics. Design thinking's inherent flexibility aligns seamlessly with this requirement.

Validation of Assumptions: Assumptions are an inherent part of entrepreneurship, but they can be risky if not validated. Design thinking encourages entrepreneurs to validate assumptions through user testing and feedback. By constantly testing assumptions, entrepreneurs can make informed decisions and pivot their strategies if necessary.

Customer-Centric Decision-Making: In the fast-paced world of entrepreneurship, it's easy to become enamored with one's own ideas. Design thinking reinforces the importance of maintaining a customer-centric perspective. Entrepreneurs who continuously seek user feedback and prioritize customer needs are better equipped to make strategic decisions that resonate with their target audience.

Data-Driven Decisions: Entrepreneurs can leverage data analytics and user insights, facilitated by design thinking methodologies, to guide their decision-making. Data-driven decisions reduce uncertainty and provide a solid foundation for strategic planning. This data-centric approach allows entrepreneurs to stay agile and responsive to market changes.

REAL-WORLD CASE STUDIES

To illustrate the practical impact of design thinking in entrepreneurship, let's explore some real-world case studies of successful entrepreneurs who have embraced this approach to innovation and problem-solving:

1. Airbnb: Airbnb disrupted the hospitality industry by applying design thinking principles to create a platform that connects travelers with unique and personalized accommodations (Guttentag, 2017). The founders conducted extensive user research, staying in their own listed properties to gain firsthand insights. This user-centric approach allowed Airbnb to refine its platform continually and tailor its services to user preferences.
2. IDEO: IDEO, a renowned design and innovation consultancy, embodies design thinking in its approach to problem-solving. IDEO has collaborated with

numerous startups and established companies to develop innovative products and services. Their emphasis on empathy, prototyping, and interdisciplinary teamwork has consistently yielded groundbreaking solutions.

3. Warby Parker: Warby Parker, a disruptor in the eyewear industry, utilized design thinking to provide affordable, stylish eyeglasses to consumers. By understanding the frustrations of traditional eyewear shopping, Warby Parker created a user-friendly online platform that allowed customers to try on glasses virtually and receive home trial kits. This innovative approach revolutionized the eyewear industry.
4. Tesla: Tesla's founder, Elon Musk, represents the spirit of design thinking by rethinking the electric vehicle industry. Musk's continuous attention on user experience, from the intuitive touchscreen interface to over-the-air software updates, has positioned Tesla distinct in the car industry. The iterative aspect of design thinking is reflected in Tesla's constant product upgrades and adaptations.

The practical applications of design thinking in entrepreneurship are far-reaching and transformative (Kurtmollaiev, 2018). From the early stages of idea generation and market research to the development of innovative products and services, design thinking provides a structured and user-centric framework for entrepreneurial success. Its iterative nature aligns with the need for agility and adaptation in the face of evolving market dynamics. Real-world case studies of successful entrepreneurs who have embraced design thinking underscore its power to disrupt industries, create user-centric solutions, and gain a competitive edge. As the entrepreneurial landscape continues to evolve, those who harness the principles and methodologies of design thinking are poised to navigate the complex terrain of innovation with empathy, creativity, and resilience, ultimately forging a path to enduring success in the ever-changing world of entrepreneurship.

THE FUTURE OF DESIGN THINKING IN ENTREPRENEURSHIP

As we stand at the verge of a new era in entrepreneurship, the role of design thinking is experiencing a fundamental transition. In this final session, we will cast our attention into the future and investigate how design thinking is poised to revolutionise the entrepreneurial landscape. With expanding technology, worldwide reach, the significance of continuing education, and the enduring worth of its principles, design thinking is ready to accelerate innovation, drive creativity, and map a road to success in the ever-evolving world of entrepreneurship.

The future of design thinking in entrepreneurship is inextricably related to the rapid evolution of technology (Clark, 2008). New frontiers like blockchain, virtual reality (VR), and artificial intelligence (AI) are poised to change sectors and offer entrepreneurs unprecedented opportunity (Johansson-Sköldberg, 2013). How might design thinking combine with these cutting-edge technologies to drive innovation and challenge existing markets?

Blockchain and Design Thinking: Blockchain technology, known for its security and transparency, is already altering industries such as finance, supply chain management, and healthcare. Entrepreneurs may utilise design thinking to discover pain spots within these industries and develop blockchain-based solutions that boost security, traceability, and trust. Design thinking approaches may influence the user-centric design of blockchain apps, ensuring they are intuitive and fit real-world needs.

Virtual Reality (VR) and Immersive Experiences: VR has the ability to transform user experiences across numerous sectors, from entertainment and education to healthcare and real estate. Entrepreneurs may employ design thinking to develop immersive and user-centered VR experiences. By empathizing with customers and understanding their aspirations for engaging and intuitive interfaces, entrepreneurs may pioneer breakthrough applications in the VR realm.

Artificial Intelligence (AI) and Personalization: AI-driven technologies are becoming increasingly integrated into our daily lives. Entrepreneurs can utilize design thinking to harness AI's capabilities for personalized user experiences. Through empathetic research and iterative prototyping, entrepreneurs can develop AI-driven solutions that anticipate user preferences, enhance decision-making, and provide tailored recommendations.

The convergence of design thinking and emerging technologies presents an exciting frontier for entrepreneurial innovation (Huq, 2017). By integrating user-centric design principles with the capabilities of blockchain, VR, and AI, entrepreneurs can unlock new avenues for disruption and create solutions that resonate with the evolving needs of a tech-savvy market. In an increasingly interconnected world, the relevance of design thinking extends beyond geographical boundaries. Its guiding principles of empathy, problem definition, ideation, and collaboration are universal and adaptable to diverse cultural contexts. As we peer into the future, it becomes evident that design thinking has the potential to transcend borders and play a pivotal role in the global entrepreneurship scene.

Cross-Cultural Innovation: Design thinking's emphasis on empathy positions entrepreneurs to navigate cultural nuances and develop solutions that resonate with international audiences. By conducting cross-cultural empathy interviews and understanding the unique needs and preferences of different markets, entrepreneurs can create products and services that bridge cultural divides.

Global Collaborations: In a world where interdisciplinary teamwork and collaboration know no borders, design thinking fosters a collaborative spirit that transcends geographic constraints. Entrepreneurs can assemble diverse, international teams that bring a rich tapestry of perspectives and expertise to tackle global challenges. This collaborative approach not only drives innovation but also opens doors to international markets.

Adaptability to Local Contexts: Design thinking's iterative nature aligns with the need for adaptability in global entrepreneurship. Entrepreneurs can use design thinking methodologies to continuously iterate on their offerings, adapting to changing market dynamics and local preferences. This flexibility ensures that entrepreneurial ventures remain relevant and competitive on a global scale.

The future of design thinking in entrepreneurship is characterized by its ability to unite cultures, foster collaboration, and enable entrepreneurs to create solutions that transcend borders (Dunne, 2006). As the world becomes increasingly interconnected, design thinking's universal principles will continue to be a driving force behind global entrepreneurial success. In the dynamic field of design thinking, staying ahead of the curve is essential for entrepreneurs seeking to maintain a competitive edge. The landscape is continually evolving, with new methodologies, tools, and trends emerging regularly. In this future-focused context, the importance of continuous education for business owners cannot be overstated. Mastering New Tools and Techniques: Design thinking is constantly evolving, with new tools and techniques being developed to enhance the innovation process. Entrepreneurs who invest in continuous education can stay abreast of these advancements and incorporate them into their entrepreneurial toolkits. Whether it's mastering the latest prototyping software or adopting cutting-edge research methods, ongoing learning is a pathway to innovation.

Adapting to Changing Trends: Entrepreneurship is subject to market trends and consumer preferences that evolve over time (Finkle, 2001). By engaging in continuous education, entrepreneurs can stay attuned to these shifts and adapt their strategies accordingly. For example, understanding the latest trends in sustainability or digital transformation can inform product development and market positioning.

Fostering a Culture of Learning: Beyond individual education, entrepreneurs can cultivate a culture of continuous learning within their organizations (Syam, 2018). Encouraging team members to pursue professional development and fostering an environment where experimentation and learning are celebrated can drive innovation and resilience in the face of change.

The future of design thinking in entrepreneurship is connected with the commitment to continuing education and adaptation (Liedtka, 2011). By embracing a philosophy of constant learning, entrepreneurs can traverse the dynamic market with agility, inventiveness, and a competitive edge. In ending our exploration of the future of design thinking in entrepreneurship, it is crucial to highlight its continuing value in the entrepreneurial process. Design thinking is not a fleeting trend; rather, it offers a timeless approach to problem-solving and innovation that will stay important in the years to come.

Unleashing Creative Potential: Design thinking allows entrepreneurs to tap into their creative potential, establishing an environment where unique ideas can flourish. By placing empathy, ideation, and cooperation at the forefront, design thinking releases the innovative spirit within entrepreneurs, propelling the creation of groundbreaking solutions.

Stimulating Innovation: Innovation is the lifeblood of entrepreneurship, and design thinking is a catalyst for continuous innovation. Its iterative nature encourages entrepreneurs to refine and enhance their offerings based on user feedback, ensuring that their ventures remain at the cutting edge of their respective industries.

A Route to Success in a Shifting Landscape: In a business environment characterized by rapid change and uncertainty, design thinking provides a reliable route to success. Entrepreneurs who embrace its principles can navigate the complexities of the entrepreneurial journey with resilience, adaptability, and a user-centric focus.

In the ever-evolving world of entrepreneurship, the future of design thinking is one of enduring relevance and transformational impact. As technology advances, markets expand, and global connections strengthen, entrepreneurs who embrace design thinking will continue to pioneer innovative solutions, disrupt industries, and create lasting value for both their ventures and the world at large. Design thinking, as a timeless approach, remains a guiding star for entrepreneurs on their journey to success in an ever-changing landscape.

CONCLUSION

Ultimately, the study of "Design Thinking and Creativity in Entrepreneurial Innovation" within the context of the book "Applying Business Intelligence and Innovation to Entrepreneurship" makes a significant contribution to our comprehension of how entrepreneurship thrives in the modern business landscape. This chapter has delved into the complex web of design thinking's theoretical underpinnings, real-world applications, difficulties, and potentials, highlighting its crucial function in fostering entrepreneurial success. Design thinking is essentially the spirit of entrepreneurship. Entrepreneurs are, by nature, dreamers who dare to see possibilities where others would only see obstacles. By creating ground-breaking goods, services, and business methods, they aim to add value. However, there are many unknowns, hazards, and significant difficulties along the way. Entrepreneurs need more than simply original ideas to effectively navigate this difficult terrain;

they also need a methodical and sympathetic approach to problem-solving. This paradigm is precisely what design thinking offers.

This chapter has carefully laid out the theoretical underpinnings of design thinking, underscoring how this methodology aligns seamlessly with the core principles of entrepreneurship. It has unveiled the intricate interplay between design thinking and the entrepreneurial process. By empathizing with end-users, defining problem statements, fostering creativity through ideation, prototyping, and testing, entrepreneurs can harness the power of design thinking to forge transformative solutions. Moreover, this chapter has explored the practical applications of design thinking in entrepreneurship. From the nascent stages of idea generation to the development of tangible products and services, design thinking provides a versatile toolkit. It equips entrepreneurs to resonate with their target audience, devise innovative solutions, and adapt rapidly in response to market feedback. Real-world case studies have illuminated how entrepreneurs, both seasoned and novice, have harnessed design thinking to pivot their ventures, disrupt industries, and secure competitive advantages.

However, we must acknowledge that the path to incorporating design thinking into entrepreneurial endeavors is not without its challenges. Entrepreneurs often face entrenched organizational cultures and resource constraints. Embracing design thinking often necessitates a cultural shift, and this chapter has offered insights into how this transformation can be navigated. Moreover, it has addressed resource limitations by discussing lean methodologies and cost-effective prototyping, making design thinking accessible to even the most resource-constrained startups. As we look toward the future, design thinking remains a beacon of hope and innovation for entrepreneurs. Emerging technologies, such as artificial intelligence and virtual reality, promise to augment the capabilities of design thinking, enabling entrepreneurs to craft even more visionary solutions. The global reach of entrepreneurship is expanding, and design thinking transcends geographical and cultural boundaries, making it a universal tool for entrepreneurs across the world. In essence, this chapter stands as a testament to the enduring relevance of design thinking in the entrepreneurial landscape. By embracing its principles and adapting them to their unique contexts, entrepreneurs can tap into their creative potential, unlock innovation, and chart a course to success amidst the dynamic currents of the business world. This chapter serves as a guidepost for all, whether aspiring entrepreneurs taking their first steps or seasoned visionaries seeking to remain at the forefront of innovation. It encourages all of us to investigate the seemingly endless opportunities that lie at the nexus of design thinking and entrepreneurial innovation. It is a call to action to inject empathy, innovation, and a relentless pursuit of value creation into our entrepreneurial journeys, ensuring that the entrepreneurial spirit continues to mould and improve the world in which we live.

REFERENCES

Amit, R., Glosten, L., & Muller, E. (1993). Challenges to theory development in entrepreneurship research. *Journal of Management Studies*, *30*(5), 815–834. doi:10.1111/j.1467-6486.1993.tb00327.x

Batat, W., & Addis, M. (2021). Designing food experiences for well-being: A framework advancing design thinking research from a customer experience perspective. *European Journal of Marketing*, *55*(9), 2392–2413. doi:10.1108/EJM-12-2020-0893

Carlgren, L., Rauth, I., & Elmquist, M. (2016). Framing design thinking: The concept in idea and enactment. *Creativity and Innovation Management*, *25*(1), 38–57. doi:10.1111/caim.12153

Clark, K., & Smith, R. (2008). Unleashing the power of design thinking. *Design Management Review*, *19*(3), 8–15. doi:10.1111/j.1948-7169.2008.tb00123.x

Dunne, D., & Martin, R. (2006). Design thinking and how it will change management education: An interview and discussion. *Academy of Management Learning & Education*, *5*(4), 512–523. doi:10.5465/amle.2006.23473212

Elkington, J., & Hartigan, P. (2008). *The power of unreasonable people: How social entrepreneurs create markets that change the world*. Harvard Business Press.

Elsbach, K. D., & Stigliani, I. (2018). Design thinking and organizational culture: A review and framework for future research. *Journal of Management*, *44*(6), 2274–2306. doi:10.1177/0149206317744252

Finkle, T. A., & Deeds, D. (2001). Trends in the market for entrepreneurship faculty, 1989–1998. *Journal of Business Venturing*, *16*(6), 613–630. doi:10.1016/S0883-9026(99)00051-8

Guttentag, D. A., & Smith, S. L. (2017). Assessing Airbnb as a disruptive innovation relative to hotels: Substitution and comparative performance expectations. *International Journal of Hospitality Management*, *64*, 1–10. doi:10.1016/j.ijhm.2017.02.003

Hannon, P. D. (2013). Why is the entrepreneurial university important? *Journal of innovation management, 1*(2), 10-17.

Huq, A., & Gilbert, D. (2017). All the world'sa stage: Transforming entrepreneurship education through design thinking. *Education + Training*, *59*(2), 155–170. doi:10.1108/ET-12-2015-0111

Ihugba, O. A., Odii, A., & Njoku, A. (2014). Theoretical analysis of entrepreneurship challenges and prospects in Nigeria. *International Letters of Social and Humanistic Sciences*, *5*(16), 21–34.

Interaction Design Foundation, Dam, R. F., & Siang, T. Y. (2021). *What is design thinking and why is it so popular*? IDF.

Johansson-Sköldberg, U., Woodilla, J., & Çetinkaya, M. (2013). Design thinking: Past, present and possible futures. *Creativity and Innovation Management*, *22*(2), 121–146. doi:10.1111/caim.12023

Kaplan, S. (2012). *The business model innovation factory: How to stay relevant when the world is changing*. John Wiley & Sons. doi:10.1002/9781119205234

Kurtmollaiev, S., Fjuk, A., Pedersen, P. E., Clatworthy, S., & Kvale, K. (2018). Organizational transformation through service design: The institutional logics perspective. *Journal of Service Research*, *21*(1), 59–74. doi:10.1177/1094670517738371

Liedtka, J. (2018). Why design thinking works. *Harvard Business Review*, *96*(5), 72–79.

Liedtka, J., & Ogilvie, T. (2011). *Designing for growth: A design thinking tool kit for managers*. Columbia University Press.

Lor, R. (2017). *Design thinking in education: A critical review of literature*.

Portnoy, L. (2019). *Designed to learn: Using design thinking to bring purpose and passion to the classroom*. ASCD.

Syam, H., Akib, H., Patonangi, A. A., & Guntur, M. (2018). Principal entrepreneurship competence based on creativity and innovation in the context of learning organizations in Indonesia. *Journal of Entrepreneurship Education*, *21*(3), 1–13.

Taajamaa, V., Kirjavainen, S., Repokari, L., Sjöman, H., Utriainen, T., & Salakoski, T. (2013, December). Dancing with Ambiguity Design thinking in interdisciplinary engineering education. In *2013 IEEE Tsinghua International Design Management Symposium* (pp. 353-360). IEEE. 10.1109/TIDMS.2013.6981258

Weerawardena, J., & Mavondo, F. T. (2011). Capabilities, innovation and competitive advantage. *Industrial Marketing Management*, *40*(8), 1220–1223. doi:10.1016/j.indmarman.2011.10.012

Welsh, M. A., & Dehler, G. E. (2013). Combining critical reflection and design thinking to develop integrative learners. *Journal of Management Education*, *37*(6), 771–802. doi:10.1177/1052562912470107

Chapter 9
Business Intelligence and Innovation Moderating Roles on Entrepreneurship and Management Using Championpreneurship Approach

Harry Orugba Ovharhe
https://orcid.org/0000-0002-3631-498X
University of Port Harcourt, Nigeria

ABSTRACT

The study explored business intelligence and innovation moderating roles on entrepreneurship and management using championpreneurship approach. The dimensions of business intelligence capture were competitive intelligence (CI) and decision support system (DSS). The innovation was focused on selected simplex innovation (product, process, service, technology, among others) and complex innovation (sustainable, transformational and systematic). The study orchestrates championpreneurship approach as entrepreneurs with championship characteristics and management acumen on entrepreneurial opportunities. This poses that entrepreneurship is a viable concept for enterprise to achieve their vision, mission, dreams, and entrepreneurial journey. In conclusion, the synchronization of entrepreneurship and management boosts the tendency of prospective and potential entrepreneurs to be equipped with spirit of championpreneurship by the intensive application of business intelligence and innovation.

DOI: 10.4018/979-8-3693-1846-1.ch009

1. OVERVIEW

Entrepreneurship is the engine house of any merchandizing activities and propeller of any nation's economic growth and development. Entrepreneurs determine the flow of new blood stream in any enterprise. While management is the coordinating force that binds all the activities to ensure there is effectiveness and efficiency to achieve the corporate goals. This means the managerial strategies will be able to fine-tune the plans, organizing, directing, motivating and control of the input resource and projected output to work its achievable concept. Unlike entrepreneurship, management exists in form of pyramid on three levels, such the strategic management (top management), tactical management (middle management) and operational management (lower management). The top management deals with long-term activities: [i.e. Director General (DG), Chief Executive Officer (CEO), Managing Director (MD) and General Management (GM)]. The middle management entails the intermediate and functional departmental activities: i.e. marketing manager, production manager, finance manager, logistic manager, sales and distribution management, personnel manager and lot more functional managerial level (Coursera, 2023). The operational management is the short-term level management that deals with daily activities. They are the supervisors and foremen in the enterprise which augment job and task functions. They are the power house of the enterprise that executes responsibilities of the workforce. In accounting, they are the book keeping, cashier, in marketing they are in charge of brand, label, pricing, advertisement. Otherwise, entrepreneurship is the propeller of innovation, skills, risk culture passion, vision, dreams and journey of the enterprise (Ovharhe, 2023a). Entrepreneur uses intrapreneurs to breed fresh thinking and idea to expand, extend, build and develop the business enterprise.

Micheal Dermer in 2023 stresses on the origin of the term 'Entrepreneur' emanates from the French word, "entreprendre" which means to start executing a generally long or complex task. In English, we translate it as "to undertake". The French word comes from Latin (in, en, + prendĕre) which means to take (Dermer, 2023).

French and English people use the same word to name the "entrepreneur." In French, the word "entrepreneur" stems from the Latin word inter prehendere, which corresponds to the verb entreprendre in French and means "to grab" or "to take control." During the Middle Age, the verb entreprendre in France used to mean "to take challenges and control with the mindset of achieving targeted goals, hence French word entreprendre could be analyzed as entre-predre. Thus; entre =go; while, predre =between. In the broad equation terms, entrepreneurs are individuals that have the ability, capability, competence, acumen and skills to go-between where there are needs and locked business opportunities with the aid to unveil it for benefits and satisfaction. Entrepreneurs have the potentials to develop risk culture with knowledge and talent to go between chaotic channel by creating possible remedies to the business world which poses challenges, competitive, dynamic, reckless and turbulent issues.

Entrepreneurship has been seen as a generic term which the definition is a matter of serious debate because of its blanket nature which enveloped and encompasses human endeavour of sustainability, survival and success. The term entrepreneurship has capture a lot of interest in various field like management science, social science, law, politics, engineering, human resource, health, philosophy among others, there remain holism of how the concept should be define (Ratten, 2023).

Seth (2023) fathoms that Howard Stevenson, known as "the godfather of entrepreneurship studies" at Harvard Business School (HBS), has defined it as the "pursuit of opportunity beyond resources controlled." HBS professor Tom Eisenmann elaborates, "'beyond resources controlled' implies resource constraints. The Stanford Center for Professional Development at Stanford University offers a somewhat simpler definition: At its most basic level, entrepreneurship refers to an individual or a small group of partners who strike out on an original path to create a new business. An aspiring entrepreneur actively seeks a particular business venture and it is the entrepreneur who assumes the greatest amount of risk associated with the project. As such, this entrepreneur also stands to benefit most if the project is a success.

Every entrepreneurs need to learn how to navigate with potentials and capabilities on the right track where there are valuable treasures of opportunities. The right track is the valuable path on the vision and mission to thread which can accomplish the entrepreneurial journey and dreams. This will enable the entrepreneur to experience new enterprise creation successfully (Yadav, Tripathi, Tripathi, Ghosal, Kumar, Mandal & Singh, 2023).

From the definition of Howard Stevenson, it could be deduce that navigation for opportunities' is paramount for the enterprise to pursuit her passion, vision, mission, dreams and entrepreneurial journey in the short-term and long-term. This is to say that opportunities are everywhere. Opportunities lies in the human, land, air, water, exploration of natural resources, artificial resource, renewable resources and lot more. All entrepreneur need is to develop and activate the wings of championship with innovation skills, creativity, business intelligence, decision support system, competitive intelligence, sensitivity and managerial acumen for pursuit and grab business opportunities. This is the pursuit that drives championship trait which boosts an entrepreneur to become 'Champiopreneur' (Ovharhe & Woko, 2024).

Navigating for opportunities is arc of entrepreneurship sustainability, survival and success in the business world. Entrepreneur need to develop business receptacle and terminals to navigate to the right direction to move with the optimal market trend. For entrepreneurs to navigate to the right direction, business intelligence, creativity and innovation skill is the key element. Without, the application of business intelligence, creativity and transformation innovation key, the success of an entrepreneur journey and the management mission are in jeopardy. An entrepreneurship opportunity is continuous improvement for business growth. Despise the emergence of climate and artificial intelligence affecting global market structure it cannot cripple entrepreneurship opportunities if entrepreneurs and management align with the intervention of business intelligence, creativity and sustainable innovation. Identifying opportunities and continuous scanning in the enterprise environment with authentic application of business intelligence, creativity and sustainable innovation would yield net cash flow on return on asset, return on equity, return on capital employed and return on investment.

Additionally, to actualize the spirit of champiopreneurship, Tom Eisenmann pointed out entrepreneurs should see 'beyond resources controlled'. This is the need for entrepreneurs to navigate beyond physical, social, emotional, mental and natural resources. For entrepreneurs to be champion, she should create and innovate beyond tangible and intangible needs to satisfy human livelihood on entity of the planet, people and profit in corroboration with the sustainable development goals (SDG). In this context, entrepreneurs should sees as creator, innovator and inventor of the future being augmented from the present. Championeurs are known for breaking edges by innovating, creating and inventing the future benefit of mankind, society at large, institutions and the entire globe. Champiopreneurship dreams could be easily accomplished if there is comprehensive application of business intelligence, creativity and innovativeness (Ovharhe & Chukwuemeka, 2023). For an individual to become a successful entrepreneur as a 'champion', he/she need to identify the potential locked within its entire being. These potentials may be talent, charisma, skills, abilities, brain storming imagination and idea generation. It may be in the concept of economical, technological, social, physical, emotional, psychological and mental. This shows how entrepreneurs are being wired (design/structure) as a competitive advantage instrumentation or weapon to become a champion. If any entrepreneurs can understand this concept, the vision and entrepreneurial journey will be easy to defined and accomplished as a champiopreneur. This is the emergence of champiopreneurship in the business world.

Champiopreneurship is the ability, capability and capacity using optimum competence to identify and take advantage of business opportunities to develop framework with business intelligence, creativity and innovation for decision to win the competition in pursuit of the business enterprise king. The pursuit of opportunities' does not underestimate any individual in the field of entrepreneurship that is desperate to be a champion because they possess sustainable innovative skills, passion, vision, dreams and risk culture to corroborate the Sustainable Development Goals (SDG) (Ovharhe, 2023a,b,c).

The psychologist strongly argued that no two individuals are wired (designed or created) the same way. Every individual have the way they are wired with unique abilities, opportunities, special gifts, talents and unending resources (Alberta, 2023). Every human are wired and locked with hundreds, thousands, millions and billions of potentials with opportunities for sustainability, survival and success. No human is born to the earth as a waste resource or automatic asset. Hence, no entrepreneur should be a liability rather a resourceful asset to be productive and fruition. There is something about every entrepreneur that enables him/her to innovate, invent and create the future from resources available around us all. Entrepreneurs need to discover and identified specific opportunities in the environment with the embedded creative skills position in him/her (Ovharhe & Saturday, 2024).

It is important to note that business intelligence, creativity and innovation are the applicable instrumentations that pivot entrepreneurs' dreams and mission to accomplish the pursuit of purpose. Business intelligence, creativity and enterprise innovativeness is the engine propeller for entrepreneur to satisfy customer, societal and institutional needs. Ovharhe (2023c) asserted from the marketing lecture of Prof A. B. Akpan (2018) which coined from Murray *et al.*, revealed that human needs are categorized into forty (40). He argued that there are twelve (12) physiological needs, while twenty eight (28) physiological needs. This posits that human psychological needs are more than human physiological needs. Physiological represent the tangible (product) needs, whereas psychological are the intangible (services) needs. Champiopreneur are the innovator, inventor and creator of the intangible and tangible needs for client or customer satisfaction. Champiopreneur can be disabilities, dwarf, unstable or deformed, but their innovative skills and creativity coupled with business intelligence changes the game of their condition or impairment (i.e. Helen Keller, Steve Wonder, Peter Dinklage; Hollywood, Nick Juvicic, Cohbam Asuquo, Akin & Pawpaw in Nollywood among others).

These are champiopreneurs that uses their disability as competitive advantage which give them edge in the competitive parity. Their condition gives them entrepreneurial opportunities as leading edge instead of bleeding edge because of the application of business intelligence, creativity and innovation. They were able to display their entrepreneurship and managerial innovation skills to conquer their business world and satisfied the needs of clients by unlocking business intelligence, creativity and innovation skills they possess (Ovharhe, 2023b; Seth, 2023; OECD, 2023).

In the tail of the above discussion, the study seeks to interface the knowledge gap that exists between business intelligence and innovation moderating roles on entrepreneurship and management using champiopreneurship approach.

2. ENTREPRENEURSHIP AND MANAGEMENT

Prima facie in the 18th century the Irish economist, Richard Cantillon dive into the term “entrepreneur”. Cantillon sees an entrepreneur as the person who buys factors services at certain prices with a view to selling its product at uncertain prices. But, Joseph Schumpeter deemed to be the father of entrepreneurship as argued by most scholars, came up with a paradigm shift with theories and concept to develop a modern features and attributes. Schumpeter averred that entrepreneurship is a process of creation of both intangible and tangible resource to generate wealth. His emphasizes was on the word ‘creation’. This is while the creative ability of every entrepreneur is to innovate, brain storm, invent and network from the past to the presence and future. This means entrepreneurs are creator of resources to satisfied human livelihood in the short-term and long-term. Being a creator makes entrepreneurs to becomes a ‘*Champion*’

In 2024 Eric Beato from Babson College, the renowned Entrepreneurship Institute with champiopreneurship trait, laid emphasis on resilience and allyship interface with champiopreneur and leaders on applying business intelligence, creativity and innovation to achieve enterprise excellence. Breato (2024) and Ovharhe (2024) inclined that these factorial elements are expected to augment vital proceedings in empowering, proliferating and advancing infant-childhood, women and youth entrepreneurs beyond now and SDG towards champiopreneurship. But, for entrepreneurs to be experience on sustainability, survival and success in the enterprise, there ought to be completive edge, business intelligence and competitive advantage. For these to be achieved certain planning, organizing, directing, motivating, staffing and control measures need to be in place. This will enable the entrepreneur to set metrics on targeted goals, strategies, policy, procedure, budget, implementation, monitoring and feedback.

This led to the synchronization between entrepreneurship and management, just as Schumpeter rings the bell of Entrepreneurship, Peter F. Drucker augment management with philosophies, theories and new terminologies even different from the founding fathers (i.e. Fredrick Taylor, Frank & Lillian Gilbert, Henry Gantt, Henry Fayol, Max Weber among others (Showkat, 2022). In this tail of these, Drucker opined management as means of delegating responsibility and fiduciary functions (Druker, 1963).

The word ‘entrepreneur’ is coined from the French word entreprendre. It means ‘to undertake’. Thus, entrepreneur is the person who undertakes the risk. This represents that actual characteristic of entrepreneur as been a risk bearer. In the same vein the term is still believes to be go or enter (Entre), between (Prendre). This portrays entrepreneurs as a change agent, problem solver and decision maker. Truly, entrepreneurs are problem solvers by taking risk in between chaos, troubles, needs, turbulence and competition to create leading edge by mitigating bleeding edge in the business world with the ability to think. Entrepreneurs have the capability and capacity to think by innovating the future for mankind comfortability, portability, accessibility and reachability of tangible and intangible resources.

Also, the term entrepreneur in the middle age (French) means to grab or take control. Entrepreneurs are made to take charge and act as change agent. Nothing should scare an entrepreneur, rather the intrapreneur should be employed for accomplishment of the entrepreneurship dreams, vision and journey. To grab means to take advantage of entrepreneurial opportunities.

The synchronization of both entrepreneurship and management is what will make the entrepreneur to be champion. Entrepreneurs is all about creating champions in the society, industry, business, religion, polity, legal, science, philosophy, catering, invent management, hospitality, health profession, engineering, technology, and lot more. To become a champion there is the need to cultivate the moderating role of business intelligence, creativity and sustainable innovation.

2.1. Type of Entrepreneurs

Entrepreneur is an individual who has a role of an industrialist and forms an organization for the commercial use. Entrepreneurs and intrapreneurs are change agent which transformative innovation instinct that focuses on client demand while creating basic alternative sources to meet their supply. Entrepreneurs are wired to invent and create customer/client satisfaction. There are several different types of entrepreneurs. Some of these types include digital entrepreneurs, home-based entrepreneurs, serial entrepreneurs, therapeutic entrepreneurs, cyber entrepreneurs, lean entrepreneurs, agile entrepreneurs, traditional entrepreneurs, social entrepreneurs, and corporate entrepreneurs (Ovharhe & Chukwemeka, 2023). But, in operations the following beneath will be discussed as types of entrepreneurs.

2.1.1. Types of Entrepreneurs in the Enterprise

The Geek (2023) community stretches tentative types of entrepreneurs in the enterprise as discussed below.

1. **Innovative Entrepreneur:** These are the ones who invent the new ideas, new products, new production methods or processes, discover potential markets and reorganize the enterprise's structure. They are the industry leader that contributes significantly towards the economic development of the country. The innovative entrepreneurs have an unusual foresight to recognize the demand for goods and services. They are always ready to take a risk because they enjoy

the excitement of a challenge, and every challenge has some risk associated with it (Manohar *et al.*, 2023)

2. **Imitating Entrepreneurs:** The imitating entrepreneurs are those who immediately copy the new inventions made by the innovative entrepreneurs. These do not make any innovations by themselves; they just imitate the technology, processes, methods pioneered by others. These entrepreneurs are found in the places where there is a lack of resources or industrial base due to which no new innovations could be made. Thus, they are suitable for the underdeveloped regions where they can imitate the combinations of inventions already well established in the developed regions, in order to bring a boom in their industry.
3. **Fabian Entrepreneurs:** Mediocrity and skeptics are the order of this entrepreneur status. They are very mild and careful; do not want to be seen making mistakes. At first they are not initiative and innovation, but spend time to study the trend of motion on event before they strike their actions in the business place. They follow the success rate of others in the invention and change transformation before they operate theirs. They strongly believe in concept testing and test marketing of their product or services and were very sure of the success and survival rate before they lunch attack on the market (Ratten, 2023).
4. **Drone Entrepreneurs:** These are more mediocrity entrepreneurs that do not want to adopt and implement change in the business environment because of their conservative nature. They strongly choreograph the rhythm of 'whatever will be, will be' in their business because they are afraid to make loss.

   Also A.B. Akpan of Ahmadu Bello University (ABU) propagates the competitive parity as supported by Ovharhe (2021, 2022) entrepreneurship form of Enterprise. These are discussed below; viz:
5. **Nichers:** These are entrepreneurs with passion but do not have the required resources or managerial acumen to capture the market. But, they decided to start from a very low scale in the business ladder trying to wait for the appropriate opportunity to grow. You see them starting with road side business before owing a business platform.
6. **Followers:** They are very strong and ready to climb to the business top at any given opportunity. They may be looking for connections on the business climax and political structure. They are always scanning in the business environment for any slight opportunity to lunch their attack. Their target in not the market nichers' rather the challengers and leaders on top the ladder in the business environment. They are not satisfied with where they are, but any mistake by those at the top, they will take over.

7. **Challengers (counter entrepreneurs):** These are the guerillas and leopards in the business environment. Their arrows are targeted to be in the control of the market share so they can occupy the first position to be the market leaders in the enterprise. Their strategy is to grab some market share, territories and sales quotas from the 'Followers', then proceed to lunch full scale attack on the market leaders. Their first priority is not profit maximization, but to gain in control of the leadership of the market. This is where the key drama of the completive parity orchestrates.
8. **Leaders:** This is where the eagle and lion exist in the business climax. There are ready to sow to any high altitude with enthusiasm, ruggedness and competitiveness to occupy the leaders ladder at all cost. They seeks to lobby and manipulate all agency, legal and politic structure, client, customer, vendor among others. They dream like the Ultrapreneurs and Extrapreneurs with resources to avail their plight.

2.1.2. Characteristics of Entrepreneur

Talent, innovation-skills and potentials are never enough to attain or experience sustainability, survival and success in entrepreneurs' field of endeavors' or interest and passion. A lot of entrepreneurs possess these traits but do not have success and never becomes champiopreneurs in their various fields. This is because they lack certain character which was never exhibited in the field of specialty.

Every entrepreneur possesses trait, feature and attributes that make them to be seen as champion in their environment. This is the reasons they are recognized as 'champiopreneur' when they attain or experience sustainability, survival and success. Just like the conventional entrepreneur, champiopreneur are characterized with charisma, spirit of enthusiasm with burning passion, visionary on focus, risk culture, creator, learning, leading the way, optimistic and opportunist of changing the future, resiliency, building the bridge and idea generator (Blessley & Mudambi, 2022; Ovharhe, 2022; 2023b, 2023c). This also means infant that are potential champion should be characterized with these attributes. Infant possesses all these characteristics as inert model wired and locked within them (Ovharhe & Woko, 2024a,b).

Figure 1. Characteristics of Champiopreneur

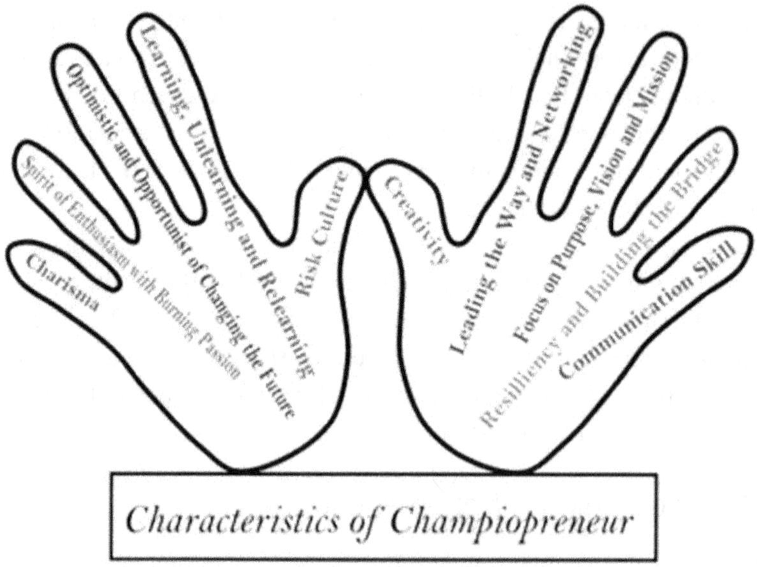

Ovharhe (2022, 2023) identified some common characteristics of entrepreneurs (champiopreneurs), which include:

1. **Charisma:** Most entrepreneurs have potentials that are like inborn talent which is very difficult for people to practice or imitate. Charisma is special gifts, skills and competence entrepreneurs possess that are priceless which makes them to be a resource and treasureable talent (i.e. singing, dancing, see the unseen by the ordinary) (Ovharhe, Woko & Ogolo, 2021). Also, these may be attributed to individuals like King David, Samson, Chinwe Achebe, Celine Dion, J. P Morgan, Rocky Feller, Joanne Rowling and Michael Jackson. We have charisma leaders in business like Nicholas Tesla, Elon Mask, Bill Gate, Steve Job etc (Ovharhe, Okolo, Woko & Igbokwe, 2022).
2. **Spirit of Enthusiasm with Burning Passion**: Strong consistence zeal that catches fire within individuals is factors that make them to stand and not discourage in turbulence and competitive time in the business world. Passion is the driver and inspiration to any entrepreneur, because in the times of high storm and dynamism in the business environment, the vital tool that is needed is the spirit of passion. Passion is the rhythm that every entrepreneur curtails to sustain, survive and succeed in business. Therapeutic passion is highly a stimulating and motivating concept which enable entrepreneurs in tough times to

withstand every catastrophe and risk in times of business turbulence especially during post covid-19 pandemic (Ovharhe, 2021, 2022a, 2023b). Passion is the architect of vision, mission and fusion for entrepreneurs to achieve their entrepreneurial journey. Passion is the pivoting fusion on innovation, creativity and perseverance (Duckworth; Biraglia & Kadile, in Ovharhe, 2023b). Passion is the anchor of entrepreneurial alert that makes entrepreneur to burn with fusion which fuels the vision and mission not to dies (Nordström, Sirén, Thorgren & Wincent; O'Keefe, Dweck & Walton in Ovharhe, 2023a).

3. **Optimistic and Opportunist of Changing the Futur**e: Entrepreneur must always have a positive mindset no matter the storms. Entrepreneurs should debunk fears at all time. They should be adaptive to change, flexibility and consistency with the mission of the enterprise. This is only how the future can be change. Changing the future is ability to invent the unseen to be seen with added benefits to the society at large (Ratten, 2023).
4. **Learning, Unlearning and Relearning**: Grossly, learning can be view in the prospect of entrepreneurship as the apt of the acquisition, storage, retention, utilization and dissemination of knowledge that transforms to a change in behavior which yield input to projected output (Ovharhe, Woko & Ogolo, 2022; Ratten, 2023). Entrepreneurial learning is generated from education, training and development programs. Learning could also be formal, semi-formal and formal. The key factor is change and transformation. All learning could lead to transformation on positive, zero or negative learning. But, the benefit is unlearning and relearning with positive result intentions. Relearning occurs when the entrepreneurs learn new strategies, tactics, patterns and approach of achieving the dream, vision and mission in the entrepreneurial journey. Whereas, unlearning is the total abandonment of the knowledge because it's obsolete, no link and supply chain of ideas.
5. **Risk Culture**: Entrepreneurs have the ability to take on a significant amount of risk with the goal of profiting from it. Risk culture is a set of standards, conformity, norms, attitudes and behaviors' related to awareness, alertness, avoidance, tolerance and absorption of risks. It shapes management and employees' day-to-day decisions and has an impact on the risks they take. The plight of every therapeutic entrepreneur is the ability to manage risk (Ovharhe, 2022a). This is the necessity of risk culture to the sense of humor that enables entrepreneurs to develop risk alert and risk awareness (Chibuike & Ovharhe, 2022). More so, risk culture is disciplinary value system with caution to deal and handle risk in the enterprise environment. Risk culture gives entrepreneur the capability of monitoring risk appetite and risk tolerance towards wealth maximization and profit maximization (Ovharhe & Igbokwe, 2021). Risk

culture could be easily analyzed by the ABC approach; risk attitude, risk behavior and risk competence (Ovharhe *et al.*, 2021, 2022, 2023).

6. **Creativity:** Entrepreneurs are seen as creator by the start-up fathers. Entrepreneurs are extremely creative problem solvers. Idea generation, thinking, innovation, invention. Innovation-skill is the ability to brainstorm and invent marketable and sellable goods and services that possess economic value and subject to scarcity. Creativity is fabricating into existence that which does not yet exists for benefits of human wellness and wellbeing. Creativity is the process of transforming certain input (tangible/intangible) into a desired output for purposes of achieving beneficial needs. In entrepreneurship, creativity must have an economic value. The fact that goods and services possess economic value means it has pricing concept and could be subject to scarcity. Thus, in this context, goods and services could be product innovation, process innovation, market innovation, idea innovation, technological innovation and administrative innovation (Ovharhe *et al.*, 2021; Manohar, Paul, Strong & Mittal, 2023). However, the skills needed for creativity and innovation process are affective skill, cognitive skill and psychomotor skill. Hence, innovation-skill and creativity can be idea, experience, tangible and intangible.
7. **Leading the Way and Networking:** Entrepreneurial leadership is very interesting features for the achievement of greatness. Entrepreneurs are potential leaders which enable them to initiate, discover and sight what the future holds. Entrepreneurs are also known for their branching network in building bond in relationship, partnership and customership. This leading tendency aids entrepreneurs for planning, organizing, coordinating, motivating, directing and controlling. Leading the way by entrepreneurs create an orientation for pace setting. All teams and intrapreneurs will be able to dive into the vision, mission, core values and propositions. The journey would be easily defined and spelt out on goals to achieve (Lim, 2023). Entrepreneurs need networking to build solid and foundation relationship to pursuit their business. Networking is of necessity in fundraising and crowd funding especially in social entrepreneurship (Mandrinos & Lim, 2023).
8. **Focus on Purpose, Vision and Mission:** Entrepreneurs should always ask the questions that will boost up the stream of focus. The first question is 'Why am I here' or 'What am I doing here'? This will answer the question of purpose. Secondly; 'What does the future holds for me' or 'What am I seeing in the future from here now'? This answer the vision parity. Thirdly; 'What is my course line of action to achieve my entrepreneurial journey' or 'What path am I threading on to arrive at my entrepreneurial dreams'? No distraction is allowed when focusing on the purpose, vision and mission. Any distraction may lead to a failure in the enterprise mission which will be aborted. This will lead to

a bleeding vision and unfertile purposed at the edge. Proper focusing enable entrepreneurs to development credible risk culture, creativity and innovation skills on learning how to drive at the right path of action and targeting best goals (Ratten, 2023).

9. **Resiliency and Building the Bridge:** Entrepreneurs should have the slogan of forward ever and backwards never in the business stream. Letting the stream of cash-flow circulating in the short-term and long-term in the entrepreneurial journey is the dream of every entrepreneurs. Entrepreneur function is to build the stream of consistent wealth creation and value creation in every business opportunity. But sometime business owners should always protect and secured their bridge at all cost (Blessley & Mudambi, 2022). A broken bridge causes a lot to repairs and maintain. Resilience strategies that will aid like competitive advantage should be of great concern to every entrepreneur as they want to sustain and survive in business. Developing fighting strategy is good, but developing resiliency and building bridges should not be taken for granted by entrepreneurs. Building solid bridges for customer, client, vendor, government, legal framework, community, institutions and stakeholders at large is of necessity. More so, this strengthens and builds strategic bonds for relationship, partnership and customership.
10. **Communication Skills:** Liaison with all stakeholders is a vital business strategy for start-up. Whether is upwards communication (from bottom-top), downward communication (top-bottom) or diagonal communication (cross-sectional) the entrepreneur must learn how to input information and get feedback. Communication also could be external virtue that must be maintained for free flow and better understanding of business. Communication is the forces that bind all entity to oneness.

Communicating the purpose, vision and mission to the organization human resource is the credibility of success and consistency in the business function. Nevertheless, effective and efficient communication to clients and customer revealed the longevity of the enterprise in the turbulence times. Thus, effective and efficient communication is a competitive advantage to the enterprise. Entrepreneurs need to learn how to generate information for effective communication. Information should be from the confident source, reliable, precise, accurate, authentic, trusted, valid, verifiable, comprehensive and meaningful. If entrepreneurs should be accurate and eloquent with information virtue they will maintain credible communication skills. The business world needs good communicators for interface with employees, management, community, external environment (government, agencies and task) vendor, customer relations and the entire supply chain management system (Yadav *et al.*, 2023).

3. CONCEPT OF BUSINESS INTELLIGENCE

The fundamental aim of business intelligence is to actualize precise, accurate and confident decision making. This is while authors argue that business intelligence is correlated to competitive intelligence and decision support system because the large amount of accurate data that has become more accessible allows business intelligence to synchronize (Huang, Savita & Zhong-jie, 2022).

Business intelligence combines analytic, data mining, data visualization, data tools, data infrastructure and best practices to help management and entrepreneurs makes more data-driven decision in the short-term and long-term (Horn, 2023). Business intelligence is also software that suggests business data and presents it in user-friendly views such as report, dashboard, chat, graph, metrics and framework. However, business intelligence could be well analyzed in entrepreneurship by integrating it with competitive intelligence and decision support system (Zhou, San, Liu & Kozyrkov, 2023).

Holori, Ahmadi, Khanmohammadi, Ranjbar and Kordlouie (2023) averred that business intelligence is a fundamental tool that assist management to evaluated business information on return on investment, return on equity, return on asset, return on capital employed, net present value, cost-benefit analysis and break-even analysis. By using the Structural Equation Model, business intelligence could yield tremendous output that boost enterprise performance in the small medium enterprise, large corporation, multinationals and conglomerates. Entrepreneur decision making should be authenticated and optimistic with the intervention of business intelligence.

The model (Figure 2) illustrated and diagrammatized the business intelligence and innovation moderating role on entrepreneurship and management explanatory paradigm in the discussion.

3.1. Competitive Intelligence

Competitive intelligence can be diagrammatized with the phrase 'know your enemy' (Baskin, 2023). Competitive intelligence is not only utilized in profit-for-making business is also adopted by the military (for defense intelligence), medical personnel (for diagnostics, clinical findings and result analytic and information storage), institution (for tracking bench marking growth and comparative analysis on activity based trend) (Cekuls, 2022). This is the essence it is also regarded as corporate intelligence because of the aid to generate data, environmental scanning, scientific systematic investigation of facts and speed in decision making (Taranu, 2023; Cloutier, 2013).

Figure 2. Business Intelligence and Innovation Moderating Roles on Entrepreneurship and Management Using Champiopreneurship Approach

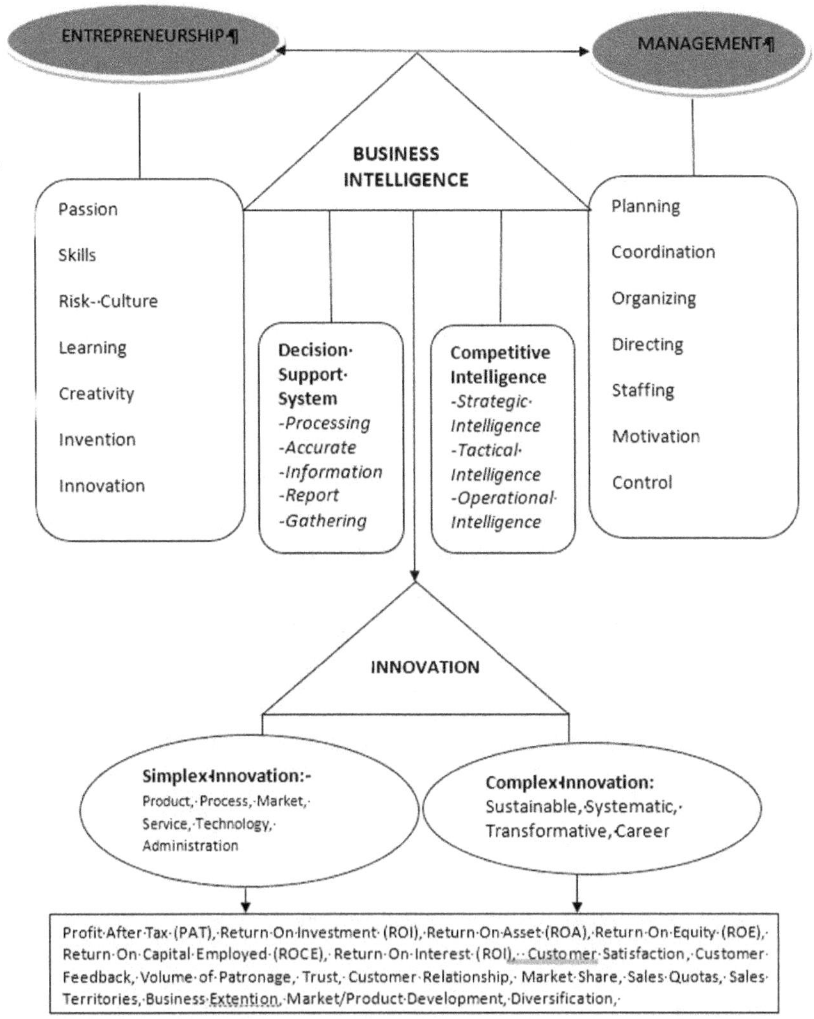

In entrepreneurship, competitive intelligence is very necessary to gather and analyze information on business risk, cost based competition, competitive pricing and new breed of innovativeness on idea, technology, market, product, process, service and administration (Dewar, Keller & Malhotra, 2022). It is on this plight that entrepreneurs and management uses competitive intelligence to align with digital model and framework for sustainability, survival and success to gain leadership edge in the market structure of the enterprise (Madureira, Popovic & Castelli, 2023).

The management at all level and in all level employed business for effectiveness and efficiency because the business environment is reckless, dynamic, competitive and turbulence (Hassani & Mosconi, 2022). No one can predict tomorrow in the business entity because of the diversities of uncertainties that lies ahead (i.e. Covid-19). But the emergence of business intelligence assists management to utilized entrepreneurial functions (risk, culture, lean entrepreneurship) on speed, continuous improvement on customer feedback and trust to gain the market leadership.

In this tail, competitive intelligence is strength based approach adopted by an enterprise prior to data scanning, gathering, coding, cleansing, analysis for the use of valuable information on competitive parity, customers and business environment which will aid the enterprise to gain competitive advantage as swift strategic implementation for business growth and development (Maluleka & Chummun, 2023).

Winning as the market leader or champion at all ramification is the bottom line of competitive intelligence. Competitive intelligence boosts the enterprise to become the leadership and championship in terms of sales territories, sales quotas, customer relationship management, market share, cost effectiveness and pricing-promotion policy. This is the entrepreneurship port folio of competitive intelligence.

The marketing mix or port folio of entrepreneurship has been expanded to 7ps for suitability of competitive intelligence. Entrepreneurs and management board need to focus on the model which should be adopted as framework in the enterprise dashboard and metrics. The model assumes a positive correlation as an impact of services of Marketing Mix 7P's through its elements (product/educational service, price, promotion, place, people, physical evidence, and process) as predictor variable, on achieving competitive advantages through its elements. This consciousness is credible for sustaining on entrepreneurial entry which mitigates entrepreneurial exist (Ovharhe & Abada, 2023a,b).

3.1.1. Elements of Competitive Intelligence

Know your enemy in entrepreneurship and managerial functions calls for serious issues and concern in the business world because of the recklessness, turbulence, dynamism and competitiveness in the market environment. Certain elementary tools are needed for competitive intelligence to design dashboard, metric and framework to mitigate any negativism in the business environment.

Applying organizational entrepreneurship paradigm, Kühn (2006) and Handfield *et al*., (2023) supported the following elements of competitive intelligence; viz:

- **Sector Intelligence**: It entails specialized data gathering, processing and analytics should be structure by expert in specific field of entrepreneurship such as in agriculture, research and development, construction, ICT, artificial intelligence, real estate management, manufacturing, sales and distribution, logistic and telecoms (Rahchamani & All, 2019).

- **Market Intelligence.** This is a surveillance gathering about the product folio or market mix (product, price, promotion and place) use to ascertain the market share, customer relationship management, market analysis and market structure (Лена, 2019).
- **Innovation Intelligence:** Innovativeness is the centre of business intelligence assurance and excellence. The key concept of competitive intelligence and business intelligence must be interface with product innovation, administrative innovation, process innovation and technology innovation as concepts that trigger transformation in the enterprise growth and development. This approach is suitable in enterprise that deals with consignment inventory system (Ahunanya, Ovharhe, Emenike & Otto, 2022a,b; Ovharhe, Ahunanya & Woko, 2022).
- **Sales Intelligence.** The forecasting of sales trend in the enterprise is a vital data analysis. Currently, big data, machine learning, data virtualization and data science can assist in computing sales quotas, sales territories and sales metric for judgment credibility and authentication. The data board shows competitive bench marking of the business failure and success. (Rahchamani & All, 2019).
- **Procurement and Supply Chain Intelligence.** This is about satisfying the client from the forward and backward integration. The procurement on enterprise resource planning and supply chain is very relevant for the sustainability, survival and success of any business (Effa, Ovharhe, Ezirim & Igwe, 2023a,b; Handfield., 2023).
- **ESG Intelligence:** This is intelligence tool which is an industry agnostic business intelligence platform, used to assist companies across all sectors monitor and report their Environmental, Social and Governance performance. It could exist in form of extranet. This is more application of strategic intelligence to analyze environmental data generation (Maune, 2022).

Generally, competitive intelligence focus on operational information and tactical analysis from various systematic sources such as news media, customer feedback and competitive parity analysis, professional experts in specific business, trade shows and conferences, symposium, government records, public filings, indexes and corporate dossier (Artur, 2020). Furthermore, competitive intelligence focuses on collecting, processing and analyzing sensitive data about your competition and client feedback to gain an advantage or leadership edge in the enterprise (Zighed *et al.*, 2023). Competitive intelligence is a process where enterprise scan, generate, gather and process information about competitors and competitive business environment, ideally using it in their policy formulation, decision-making and planning process, with the corporate goal of adjusting activities to improve performance (Cloutier, 2013).

3.1.2. Level of Competitive Intelligence

Challenges in business growth vary on certain factors that need interventions with competitive intelligence. Certain factors are environment issues, type of business and services, season of the business or services, capital formation and human resource constraint. Though, be it SMEs or large enterprise all have their own peculiar challenges. Also certain challenges in business are exigencies, hazards; security, pandemic, exchange rate, inflation rate and interest rate and lots more are critical issues and bottlenecks that have resultant effect on business growth. But, certain challenges could be mitigated by the application of Boston Matrix, Ansoff Matrix, SWOT Analysis, Entrepreneurship Profile, Customer Profile and Managerial Grid (Ovharhe, 2024a,b).

Ovharhe and Igbokwe (2021) identify certain pitfall and bottleneck that faces an enterprise as challenges. These can be operational challenges, tactical challenges and strategic challenges; they are daily activities that flow with the activities of work. They are so enormous based on the specific field such as engineering, production, audit, account, telecoms, and administration etcetera. However, in entrepreneurship the following itemized below could be actualized.

a. Operational Intelligence

These are short-term challenges that occur within the period of one year which deals with day to day functions. They are problems encountered with the foremen or line operations that deal with intrapreneurs for executorships of the enterprise activities. These challenges include inventory control, repairs and maintenance, payment of allowances, customer satisfaction, market-cost pricing, product mix or company port-folio analysis, capital formation and fund raising, hiring and firing, fintech startup, crypto-currency, blockchain, creativity and sustainable innovation etcetera (Corsaro & D'Amico, 2022). For smart motion to be activated in the business enterprise, the short-term intelligence is of basic necessity to actualized goals and objectives in the mission.

In the ever-evolving landscape of navigating human intelligence, artificial intelligence and business intelligence are the realms of operational intelligence which stand at the forefront of innovation and creativity with availability of business opportunities in the business world. As business enterprise navigates into future prospect with complex intelligence as shaped by data-driven decisions support and heightened operational intelligence, the pursuit of champiopreneurs dreams and missions seems possible for accomplishment of statuary corporate goals and targets (Davinsi, 2024).

Let it be known to all business enterprise that operational intelligence also known as counter-intelligence is the frontiers of organization guerrilla combat instrument employed to mitigate problems in the tough competitive parity especially during pandemic, disaster, turbulence, uncertain riskiness of monetary and fiscal policy (high inflation rate, exchange rate, interest rate and taxes) (Business Research Insight, 2024). Interesting to know, Business Research Insight (2024) opines that the pre-post pandemic era will experience organizational healthiness of business opportunities on application of operational intelligence. The business platforms, market size, share and growth has an optimistic prediction for the post pandemic era 2024-2031 to exhibit positive increases, because the application of operational intelligence has make the enterprise to overcome the shock and trauma from the pre-pandemic era.

b. *Tactical Intelligence*

These are intermediate or functional issues and concern for department level challenges: agile factors (changes to new technology and artificial intelligence), intermittent cash flow analysis on inflow and outflow. New idea generation, market development, forecasting, product development, leasing and procurement of sophisticated devices, machinery and equipment, sales quotas, lunching of new prototype, test marketing, concept testing, expansion of market share, sales territories, service quality delivery etcetera (Lim, 2023).

Tactical intelligence is the middle field and heart of combat intelligence of creative and innovative information required for decision support system in the competitive parity which orchestrates sustainability, survival and success in the business enterprise. Britannica (2024) pointed out that tactical intelligence primarily respond to the plans of the business enterprise need to executes for positive resultant outcome in the competitive parity by employing the most appropriate actions.

Tactical intelligence is specific information about a target to accomplish mission and corporate goals on departmental or functional level in the business enterprise, such as in production, telecommunication, purchasing and supply, logistics, marketing and finance. Tactical intelligence is medium-term or intermittent period which gives credible knowledge storage, knowledge memory and knowledge dissemination of business enterprise at all parameters. It is the fundamental based of the decision support system of the business enterprise (Wakuthii, 2024).

Tactical intelligence is focused on support to marketplace operations at the functional level of the business enterprise where the competitive parity is tense. Tactical intelligence is in liaison with the units or group level of the business enterprise to smoothen and swing into action for revenue generation, frequency of patronage, return on asset, return on investment and return on equity, customer satisfaction and feedback (ScienceDirection, 2024). This is the reasons most conglomerates, large corporation, multinationals sees tactical intelligence as secret and mysteries intelligence, because of the roles in secretly generated wisdom beyond the limits of formal reasoning that makes uncertain estimates less to be certainty, and consequently generates political, business, economical, strategic and operational advantages in the market competition. (STRATAGEM, 2024).

c. Strategic Intelligence

These are the remedies to long-term bottles and pitfalls that surround the business enterprise. It is anchor by top leadership functions of the enterprise as highest executive order. The challenges can be merger and acquisition, reconstruction, take-over, conglomerate diversification, vertical integration, horizontal integration, forward integration, backward integration, enterprise resource planning, ESG intelligence, strategic intelligence, supply chain management system, bench-marking, pension and gratuity, building of new industries, franchising, licensing, consignment inventory system and automation/robotic/artificial intelligence (Alqahtani & Uslay, 2023).

Britannica (2024) postulate that strategic intelligence is long-term information and decision making which is used to formulate policy and plans at interfacing the global networking. Strategic intelligence is the outlook for the future prospect of the business enterprise which authenticates the business excellence, climate change, artificial intelligence, machine learning, data virtualization, big data analytics, data science, leadership and champiopreneurship (World Economic Forum, 2024, Ovharhe & Woko, 2024a). Entrepreneurs are more concern about the integration of strategic intelligence outlook on innovation skills, creativity, customer feedback, new business opportunities, growth and development (Emergent Risk International, 2024).

3.2 Decision Support System

Entrepreneurs cannot function effectively and efficiently without conceptualized decision making to accomplish her corporate goals. The enterprise depends on its long-term and short-term decision making to regulate statutory framework for flow of fiduciary responsibilities and oriented task (Kozyrkov, 2023). In managerial expression, the short-term decision making can also be regarded as operational or programmable decisions, while the long-term decision making can be view as strategic or non-programmable decisions. Programmed decisions are functions conducted by operational (low level) management like the supervisors and foremen which can be utilized by entrepreneurs in the short-term as repetitive and routine merchandizing activities to solve through clear-cut mechanical procedures, such as applying the formidable rules and sound judgment to find the best solution and possible remedies within the specific available time frame (O'Callaghan, 2023). Majority of management decisions entrepreneurs need in start-up operations are programmed in the enterprise because of its implication on daily operational activities. On the contrary, non-programmed decisions deals with functions that are exceptional or nonrecurring to management, and they are often made under strategic conditions which involve so much ambiguity that specific procedures or programs are not available. These are done by the strategic (top level) management like the chief executive officer (CEO), general management (GM), director general (DG), chief medical director [CMD (in hospitals)], chairman medical advisory committee [CMAC (in hospitals)], among others (Dewar *et al.*, 2022). Therefore, managers who must make non-programmed decisions rely on tough judgment, cognitive innovativeness, brain storming, creativity and strategic intuition (Reeves & Whitaker, 2022).

Decision making is an operational and strategic process of initiating ideas, design framework and analyzing basic alternatives with possible remedies to make a best choice from selective outcomes. Most decisions are made in response to a problem that requires high level of intelligence. These might be in need of sales intelligence, market intelligence and production intelligence (Ovharhe & Odepeli, 2024).

Zhou et al., (2023) posit chaotic processes that fathom entrepreneurs and management to invoke concept of decision support system being buttress by business intelligence applications and complex innovations. Decision support system is a computerized program used to support determinations, unbiased sound judgments and analytic courses of action in a business enterprise.

Decision support system (DSS) is synchronized information system that supports enterprise decision-making functions in merchandizing activities. DSSs serve the management, operations and planning levels of an enterprise which help entrepreneurship and managerial decision making about remedies to problems solving that may be rapidly changing and not easily specified in advance (i.e., structural, unstructured and semi-structured decision problems). Decision support systems can be either fully computerized or human-powered, or a combination of both (Kozyrkov, 2023).

While academics have perceived DSS as a tool to support decision making processes, DSS users it as decision intelligence on a dashboard tool to facilitate enterprise processes (O'Callaghan, 2023). DSS include any systematic phenomena that might boost decision making and some DSS include a decision-making software component. Sprague (1980)https://en.wikipedia.org/wiki/Decision_support_system-cite_note-sprague1980-2 defines a properly termed DSS as follows:

1. DSS tends to be aimed at the less well structured, underspecified problem that upper level managers typically face;
2. DSS attempts to combine the use of models or analytic techniques with traditional data access and retrieval functions;
3. DSS specifically focuses on features which make them easy to use by non-computer-proficient people in an interactive mode; and
4. DSS emphasizes flexibility and adaptability to accommodate changes in the enterprise environment and the decision making approach of the user.

4. DEXTERITY OF INNOVATION ON ENTREPRENEURSHIP AND MANAGEMENT

The field of entrepreneurship is the iota of innovation. The entrepreneurs are the steering that drives innovation into high depth of competitiveness in the business world. Every firm's innovative management team is dependent to entrepreneurship orchestration to push and pull the trigger of the market forces competitive parity string. Innovation in the plight of entrepreneurship can be categories to the two instrumentations which regarded as the *simplex innovation and complex innovation.* The simplex innovation can also be referred to as *'Content Innovation'* Hence, the complex innovation is perceived as *Context Innovation.* Both are the anchor of the instrumental strings that push and pull the resultant outcome of innovation in the competitive market environment because the business intelligence of an enterprise is revealed on its ability, capability and capacity of innovation (Reeves & Whitaker, 2022)

The simplex innovation can also be called the 'content innovation' which are instrumental strings of component that are unique concept such as the product innovation, process innovation, service innovation, administrative innovation, market innovation and technology innovation. Whereas, the complex innovation can also be seen as the 'context innovation' consist of digital innovation, sustainable innovation and transformative innovation. The instrumental components are drawn to augment the simplex innovation or content innovation. It is applied on specific task as hybrid or aggregate entrepreneur. For example, the digital innovation can be use by the entrepreneurs to promote data science, analytic, processing, report and feedback loop which is in liaison with the digital entrepreneurship. Though, with the advent of business competitiveness digital entrepreneurship is sky rocking towards massive total adoption of artificial intelligence, fintech startup and crypto-currency and blockchain (Anderbjork & Martell, 2021). While, the sustainable innovation embraces the triple P's concept on people, planet and profit that is in alignment with green entrepreneurship. Basically, the sustainable innovation pursuit the Sustainable Development Goals (SDG) seventeen fundamentals focus of the United Nation. Moreover, the entrepreneurs are always struggling for cost-leadership, price-leadership, and market share leadership; the truth is that innovation makes the difference. Thus, the nexus of innovation is centered on content innovation and context innovation that boost entrepreneur in the market survival operationally and strategically.

4.1. Innovation

Entrepreneurship deals with the art and science of creation, idea generation, invention of the future to the present and innovation of tangible and intangible beneficial resources to mankind. Oyinlola *et al.*, (2023) argued strongly that the business process can only be achieved through innovation. Ovharhe (2023a,b) opined that innovation is the practical implementation of corporate and beneficial ideas that result in the introduction of new tangible and intangible or improvement in offering goods or services that have value and treasure. He further categorized innovation into simplex and complex innovation. The simplex for example is the product, process, service, administrative, market, digital, social and lot more. While the complex are transformation, systematic, sustainable and other form of hybrid and multi-dimensional innovation. Innovation is the new life blood flow of entrepreneurship, meaning if there is no innovation, there is no concept of entrepreneurs that will be in existence. The passion, vision, mission and fusion propelling force of entrepreneurship are pivoted on innovation (Ovharhe, 2023; Kanyi, Wanjau & Kyalo, 2023).

La Venre (2023) as supported by Drucker pointed out that innovation is the driving force behind progress in any industrial transformation and systematic process. It is the process of developing new and better ways of doing things, from developing new tangible and intangible ideas implementation to improving existing ones. Innovation can be sparked by a variety of factors, including new technologies, changing customer needs, and emerging market trends in the business world, institutions and society at large. Though, entrepreneurship is the process of turning innovative idea into sustainable and successful business enterprise. It involves identifying a market need, developing a product, process, technology, structure and service that meet need, and then creating a business model that allows the product or service to be sold and scaled. Entrepreneurs are the individuals who take on the risks and challenges of starting a new business, and they are the ones who bring new products and services to market.

Jain (2023) said innovation is the process of bringing about new ideas, methods, products, services, or solutions into valuable existence that have a significant positive impact and value. It involves transforming creative concepts into tangible outcomes that improve efficiency, and effectiveness, or address unmet needs.

Innovation is not limited to technological advancements and encompasses novel approaches to problem-solving, processes, organizational practices, or business model innovations. At its core, innovation involves challenging the status quo, thinking outside the box, and taking calculated risks to drive progress and achieve breakthrough outcomes (Ntandoyenkosi, 2023).

Innovation is driven by a combination of factors, including curiosity, creativity, and the desire for improvement. It requires a mindset that embraces change, welcomes ideation, and encourages experimentation. Innovation can occur in various contexts, such as business, science, technology, social sectors, or public services. It can lead to economic growth, social progress, improved quality of life, and sustainable development (Kanyi, Wanjau & Kyalo, 2023).

Jain (2023) later portray that innovation can take various forms, and different types of innovation serve as discussed beneath.

- Product Innovation: This involves developing new or improved products or services. It can include innovations in functionality, features, design, performance, or packaging. It aims to create value for customers by addressing their needs, solving problems, or introducing novel and desirable offerings.
- Process Innovation: This is improving the efficiency, effectiveness, or quality of internal processes within an organization. It involves rethinking and redesigning workflows, technologies, and systems to streamline operations, reduce costs, enhance productivity, or improve the delivery of products or services. Process innovation often leads to increased operational efficiency and competitive advantage.
- Service Innovation: This anchor developing new or improved services, delivery methods, or customer experiences. It focuses on enhancing the value and satisfaction customers derive from service interactions. Service innovation can include innovations in service design, customization, accessibility, convenience, or personalization. It aims to meet evolving customer expectations and create a competitive edge.
- Sustainable Innovation: This orchestrates developing and implementing new products, services, technologies, or business models that have a positive environmental, social, and economic impact. It involves finding creative and efficient solutions to address pressing challenges, such as climate change, resource depletion, pollution, inequality, and poverty.
- Social Innovation: This fine-tuned the development and implementation of novel solutions to address social, cultural, economic, or environmental challenges. It involves the creation and adoption of new ideas, products, services, or approaches that result in positive societal impact and sustainable change.

- Technology Innovation: This refers to the creation, adoption, and utilization of new or improved technologies to drive progress and improve outcomes in various domains. It encompasses advancements across a wide range of technological fields, including but not limited to information technology, biotechnology, renewable energy, nanotechnology, robotics, materials science, and telecommunications.

4.2. Creativity

Every entrepreneur needs instruments to achieve her championship goals to maintain sustainability at the top of the business enterprise. This is what propels champiopreneurship in the long-term. Peek (2024) buttressed that creativity and innovations are the two key words that entrepreneur constantly thrown around in business intelligence, decision support system and competitive intelligence. Champiopreneur needs creativity and innovations to survive and sustain the recklessness, competitive, turbulence and dynamism in the business (Ovharhe & Saturday, 2024).

Peek (2024) supported that creativity is the intuition to think in new ways, new patterns, new styles and apply fresh generated ideas to solve problems. Shawn Hunter, author of Out Think: How Innovative Leaders Drive Exceptional Outcomes (Wiley, 2013), haphazardly sees creativity as the capability, capacity and ability or act of conceiving something original or unusual (Ovharhe and Chibuike, 2024). It is a critical, tactical and logical skill in business competitive parity that enables stakeholders to adapt, bench mark and create unique approaches that may be even better suited than tried-and-true methods.

Peeks (2024) streamline a research conducted by Arne Dietrich, at the American University of Beirut, Lebanon which segmented creativity into four types: deliberate and emotional, deliberate and cognitive, spontaneous and emotional, and spontaneous and cognitive. Despite the professional field of endeavor, champiopreneurship needs these four types of creativity to function effectively. Deliberate and cognitive creativities use focused attention and formed connections between information stored in the brain and rely on the prefrontal cortex, while emotional and spontaneous creativities stem from the amygdala and tend to be more instinctive. People who are good at taking insights derived from creativity excel at thinking outside the box and applying new approaches to their work (Stanford Center For Professional Development, 2024). Peeks (2024) boils that creativity is the spontaneous development of new ideas and out-of-the-box thinking and brainstorming. Creativity is a necessary prerequisite for innovation, but they are not the same thing.

4.2.1. Creativity and Innovation

To boost creativity in your organization, consider giving employees flexibility within their workday to try out new things or explore different avenues of thinking. Create a company culture where thinking outside the box is encouraged and rewarded in order to spur your most creative thinkers to do their best work (Stanford Center For Professional Development, 2024).

Innovation is the action of putting things into practical reality, despite challenges and resistance, rather than just contemplating. It takes creative thinking, planning and implementation of new ideas to constitute innovation (Mark, 2024).

Innovation is a practical application of creativity to bring generated idea into reality of tangible and intangible marketable goods, in which the spark of the new idea is turned, furbished and fabricated into a possible remedies and active solution or process. Hunter in Peek (2024) weighs in his own view that innovation is the implementation or creation of something new that has realized value to the business (Mark, 2024).

Innovation is generic not tied specifically to humans, but to other species. For example bird created nest, rabbit, rats, ants digs hole to live survived. Innovation is attributed to using creative ideas to solve problem. Innovation with business intelligence of the enterprise modifies the creative ideas into branded product and services for the benefits to client during patronage. An innovation makes a demonstrable, often disruptive branding differentiation in a product, service or industry. It is a fundamentally new, tangible shift and departure from the conventional.

Champiopreneur uses creativity and innovations to transform organization on leading edge at the competitive marketplace from stagnating that catapult the enterprise to mission target (Ovharhe & Woko, 2024a). Champiopreneur should always bear in mind that creativity precedes innovation. Creativity is the first phrase of business enterprise for the assurance that something can be possible, but an action is needed to activate that creativity into existence. Mark (2024) fine-tunes the concept of creativity by expressing that, if entrepreneur have multifaceted brainstorming new ideas, then the entrepreneurs displayed creativity, but cannot be called a champiopreneur until there is an implementation of the idea into reality that benefits the client and the enterprise. Also, champiopreneur do not create something just to sell, rather they created something which consumers/client are propel to buy.

Hunter in Peek (2024) noted that many business leaders and mere entrepreneurs emphasize generating creativity on demand instead of building the conditions that enable ongoing creative thinking, which can ultimately lead to innovative development. This is the credible difference between champiopreneurs and entrepreneurial leaders. Champiopreneurs tries to see the end from the beginning, not just from the impulses of client or customer, but from the overall interest of the planet, people and profit.

The business intelligence of entrepreneurs is synchronized greater to orchestrate function suitable for the client, enterprise, society and market structure.

4.3. Entrepreneurship Opportunities

In the mindset of business opportunity framework, it is important to note that an entrepreneur should not produce what he/she can manufacture, or produce what he/she can sell, but should produce what customer can buy. This is what makes the difference among successful entrepreneurs that makes them to be champions. Is it not about innovation and creativity but want the customer needs or customer focus and feedback (Dieffenbacher, 2023).

Ovharhe and Woko (2024) argues that entrepreneurship is scanning for business opportunities, identifying business opportunity, chasing business opportunities and grabbing business opportunity. It is about focusing and pursuit business opportunity in the business environment by taking advantage of the untouched, unmet needs, re-positioning and non-utilized aspect of the business.

Business opportunity can be defined as the searching and pursuit of the unmet need and positioning the product to the underserved or over-served market with new styles and patterns to satisfy the customer with optimistic feedback. Eckhardt and Shane (2003) identify four elements that elaborate business opportunity. These four elements are:

- A specific or define need
- The means, venture and risk culture to accomplish the need
- A method, style and pattern to apply the means to fulfill the need and;
- A method, style and pattern to analyze cost-benefit to reward the enterprise.

A champiopreneur creativity and innovation is needed to close the gap peradventure any of the named element is missing maybe in the short-term or long-term. This gap may be use as a competitive advantage of leading the edge in the business because this is what champiopreneurship is equipped to do (Shane & Venkataraman, 2000).

Harvard Business School Professor Clayton Christensen, who teaches in-depth fact and theoretical framework on business opportunities for aspiring entrepreneurs proposed for startup to begin with an idea for a new business, fulfill a market need, solve a customer pin point, or improve an existing product. cote (2022) as coined by Christensen identifies three types of business opportunities to search for entrepreneurial sustainability, survival and success. These are discussed underneath as follows; viz:

1. Jobs to Be Done

Innovating and creating the unmet needs suitable to customer satisfaction calls for a serious job entrepreneurs should carry out daily until there is a prototype which propel them to get positive feedback from client/customers that will benefit the enterprise.

2. Low-End Market Opportunities

This is when the entrepreneur avoids much competition by using penetration pricing strategy but with the lower segment and low pricing. Here, he can get the market with its product and services that will enable her to built momentum and navigate with its tentacles which enable her to spread to broad market with higher profit to combat with those leading in the competitive parity. Entrepreneurs at the level should invoke the doctrines of lean entrepreneurship (Ovharhe, 2023).

3. New Market Opportunities

This occurs when entrepreneur creates a new segment in an existing market. The entrepreneur capitalized on the weaknesses which threaten the competitor existing product and services. The entrepreneurs match in with new style and patterns the customers have not seen that energizes her to network the market into possession and progression. With enough business intelligence adopted, the entrepreneur should create and innovate low pricing not rapid pricing skimmed to capture and utilized maximum used of the business opportunity in the new segment.

Smart action need to be made with business intelligence in the marketplace when there is tough competitive parity. Talent is never enough with just creativity, innovation skills and business potentials to cope in the turbulence times, rather competitive intelligence and decision support system in this modern times calls for alignment on how to chase business opportunities. Tough actions are needed to chase business opportunities because of the negation factors affecting enterprise such as the pandemic, turbulence, recklessness and competitiveness to win as the champion (Ovharhe & Woko, 2024b).

Entrepreneurship is not just about innovation, creativity and invention, entrepreneur need to go further to become champiopreneurs in the industries. Someone manufactures the computer, but another is learning the computer as skills for earnings, someone manufactures the vehicle but another is using it as a source of livelihood, someone manufactures the musical instrument, whereas others use it to make melodies. In all this supply chain system, entrepreneurs can be outstanding as champion, because there are business opportunities for creativity and innovation to become a champiopreneur (Thompson, 2009). Champiopreneurs are the 'creator' and 'innovator' when it comes to achieving business opportunities.

5. BUSINESS INTELLIGENCE AND INNOVATION MODERATING ROLE ON ENTREPRENEURSHIP AND MANAGEMENT

Business intelligence is synonymous with competitive intelligence and decision support system in practical implementation phrases. Competitive intelligence is structured on strategic intelligence, tactical intelligence and operational intelligence. Strategic intelligence focus on long-term activities of the enterprise such as mergers, reconstruction, takeover, diversification, new product development, launching a new product, make or buy decision etcetera. Strategic decision is convey by the top management of the enterprise such as the managing director, general manager, director general etc. In the same vein, tactical intelligence is centered on the middle, functional and intermediate management of the enterprise. This is anchors on medium term corporate affairs of the enterprise management that deals with sales on revenue generation, production forecasting, market territories, market quotas, supply chain management system and telecoms choice decision (Ahunanya *et al.*, 2022a,b) This is conveying by the accounting management, production manager, marketing manager and sales manager. Sustainably, the operational intelligence is the daily activities and operation of the enterprise. This is short-term operations which involve payment of monthly salaries, buying and procurement of utilities, repairs, maintenance and frequency of patronage, time of patronage and volume of patronage, profitability, return on investment, break even analysis and lots more. More so the operational intelligence is the foremen, supervisors and low executive of the enterprise.

Business intelligence is needed at all level of management for her to achieve short-term goals and long-term goals because innovations occur at all ramifications. Business intelligence is the added competitive advantage of entrepreneurs.

In the essence, expressing the integration of entrepreneurship and management could be seemed as a CHAMPIOPRENEUR.

5.1. Concept of Champiopreneurship

The world is rule by champions in all ramifications of industries and organizations, be it in sport, military, academic, entertainment, movie, news, academic, technology, engineering, music, manufacturing, logistics, online business, crypto etcetera. Entrepreneurs is the plight of champions in the business world are been seen as champiopreneurs. The operational system of champiopreneur's performance in its enterprise merchandizing function is regarded as championpreneurship. The term championpreneurship is embrace to business intelligence, innovation skills and creativity in respective field. The application of business intelligence depends on the enterprise ability to recognize and grabs the available business opportunities (Ovharhe & Woko, 2024a). When business opportunity is recognized, pursue and utilize, there will be need to apply competitive intelligence and decision support system to authenticate the process to achieved optimum goals. The success of every enterprise to achieved goals lies on the entrepreneurship to adopt the spirit of championship known as 'champiopreneurship'.

Champiopreneurship is coined from the prefer (champion) and suffix (entrepreneur). The simple algebraic expression:

```
Champiopreneur= Champion + Entrepreneur
Let, Champion=Champio (prefix from Medieval Latin)
Where, Entrepreneur= Preneur (suffix from Middle Age French)
Thus, Champio-preneur= Champio + Preneur
Therefore= Champio-preneur= Champiopreneur (synchronization of
compound word)
However, Champiopreneurship= Championship + Entrepreneurship
Hence, Champiopreneurship= Ship (Champio + Preneur)
```

Nevertheless, base on corresponding, alternate usage and application of words;

```
Furthermore, Champiopreneur ≡ Champiopreneurship
```

The term 'Champion' emanates from the Latin word 'campionem' meaning gladiator, fighter." Also, means to fight or grab for an opportunity. Champions do not just fight, there must be an opportunities to take advantage (Vocabulary.com, 2024). For business opportunities to be accomplish, champion should have insight of competitive advantage before the swing into action, Where entrepreneurial champion sense an opportunity, it shows there is a need for grabbers, chasers and achievers which creates room for entrepreneurs to become Champiopreneur. Champiopreneurs are equipped with innovation skills and creativity to grab business opportunities by application of business intelligence (competitive intelligence and decision support system) to achieve long-term goals and short-term goals in the business world. This posits that a champiopreneur has the ability, capacity and capability to defeat opponent and win in the marketplace (Collin, 2024).

Etymonline (2024) went further to explain the meaning of champion from French, Frankish, German, Hebrew and Greek as fighter, combat soldier, to battle and to campaign. This means for individual to sustain, survive and become successful as a champion he/she should have innovative skills and creativity to conquer in the battlefield during the combat. A champion must learn how and when to raise a campaign field using strategic intelligence, tactical intelligence, operational intelligence and decision making system in the marketplace because the competitors are not sleeping. Intelligence modality in business should be strategized to seize the opportunities in the marketplace using swift campaigning (promotional) modalities. Signals of communication should be imbibes to capture and sustain the opportunities in the business environment.

The champiopreneur should know that he/she holds the whistle to blow the campaigning signal that will authorized the action, because in the business battle, timing and environment is very important. A champiopreneur is an individual that possesses intelligence, ability, innovation skills and creativity to win luxury prize in a competition, contest, or combat (Merriam-Webster, 2024).

Champiopreneur should know ten metric that will guide them in competition, contest and combat in the marketplace; viz:

1. Lunching of the product and services should be sensitive with customer focus and feedback,
2. Entry and exit point should be easily articulated and comprehensive
3. Positioning (i.e. market, product, logistics etc) must be well design
4. Prototype of the product or services should be well cultivated
5. Systemization of experiential practice should be tactical and strategic
6. Gravity of startup process must be authenticated with risk culture
7. Test-Marketing and Product-Testing must be quick and satisfactory
8. Team spirit should be magnetized with competence on possible feedback
9. Error correction model must be loop in place with immediate action
10. Intrinsic and extrinsic reward must be in place to act as tactic for game changer

For champiopreneur to be successful, the above should be adhering to. The drive a champiopreneur has may not correspond with other resource individuals in the team. Hence, to achieve sustainable championship in the merchandizing functions the ten metrics should be in momentum. To crown it all the Britannica (2024) stresses that champion are corresponding terms that represents monarch, royalty and nobility. This can easily be said that champiopreneurs are king in the marketplace. They possess the character of greatest kingship and leadership in the business world.

5.2. Nexus of Champiopreneurship

Every champion can be a winner of crown, trophy or scepter but remain poor. The essence of champiopreneurship is to learn how to acquire wealth with the trophy, corporate image and goodwill. Champiopreneur are groom to benefits wealth from their pursuit or wins.

In the spirit of championship, entrepreneurship is the process of scanning for opportunities, identifying opportunities, chasing opportunities and grabbing opportunities via transformation intelligence to mankind with meaningful sustainable growth and benefits. This is about seeing, pursuit and exploiting opportunities that makes someone enterprising as entrepreneur yielding to champiopreneur (Ovharhe & Woko, 2024b).

Champiopreneurship is about 'visionary of the future', 'embarking on the mission impossible' with 'dynamic competitive spirit'. You cannot be a champion, without winning any battle in the business world. Champiopreneur are leaders that win the battle because, the business enterprise is reckless, troublesome, dynamic and competitive. Champiopreneurs are champions of business leaders. They are the king of business rivals, challengers and followers with leading competitive edge not bleeding edge. Champiopreneur has strong spirit of resilience. Every field of industries needs who to conquer as the market leader to be the champions. Creating, innovating and inventing the future of tangible and intangible sustainable goods to be position in the market is an attribute of the champiopreneur. The consciousness of the champiopreneur is to be the first or overtake to be the first with stability of apex business opportunities (Ovharhe & Woko, 2024a).

Champiopreneur are all over the business globe industries; business market, music, movie, sport, cattery, academic, technology, ICT, banking and finance, politics, health, medical, engineering, theater art, fine art and any business with games changers. For example, Koblin (2024) insight of the super bowl viewership which rose to 123.4 million, shows a magnificent record on the entertainment industrial as edge of championship position.

Cristiano Ronaldo and Lionel Messi are champiopreneur in the football sport industries. Michael Jackson, Dolly Parton, Beyonce are in the music industries with their exclusive branding styles and pattern (Baysinger, 2024). Every champiopreneur should posses its special styles and pattern that is charismatic. This charismatic trait, whether known or unknown, gives a competitive edge when an opportunity arises. Elon Musk (X, Tesla), Mark Zuckerberg (Facebook), Bill Gates (Micro Soft), Amazon, Google etcetera are all champions in their various area of specialty, just as Coke-Cola is the champion in the soft drink industries. In the civil construction industries in Nigeria and most Africa countries, Julius Berger is the champiopreneur (Ovharhe & Woko, 2024a,b). The most important questions is; Who's next?

The good thing about champiopreneur is the ability to create, invent and innovates the future with any slight business opportunities. Champiopreneur uses their charismatic styles and patterns in visualizing, pursuit and grabbing opportunities which reveal the skillful value added competitive advantage they possess. They are not just satisfied in the leadership position but want to use the slogan of CNN; 'Be the First to Know' in the broadcasting industries. 'All champiopreneur are leaders, but not all leaders are champiopreneurs;' It could be formal or informal leadership. Some leaders make themselves to be champion of the team. Some people make the leaders in the team; also make them to be champions. In this scenario, the championship does not last.

Shawn (2023) posit that leader guides, influence, direct, motivate and inspires with framework establish by the enterprise to achieve common goal. Whereas, a champion is someone like an intrapreneur or entrepreneur who has already achieved success in a competitive settings, being recognized for their accomplishments and are seen as a role model, change agent, pace setters and record breaker for others to follow the landmark **(Fernando,** 2024). Hence, champiopreneur is a role model with charismatic experiential knowledge for other entrepreneurs to achieve growth to the journey of champiopreneurship.

Nilima (2024) argued that there is a big difference between a champion and a leader. A champion works for notion as revolutionized trend or game changers, while a leader works for others with structural framework. A leader takes responsibility, is of service to his environment and people. He helps them in every way. People look up to him, love him and respect him. On the other hand, a champion is a star. He makes people proud by winning laurels for the country or the team and enterprise he belongs to. But initially he has to train himself, unlike the leaders who depend on the organization. Thus, a leader ought to look after his own self to become a champion. He has to become famous by giving his best.

Championship have a trait to innovate and create patterns of maintaining the business opportunities of be the first. In the News industries like; Aljazeera, BBC, SKY News and ABC News are all leaders but someone must be the Champiopreneur. The Olympic is the determinant of championship for who win and hold the trophy with the accurate compliance to the disciplinary rule of the game. Champiopreneurship is about who is the game changer (Ovharhe & Woko, 2024a).

Champiopreneur does not just think about survival and success, rather who is the game changer and more concern about sustainability. This is the reasons champiopreneur need to integrate business intelligence, creativity and innovation as paramount plight. Champiopreneurs need team (intrapreneurs) for decision making and competitive intelligence to actualize her business intelligence.

J. B. Say fathoms that entrepreneurs are creator, while Peter F. Drucker entrepreneurs opined they are innovator which were supported by Joseph Schumpeter and Christenson, The International Risk Management entity in Ovharhe *et al.*, (2021) agreed that entrepreneurs has the potency risk culture. In the algebraic expression using simple linear function can be stated below; viz:

Let Creator = CTR
Innovator= IVT
Business Opportunities = BOT
Charisma = CRM
Risk Culture= RCT
Business Intelligence= BIG
Using linear equation
Thus Champiopreneurship (CPP)= f(CTR,IVT,BOP,CRM)
Hence: $Y= a + b(x_{i,}\ x_{i,}\ x_{i,}\ x_{i,,}\ x_{i\ldots\ldots}\ x_{n})$.

Where Y= criterion or dependent variable {Champiopreneurship (CPP) i.e. win, growth, profit, benefit, client satisfaction}.

But:

a= constant= RCT
b=co-efficient of x=BIG
x= predictor or independent variable.

Therefore:

Champiopreneurship = Risk Culture + Business Intelligence (Creator, Innovator, Business Opportunity, Charisma)
When: CPP= RCT + BIG (CRT, IVT, BOT, CRM)

Though, in the practice of credible culture and business intelligence, committed and enthusiastic leaders can develop themselves to become champion. Leaders that cannot grow to become champion may experience injelititis and cynicism (Ovharhe, 2023). The injelititis and cynicism occurs as a result of inability to explore innovation skills, creativity, business opportunities and business intelligence. This leads to enterprise paralysis because the business will experience epileptic growth. It would be observe that there are lack of creativity, risk culture, business intelligence, opportunities and innovation that degenerate to the state of injelititis and cynicism in the enterprise.

6. THEORETICAL PARADIGM

The paradigms adopted in the study are BCG Matrix and Blake and Mouton Managerial Grid.

A. BCG Matrix Analysis

The prolific strategic firms in the USA came up with a tactical model to manage the product portfolio of enterprise. The tactical model is known as Boston Consulting Group (BCG) Matrix. BCG's founder, Bruce Henderson, popularized the concept in his essay *The Product Portfolio*, in 1970. The champiopreneur BCG's Alan Zakon created a trophy in this plight. While Revees & Moose (2023) breathe a fresh breathe on the matrix in collaboration with the team.

The matrix is a simplex graphical instrumental tools use to cross-examine and evaluate the product portfolio of the different enterprise product and services the firm is willing to offer for sales in the competitive parity. This is expressed in simplex form called the strategic business units (SBU) in synchronization of the market share and business growth of the enterprise. It shows relatively how the market share expands or contrasts in alignment with the business growth rate. It is perceived by the management as two dimensional analyses among the market share and business growth of the SBU's (Strategic Business Unit).

The expression can be seen as stated beneath as stipulated per annum comparison of base and preceding.

```
Relative Market Share = Strategic Business Unit (SBU) Sales
leading in the competitive parity.
Market Growth Rate = Industry sales per annum now - Industry
sales per annum last year.
```

The BCG matrix has four compartment cells which can easily be understood in the horizontal axis expression and vertical axis expression with the strategic business unit (SBU).

The four compartment cells of the BCG matrix are the Stars, Cash Cows, Question Marks and Dogs as illustrated in Figure 3.

BCG Matrix

From the above illustration in the diagram the explanation of the concept is discussed.

1. **Stars:** Stars represent business units among the enterprise portfolio that have rapid growth rate and cash generating income stream with large market share in a fast growing business environment. They are high perceived products in the port folio which generate cash with fast growth rate with the relative market share. Though, because of the fast growth in the industry, stars product requires flow of huge investment to sustain the business unit. Overhead and

Figure 3. Boston Consulting Group Matrix
Credit: Ovharhe, O. H. (2023d). The entrepreneur: Thinking globally and acting locally. FUPRE EntrepreneurshipTraining Programme; Module 9, 1-34.
Source: Stern, C. W., & Deimler, M. S. (2006).

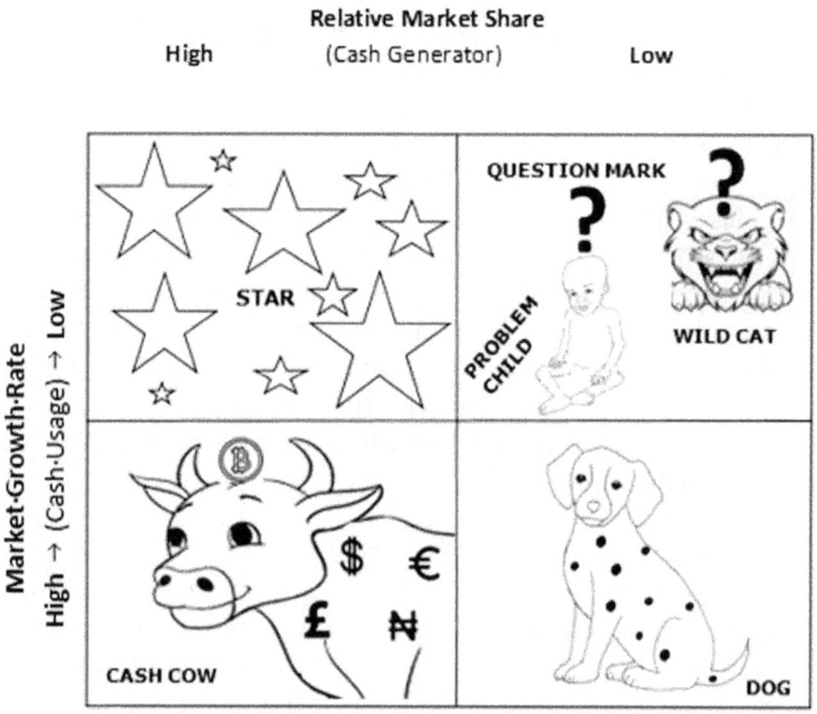

capital expenses are needed consistent and simultaneously keep the stream of income flowing in relationship with the customer frequency and volume of patronage. Star products give the enterprise huge competitive advantage over the competition because their threats are like arrow in the market environment. They give hope and pride to the enterprise with good corporate image and strong perceived good will. Entrepreneurs uses stars product to boost their reputation and corporate identity with business world (Alqahtani & Uslay, 2023).

Entrepreneur seeks to be called a champion. The championship entrepreneurs profile is all about becoming the market leader. The struggle and fight encountered by the champiopreneur to win the market share, sales territories and sales quotas is enveloped in capturing the business units to be the star in the marketplace. Star product needs a lot of advertisement which in the process publicized the enterprise other products or business units (Yadav, Tripathi, Tripathi, Ghosal, Kumar, Mandal & Singh, 2023). The net cash flow is spontaneous and precise because the cash outflow inflow (income) outsmarts the cash outflow (expenditure) because of high volume and frequency of patronage of the star product.

2. **Cash Cows:** Cash Cows identify products and services of the enterprise or business units that possesses extensive profane market share in the competitive mature stage. Whereas there is slow market growth but less investment capital or seed capital unlike the Star business units (Lim, 2023). Hence, Cash cow seems to generate rapid inflow of income, with tremendous net cash flow in the enterprise. The cash cow products are the bedrock or strength based of the enterprise. With the horn of the cash cow its can harm and attacked another product or business units that seems to be threat in the entire product port folio of the competition. When the cash cow is close to the end of the maturity stage or decline stage of the business cycle, an aggressive product rejuvenization strategy should be integrated to be the champiopreneurship (Ovharhe *et al.*, 2022).

   Entrepreneurs use the horn of cash cow business units to protect and support offspring of new product lunched into the market industry. The cash cow can be use to feed problem children or wild cat (question mark) product to develop to star and cash cow before they can develop their horn to be self-defendant in the business fight. This is because the horn of the cash cow is very aggressive and dangerous in the business world during combat; it is like fighting in battle of the guerilla warfare. Every entrepreneur that wants to be champion leaders needs the horn to be alert to survive in the business world.

3. **Question Marks:** There are product or business units in enterprise portfolio that are behaving like wild cat or problem children. This is range of business unit which are tagged with questions marks. The enterprise is in tough dilemma phrase on what to do or how to cope with them. The problem is that entrepreneur and intrapreneur are always faces with doubt and worries about what to do with them. The questions every entrepreneur or intrapreneurs ask are that; should we stay here with it? Should we go forwards or retrench? This is because the question marks (business units) have very low relative competitive market share with responses to high business growth rate. The question mark or wild cat product required huge investment capital to sustain and survive her for success to expand the market share intensively (Ratten, 2023). This can calls for the champiopreneurship for sustainability, survival and success to holds the business units to illuminate the market.

   Entrepreneurs need more attention and market research to uphold the business units of the questions mark. This is while it is also called problem children business units or product. Problem child is perceived to be very sick, needs diagnostic intervention and immunization for survival. Entrepreneurs are worried for how long to continued this intervention because it's a drain of human, material, financial and physical resources. But the good news is that most entrepreneurial journey and dreams begin with the question mark product before they start nurturing is for growth before building extensive market share in the business environment. If entrepreneurs and intrapreneurs ignore the problem children (questions mark) they will just be looking and behaving like wild cat and eventually turn to dogs, which might be a total loss or failure for the entrepreneur. Hence the lean startup principles need to be in place before commencement by champiopreneurs (Ovharhe, 2023a,b,c).

4. **Dogs:** The cannibalistic products or vampire business units that drain the life cycle of the enterprise as proscribe to be 'dogs'. When a product drains the organizational life cycle it can eventually sink the boat of the enterprise in the deep ocean without safety instrumental tools. Dogs are vampire products because they feed on the flesh and new bleed of the enterprise port folio. Entrepreneur should be very careful in dealing with this kind of business units (dogs) that make them to have low market share, high debt leverage, poor turnover, non-customer feedback/relation and no patronage (Ovharhe *et al.*, 2022).

   Dogs are epileptic and paralytic products that do feed on their host until they drain it to death. Dogs are business unit with weak market shares and market growth that do not generate cash and attract capital formation for investment venture in the business environment. It is advisable to invoke the *prunal* of the product line when any business units are perceived to be dogs. This calls for retrenchment or take a shot at the dogs. Hence, such livelihood of the cycle of dogs should not exist because it is at the expense of the enterprise that if such product will survive which required huge cash flow expenditure, it is only favorable to the competition at the expense of the enterprise.

   Dogs are usually from factors of dying product and bad company name. Thus a lot need to be done before saving the life of the product because the competitor might use it as competitive advantage to attack the enterprise weakness. Sometimes what need to be done is do nothing strategy to await an entrepreneurship opportunities that will yield momentum in short-term. But for some exceptional and strategic reasons some dogs product life are sustain by some enterprise, cooperation or conglomerate (Mandrinos & Lim, 2023).

B. Blake-Mouton's Managerial Grid Theory

The managerial grid is an exceptional instrumental strategic tool use to appraised leadership competence and concern in management of people and productivity in

Figure 4. Blake and Mouton Managerial Grid
Credit: *Ovharhe, O. H. (2023d). The Entrepreneur: Thinking globally and acting locally. FUPRE Entrepreneurship Training Programme; Module 9, 1-34*

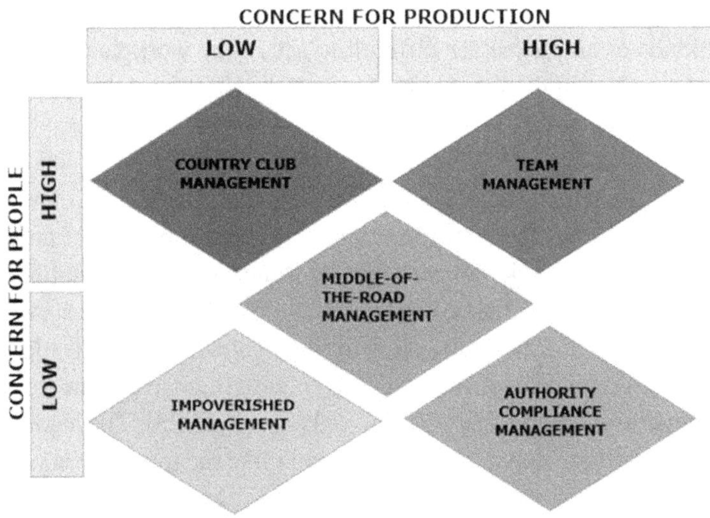

the workplace. This is very vital for the intrepreneur and entrepreneur relationship evaluation on how the enterprise can move forward for growth especially for lean start-up and growth. The managerial grid Theory was developed R. R. Blake and J. S. Mouton which helps leaders and entrepreneurs in the enterprise to optimized leadership style best fit for business intelligence, creativity and innovation (Blake & Mouton, 1964).

As shown in the Figure above, the managerial grid is enveloped on two dimensions, firstly; Concern for People secondly; Concern for Production. The managerial grid managers intrapreneurs and entrepreneur to identify best fit pattern of five basic leadership style; (a) Country Club Management, (b) Authority-Compliance Management, (c) Impoverished Management, (d) Middle-of-the-road Management, and (5) Team Management.

1. Country Club Management (1,9): This demonstrates how leaders are more concerned for the people rather than the job functions. This further shows how leaders are more concern of their staff welfare such as when they are sick or have birth days, huge concern for the bereaved, delivery of offspring and social requirements which motivate positive emotions innovation skills, creativity, strategic intelligence, tactical intelligence and operational intelligence. This poses a workplace friendliness which most employees might take such

opportunities for granted that leads to deficiency in organization growth and low productivity. This leadership style pattern could be advisable when the employee are self-starter, self-motivated and self-monitored because of self–oriented competence and goal driven individuals attitude at the workplace. But such kinds of employee are difficult to see in the workplace; even those that possess such attitude may not be interested in high social lifestyle (Helmold, 2021; Ovharhe & Chukwuemeka, 2023).

2. Authority-Compliance Management (9,1): This type of leadership style dramatized where the leader of the enterprise is focused more concerned about productivity rather than the emotional and social premium of employee. The leaders in this sense do not care for about individual lifestyle pattern. This is a game of hiring and firing kind of leadership if anyone messes up with the strict rules and fundamental policy of the organization. The leader talks more about man-hour and instrumentations (i.e. device, machine, material, finance) on productivity (Northouse, 2018); Yadav *et al.,* 2023). The leader attitude is; 'it's cool out there down town', if you don't like the job and leadership pattern you quit.

   This kind of job may not be favorable for intrapreneurs and entrepreneur that have huge competition because there might be lack of business intelligence, innovation, creativity and business opportunities, perhaps their opposition might use it as attacked against them. Entrepreneurs with this attitude which is a starter might not survive in the long-term. This kind of leadership style is for lean startup or SME's, but favorable where the entrepreneur want to sustain is business growth with huge compensation and enormous fringe benefits with bonus tighten to the job functions, despise the autocratic nature of the leadership style the enterprise might succeed (Alqahtani & Uslay, 2023).

3. Impoverished Management (1,1): This pattern of leadership is the unexpected in any workplace because it ruins the entire enterprise from the roof to the foundation. It poses negation attributes in all ramifications because the concern for people is very poor and the concern for productivity is much obscured. It is a type of leadership style which occurs where there are high needs for distributive or decentralized forms on management. The task, responsibility and job function is specified to certain work scope without much interference from the centre. This can occurs in holdings and subsidiaries, religious organizations and large conglomerate with multi-nationals. This is good for leader where they may be community disturbance, turbulence, hazards, pandemic and inconsistency in exchange rate, inflation rate and interest rate (Helmold, 2021; Ovharhe et al., 2021). This kind of leadership style does not follow the steam of any entrepreneurship pattern, talk less of champiopreneurship.

4. Middle-of-the-road Management (5,5): This illustrates where there are mediocrity concerns on the management of an enterprise in terms of employee welfare and productivity. The leadership perception is on boomerang and fictitious profit been generated from another market environment, hence the leaders seems to display the attribute of 50-50 ratio on concern for people and productivity. It is done sometimes just to keep the ball rolling in the business enterprise. Much energy is not enacted because the portfolio in another sales quotas and sales territories is very high. Thus, they will averagely concern about the market and employee in the place of 50-50 provided they just keep generating wealth for the stakeholders (Northouse, 2018; Yadav et al., 2023). This somehow happens to entrepreneurs that discovered new business unit with high profit market and net cash flow. The income stream seems to be very beneficial. This is practice of most serial extrepreneurs, ultrapreneurs and extrapreneurs (Ovharhe, 2023).
5. Team Management (9,9): this is the best posited leadership that orchestrate high proficiency of concern for people and concern for productivity. Here, there will be high spirit of motivation to accomplish task with target with pursuit of business opportunities, business intelligence, creativity and innovation (Helmold, 2021). The entrepreneurial dreams and journey will experience upwards smooth slope movement despise the turbulence, hazard, pandemic and recklessness in the business environment. There will be upward impression management and affective commitment, job satisfaction. Employee satisfaction will be experiential compare to employee turnover, intention to stay, normative commitment with enterprise. Mush attributes of organizational citizenship behavior will be experience (altruism, civic virtue sportsmanship courtesy and conscientiousness) (Ovharhe & Chukwuemeka, 2023).

   This type of leadership style promotes team spirit, cohesiveness standard, norms and industrial harmony among workforce. Grievances that resulted to strike and industrial dispute will be handled amicable. The concern for the employee to meet up target is at large; also the compensation and benefit of the employees are in the heart of the management at all times. The competition will be afraid to the arrow and threat on the business portfolio because they will see the corporate image and identify of the enterprise (Ratten, 2023).

The managerial grid matrix indicated the model of paradigm shift among managers, entrepreneurs, intrapreneurs, social entrepreneurs, serial entrepreneurs, ultrapreneurs and extrapreneur is their mode of operation towards the concern of workforce and productivity. Though, the managerial grid do not covers vast aspect of management. This dealt most with concern for workforce and productivity whereby call for business intelligence, creativity and innovation with ability to grab business opportunities. But, the grid can be use as a paradigm shift of extension to gross function of leadership style (Islam, 2023).

7. CONCLUSION

Entrepreneurship is the engine house of any merchandizing activities and propeller of any nation's economic growth and development. Entrepreneurs determine the flow of new blood stream in any enterprise. Whereas, management is the coordinating force that binds all the activities to ensure there is effectiveness and efficiency. This means the managerial strategies will be able to fine-tune the plans, organizing, directing, motivating and control of the input resource and projected output to work in achievable concept.

Every entrepreneurs need to learn how to navigate with potentials and capabilities on the right track where there are valuable treasures of business opportunities. The right track is the valuable path on the vision and mission to thread on which can accomplish the entrepreneurial journey and dreams. This will enable the entrepreneur to experience new enterprise creation successfully through the application of business intelligence (competitive intelligence, decision support system), creativity and innovation.

The business intelligence was adopted to enhance the return on asset (ROA), return on investment) ROI, return on capital employed (ROCE) and return on equity (ROE). The business intelligence is anchored with strategic intelligence, tactical intelligence, operational intelligence and decision support system that give the enterprise competitive advantage and championship edge in the market structure. However, the enterprise growth and development cannot be achieved without these concepts that give new blood life stream flow in the enterprise that is fathom as creativity, innovation and entrepreneurship opportunities. This is the store house of idea generation, networking and brain storming that enables entrepreneurship to be on the leading edge rather that bleeding edge over the artificial intelligence, data science, data virtualization, machine learning and big data emergence.

Entrepreneurship opportunities, creativity and innovation are fruition to the management of any enterprise in the short-term and long-term in her merchandizing activities. With the application of entrepreneurship innovation skills, the managerial policy, decision making and budgetary control implementation, the enterprise will experience business excellence in sustainability, survival and success. This calls for champiopreneurship approach which possesses ability, capability and capacity to control turbulence, post-pandemic and competitive parity in the business world. Champiopreneuship is the key to enterprise growth and development.

ACKNOWLEDGMENT

Crystallized appreciation to my Shuddie; Wife and my Exponential Champions; Terry, Kerry and Jerry.

REFERENCES

Лена, M. (2019). Marketing intelligence as a tool for strategic enterprise management. *International Journal of Psychosocial Rehabilitation*, *24*(8), 7. doi:10.37200/IJPR/V24I8/PR281089

Zighed Rahma., & Sabri Mekimah. (2023). The role of competitive intelligence in improving performance through organizational learning, A case study Start-ups in Algeria. Journal of Intelligence Studies in Business, 13(1), 53-64. DOI: doi:10.37380/jisib.v13i1.991

Ahunanya, V., Ovharhe, O. H., Emenike, C. G., & Otto, G. (2022a). Consignment inventory system and entrepreneurial success among micro warehousing firms. *International Journal of Social Science & Management Research*, *8*(5), 18–28. doi:10.56201/ijssmr.v8.no5.2022.pg18.28

Ahunanya, V., Ovharhe, O. H., Emenike, C. G., & Otto, G. (2022b). Consignment inventory system and obsolescence management in the drilling fluid firms in Nigeria. *International Journal of Social Science & Management Research*, *8*(5), 1–27. doi:10.56201/ijssmr.v8.no5.2022.pg1.17

Alberta.alis (2023). *Career insight: Know yourself.* Alis. https://alis.alberta.ca/careerinsite/know-yourself/skills-quiz/

Alqahtani, N., & Uslay, C. (2023). *Marketing/entrepreneurship interface research priorities (2023–2026). Journal of Research in Marketing and Entrepreneurship.* Emerald Insight.

Amjad, M. (2023). *7 Promising Areas for Entrepreneurship in 2023*. LinkedIn. https://www.linkedin.com/pulse/7-promising-areas-entrepreneurship-2023-maheen-amjad

Anderbjork, G., & Martell, J. (2021). *Gardens of intelligence: Designing robust digital market and competitive intelligence platforms* (1st ed.). Technics Publications.

Apostolopoulos, N., Ratten, V., Petropoulos, D., Liargovas, P., & Anastasopoulou, E. (2021). Agri-food sector and entrepreneurship during the COVID-19 crisis: A systematic literature review and research agenda. *Strategic Change*, *30*(2), 159–167. doi:10.1002/jsc.2400

ArturV. (2020). Competitive intelligence concepts and definitions. *Management and leadership*. DOI: doi:10.13140/RG.2.2.14667.34087

Baskin, K. (2023). How to use competitive insight. *MIT Sloan*. https://mitsloan.mit.edu/ideas-made-to-matter/how-to-use-competitive-insight

Baysinger, T. (2024). *Sony said to pay around $600M for Michael Jackson catalog deal*. Axios. https://www.axios.com/2024/02/12/sony-michael-jackson-catalog

Beato, E. (2024). 2024: A year of collaboration and innovation at the blank school. *https://entrepreneurship.babson.edu/2024-blank-school/*

Blake, R., & Mouton, J. (1964). *The Managerial Grid: The key to leadership excellence*. Gulf Publishing Co.

Blessley, M., & Mudambi, S. M. (2022). A trade way and a pandemic: Disruption and resilience in the food bank supply chain. *Industrial Marketing Management*, *102*, 58–73. doi:10.1016/j.indmarman.2022.01.002

Britannica. (2024). *Champion: Monarch, royalty & nobility*. Britannica. https://www.britannica.com › champion-English-history

Business Research Insight. (2024). Operations Intelligence platforms market report overview. https://www.businessresearchinsights.com/market-reports/operations-intelligence-platforms-market-103984

Cekuls, A. (2022). Expand the scope of competitive intelligence. *J Intell Stud Bus*, *12*(1), 4–5. doi:10.37380/jisib.v12i1.924

Chibuike, C. U., & Ovharhe, O. H. (2022). Emergence of risk culture and lean culture in Nigeria during pandemic and crisis era: Using confirmatory analysis. *International Journal of Multidisciplinary Research and Growth Evaluation*, *3*(1), 263–271. doi:10.54660/anfo.2021.3.1.14

Chibuike, C. U., Ovharhe, O. H., & Abada, A. M. (2022). Synchronization of lean accounting alert and entrepreneurial sustainability among micro firms in Nigeria during pandemic and catastrophe: Using confirmatory factor analysis. *International Journal of Business and Management*, *10*(1), 1–13. doi:10.54660/anfo.2021.2.6.15

Christensen, C. M. (1997). *The innovator's dilemma: When new technologies cause great firms to fail*. Harvard Business School Press.

Cloutier, A. (2013). Competitive intelligence process integrative model based on a scoping review of the literature. *International Journal of Strategic Management*, *13*(1), 57–72. doi:10.18374/IJSM-13-1.7

Cole, C. (2022). *How to identify business and market opportunities.* Harvard Business School Online.

Collin (2024). Champion. https://www.collinsdictionary.com/dictionary/english/champion

Corsaro, D., & D'Amico, V. (2022). How the digital transformation from COVID-19 affected the relational approaches in B2B. *Journal of Business and Industrial Marketing*, *37*(10), 2095–2115. doi:10.1108/JBIM-05-2021-0266

Coursera, S. (2023) What Is management? Definition, types, skills, and careers. *https://www.coursera.org/articles/management*

Dana, L.-P., & Vorobeva, E. (2021). Understanding the term "minority entrepreneurship". In T. M. Cooney (Ed.), *The Palgrave handbook of minority entrepreneurship* (pp. 15–32). Palgrave Macmillan. doi:10.1007/978-3-030-66603-3_2

Darwiesh, A., Elhoseny, M., Atassi, R., & El-Baz, A. H. (2023). A business intelligence system for governing risks in SMEs. In R. El Ayachi, M. Fakir, & M. Baslam (Eds.), *Business Intelligence. CBI 2023. Lecture Notes in Business Information Processing, 484*. Springer. doi:10.1007/978-3-031-37872-0_1

Davinsi Lab. (2024). Mavigating tomorrow: The future outlook of operational intelligence and security in 2024. *https://davinsi.com/en/news/navigating-tomorrow-future-outlook-operational-intelligence-and-security-2024*

Dermer, M. (2023). *Etymology of entrepreneur.* [Video]. Facebook. https://web.facebook.com/watch/?v=602542661584141

Dewar, C., Keller, S., & Malhotra, V. (2022). *CEO excellence: the six mindsets that distinguish the best leaders from the rest* (1st ed.). Scribner.

Dieffenbacher, S. F. (2023). *Creativity and Innovation: Differences, Examples & Definitions*. Digital Leadership. https://digitalleadership.com/blog/creativity-and-innovation/

Drucker, P. F. (1993). *Innovation and entrepreneurship practice and principles.* HarperCollins Publishers Inc.

Eckhardt, J. T., & Shane, S. A. (2003). Opportunities and entrepreneurship. *Journal of Management, 29*(3), 333–349. doi:10.1177/014920630302900304

Effa, G. A., Ovharhe, O. H., Ezirim, A. C., & Igwe, S. (2023a). Procurement sustainability policy and logistics performance in Nigeria. [IJMCS]. *International Journal of Marketing and Communication Studies, 7*(1), 56–72. doi:10.56201/ijmcs.v7.no1.2023.pg56.72

Effa, G. A., Ovharhe, O. H., Ezirim, A. C., & Igwe, S. (2023b). Strategic procurement initiatives and logistics performance in Nigeria. [IJMCS]. *International Journal of Marketing and Communication Studies*, *7*(1), 38–55. doi:10.56201/ijmcs.v7.no1.2023.pg38.55

Elia, G., Margherita, A., & Passiante, G. (2020). Digital entrepreneurship ecosystem: How digital technologies and collective intelligence are reshaping the entrepreneurial process. *Technological Forecasting and Social Change*, *150*, 119791. doi:10.1016/j.techfore.2019.119791

Emergent Risk International (2024). Strategic Intelligence Estimate 2024: Global disruptors. *https://emergentriskinternational.com/event/strategic-intelligence-estimate-2024 global-disruptors/*

Etymonline (2024). *Etymology of champion by etymonline*. Etymonline. https://www.etymonline.com › word › champion

Farradinna, S., Syafitri, N., Herawati, I., & Jayanti, W. (2023). An exploratory factor analysis of entrepreneurship psychological readiness (EPR) instrument. *Journal of Innovation and Entrepreneurship*, *12*(1), 66. doi:10.1186/s13731-023-00314-y

Fernando, G. (2024). *The champion: A model for 21st century strategic leadership*. Tough Nickle. https://toughnickel.com/business/The-Champion

Geeks for Geeks. (2023). Types of entrepreneurs: Innovating, imitative, fabian and drone entrepreneurs. Geeks for Geeks. https://www.geeksforgeeks.org/types-of-entrepreneurs-innovating-imitative-fabian-and-drone-entrepreneurs/

Gianinazzi, W. (2018). Penser global, agir local. Histoire d'une idée, EcoRev'. Revue critique d'écologie politique, 46. doi:10.3917/ecorev.046.0019

Gupta, P., & Bamel, U. (2023). Need for metacognition and critical thinking in the e-learning ecosystem: The new normal in post Covid era. *Global Business and Organizational Excellence*, *43*(1), 104–120. doi:10.1002/joe.22208

Gurcan, F., Ayaz, A., Dalveren, M. G. G., & Derawi, M. (2023). Business intelligence strategies, best practices, and latest trends: Analysis of scientometric data from 2003 to 2023 using machine learning. *Sustainability (Basel)*, *15*(13), 9854. doi:10.3390/su15139854

Handfield, B. R., Petersen, K., Cousins, P.N., & Lawson, B. (2023). An organizational entrepreneurship model of supply management integration and performance outcome. *International Journal of Operations &Production Management, 29* (2), 100-126. Emerald Group Publishing Limited0144-3577DOI doi:10.1108/01443570910932011

Handfield, R., Petersen, K., Cousins, P., & Lawson, B. (2009). An organizational entrepreneurship model of supply management integration and performance outcomes. *International Journal of Operations & Production Management*, *29*(2), 100–126. doi:10.1108/01443570910932011

Hassani, A., & Mosconi, E. (2022). Social media analytics, competitive intelligence, and dynamic capabilities in manufacturing SMEs. *Technological Forecasting and Social Change*, *175*(1), 1–11. doi:10.1016/j.techfore.2021.121416

Holori, R. B., Ahmadi, F., Khanmohammadi, M., Ranjbar, H. M., & Kordlouie, H. (2023, Autumn). Development and assessment of a business intelligence-based management accounting information system model: A structural equation modeling approach. *International Journal of Finance and Managerial Accounting*, *8*(31).

Horn, J. (2023). *Inside the competitor's mindset: how to predict their next move and position yourself for success* (1st ed.). The MIT Press. https://mitpress.mit.edu/9780262047883/inside-the-competitors-mindset/ doi:10.7551/mitpress/14628.001.0001

Hossain, M. S., Islam, M. A., Hosen, M., Mohd, T., & Thaker, H. (2023). Missing catalysts of female entrepreneurship success: Evidence from an emerging economy. *Global Business and Organizational Excellence*, *42*(5), 50–64. doi:10.1002/joe.22201

Huang, Z., Savita, K. S., & Zhong-jie, J. (2022). The business intelligence impact on the financial performance of start-ups. *Information Processing & Management*, *59*(1), 102761. doi:10.1016/j.ipm.2021.102761

Islam, M. N. (2023). Managing organizational change in responding to global crises. *Global Business and Organizational Excellence*, *42*(3), 42–57. doi:10.1002/joe.22189

Koblin, J. (2024). *Super bowl viewership rose to 123.4 million, a record high. https://www.nytimes.com/2024/02/12/business/media/super-bowl-ratings-record.html*

Jain, N. (2023). *What is innovation? Definition, types, examples and process*. Ideascale.

Kanyi, J. M., Wanjau, K. L., & Kyalo, T. N. (2023). The role of product innovation and entrepreneurial passion on performance of manufacturing pharmaceutical companies in Kenya. *International Journal of Arts and Social Science*, *6*(8), 282.

Knezović, E. (2023). Self-perceived employability and entrepreneurial and intrapreneurial intentions: Evidence from six countries. *Global Business and Organizational Excellence*, joe.22205. doi:10.1002/joe.22205

Kozyrkov, C. (2023). What is decision intelligence? *Medium*. https://towardsdatascience.com/introduction-to-decision-intelligence-5d147ddab767.

Kühn, M. L. (2006). Parts of competitive intelligence: Competitor intelligence. *South African Journal of Information Management*, *8*(1). doi:10.4102/sajim.v8i1.209

La Verne. (2023). *The difference between innovation and entrepreneurship*. La Verne. https://laverne.edu/entrepreneurship/wp-content/uploads/sites/81/2023/04/The-difference-between-innovation-and-entrepreneurship.pdf. University of La Verne

Lim, M.W. (2023). Transformative marketing in the new normal: A novel practice-scholarly integrative review of business-to-business marketing mix challenges, opportunities, and solutions. *Journal of Business Research*, *160*, 113638. Elsevier Inc.

Loizos, C. (2011). *Lean Startup' evangelist Eric Ries is just getting started.* PeHUB. https://www.scribd.com/document/377073019/Lean-Startup

Madureira, L., Popovic, A., & Castelli, M. (2023). Competitive intelligence maturity models: Systematic review, unified model, and implementation frameworks. *J Intell Stud Bus*, *13*(1), 1–29. doi:10.37380/jisib.v13i1.988

Maluleka, M. L., & Chummun, Z. B. (2023). Competitive intelligence and strategy implementation: Critical examination of present literature review. *South African Journal of Information Management*, *25*(1). https://sajim.co.za/index.php/sajim/article/view/1610. doi:10.4102/sajim.v25i1.1610

Mandrinos, S., & Lim, W. M. (2023). De-internationalization: An organizational institutionalism perspective. *Global Business and Organizational Excellence*, *42*(3), 58–73. doi:10.1002/joe.22195

Manohar, S., Paul. J., Strong, C., & Mittal, A. (2023). Generalized scale for perceived service innovation. *Journal of Business Research*, *160*, 113723.

Mark, T. R. (2024). *Importance of creativity & innovation in entrepreneurship 2024*. Nexford. https://www.nexford.edu/insights/creativity-innovation-in-entrepreneurship

Martins, M. J., Shahzad, F. M., & Xu, S. (2023). Factors influencing entrepreneurial intention to initiate new ventures: Evidence from university students. *Journal of Innovation and Entrepreneurship*, *12*(1), 63. doi:10.1186/s13731-023-00333-9

Maune, A. (2022). Mobile applications adoption and use in strategic competitive intelligence: A structural equation modelling approach. *Journal of Intelligence Studies in Business*, *12*(1).

Merriam-Webster. (2024). *Champion definition & meaning*. Merriam-Webster. https://www.merriam-webster.com › dictionary › cham.

Musabayana, T. G., Mutambara, E., & Ngwenya, T. (2023). Establishment of a Zimbabwe National SME sector: A major priority to enhance the performance of the national economy. *Journal of Innovation and Entrepreneurship, 2023*(12), 65. doi:10.1186/s13731-023-00329-5

Nightingale, P., & Coad, A. (2013). Muppets and Gazelles: Political and Methodological Biases in Entrepreneurship Research. (SPRU Working Paper Series 2013-03). SPRU - Science and Technology Policy Research, University of Sussex.

Nilima (2024). What makes a person a leader and another a champion: *https://www.quora.com/What-makes-a-person-a-leader-and-another-a-champion#:~:text=There%20is%20a%20big%20difference,to%20his%20environment%20and%20people*

Ntandoyenkosi, S. (2023). Entrepreneurship education. *Journal of Entrepreneurial Innovations, 4*(SI). doi:10.14426/jei.v4iSI.1674

O'Callaghan, M. (2023). *Decision intelligence: human–machine integration for decision-making* (1st ed.). CRC Press/Taylor & Francis. doi:10.1201/b23322

OECD. (2023). *Financing SMEs and Entrepreneurs: An OECD Scoreboard, 2023 Highlights.* OECD Publishing, Paris. doi:10.1787/f493861e-en

OECD. (2023). Job Creation and Local Economic Development 2023: Bridging the Great Green Divide, OECD Publishing, Paris. doi:10.1787/21db61c1-en

OECD (2023). *Risks and opportunities of reshaping global value chains.* OECD Economics Department, Working Party No. 1 on Macroeconomic and Structural Policy Analysis (CPE/WP1(2023)8).

OECD. (2023). *SME and Entrepreneurship Papers, No. 36*. OECD Publishing. doi:10.1787/a8d13e55-

Okhrimenko, I., Stepenko, V., Chernova, O., & Zatsarinnaya, E. (2023). The impact of information sphere in the economic security of the country: Case of Russian realities. *Journal of Innovation and Entrepreneurship, 12*(1), 67. doi:10.1186/s13731-023-00326-8

Opuala-Charles, O. S., & Oshilike, I. V. (2023). Entrepreneurship, public policy and economic development in Nigeria. *Journal of Economics &Management Research.* 4(2), 4-77. *SRC, JESMR-210*. doi:10.47363/JESMR/2023(4)173

Ovharhe, O. H. (2022a). Sustainable development goals: Multicollinearity between therapeutic entrepreneurship and rehabilitation therapy among African nations. *International Journal of Small Business and Entrepreneurship Research, 10*(3), 1–59. doi:10.37745/ijsber.2013/vol10n3157

Ovharhe, O. H. (2022b). Sustainable development goals: Therapeutic entrepreneurship and entrepreneurship Injelititis among West Africa Countries. [WJEDS]. *World Journal of Entrepreneurial Development Studies*, *7*(1), 87–113. doi:10.56201/wjeds.v7.no1.2022.pg87.113

Ovharhe, O. H. (2023). *Champiopreneurship: Lean start-Up and business growth.* Impress.

Ovharhe, O. H. (2023). *Light entrepreneurship and customer funded business: Simplified.* Lambert Academic Publishing.

Ovharhe, O. H. (2023). The entrepreneur: Thinking globally and acting locally. FUPRE EntrepreneurshipTraining Programme [Chapters]. *Module*, *9*, 1–34.

Ovharhe, O. H., & Abada, A. M. (2023). IFRS: Entrepreneurial Exit and Entrepreneurial Entre. *American Journal of Social Development and Entrepreneurship*, *2*(2), 1–8. doi:10.54536/ajsde.v2i2.1578

Ovharhe, O. H.., & Abada, A. M. (2023). IFRS adoptions on entrepreneurship entry and entrepreneurship exit: The Nigeria experience from 2006-2017. *American Journal of Social Development and Entrepreneurship, 2*(2). https://doi.org/ doi:10.54536/ajsde.v2i2

Ovharhe, O. H., Ahunanya, V., & Woko, E. B. (2022). Consignment inventory system and entrepreneurial survival in Lagos State. *International Journal of Social Science & Management Research*, *8*(5), 29–42. doi:10.56201/ijssmr.v8.no5.2022.pg29.42

Ovharhe, O. H., Chibuike, C. U., & Abada, A. M. (2023). Lean Accounting And Lean Entrepreneurship. *American Journal of Social Development and Entrepreneurship*, *2*(2), 1–8. doi:10.54536/ajsde.v2i2.1578

Ovharhe, O. H., & Chukwuemeka, S. P. (2023). Sustainable Development Goals: Therapeutic Entrepreneurship and Mental Health Conditions. *British Journal of Multidisciplinary and Advanced Studies*, *4*(1), 81–119. doi:10.37745/bjmas.2022.0107

Ovharhe, O. H., & Igbokwe, E. L. (2021). Analytical intervention of remote working correlates on risk culture and entrepreneurial adaptability in South-South Geopolitical Zone, Nigeria: Covid-19 Perspective. *Journal of Education and Practice, IISTE, 12*(3), 34–44. doi:10.7176/JEP/12-34-05

Ovharhe, O. H., & Okolo, B. S. (2022). Sustainable development goals: Lean entrepreneurship and Green entrepreneurship. *International Journal of Research and Scientific Innovation, 9*(10), 59-71.

Ovharhe, O. H., Okolo, B. S., Woko, E. B., & Igbokwe, L. (2022). Light entrepreneurship and customer funded business model. *International Journal of Social Sciences and Management Research*, *8*(5), 87–106. doi:10.56201/ijssmr.v8.no5.2022.pg87.106

Ovharhe, O. H., & Saturday, O. (2024b). Environmental pollution and maternal mortality among female entrepreneurs. *ABC Index.* https://explore.abcdindex.com/ai_portal/login.php.

Ovharhe, O. H., & Woko, B. E. (2024a). Environmental pollution and life expectancy among intrepreneurs. Journal of Economics and Management; JEM .

Ovharhe, O. H., & Woko, B. E. (2024b). Environmental pollution and infant mortality on entrepreneurial opportunities: A champiopreneurship approach. *ABC Index.* https://explore.abcdindex.com/ai_portal/login.php.

Ovharhe, O. H., Woko, E. B., & Ezeocha, V. U. (2021). Remote working: Entrepreneurial risk and entrepreneurial survival in the micro firms in Niger-Delta, Nigeria (COVID-19 Pandemic Prospects). *International Journal of Small Business and Entrepreneurship Research*, *9*(4), 11–28. doi:10.37745/ijsber.2013/vol9n11-28

Ovharhe, O. H., Woko, E. B., & Ogolo, T. M. (2021). Competitive risk strategy and entrepreneurial satisfaction among fast moving consuming goods in Nigeria during covid-19 pandemic using confirmatory factor analysis. *International Journal of Multidisciplinary Research and Growth Evaluation*, *2*(6), 267–272. doi:10.54660/anfo.2021.3.1.14

OyinlolaM.KoladeO.OkoyaS. A.AjalaO.AdefilaA.AdedijiA.BabaremuK.TijaniB.AdejuwonJ.WambuiF.AkinlabiE. (2023). Entrepreneurship and Innovation in Nigerian Universities: Trends, Challenges and Opportunities. SSRN. doi:10.2139/ssrn.4419457

Peek, S. (2024). Creativity is not innovation (but you need the both). *Business News Daily.* https://www.businessnewsdaily.com/6848-creativity-vs-innovation.html

Rahchamani, A., & All, E. (2019). The impact of marketing intelligence and business intelligence on acquiring competitive advantage. *Revista Gestão & Tecnologia*, *19*(5), 52–70. doi:10.20397/2177-6652/2019.v19i5.1794

Ratten, V. (2023). Entrepreneurship: Definitions, opportunities, challenges, and future directions. *Global Business and Organizational Excellence*, *42*(5), 79–90. doi:10.1002/joe.22217

Ratten, V. (2023). Entrepreneurship: Definitions, opportunities, challenges, and future directions. *Global Business and Organizational Excellence*, *42*(5), 79–90. doi:10.1002/joe.22217

Reddit (2023). Etymology. https://www.reddit.com/r/etymology/

Reeves, M., & Whitaker, K. (2022). Innovating management innovation. *Strategic Management Review*, *3*(1), 157–167. doi:10.1561/111.00000040

Revees, M., & Moose, S. (2023). *Boston consulting group matrix*. BCG. https://www.bcg.com/about/overview/our-history/growth-share-matrix

Ries, E. (October 17, 2017). The startup way: How modern companies use entrepreneurial management to transform culture and drive long-term growth (Unabridged ed.). Random House Audio.

ScienceDirect.com. (2024). Tactical intelligence. *https://www.sciencedirect.com/topics/computer-science/tactical-intelligence*

Seth, S. (2023). *Why entrepreneurship is important to the economy. The Business Post: 118-121*. TejgaonI/A.

Shane, S., & Venkataraman, S. (2000). The promise of entrepreneurship as a field of research. *Academy of Management Review*, *25*(1), 217–226. doi:10.5465/amr.2000.2791611

Shawn, M. (2023). The content authority. https://thecontentauthority.com/blog/leader-vs-champion

Shevlin, H. (2022, October 21). The artist is dead, AI killed them. *IAI News.*

Shobhit, S. (March 16, 2023). *As in the definition of entrepreneurship*.https://www.google.com/search?q=Shobhit+Seth+(March+16%2C+2023).&oq=Shobhit+Seth+(March+16%2C+2023).+&gs_lcrp=EgZjaHJvbWUyBggAEEUYOTIHCAEQABiiBNIBCTM0NDVqMGoxNagCALACAA&sourceid=chrome&ie=UTF-8

Showkat, A. D. (2022). The relevance of Taylor's scientific management in the modern era. *Journal of Psychology and Political Science*, *24*(2) https://doi.org/. doi:10.55529/jpps

Sprague, R. H. (1980). A framework for the development of decision support systems. *Management Information Systems Quarterly*, *4*(4), 1–26. https://www.jstor.org/stable/248957. doi:10.2307/248957

Stanford Center For Professional Development. (2024). *Creativity and innovation management: How to inspire original ideas*. Stanford University. https://online.stanford.edu/creativity-and-innovation-management

Stern, C. W., & Deimler, M. S. (2006). *The boston consulting group on strategy: Classic concepts and new perspectives* (2nd ed.). John Wiley & Sons, Inc.

STRATAGEM. (2024). Understanding as a term in tactical intelligence - PART 2. *https://www.stratagem.no/understanding-as-a-term-in-tactical-intelligence-part-2/*

Taranu, S. (2023). Measuring the added value of competitive intelligence in business. *Proceedings of the 17th International Conference on Business Excellence*, 1328-1336. , ISSN 2558-9652. 2023. doi:10.2478/picbe-2023-0119

Thompson, M. (2009). *Organizational champions: How to develop passionate change agents at every level*. McGraw-Hill.

Vocabulary.com. (2024). Champion: definition, meaning & synonyms. Vocabulary.com

Wakuthii, S. (2024). Tactical intelligence mastery: Effective knowledge management in the military. https://www.linkedin.com/pulse/tactical-intelligence-mastery-effective-knowledge-sarah-wakuthii

World Economic Forum. (2024). Strategic Intelligence Outlook: What's in store for 2024. https://www.weforum.org/agenda/2023/12/strategic-intelligence-outlook-climate-economy-forecast-2024/

Yadav, S. U., Tripathi, R., Tripathi, A. M., Ghosal, I., Kumar, A., Mandal, M., & Singh, A. (2023). Digital and innovative entrepreneurship in the Indian handicraft sector after the COVID-19 pandemic: Challenges and opportunities. *Journal of Innovation and Entrepreneurship, 12*(1), 69. doi:10.1186/s13731-023-00337-5

Yugandhara, R. Y. (2023). Business intelligence market size 2023-2030 (US$ in Bn). *Business Intelligence Market Growth Drivers & Analysis 2023*. Research Gate. https://www.researchgate.net/publication/369595866_Business_Intelligence_Market_Growth_Drivers_Analysis_2023

Zhou, J., San, O. T., & Liu, Y. (2023). Design and Implementation of enterprise financial decision support system based on business intelligence. *International Journal of Professional Business Review, 8*(4), e0873. doi:10.26668/businessreview/2023.v8i4.873

Chapter 10
Impact of Board of Directors Composition, Activity, and Compensation on the ESG Performance in an International Context

Tijani Amara
Higher Institute of Business Administration, University of Gafsa, Tunisia

Ali Ahmadi
https://orcid.org/0000-0002-2170-941X
Higher Institute of Business Administration, University of Gafsa, Tunisia

ABSTRACT

A growing body of research suggests that the Board of Directors Composition, Activity, and Compensation can influence its environmental, social, and governance (ESG). This chapter seeks to fill this gap in the literature by testing the impact of board size, board meetings, women on the board, executive compensation, and ESG controversies on ESG performance. Using one of the largest datasets to date, consisting of an unbalanced panel dataset consisting of 31040 firm-year observations from 5500 listed firms, covering a period of 16 years (2002–2017) from 60 countries around the world, these findings are fivefold. First, these results suggest that board size is positively associated with ESG performance. Second, the authors show that the number of meeting of the board per year is positively related to the environmental, social and governance score. Third, the main empirical evidence shows that the relationship between women on the board of directors and a firm's ESG performance is a strongly significant. Fourth, these results reveal that executive compensation has a positive effect only for some geographic areas. Fifth, there is a negative link between ESG performance and ESG controversies.
DOI: 10.4018/979-8-3693-1846-1.ch010

INTRODUCTION

A company's performance essentially depends on the board of directors (Merendino, & Melville, 2019), given that they are responsible for approving and overseeing the implementation of strategic goals, the system of governance and creating company culture (Castellanos, & George, 2020). A successful board of director will also make an emphasis on business ethics and corporate responsibility (Qa'dan,& Suwaidan, 2019). An increasing amount of research finds a strong positive relationship between a firm's sustainability performance and profitability: companies with high sustainability ratings significantly out perform their counterparts both in terms of stock market value and accounting performance (Birindelli et al., 2018). In other terms, adopting environmental, social and governance (ESG) best practices leads to a long-term competitive advantage.

Based on these considerations, this study aims to identify the characteristics of the board of directors, which raise environmental social governance performance. More specifically, according to the existing literature (Qa'dan,& Suwaidan, 2019; Xie et al., 2019; Arayssi et al., 2020; Armstrong, 2020; Harjoto, & Wang, 2020) our analysis examines the impact of a board's characteristics (gender diversity, size, activity, compensation and ESG controversies) on ESG performance in a sample of 31.040 observations from 60 countries from 2002 to 2017. Our focus on this sample allows for a more homogeneous reference population and is important because these high number a firms present one of the main economic drivers in their economies which can enhance the transition towards a more inclusive and sustainable economy Rajesh, (2020). To proxy a firm's sustainability performance, we use Thomson Reuters' ESG Asset4 score, a broad and verified measure of CSR performance adopted by scholars both for financial (Hübel, & Scholz, 2020; Kiriu, & Nozaki, 2020) and non-financial firms (Jackson et al., 2020; Beretta et al., 2020; Hedqvist, & Larsson, 2020; Jahmane, & Gaies, 2020; Arayssi et al., 2020).

Our main empirical evidence shows that there is a non-linear relationship between women on the board of directors and a firm's ESG performance. This study contributes both to academic literature and to firm practices in several aspects. Indeed, current literature on the topic (relationship between board composition and ESG performance) primarily concentrates on non-financial firms (Qa'dan, & Suwaidan, 2019; Arayssi, et al., 2020; Wong et al., 2020, Plastun et al., 2020; Alessandrini, & Jondeau, 2020; Ng et al., 2020).

The remainder of the paper is organized as follows. Section 2 presents the literature review and the research hypotheses. Section 3 discusses the research method, including the sampling procedure, the measurement of dependent and independent variables and the methodology used. Section4shows and discusses the results, and finally, Section5presents the conclusions.

LITERATURE REVIEW AND HYPOTHESES DEVELOPMENT

The variables most widely used in the literature to describe the impact of corporate governance on ESG performance are related to board size, board gender diversity, the number of board meetings per year, board compensation, and the score of ESG controversies. In the sub-sections below, we develop our hypotheses for each of these characteristics of corporate governance.

Board Size

Board size has mostly been studied as to its relationship to firm performance. Empirical studies can be classified into two categories: a first stream of research is in favour of smaller boards, whereas a second school of thought advocates larger boards. Since the firms in our sample are listed, and are therefore large and complex financial institutions that work in a context of intense regulation, we expect that larger boards will be more efficient, especially in terms of workload and responsibility allocation, and of greater diversity in terms of stakeholder representation, when and improving ESG performance (Albitar et al., 2020; Zubeltzu-Jaka et al., 2020; Arayssi et al., 2020). Our hypothesis agrees with the findings of previous studies that show a positive relationship between board size and the breadth of sustainability practices (Baraibar-Diez, & Odriozola, 2019; Harjoto, & Wang, 2020; Albitar et al., 2020). Based on the previous considerations, the following hypothesis is proposed for testing:

Hypothesis 1. *Board size affects positively the ESG performance.*

Board Meetings

For the number of board meetings per year, which is usually used as a proxy for the level of board activity and board diligence (Baraibar-Diez, & Odriozola, 2019; Bravo, & Reguera-Alvarado, 2019), there is also no consensus about impact on non-financial performance. Since the firms in our sample work in a dynamic business environment, which requires increased meeting frequency to ensure legitimacy, legitimacy theory provides the basis for proposing a positive relationship between board meeting frequency and ESG performance. Our hypothesis aligns with the studies that find a positive relationship between the number of board meetings and sustainability practices (Ismail, et al., 2019; Bravo, & Reguera-Alvarado, 2019; García Martín, & Herrero, 2020). Based on the previous considerations, the following hypothesis is tested:

Hypothesis 2. *The number of board meetings affects positively the ESG performance.*

Women on the Board

Interpretations of the relationship between women on the board and ESG performance are connected to the various features of the women themselves. There seems to be a general consensus in the literature regarding the positive impact of female directors on sustainability performance. More in detail, women on boards positively impact the firm's charitable contributions (Bettinelli et al., 2019; Furlotti et al., 2019; Abd Rahman et al., 2019), apprehension for climate change (Birindelli, et al., 2019) and reputation-based CSR measures (Ajaz, et al., 2020). Similarly, many studies find that board gender diversity increases the extent of social and environmental reporting and decreases environmental lawsuits (Yuan et al., 2019; Peng, 2020). A likely explanation of these inconsistent results could be the presence of a non-linear relationship between board gender diversity and social and environmental performance. Based on their findings, some studies such those of (Birindelli et al., 2019; Furlotti et al., 2019; Ajaz et al., 2020; Peng, 2020) point out that a high level of presence of women on the board improve the ESG performance. In consideration of this evidence, we advance the following hypothesis:

Hypothesis 3. *I high level of gender diversity affects positively the ESG performance*

Executive Compensation

The provision of ESG based sustainable compensation policy is likely to play a critical role in motivating corporate executives to undertake carbon initiatives, which can in turn enhance both organizational legitimacy and market value. As part of sustainable corporate strategies, corporations are increasingly using sustainable compensation policy to motivate executives to pursue social and environmental projects. Empirically, Baraibar-Diez et al., (2019); Eklund, (2019); Haque, & Ntim,. (2020) find that sustainable compensation schemes improve the ESG performance. We argue, therefore, that in the presence of a sustainable compensation policy, the board of directors and the compensation committee of the board might be in a better position to evaluate the environmental, social and governance attributes of a firm to design a more effective which may enhance corporate carbon performance. Therefore, any symbolic ESG compensation policy, without requiring explicit guidelines and mandatory emission reduction targets, might enhance process-oriented ESG performance of the firm (Westling, & Mazhari, 2019; Baraibar-Diez et al., 2019). Thus, we advance the following hypothesis:

Hypothesis 4.: *Executive compensation affects positively the ESG performance*

ESG Controversies

ESG score is traditionally seen as a tool to influence stakeholders. The topic of the ESG controversies related to environmental, social and governance issues was investigated in the literature because of the assumed negative impact that the ESG problems or weaknesses may have on the corporate financial results and the need to deal with them (Iamandi et al., 2018; Markopoulos et al., 2020; Li et al., 2020). The more a company is seen as virtuous, the more likely it is to be appreciated by consumers, employees, and investors. Most importantly, when such virtues are disclosed by external sources such as the media, they build both reputation and credibility (Javedt et al., 2020). The ESG controversies are usually based on public or media disclosure of ESG-related corporate scandals, Utz, (2019); Aouadi, & Marsat, (2018) interestingly found a negative impact of ESG controversies over the firm ESG performance. Taking as a whole, one could expect the following hypothesis.

Hypothesis 5.: *ESG controversies have a negative impact ESG performance*

RESEARCH METHODOLOGY

Sample Selection and Data Sources

Our initial sample was based on the availability of ESG data in the Thomson Reuters Asset4 database and Thomson Reuters Eikon. We started with all the available sample of 35000 firm-year observations from nonfinancial firms listed on the main stock exchanges of 60 countries included in the panel A of table 1. We then removed 4960 observations with missing firm-level data relating to the dependent or independent variables used in our explanatories models. Our final sample is based on an unbalanced panel dataset consisting of 31040 firm-year observations from 5500 listed firms, covering a period of 16 years (2002–2017). Table 1 shows the annual- and country-wise distribution of the sample. We used the Asset4 dataset and the Thomson Reuters Eikon to collect ESG score and corporate governance data. The ASSET4 database from Thomson Reuters is utilized in our research because it is readily available for many investors and scholars.

Dependent Variable

To test our hypotheses, we used data on ESG performance (ESG SCORE) from Asset4. This score is based on three dimensions: environmental, social and corporate governance. ESG performance measures a company's capacity to reduce environmental emissions, to efficiently use natural resources in the production

Table 1. Sample distribution

Firms	Number of observations per country	Percent (%) per country
Panel A. Distribution of the sample by country		
Argentina	4	0,01%
Australia	2242	7,22%
Austria	127	0,41%
Bahrain	2	0,01%
Belgium	125	0,40%
Bermuda	510	1,64%
Brazil	225	0,72%
Canada	2103	6,77%
Chile	92	0,30%
China	413	1,33%
Colombia	35	0,11%
Cyprus	15	0,05%
Czech	20	0,06%
Denmark	275	0,89%
Egypt	33	0,11%
Finland	301	0,97%
France	792	2,55%
Germany	490	1,58%
Greece	64	0,21%
Hong Kong	425	1,37%
Hungary	27	0,09%
India	514	1,65%
Indonesia	226	0,73%
Ireland	298	0,96%
Italy	195	0,63%
Japan	3180	10,24%
Jordan	7	0,02%
Kazakhstan	8	0,03%
Kuwait	23	0,07%
Luxembourg	74	0,24%
Malaysia	348	1,12%
Malta	2	0,01%
Mauritius	10	0,03%
Mexico	127	0,41%

continued on following page

Table 1. Continued

Firms	Number of observations per country	Percent (%) per country
Morocco	1	0,00%
Netherlands	424	1,36%
New Zealand	195	0,63%
Nigeria	4	0,01%
Norway	153	0,49%
Oman	16	0,05%
Peru	37	0,12%
Philippines	120	0,39%
Poland	171	0,55%
Portugal	81	0,26%
Saudi Arabia	8	0,03%
Qatar	12	0,04%
Singapore	365	1,17%
South Africa	644	2,08%
South Korea	256	0,83%
Spain	428	1,38%
Sri Lanka	8	0,03%
Sweden	554	1,78%
Switzerlan	627	2,02%
Taiwan	783	2,52%
Thailand	152	0,49%
Turkey	56	0,18%
United Arab Emirates	24	0,08%
United Kingdom	2780	8,95%
United Stated	9804	31,63%
Zimbabway	5	0,02%
Total	31040	100,00%
Panel B. Distribution of the sample by geographic area		
Africa	688	2,217%
America	12448	40,103%
Asia	6873	22.142%
Australia	2437	7,851%
Europe	8594	27,686%
Total	31040	100,00%

processes and to support the research and development of eco-efficient products and services. Social performance measures a company's capacity to generate trust and loyalty in its workforce, to respect the fundamental conventions on human rights, to be a good citizen, to protect public health, to respect business ethics and to create value-added products and services.

Following the literature Dalal, & Thaker, (2019); Eliwa et al., (2019); Lopez de Silanes et al., (2019) our study measures the level of ESG performance by calculating the arithmetic mean of the three scores: social, environmental and corporate governance. The overall ESG SCORE is expressed as a percentage ranging from 0 to 100 percent. In an attempt to capture the impact of board characteristics on ESG performance with time for the effects to appear and lessen endogeneity problems, governance variables of any year are related to the ESG measure of the following year.

Independent Variables

The independent variables included in our econometric models are the board size, the share of women on the board of directors, executive compensation, number of board meetings per year and the ESG controversies score.

The next section will test the hypotheses regarding the effect of the board characteristics on the ESG SCORE, using panel data analysis. We estimate the following models to measure the relationship between ESG performance and independent variables:

Table 2. A summary of the measurement and the expected relationship with ESGSCORE

Variable	Measurement	Expected sign with ESG SCORE
ESG performance (ESGSCORE)	This score is based on three dimensions: environmental, social and corporate governance	Dependent variable
Board size (BOARDS)	Total number of directors on the bank's board	Positive
Board meetings (BOARDM)	Number of board meetings per year	Positive
Gender diversity (GENDERD)	Total number of women on the board of directors divided by the total number of board members	Positive
Executive Compensation (ECOMPENS)	Total compensation (in USD) as paid to all senior executives as reported by the firm.	Positive
ESG Controversies (ESGCONTR)	ESG controversies score	Negative

$$ESGSCORE\ it = \beta 0 + \beta 1\ BOARDS + \beta 2\ BOARDM + \beta 3\ GENDERD + \beta 4\ ECOMPENS + \beta 5\ ESGCONTR + \varepsilon$$

EMPIRICAL RESULTS AND DISCUSSION

Descriptive Statistics

The Panel A of table 3 illustrates the descriptive statistics for both the dependent and independent variables. The descriptive statistics table includes the minimum, maximum, mean and standard deviation. The average level of ESG performance (ESG SCORE) of firm analysed is 51,4%, with a maximum equal to 98%. This reveals that the firms' sustainability performance for the period 2002–2017 was very satisfactory by the standards of the score definition. On the contrary, the average number meetings of boards seem inadequate, considering that some firm boards have no meeting per year (the minimum value is equal to zero). Similarly, the women mass (the proportion of female gender on the board) reaches an average value of (10.4%) and the maximum value is 100%, seems it still low but suggesting that there are firms of which board members are all women. In addition, executive

Table 3. Summary statistics of ESG SCORE and explanatory variables

Panel A. Descriptive statistics						
Variable	**Obs**	**Mean**	**Std. Dev.**	**Min**	**Max**	
esgscore	31040	51.4273	17.90952	6.785546	98.01675	
boards	31040	10.02432	3.305228	1	39	
boardm	31040	7.528337	3.824497	0	37.35	
genderd	31040	10.39885	12.28903	0	100	
ecompens	31040	1.28e+07	7.50e+07	500000	9.33e+09	
esgcontr	31040	49.26388	21.55324	.08726	87.5	
Panel B. Metrix of correlation						
	esgscore	boards	boardm	genderd	tcompens	esgcontr
esgscore	1.0000					
boards	0.3334	1.0000				
boardm	0.4905	0.0202	1.0000			
genderd	0.2863	0.0607	0.1776	1.0000		
ecompens	0.0041	-0.0038	-0.0040	-0.0092	1.0000	
esgcontr	-0.3368	-0.1903	-0.2183	-0.0937	0.0004	1.0000

compensation values range from 500000 dollars to 9.33e+ dollars, with a mean value of 1.28e+07 and a standard deviation of 7.50e+07. It is also evident that the mean value of ESG controversies is 49%, with a standard deviation of 21,5%.

The correlation matrix (Panel B Table 3) highlights very important relationships between the main variables of the study. More specifically, ESG SCORE is found to be positively associated with board size, number of meetings and gender diversity. These relationships show that more ethical and responsible firms tend to appoint more women to their boards and more frequently number of meeting of board of directors dedicated solely to sustainability. Interestingly, a high proportion of women on the board are positively associated with bank board meeting, suggesting that firms of which boards are served by more female directors have a larger number of meetings per year. Contrary, ESG controversies are negatively related to the firm's board size and number of meeting per year.

This table shows the summary statistics of ESG SCORE and explanatory variables. The number of firm-year observations is 31040 for all the variables. Data source: Thomson Reuters Asset4 and Datastream. Significant correlation coefficients are indicated by the usual significance levels: ***, 1%; **, 5%; *, 10%.

Regression Results and Discussion

Table 4 shows the estimation results of Equation (1) which can address our hypotheses relating to the impact of board composition, Activity and Compensation on ESG performance of a sample of 31040 observations from 60 countries. Hypothesis 1 predicts that a board size has a positive effect on a firm's ESG performance. In our Model (Table 4), BOARDS is significant and positively related to ESG performance for the full set of sample and for all the different geographic area. When interactions are involved, the final sign of the effect of a predictor is immediately readable from an estimation table. Indeed, the coefficients related to the BOARDS present significant effects an increasing board size exerting a positive effect on ESG SCORE (Baraibar-Diez, & Odriozola, 2019; Harjoto, & Wang, 2020; Albitar et al., 2020). It is more likely that larger boards are served by directors with different skills and attitudes, including directors characterized by a strong propensity towards a culture of sustainability. Therefore, this result does corroborate Hypothesis 1.

Hypothesis 2 predicts a relationship between independent number of meetings board and ESG performance, even though the sign is certain. In other terms, according to existing literature, the number of meetings positively affects the ESG performance. Our results show a positive relationship: the coefficient related to BOARDM is positive and significant in all geographic areas. This result is in line with the studies of (Ismail, et al., 2019; Bravo, & Reguera-Alvarado, 2019; García Martín, & Herrero, 2020). It is likely that an excessive number of meetings of board of directors act as improving components increasing the firm's ESG performance. Therefore, this result does corroborate Hypothesis 2.

Hypothesis 3 predicts a positive relationship between gender diversity and ESG performance. In this case, the hypothesis seems to be confirmed. In all Models presented in the (Table 4), GENDERD is significant and positively related to ESG SCORE. Hence, consistent with correlation results (see Table 3), the econometric model indicates that the high shares of female in the board are associated with better sustainability performance. This positive effect is broadly consistent with the findings of (Birindelli et al., 2019; Furlotti et al., 2019; Ajaz et al., 2020; Peng, 2020). It is more likely that higher share of gender diversity are served by female with different skills and attitudes, including directors characterized by a strong propensity towards a culture of sustainability. Therefore, this result does corroborate Hypothesis 3.

On the contrary, we reject Hypothesis 4, which predicts a positive relationship between the executive compensation and the extent of sustainability performance. In our regression results (Models Full set, America and Australia), ECOMPENS shows a positive coefficient, but it is never significant for these contexts. For the area of African, Asian and European countries, the hypothesis 4 is verified very strongly (Westling, & Mazhari, 2019; Baraibar-Diez et al., 2019).

Table 4. Results of regression models of ESG SCORE

esgscore	Full set	Panel regression models of ESG SCORE by geographic area				
		Africa	**America**	**Asia**	**Australia**	**EU countries**
boards	62.95*** (1.520443)	11.35*** (1.728296)	38.98*** (1.723875)	2.65*** (.1080139)	38.55*** (3.395974)	41.67*** (1.65843)
boardm	91.32*** (1.941201)	16.55*** (2.285925)	51.86*** (1.753598)	14.55*** (.6409793)	32.63*** (1.94613)	55.26*** (1.937374)
genderd	40.22*** (.2610001)	2.76*** (.0913684)	18.07*** (.1890879)	79.01*** (1.125829)	6.84*** (.1102734)	5.71*** (.0651734)
ecompens	0.09 (9.82e-11)	4.53*** (1.08e-06)	0.30 (3.20e-10)	3.73*** (1.28e-07)	0.82 (6.42e-08)	9.44*** (1.67e-07)
esgcontr	-38.59*** (-.1464147)	-5.34*** (-.1226537)	-30.76*** (-.1758814)	-6.81*** (-.0519039)	-8.30*** (-.1070479)	-19.61*** (-.1251948)
N. of obs	31040	688	12448	6873	2437	8594
F(5, 31034)	4268.29	104.60	1572.39	2360.10	771.94	1365.36
Prob > F	0.0000	0.0000	0.0000	0.0000	0.0000	0.0000
R-squared	0.4075	0.4340	0.3872	0.6321	0.6136	0.4429
Adj R-squared	0.4074	0.4299	0.3870	0.6319	0.6128	0.4425

Finally, Hypothesis 5 is verified very strongly: the verification of the ESG controversies seems to negatively impact a firm's ESG performance (see Table 4). The ESG controversies are usually based on public or media disclosure of ESG-related corporate scandals, Aouadi, & Marsat, (2018); Utz, (2019) interestingly found a negative impact of ESG controversies over the firm ESG performance. This occurs because the bad news of such controversies is critical in ESG issues]. Finally, although it does refer to the ESG controversies discourages firms to improve the ESG performance or to increase the efficiency and allow deeper focus in specific areas. Therefore, the same Results are highlighted for all geographic areas, (Aouadi, & Marsat, 2018; Iamandi et al., 2018; Utz, 2019; Markopoulos et al., 2020; Li et al., 2020), the hypothesis 5 is verified very strongly.

This table shows the results regression for all set of a sample of 31040 observation and those by geographic areas. Data source: Thomson Reuters Asset4 and Datastream. Significant coefficients are indicated by the usual significance levels: ***, 1%; **, 5%; *, 10%

CONCLUSION

Based on prior literature demonstrating that boards play a key monitoring role in financial institutions, this study investigates the relationship between board composition (size, activity, gender diversity and compensation) and sustainability performance in a large sample of 31040 observations for 5500 listed firms for the period 2002–2016.

Main findings reveal that size, activity, gender diversity and compensation are positively impacts a firm's ESG performance for all models regression for the whole the sample full set either for each geographic area. For this reason, we support the critical perspective that emphasizes board characteristics, such as board size, number of meetings, share of women in the board and executive compensation are very important to enhancing a firm's ESG performance. The empirical results of this research present a significant effect of ESG controversies on the ESG performance. This shows that the importance of this variable on ESG performance would be even more pronounced if the region were to implement stronger corporate governance measures. Since this variable is significant in forming a good reputation and encouraging the firm to be more involved in societal, environmental and governance activities and performance, firms should strive to increase their ESG score.

This study has important implications, especially for managers and regulators. From a managerial point of view, our work suggests that managers and CEOs should pay more attention to the number of meetings per year, the board size and gender diversity of their boardrooms. To enhance sustainability performance, it is important to appoint a number of women to the board and ensure a high number of meetings. Since larger boards positively influence ESG performance, firm managers should select both male and female directors to increase board size. Contrary, our study suggests evidence to support the effect of executive compensation but not for all geographic areas as a strategic tool that demonstrates the firm's strong commitment toward ESG performance.

Our study did not investigate the CRS committee, the emission score or environmental innovation, but future research could go in this direction. Recent empirical evidence for non-financial firms shows that a CSR committee is more effective in improving a firm's corporate social responsibility when it is characterized by a larger proportion of independent directors, by a female chair and a smaller size.

REFERENCES

Abd Rahman, I. M., Jamil, N. N., & Ismail, K. N. I. K. (2019). Does Political Connection Moderate Women Directors' Effect on CSR Disclosure? Evidence from Malaysia. *Asian Journal of Accounting and Governance, 11*.

Ajaz, A., Shenbei, Z., & Sarfraz, M. (2020). Delineating the influence of boardroom gender diversity on corporate social responsibility, financial performance, and reputation. *LogForum, 16*(1).

Albitar, K., Hussainey, K., Kolade, N., & Gerged, A. M. (2020). ESG disclosure and firm performance before and after IR. *International Journal of Accounting & Information Management*.

Alessandrini, F., & Jondeau, E. (2020). Optimal Strategies for ESG Portfolios. *Swiss Finance Institute Research Paper*, (20-21).

Aouadi, A., & Marsat, S. (2018). Do ESG controversies matter for firm value? Evidence from international data. *Journal of Business Ethics*, *151*(4), 1027–1047. doi:10.1007/s10551-016-3213-8

Arayssi, M., Jizi, M., & Tabaja, H. H. (2020). *The impact of board composition on the level of ESG disclosures in GCC countries*. Sustainability Accounting, Management and Policy Journal. doi:10.1108/SAMPJ-05-2018-0136

Armstrong, A. (2020). Ethics and ESG. *Australasian Accounting. Business and Finance Journal*, *14*(3), 6–17.

Baraibar-Diez, E., & Odriozola, D, M. (2019). CSR Committees and Their Effect on ESG Performance in UK, France, Germany, and Spain. *Sustainability*, *11*(18), 5077. doi:10.3390/su11185077

Baraibar-Diez, E., Odriozola, M. D., & Fernández Sánchez, J. L. (2019). Sustainable compensation policies and its effect on environmental, social, and governance scores. *Corporate Social Responsibility and Environmental Management*, *26*(6), 1457–1472. doi:10.1002/csr.1760

Beretta, V., Demartini, M. C., & Trucco, S. (2020). Tone at Top in Integrated Reporting: The Role of Non-Financial Performance. In *Non-Financial Disclosure and Integrated Reporting: Practices and Critical Issues*. Emerald Publishing Limited. doi:10.1108/S1479-351220200000034009

Bettinelli, C., Del Bosco, B., & Giachino, C. (2019). Women on boards in family firms: What we know and what we need to know. In *The Palgrave handbook of heterogeneity among family firms* (pp. 201–228). Palgrave Macmillan. doi:10.1007/978-3-319-77676-7_9

Birindelli, G., Dell'Atti, S., Iannuzzi, A. P., & Savioli, M. (2018). Composition and activity of the board of directors: Impact on ESG performance in the banking system. *Sustainability (Basel)*, *10*(12), 4699. doi:10.3390/su10124699

Birindelli, G., Iannuzzi, A. P., & Savioli, M. (2019). The impact of women leaders on environmental performance: Evidence on gender diversity in banks. *Corporate Social Responsibility and Environmental Management*, *26*(6), 1485–1499. doi:10.1002/csr.1762

Bravo, F., & Reguera-Alvarado, N. (2019). Sustainable development disclosure: Environmental, social, and governance reporting and gender diversity in the audit committee. *Business Strategy and the Environment*, *28*(2), 418–429. doi:10.1002/bse.2258

Castellanos, J. D., & George, B. (2020). Boardroom leadership: The board of directors as a source of strategic leadership. *Economics and Business Review*, *6*(1), 103–119. doi:10.18559/ebr.2020.1.5

Dalal, K. K., & Thaker, N. (2019). ESG and corporate financial performance: A panel study of Indian companies. *IUP Journal of Corporate Governance*, *18*(1), 44–59.

Eklund, M. A. (2019). Compensation for Non-financial Performance (ESG Scores). In *Fairness of CEO Compensation* (pp. 67–74). Springer. doi:10.1007/978-3-030-33554-0_4

Eliwa, Y., Aboud, A., & Saleh, A. (2019). ESG practices and the cost of debt: Evidence from EU countries. *Critical Perspectives on Accounting*, 102097.

Furlotti, K., Mazza, T., Tibiletti, V., & Triani, S. (2019). Women in top positions on boards of directors: Gender policies disclosed in Italian sustainability reporting. *Corporate Social Responsibility and Environmental Management*, *26*(1), 57–70. doi:10.1002/csr.1657

García Martín, C. J., & Herrero, B. (2020). Do board characteristics affect environmental performance? A study of EU firms. *Corporate Social Responsibility and Environmental Management*, *27*(1), 74–94. doi:10.1002/csr.1775

Haque, F., & Ntim, C. G. (2020). Executive compensation, sustainable compensation policy, carbon performance and market value. *British Journal of Management*, *31*(3), 525–546. doi:10.1111/1467-8551.12395

Harjoto, M. A., & Wang, Y. (2020). Board of Directors Network Centrality and Environmental, Social and Governance (ESG) Performance. *Corporate Governance: An International Journal of Business in Society [Forthcoming 2020]*.

Hedqvist, L., & Larsson, A. (2020). *ESG or Financial Performance-Does It Have to be a Choice?: A Regression Analysis of Thomson Reuters ESG scores and Financial Performance in Sweden and the UK.*

Hübel, B., & Scholz, H. (2020). Integrating sustainability risks in asset management: The role of ESG exposures and ESG ratings. *Journal of Asset Management*, *21*(1), 52–69. doi:10.1057/s41260-019-00139-z

Iamandi, I. E., Constantin, L. G., Munteanu, S. M., & Cernat-Gruici, B. (2019). Mapping the ESG Behavior of European Companies. A Holistic Kohonen Approach. *Sustainability (Basel)*, *11*(12), 3276. doi:10.3390/su11123276

Ismail, A. M., Adnan, Z. H. M., Clark, C., & Said, J. (2019). Impact of Board Capabilities on Environmental and Social Governance (ESG) Practices: Evidence from Malaysia. *International Journal of Business & Management Science*, *9*(2).

Jackson, G., Bartosch, J., Avetisyan, E., Kinderman, D., & Knudsen, J. S. (2020). Mandatory non-financial disclosure and its influence on CSR: An international comparison. *Journal of Business Ethics*, *162*(2), 323–342. doi:10.1007/s10551-019-04200-0

Jahmane, A., & Gaies, B. (2020). Corporate social responsibility, financial instability and corporate financial performance: Linear, non-linear and spillover effects–The case of the CAC 40 companies. *Finance Research Letters, 34*, 101483. doi:10.1016/j.frl.2020.101483

Javed, M., Rashid, M. A., Hussain, G., & Ali, H. Y. (2020). The effects of corporate social responsibility on corporate reputation and firm financial performance: Moderating role of responsible leadership. *Corporate Social Responsibility and Environmental Management, 27*(3), 1395–1409. doi:10.1002/csr.1892

Kiriu, T., & Nozaki, M. (2020). A Text Mining Model to Evaluate Firms' ESG Activities: An Application for Japanese Firms. *Asia-Pacific Financial Markets, 27*(4), 1–12. doi:10.1007/s10690-020-09309-1

Li, P., Zhou, R., & Xiong, Y. (2020). Can ESG Performance Affect Bond Default Rate? Evidence from China. *Sustainability (Basel), 12*(7), 2954. doi:10.3390/su12072954

Lopez de Silanes, F., McCahery, J. A., & Pudschedl, P. (2019). *ESG performance and disclosure: A cross-country analysis*. European Corporate Governance Institute-Law.

Markopoulos, E., Kirane, I. S., Gann, E. L., & Vanharanta, H. (2020, April). A democratic, green ocean management framework for Environmental, Social and Governance (ESG) compliance. In *International Conference on Human Interaction and Emerging Technologies* (pp. 21-33). Springer, Cham. 10.1007/978-3-030-44267-5_4

Merendino, A., & Melville, R. (2019). The board of directors and firm performance: empirical evidence from listed companies. *Corporate Governance: The international journal of business in society.*

Ng, T. H., Lye, C. T., Chan, K. H., Lim, Y. Z., & Lim, Y. S. (2020). Sustainability in Asia: The Roles of Financial Development in Environmental, Social and Governance (ESG) Performance. *Social Indicators Research, 150*(1), 1–28. doi:10.1007/s11205-020-02288-w

Peng, C. W. (2020). The role of business strategy and CEO compensation structure in driving corporate social responsibility: Linkage towards a sustainable development perspective. *Corporate Social Responsibility and Environmental Management, 27*(2), 1028–1039. doi:10.1002/csr.1863

Plastun, A., Makarenko, I., Khomutenko, L., & Shcherbakov, P. (2020). SDGs and ESG disclosure regulation: Is there an impact? Evidence from Top-50 world economies. *Problems and Perspectives in Management, 18*(2), 231–245. doi:10.21511/ppm.18(2).2020.20

Qa'dan, M. B. A., & Suwaidan, M. S. (2019). Board composition, ownership structure and corporate social responsibility disclosure: The case of Jordan. *Social Responsibility Journal.*

Rajesh, R. (2020). Exploring the sustainability performances of firms using environmental, social, and governance scores. *Journal of Cleaner Production, 247*, 119600. doi:10.1016/j.jclepro.2019.119600

Utz, S. (2019). Corporate scandals and the reliability of ESG assessments: Evidence from an international sample. *Review of Managerial Science, 13*(2), 483–511. doi:10.1007/s11846-017-0256-x

Westling, M., & Mazhari, M. (2019). *Sustainability and senior executive compensation: A study of the relationship between sustainability and senior executive compensation in the Nordics.*

Wong, W. C., Batten, J. A., Mohamed-Arshad, S. B., Nordin, S., & Adzis, A. A. (2020). Does ESG certification add firm value? *Finance Research Letters*, 101593.

Xie, J., Nozawa, W., Yagi, M., Fujii, H., & Managi, S. (2019). Do environmental, social, and governance activities improve corporate financial performance? *Business Strategy and the Environment, 28*(2), 286–300. doi:10.1002/bse.2224

Yuan, Y., Tian, G., Lu, L. Y., & Yu, Y. (2019). CEO ability and corporate social responsibility. *Journal of Business Ethics, 157*(2), 391–411. doi:10.1007/s10551-017-3622-3

Zubeltzu-Jaka, E., Álvarez-Etxeberria, I., & Ortas, E. (2020). The effect of the size of the board of directors on corporate social performance: A meta-analytic approach. *Corporate Social Responsibility and Environmental Management, 27*(3), 1361–1374. doi:10.1002/csr.1889

Chapter 11
Sustainability in Transformational and Transactional Leadership:
Turkish Textile Industry Example

Korhan Arun
https://orcid.org/0000-0001-7494-9591
Namık Kemal Üniversitesi, Turkey

ABSTRACT

The relationship between leadership and sustainability in organizations is a topic of significant interest, focusing on the impact of transformational and transactional leadership styles on organizational sustainability. This study emphasized the importance of transformational and transactional leadership in driving sustainable practices and outcomes, addressing the gap between leadership styles and sustainability. Path analysis results show that transformational and transactional leadership styles significantly influence sustainability. However, interestingly, transformational leadership decreases sustainability expenditures, and both leadership styles increase nitrogen emissions. The relationship between transformational leadership and negative outcomes for sustainability needs to be directly addressed in the available literature. In the textile industry in developing countries, both transformational and transactional leadership and environmental sustainability have negative correlations, and transformational leaders may decrease environmental expenditures.

DOI: 10.4018/979-8-3693-1846-1.ch011

INTRODUCTION

The topic of the relationship between Leadership and sustainability in organizations has garnered significant interest in recent times. According to Metcalf and Benn (2013), Leadership plays a critical role in driving sustainable practices and outcomes. While the literature suggests that effective Leadership is crucial for promoting sustainability and achieving sustainable outcomes in organizations, there is a dearth of studies that directly address this relationship. As a result, this chapter aims to bridge the gap between transformational and transactional leadership styles on organizational sustainability. It delves into the nuances of these leadership styles and their impact on sustainability outcomes, providing a more comprehensive understanding of the relationship between Leadership and sustainability.

Many studies found a relationship between transformational Leadership and sustainability. Kafetzopoulos and Gotzamani (2022) studied the effect of leadership styles on firms' sustainable performance. They found that transformational and transactional leadership styles significantly influence social and environmental sustainability performance. Moreover, Jiang et al. (2017) explored the impact of transformational leadership on employees' sustainable performance. They suggested that transformational Leadership positively influences organizational citizenship behavior, which, in turn, contributes to sustainable performance. Muralidharan and Pathak (2018) studied the role of transformational Leadership in promoting sustainability. On the other hand, Quinn and Dalton (2009)studied the need for Leadership that focuses on sustainability, but they should have focused on a particular style.

Bass et al. (2003) proposed that transactional Leadership predicts short-term outcomes, while transformational Leadership exhibits stronger predictions over a longer period. On the other hand, Gorgulu (2020)mentions that transactional leaders aim to increase productivity through effective reward mechanisms. While not explicitly focused on sustainability, rewards and incentives can motivate employees to engage in sustainable behaviors. So, the impact of transactional Leadership on sustainability may vary depending on the specific context and organizational factors. Further research is needed to explore the direct relationship between transactional leadership style and organizational sustainability outcomes.

HYPOTHESES DEVELOPMENT

Proxies of Environmental Sustainability in Organizations: Sustainability Expenditures and Measurement of Nitrogen Emissions

Wang et al. (2022) considered the yearly increase in environmental protection spending as a proxy variable for environmental protection investment, indicating a potential link between education and environmentally friendly behaviors among CEOs. Moreover, Lu et al. (2020) highlighted the significance of leveraging the synergistic effect of environmental protection investment and technological innovation to promote corporate performance, underscoring the strategic implications of integrating environmental protection expenditure with innovation efforts.

Yang et al. (2020) found that organizational management has a significant positive impact on enterprise environmental protection investment and financial performance, emphasizing the importance of leadership in driving environmental protection expenditure.

The production-based nitrogen emissions of the textile industry have a significant impact on environmental sustainability. This sector faces considerable challenges due to the substantial emissions of sulfur dioxide and nitrogen oxide during the production phases. These emissions can have negative effects on air quality, climate change, and human health. Therefore, it is essential to address these issues and work towards sustainable and eco-friendly production methods in the textile industry.Guo et al. (2023) emphasize the environmental significance of nitrogen emissions in textile manufacturing. Knowledge-based nitrogen management is crucial in mitigating greenhouse gas emissions and reactive nitrogen pollution. Xia et al. (2017) found the significance of this approach for environmental sustainability in agricultural systems. This understanding can be applied to the textile sector, as effective nitrogen control can help lessen negative environmental effects (Qian and colleagues. Qian et al. (2020) examined how textile products affected the environment and stressed the need to evaluate and account for the chemical footprint—including nitrogen emissions—during the production phase of the textile life cycle.

Effects of Transformational Leadership on Environmental Sustainability

The role of leadership in promoting sustainability extends beyond the internal organizational environment. It has been suggested that leadership support can compensate for a lack of clear sustainability goals and direction, emphasizing the crucial role of leadership in driving sustainability strategies (Wolf, 2011). In sustainable competitive advantage, good leadership and effective strategy implementation have been proposed as key factors that can lead corporate environmental activities to sustainable competitive advantage (Amoako, 2019).

Suphattanakul (2017) identified the impact of transformational leadership on organizational performance and its role in creating strategic organizational change, emphasizing its relevance for strategic implementation. Additionally, Schlosser and Volkova (2022) emphasized the alignment of transformational leadership with the greater good, indicating its potential to drive strategic leadership practices that deliver shared value. Transformational leadership has the potential to influence strategic outcomes within firms, and transformational leadership also influences the environmental sustainability outcomes of the firms.

Transformational leadership is in the figure gathered under the so-called four I's. These five I's (Idealized Influence (II), Inspirational Motivation (IM), Intellectual Stimulation (IS), and Individual Attention (IO)) in transformational leadership are effective in environmental sustainability.

Idealized Influence (II) (Attribution and behavior) contains charisma or idealized influence. Idealized Influence, a key component of transformational leadership, has significantly influenced environmental sustainability within organizations (Singh et al., 2020). Furthermore, Zong-Bo et al. (2020) emphasized the role of environmentally specific transformational leaders in acting as role models for employees by demonstrating environmental sustainability ideas and encouraging environmentally friendly actions, which aligns with the concept of idealized influence (Li et al., 2020). As a result, leadership support by transformational leaders, including actively demonstrating the importance of sustainability by managers-attribution, impacts pro-environmental behavior in the workplace, indicating the potential influence of idealized influence on promoting environmental sustainability (Wesselink et al., 2017).

The relationship between Inspirational Motivation (IM) and environmental sustainability has been a topic of interest in the literature. Xenikou and Simosi (2006) emphasized the indirect positive impact of transformational leadership on performance, suggesting its potential influence on environmental sustainability through IM. Additionally, some writers proposed that environmental innovation indirectly impacts sustainable leadership on environmental performance, suggesting the potential contribution of IM to the promotion of environmental innovation and, by extension, sustainability (Cho & Kao, 2022; Iqbal et al., 2021). Additionally, they discovered that transformational leadership has a strong positive impact on organizational commitment, which may use IM to support environmental sustainability (Cho & Kao, 2022). Furthermore, Erat et al. (2020) emphasized the connection between sustainable organizational identity and transformational leadership, suggesting that IM may impact forming organizational values that align with sustainability.

Intellectual Stimulation (IS) means that the manager stimulates employees to become more creative and innovative through, among other things, linguistic guidelines. The intricate and diverse topic of the relationship between individual creativity and environmental sustainability has attracted interest from a wide range of academic fields. Awan et al. (2019) emphasized the critical role of creativity in addressing environmental sustainability, particularly in the context of green innovation. They offer a broadly applicable paradigm that illustrates how creativity fosters green innovation and can positively impact sustainability. This suggests that individual creativity, when integrated into organizational practices, can contribute significantly to environmental sustainability (Souto, 2022). Additionally, Moraru (2021) (Moraru, 2021) highlights the potential link between individual creativity and environmental sustainability, suggesting that creativity can be linked to environmental and economic sustainability and the dimensions of social and human sustainability. In conclusion, Intellectual Stimulation (IS) can positively impact environmental sustainability, highlighting the potential of individual creativity as a driver for sustainable development.

Individual Attention (IO) is about individual attention and seeing the employees. Transformational leaders focus on employees' needs for growth and development by acting as mentors or coaches. In that sense, mentorship plays a crucial role in fostering environmental sustainability within organizations. Reddy et al. (2021) emphasized the importance of peer-to-peer or collaborative mentorship relationships in promoting sustainable practices among employees. Similarly, Erhabor (2018) underscores the integral role of mentorship programs in developing effective environmental leaders, indicating the potential of mentorship in cultivating individuals who can drive sustainability initiatives within organizations. These references collectively suggest that mentorship, particularly in peer-to-peer or collaborative relationships, is instrumental in influencing employee adoption of sustainability practices.

Furthermore, the literature in this chapter suggests that transformational leadership can indirectly affect organizational performance through various mediating variables. For example, Çop and friends (2021) emphasized that transformational leaders provide environmentally sustainable results by engaging employees in both the organization's activities and the environment. Moreover, Suliman et al. (2023) found that transformational leadership increases the total environmental sustainability performance of the organizations; however, they did not specify the environmental performance indicators.

H1: Transformational leadership increases environmental sustainability in organizations. More clearly, TL increases environmental protection expenditures and decreases Production-based nitrogen emissions in organizations.

Effects of Transactional Leadership on Environmental Sustainability

Transactional leadership has been the subject of extensive research concerning its impact on organizational performance and employee behavior. The findings of Kafetzopoulos and Gotzamani (2022) indicate that this leadership style has a positive influence on talent work motivation and performance. However, Khan and Jantan (2022) discovered that transactional leadership has adverse effects on innovative work behavior. Moreover, Chủan's (2022) research revealed that the use of this leadership style results in negative consequences for non-financial performance in the multi-level marketing industry. These studies emphasize the importance of considering the pros and cons of transactional leadership carefully.Additionally, Tanveer et al. Tanveer et al. (2021) explored the impact of environmental sustainability and financial resource utilization on firms' financial performance, indicating the mediating role of leadership styles, including transactional leadership. Additionally, some authors discovered that transactional leadership enhanced the link between stress and unfavorable conduct, lessening the environment's impact on workplaces (Yao et al., 2014).

The references provided in this chapter collectively suggest that the effects of transactional leadership on environmental sustainability and organizational performance are complex, with both positive and negative impacts. The influence of transactional leadership on employee behavior, talent motivation, and organizational performance varies across different contexts and industries.

H2: Transactional leadership increases environmental sustainability in organizations. More clearly, TL increases environmental protection expenditures and decreases Production-based nitrogen emissions in organizations.

METHODOLOGY

Sample and Measures

To measure these relationships, the structural equation model is used for the path model of hypotheses. Production-based nitrogen emissions (kg/capita) data was gathered from the Sustainable Development Report 2023 (www.sdgindex.org). Reactive nitrogen is released while manufacturing goods imported or used locally. Reactive nitrogen is associated with emissions to the atmosphere of ammonia, nitrogen oxides, nitrous oxide, and reactive nitrogen that may be exported to aquatic environments. These pollutants can harm human health and the environment (Sustainable et al., 2023).

Environmental protection expenditure by domains, 2013-2021, is gathered from TurkStat, Environmental Protection Expenditure Statistics, 2021, from TUIK (Turkish Statistical Institute) (TUIK, 2023a). A leadership survey is gathered from the highest manager of each textile company from the Thrace region in Turkey. The textile industry has the fourth highest share by sales value of the four highest industries in Turkey (TUIK, 2023b).

Due to its strategic location at the crossroads of several regions, including the Middle East, Asia, North Africa, Eastern Europe, and Russia, the Turkish textile industry is significant (Kaya et al., 2019). The industry primarily focuses on labor and exports, with small and medium-sized businesses making up more than 90% of the sector (SMEs)(Divrik & Baykal, 2023). However, the sector needs help with environmental sustainability, energy management, nitrogen emissions, energy consumption, and pricing. However, the sector needs help concerning environmental sustainability, energy management, and nitrogen emissions, as well as energy consumption and pricing (Alkaya & Demirer, 2015; Divrik & Baykal, 2023; Hasanbeigi & Price, 2012). Despite experiencing periods of recession, the Turkish textile industry's economic significance is seen in its contribution to the country's economy (Bilgin et al., 2011; Duran & Temíz Dínç, 2016). Global occurrences like the COVID-19 epidemic have also affected the sector, causing changes in manufacturing and economic problems (Sutrisno, 2022). Analysis has been done on the sector's development, productivity, and competitiveness, which reflects how dynamic the Turkish textile industry is (Başkol, 2018; Karabag et al., 2014) (Karabag et al., 2013; Başkol, 2018; Alvan & Ghosh, 2010). In addition, research and concern have focused on the industry's effects on the environment, waste management, and energy conservation, underscoring the necessity of sustainable practices and technological developments (Gümüş & Akbal, 2011; Qingfen et al., 2023; Tunc et al., 2016). The textile industry's importance to the Turkish economy and beyond is further highlighted by its position in trade, intra-industry dynamics, and effects on other sectors like tourism and agriculture (Jain, 2022; Permata Sari et al., 2019; Tokel et al., 2022).

Moreover, the Thrace Region is the locomotive region of our country's textile and textile product manufacturing, mainly concentrated in the city of Tekirdağ. According to the 2018 SSI database, 488 businesses in the Thrace Region are active in the textiles industry, and 56,799 people are employed within the industry (Invest in Trakya-Tekirdağ, Edirne Kirklareli, 2023). The online survey was sent to 472 textile manufacturing firms; 341 returned, but 322 were found suitable for the analysis. Turkish validated scale by Demir and Okan (2008) of transformational and transactional leadership survey is used for the research. In this version of the scale, transformational leadership has 12 questions, and transactional Leadership has 10 questions. Transformational Leadership has sub-dimensions: idealized influence

Table 1. Correlations

	(1)	(2)	(3)	(4)	(5)	(6)	R square adjusted
1. MBE active	1						0.234
2. MBE passive	0.096	1					0.515
3. Production-based nitrogen _emissions	0.056	0.01	1				0.003
4. Transactional leadership	0.486	0.719	0.037	1			
5. Transformational Leadership	0.012	0.021	0.089	0.032	1		1
6. environmental protection _ expenditure	0.02	0.074	-0.311	0.126	-0.018	1	0.01

(attribute), idealized influence (behavior), inspirational motivation, intellectual stimulation, and individualized consideration. Transactional Leadership has three subdimensions, namely contingent rewards, management by exception (active), and management by exception (passive) (Dhammika et al., 2014; Ismail et al., 2010; Yukl & Gardner, 2020).

Table 1 shows the correlations between variables in the model and R square adjusted. An important statistical metric that considers a regression model's number of predictors and offers a more precise evaluation of the model's goodness of fit is the adjusted R-squared (R2). It is especially crucial in regression analysis since it modifies the R-squared value according to the number of predictors, providing a more accurate picture of the percentage of the dependent variable's variance that can be accounted for by the independent variables. The adjusted R-squared value is significant because it can handle the possible problem of overfitting in regression models with several predictors. The adjusted R-squared provides a more realistic assessment of the model's explanatory power by considering the impact of adding predictors and penalizing the inclusion of irrelevant variables, in contrast to the standard R-squared, which tends to increase with more predictors. When used for research and data analysis, a higher adjusted R-squared value means that the model minimizes the risk of overfitting while accounting for the significant factors and better fitting the data. This is essential to guarantee the validity and dependability of regression models, particularly when drawing conclusions or forecasts from the model's output. Thus, to evaluate the reliability and validity of regression models, researchers and analysts can benefit greatly from the modified R-squared, which eventually enhances the accuracy and robustness of statistical studies. Leadership can explain environmental protection expenditures more significantly than production-related nitrogen emissions, based on R^2 corrected values in Table 1 and Figure 1. Thus, transformational and transactional leaders in Turkiye are still more focused on macro management factors, like expenditures, than micro or meso management factors, like production lines.

Figure 1. Path model analysis of the hypothesis model by structural equation modeling

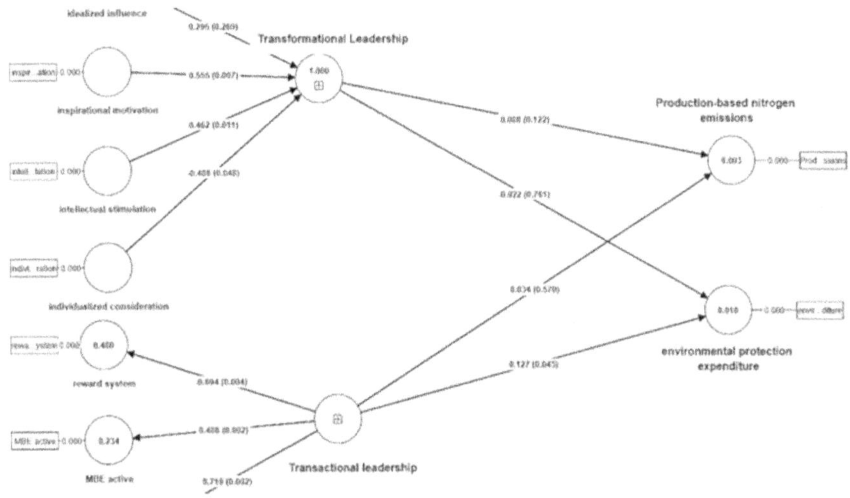

Structural Equation Modeling (SEM) holds significant importance in social sciences research because it analyzes complex relationships among observed and latent variables. The substantive use of SEM in psychology and social sciences highlights its growing importance in empirical research (Anderson & Gerbing, 1988). Moreover, SEM emerged as a key statistical tool in social sciences and medical research, indicating its widespread adoption for improved analysis (Shaheen et al., 2017). Moreover, recent research highlights the wide usage of SEM in social sciences research, particularly in attitudes, behavior, and performance measurement (Al-Qadasi et al., 2021; Ehidiamen et al., 2023). Some authors also discussed the methodological advancements and guidelines for using SEM, such as the updated guidelines for using PLS path modeling in new technology (Ali et al., 2018; Hair, 2017; Henseler et al., 2016). These methodological advancements contribute to refining and standardizing SEM practices in social sciences research. Thus, the application of SEM in exploring and validating performance measurement domains and modeling predictors of environmental sustainability by forming path analysis demonstrates its versatility and relevance in this research.

Table 2 shows the path model results and other statistics.

According to path coefficients, Table 2, only transactional Leadership is effective on the environmental protection expenditure. The path coefficient is 0.127, which proposes that there is a positive relationship between transactional Leadership and environmental protection expenditures. Interestingly, in the textile sector, transformational Leadership is not significantly effective on sustainability (p values are greater than 0.005).

Table 2. Path model results

	Sample mean (M)	Standard deviation (STDEV)	P values	Path coefficients
Transactional Leadership -> Production-based nitrogen _emissions	0.037	0.06	0.57	0.034
Transactional Leadership -> environmental protection _expenditure	**0.117**	**0.063**	**0.043**	**0.127**
Transformational Leadership -> Production-based nitrogen _emissions	0.08	0.057	0.122	0.088
Transformational Leadership -> environmental protection _expenditure	-0.017	0.072	0.761	-0.022

DISCUSSION AND CONCLUSION

Initial analysis of this study shows that transformational Leadership is not significant, and transactional leadership style is partially significant in sustainability. Even if the studies have shown that transformational and transactional leadership approaches positively impact the environmental aspects of firms (Changar & Atan, 2021; Tanveer et al., 2021), our results differ from the literature.

According to a study conducted by Kafetzopoulos and Gotzamani in 2022, there is a significant correlation between transactional leadership and sustainable organizational performance. While the study does not specify the exact environmental factors involved, it suggests that transactional leadership can have a positive effect on sustainability outcomes. In contrast, leaders who focus on environmental transformation can indirectly influence their organizations, as noted by Robertson and Carleton in 2018. Moreover, one study found that the degree of influence of transformational leadership on employees' sustainable performance depends on organizational members' citizenship behavior. This research supports this study's results that in the textile sector in Turkey, transformational leaders have a harmonious passion for the environment; however, influencing employees' voluntary pro-environmental behavior could not be changed easily.

REFERENCES

Al-Qadasi, N., Zhang, G., & Al-Jubari, I. (2021). Attitude of youth towards self-employment: Evidence from university students in Yemen. *PLoS One*, *16*(9), e0257358. doi:10.1371/journal.pone.0257358 PMID:34516592

Ali, F., Rasoolimanesh, S. M., Sarstedt, M., Ringle, C. M., & Ryu, K. (2018). An assessment of the use of partial least squares structural equation modeling (PLS-SEM) in hospitality research. *International Journal of Contemporary Hospitality Management, 30*(1), 514–538. doi:10.1108/IJCHM-10-2016-0568

Alkaya, E., & Demirer, G. N. (2015). Sectoral assessment of the Turkish textile industry for the diffusion of sustainable production approach. *Journal of the Textile Institute, 106*(11), 1212–1225. doi:10.1080/00405000.2014.985880

Amoako, G. K. (2019). A conceptual framework: Corporate environmental management activities and sustainable competitive advantage. *Management of Environmental Quality, 31*(2), 331–347. doi:10.1108/MEQ-09-2019-0187

Anderson, J. C., & Gerbing, D. W. (1988). Structural equation modeling in practice: A review and recommended two-step approach. *Psychological Bulletin, 103*(3), 411–423. doi:10.1037/0033-2909.103.3.411

Awan, U., Sroufe, R., & Kraslawski, A. (2019). Creativity Enables Sustainable Development: Supplier Engagement as a Boundary Condition for the Positive Effect on Green Innovation. *Journal of Cleaner Production, 226*, 172–185. Advance online publication. doi:10.1016/j.jclepro.2019.03.308

Başkol, M. O. (2018). INTERNATIONAL COMPETITIVENESS IN TURKISH TEXTILE AND CLOTHING SECTOR. *International Journal of Management Economics and Business, 14*(3), 0–0. doi:10.17130/ijmeb.2018343115

Bass, B. M., Avolio, B. J., Jung, D. I., & Berson, Y. (2003). Predicting unit performance by assessing transformational and transactional leadership. *The Journal of Applied Psychology, 88*(2), 207–218. doi:10.1037/0021-9010.88.2.207 PMID:12731705

Bilgin, M. H., Demir, E., Lau, M. C. K., Kin-Man To, C., & Zhang, Z. (2011). The Turkish handmade carpet industry: An analysis in comparison with select Asian countries. *Journal of the Textile Institute, 102*(6), 514–526. doi:10.1080/00405000.2010.498171

Changar, M., & Atan, T. (2021). The Role of Transformational and Transactional Leadership Approaches on Environmental and Ethical Aspects of CSR. *Sustainability (Basel), 13*(3), 1411. doi:10.3390/su13031411

Cho, C.-C., & Kao, R.-H. (2022). Developing sustainable workplace through leadership: Perspectives of transformational leadership and of organizational citizenship behavior. *Frontiers in Psychology, 13*, 924091. doi:10.3389/fpsyg.2022.924091 PMID:35959035

Çop, S., Olorunsola, V. O., & Alola, U. V. (2021). Achieving environmental sustainability through green transformational leadership policy: Can green team resilience help? *Business Strategy and the Environment*, *30*(1), 671–682. doi:10.1002/bse.2646

Demir, H., & Okan, T. (2008). Etkileşimsel ve Dönüşümsel Liderlik: Bir Ölçek Geliştirme Denemesi. *Yönetim Dergisi:İstanbul Üniversitesi İşletme Fakültesi İşletme İktisadı Enstitüsü, 19*(61), Article 61.

Dhammika, K. A. S., & Ahmad, F. bin, Sam, T. L., & Lanka, S. (2014). *Measurement of Transactional and Transformational Leadership: Validity and Reliability in Sri Lankan Context*. Semantic Scholar. https://api.semanticscholar.org/corpusid:55822458

Divrik, B., & Baykal, E. (2023). Relation Of Digitalization And Internationalization For Smes; Evidence From Turkish Textile And Clothing Industry. *Journal of Global Strategic Management*, *16*, 16. doi:10.20460/JGSM.2023.318

Duran, A., & Temíz Dínç, D. (2016). Türk Tekstil ve Hazır Giyim Sanayisinin Yapısı: Gümrük Birliği Anlaşması'nın Öncesi ve Sonrası. *İnsan ve Toplum Bilimleri Araştırmaları Dergisi, 5*(3), 505. doi:10.15869/itobiad.74629

Ehidiamen Oamen, T., & Moshood Lawal, B. (2023). Exploring and Validating Performance Measurement Domains of Community Pharmacists Using Structural Equation Modeling: Implications and Recommendations for Research. *Journal of Scientific Research and Reports*, 38–47. doi:10.9734/jsrr/2023/v29i11726

Erat, S., Kitapçı, H., & Akçin, K. (2020). Managerial Perception and Organizational Identity: A Comparative Analysis. *Sustainability (Basel)*, *12*(6), 2278. doi:10.3390/su12062278

Erhabor, N. I. (2018). Developing Leaders Through Mentoring in Environmental Education. *Electronic Green Journal*, *1*(41). doi:10.5070/G314134454

Görgülü, V. (2020). Case studies on the downside of transactional and authoratitative organizational leadership styles during crisis management. *Turkish online journal of design art and communication*, *10*(4), 597–611. doi:10.7456/11004100/020

Gümüş, D., & Akbal, F. (2011). Photocatalytic Degradation of Textile Dye and Wastewater. *Water, Air, and Soil Pollution*, *216*(1–4), 117–124. doi:10.1007/s11270-010-0520-z

Guo, Y., Zhu, L., Ye, X., Wang, X., Xu, Y., Qian, G., & Wang, L. (2023). Toxicity Impact Assessment of Nitrogen Oxide and Sulfur Dioxide Emissions in China's Textile Industry With Chemical Footprint Method. *AATCC Journal of Research, 10*(4), 232–240. doi:10.1177/24723444231161744

Hair, J. F. (Ed.). (2017). *A primer on partial least squares structural equation modeling (PLS-SEM)* (2nd ed.). Sage.

Hasanbeigi, A., & Price, L. (2012). A review of energy use and energy efficiency technologies for the textile industry. *Renewable & Sustainable Energy Reviews, 16*(6), 3648–3665. doi:10.1016/j.rser.2012.03.029

Henseler, J., Hubona, G., & Ray, P. A. (2016). Using PLS path modeling in new technology research: Updated guidelines. *Industrial Management & Data Systems, 116*(1), 2–20. doi:10.1108/IMDS-09-2015-0382

Invest in Trakya-Tekirdağ. (2023). *Textile Sector—Sectors—Invest in Trakya*. Invest in Trakya - Tekirdağ, Edirne, Kırklareli. https://www.investintrakya.org.tr/en/36635/Textile-Sector

Iqbal, Q., Ahmad, N. H., & Li, Y. (2021). Sustainable Leadership in Frontier Asia Region: Managerial Discretion and Environmental Innovation. *Sustainability (Basel), 13*(9), 5002. doi:10.3390/su13095002

Ismail, A., Mohamad, M., Mohamed, Hj. H. A.-B., Rafiuddin, N., & Zhen, K. (2010). Transformational and Transactional Leadership Styles as a Predictor of Individual Outcomes. *Theoretical and Applied Economics, 6*(547), 89–104.

Jain, D. (2022). Human resource issues and challenges prevailing in Indian textile & garment industry. *International Journal of Home Science, 8*(3), 227–232. doi:10.22271/23957476.2022.v8.i3d.1378

Jiang, W., Zhao, X., & Ni, J. (2017). The Impact of Transformational Leadership on Employee Sustainable Performance: The Mediating Role of Organizational Citizenship Behavior. *Sustainability (Basel), 9*(9), 1567. doi:10.3390/su9091567

Kafetzopoulos, D., & Gotzamani, K. (2022). The effect of talent management and leadership styles on firms' sustainable performance. *European Business Review, 34*(6), 837–857. doi:10.1108/EBR-07-2021-0148

Karabag, S. F., Lau, M. C. K., & Suvankulov, F. (2014). Determinants of firm competitiveness: Case of the Turkish textile and apparel industry. *Journal of the Textile Institute, 105*(1), 1–11. doi:10.1080/00405000.2013.811787

Kaya, Y., Karakan, G. G., & Visileanu, E. (2019). The impact of foreign exchange movements on Turkish textile sector. *Industria Textila (Bucuresti)*, *70*(03), 291–296. doi:10.35530/IT.070.03.1591

Khan, A. Md., & Jantan, A. H. B. (2022). Moderating Role of Psychological Empowerment on the Relationship between Transactional Leadership and Individual Innovation: Evidence from Banking Sector of Bangladesh. *Journal of International Business and Management*, *5*. doi:10.37227/jibm-2022-09-5488

Li, Z., Xue, J., Li, R., Chen, H., & Wang, T. (2020). Environmentally Specific Transformational Leadership and Employee's Pro-environmental Behavior: The Mediating Roles of Environmental Passion and Autonomous Motivation. *Frontiers in Psychology*, *11*, 1408. doi:10.3389/fpsyg.2020.01408 PMID:32670165

Lu, C., Wang, H., & Li, J. (2020). Research on the Synergistic Effect of Environmental Protection Investment and Technological Innovation on Corporate Performance. *European Journal of Business and Management*, *12*(11), 1–13.

Metcalf, L., & Benn, S. (2013). Leadership for Sustainability: An Evolution of Leadership Ability. *Journal of Business Ethics, 112*(3), 369–384. *Scopus*. Advance online publication. doi:10.1007/s10551-012-1278-6

Moraru, G.-M. (2021). The Creativity Of Future Engineers, An Insufficiently Exploited Resource In Romanian Organizations. *Management of Sustainable Development*, *13*(1), 21–25. doi:10.54989/msd-2021-0004

Muralidharan, E., & Pathak, S. (2018). Sustainability, Transformational Leadership, and Social Entrepreneurship. *Sustainability (Basel)*, *10*(2), 567. doi:10.3390/su10020567

Permata Sari, R. Y., Yuliati, L., & Komariyah, S. (2019). Intra-Industry Trade in Indonesia: A Case of the Textile and Textile Product Industry. *Journal of International Business. Economics and Entrepreneurship*, *4*(1), 47. doi:10.24191/jibe.v4i1.14416

Pultz Schlosser, K., & Volkova, T. (2022). Social Enterprise Strategic Leadership For Delivering Shared Value. *Journal of Business and Management*, *20*, 36–56. doi:10.32025/JBM22002

Qian, J.-H., Qiu, Y.-Y., Yang, Y.-D., Li, Y., Xu, P.-H., & Wang, L.-L. (2020). Accounting and evaluation of chemical footprint of cotton woven fabrics. *Industria Textila (Bucuresti)*, *71*(03), 209–214. doi:10.35530/IT.071.03.1678

Qingfen, Z., Wei, G., & Yuwen, Z. (2023). *Temporal and Spatial Trajectories of the Economic and Pollution Emission Focus of China's Textile Industry*. World Journal of Management Science and Technology., doi:10.57237/j.wjmst.2022.01.006

Quinn, L., & Dalton, M. (2009). Leading for sustainability: Implementing the tasks of leadership. *Corporate Governance (Bradford)*, *9*(1), 21–38. doi:10.1108/14720700910936038

Reddy, S. M. W., Torphy, K., Liu, Y., Chen, T., Masuda, Y. J., Fisher, J. R. B., Galey, S., Burford, K., Frank, K. A., & Montambault, J. R. (2021). How Different Forms of Social Capital Created Through Project Team Assignments Influence Employee Adoption of Sustainability Practices. *Organization & Environment*, *34*(1), 43–73. doi:10.1177/1086026619880343

Robertson, J. L., & Carleton, E. (2018). Uncovering How and When Environmental Leadership Affects Employees' Voluntary Pro-environmental Behavior. *Journal of Leadership & Organizational Studies*, *25*(2), 197–210. doi:10.1177/1548051817738940

Shaheen, F., Ahmad, N., Waqas, M., Waheed, A., & Farooq, O. (2017). Structural Equation Modeling (SEM) in Social Sciences & Medical Research: A Guide for Improved Analysis. *International Journal of Academic Research in Business & Social Sciences*, *7*(5), 132–143. doi:10.6007/IJARBSS/v7-i5/2882

Singh, S. K., Giudice, M. D., Chierici, R., & Graziano, D. (2020). Green innovation and environmental performance: The role of green transformational leadership and green human resource management. *Technological Forecasting and Social Change*, *150*, 119762. doi:10.1016/j.techfore.2019.119762

Souto, J. E. (2022). Organizational creativity and sustainability-oriented innovation as drivers of sustainable development: Overcoming firms' economic, environmental and social sustainability challenges. *Journal of Manufacturing Technology Management*, *33*(4), 805–826. doi:10.1108/JMTM-01-2021-0018

Suliman, M. A., Abdou, A. H., Ibrahim, M. F., Al-Khaldy, D. A. W., Anas, A. M., Alrefae, W. M. M., & Salama, W. (2023). Impact of Green Transformational Leadership on Employees' Environmental Performance in the Hotel Industry Context: Does Green Work Engagement Matter? *Sustainability (Basel)*, *15*(3), 2690. doi:10.3390/su15032690

Suphattanakul, O. (2017). Role of Transformational Leadership in Effective Strategic Implementation with the Moderating Effect of Organizational Culture. *Journal of Business and Social Review in Emerging Economies*, *3*(2), 253–262. doi:10.26710/jbsee.v3i2.80

Sustainable development report. (2023). SDGIndex. https://dashboards.sdgindex.org/

Sutrisno, A. (2022). Textile Industry in Indonesia Amidst the Impact of the Covid-19 Coronavirus Pandemic. *Kybernology : Journal of Government Studies*, *2*(1), 1–8. doi:10.26618/kjgs.v2i1.7853

Tanveer, A., Anwer, M. A., & Umar, M. (2021). The Impact of Environmental Sustainability and Financial Resources Utilization on Firm Financial Performance: The Mediating Role of Leadership Styles. *ANNALS OF SOCIAL SCIENCES AND PERSPECTIVE*, *2*(2), 389–407. doi:10.52700/assap.v2i2.46

Tokel, D., Dogan, I., Hocaoglu-Ozyigit, A., & Ozyigit, I. I. (2022). Cotton Agriculture in Turkey and Worldwide Economic Impacts of Turkish Cotton. *Journal of Natural Fibers*, *19*(15), 10648–10667. doi:10.1080/15440478.2021.2002759

TUIK. (2023a). *TÜİK - Veri Portalı*. Data Portal for Statistics. https://data.tuik.gov.tr/Kategori/GetKategori?p=Cevre-ve-Enerji-103

Tunc, M., Kaplan, K., Sisbot, S., & Camdali, U. (2016). Energy management and optimization: Case study of a textile plant in Istanbul, Turkey. *World Journal of Engineering*, *13*(4), 348–355. doi:10.1108/WJE-08-2016-046

Wang, C., Gou, L., & Li, X. (2022). Is Education Beneficial to Environmentally Friendly Behaviors? Evidence from CEOs. *International Journal of Environmental Research and Public Health*, *19*(18), 11391. doi:10.3390/ijerph191811391 PMID:36141663

Wesselink, R., Blok, V., & Ringersma, J. (2017). Pro-environmental behaviour in the workplace and the role of managers and organisation. *Journal of Cleaner Production*, *168*, 1679–1687. doi:10.1016/j.jclepro.2017.08.214

Wolf, J. (2011). Sustainable Supply Chain Management Integration: A Qualitative Analysis of the German Manufacturing Industry. *Journal of Business Ethics*, *102*(2), 221–235. doi:10.1007/s10551-011-0806-0

Xenikou, A., & Simosi, M. (2006). Organizational culture and transformational leadership as predictors of business unit performance. *Journal of Managerial Psychology*, *21*(6), 566–579. doi:10.1108/02683940610684409

Xia, L., Lam, S. K., Chen, D., Wang, J., Tang, Q., & Yan, X. (2017). Can knowledge-based N management produce more staple grain with lower greenhouse gas emission and reactive nitrogen pollution? A meta-analysis. *Global Change Biology*, *23*(5), 1917–1925. doi:10.1111/gcb.13455 PMID:27506858

Yang, L., Qin, H., Gan, Q., & Su, J. (2020). Internal Control Quality, Enterprise Environmental Protection Investment and Finance Performance: An Empirical Study of China's A-Share Heavy Pollution Industry. *International Journal of Environmental Research and Public Health*, *17*(17), 6082. doi:10.3390/ijerph17176082 PMID:32825596

Yao, Y.-H., Fan, Y.-Y., Guo, Y.-X., & Li, Y. (2014). Leadership, work stress and employee behavior. *Chinese Management Studies*, *8*(1), 109–126. doi:10.1108/CMS-04-2014-0089

Yu Chuan, Y. (2022). The Impact of Scenario Planning and Leadership on Non-Financial Performance in the Multi-Level Marketing (MLM) Industry. *International Journal of Accounting Finance in Asia Pasific*, *5*(3), 17–38. doi:10.32535/ijafap.v5i3.1728

Yukl, G. A., & Gardner, W. L. (2020). *Leadership in organizations* (9th ed.). Pearson Education, Inc.

Chapter 12
A Study on the Interaction Between Civil Business Groups and the State From the Perspective of Public Sphere Theory:
A Comparison Between the Shangha

Wei Yao
Nanjing University, China

Yuhong Li
https://orcid.org/0000-0002-3544-4475
Nanjing University, China

Tingxuan Liu
Nanjing University, China

ABSTRACT

This chapter attempts to use public sphere theory as a starting point to compare the behavior of the British government in protecting the interests of British business in China in the 19th century with the Chinese government's neglect of the interests of Chinese business in the Philippines. This chapter uses the Shanghai Branch of the China Association and Philippine Chinese Charitable Association Inc. as representatives of private business groups in the UK and China. For the UK, due to the public sphere of competition with the central government within the UK, private business groups must consult with relevant private business groups when

DOI: 10.4018/979-8-3693-1846-1.ch012

implementing any economic foreign policy. This process promotes consensus between the British government and society and promotes the British government's determination to maintain British business in China. However, for China, due to the absence of a public sphere where the central government interacts with society, even though Chinese private business groups have huge interests overseas, the state and society have always been unable to form a positive interaction. At the same time, this situation also results in Chinese businesses in the Philippines having to rely on their abilities to maintain their local interests.

INTRODUCTION

For a long time, the interaction between the state and society has been a concern of most scholars, and the political decisions or foreign policies made by the central government as a representative of the state have more or less influenced the interests of different groups in society. Especially in the economic aspect, whether the state takes into account the interests of private business groups in the "public interest" is the key to positive interaction. Generally speaking, 'public interest' is considered a national interest. If a state wants to effectively mobilize its members of society, it must have the ability to take into account the "public interest" of the majority of its members. According to Mike Feintuck's discussion of "public interest", it can be found that "public interest" roughly has three functions. The first function, public interest, is as a means of legitimizing intervention in private behavior. To shape citizens who are highly bound to their relationships, the state will attempt to change their living conditions to possess the core values of the state. The second type of governance and function, "public interest", is the function of the "arena", that is, the ability of the "public interest" represented by national interests. In other words, to what extent do national interests represent the 'public'? The third function is whether social actors can consciously represent the "public interest" and interact with the state (Feintuck, 2014). However, if we consider private business groups as a part of society. So why do some countries strongly support this group, so that the interests of the state and society are effectively bound together? However, in some countries, conflicts between the state and society arise due to differences in their interests and private business groups.

During the period from the 19th century to the early 20th century, as one of the most important countries in the world at that time, Britain not only could safeguard national interests overseas but also greatly protected the interests of British business in China. For example, when discussing the issue of raising tariffs on China with the Chinese government, the British government not only solicited opinions from British business organizations in China, such as the Shanghai Branch of the China

Association. The British government is also actively negotiating with other private chambers of commerce in its home state to ensure the maximization of 'public interest'. On the contrary, China is not only unable to safeguard the basic sovereignty interests of the state on its territory but also unable to safeguard the interests of Chinese businessmen in Southeast Asia. For example, the Philippine Chinese Charitable Association Inc., a Chinese business association in the Philippines, actively sought help from the Chinese government in the face of the Spanish-American War, hoping to gain national support, but still had to rely on its own self-supporting.

Why did Chinese and British private business groups receive different feedback from the state on similar interest demands at the same time? Why is there such a huge difference in the attitude of the Chinese government and the British government towards domestic business groups? This article will use this as the starting point for discussion.

RESEARCH HYPOTHESIS & THEORY

Throughout the international environment of the 19th century, whether it was the British Chamber of Commerce in China or the commercial activities of Chinese businessmen in Southeast Asia, they were all spontaneous commercial organizations among the people. They are a part of society exercising civil rights, and they are also pioneers of the state's interests overseas. To explain the relationship between the interaction between the state and society and "private business organizations", this article will be revised based on Habermas' theory of the "public sphere" as the framework. Habermas believes that the Public sphere is such a platform. A part of the public sphere consists of various dialogues. Every dialogue between actors promotes their aggregation into a public group, and at this point, a portion of the Public sphere is formed.

When actors (including the state) engage in dialogue and interaction regarding their interests, issues related to private interests become public issues, resulting in an interactive field that affects the relationships and cognition between actors. The public sphere is a field of mediation between the state and society, in which the state and society will engage in a game of "publicity" and "public principles" to reach a consensus (Habermas 1999). Although Habermas well explains the process of the game between the state and society, his insufficient explanation is that if there is an interactive platform between the state and society, there should be no (too many) contradictions in the interaction between the state and society. However, the fact is that some countries do not have a "public sphere" in their interaction with society; Some countries and societies may have a 'public sphere', but this may not necessarily have a 'consensus'.

Regarding the relationship between the "public sphere" and "consensus", Habermas well explains the formation of consensus between the state and society. A 'consensus' will be formed, which represents the' trust 'relationship between the state and society. Consensus, as a state of mutual trust, can help civil society trust the behavior of the central government representing the state, Cancelling obstacles in governing society. At the same time, the 'Public sphere' is also a type of 'rites d institution'. The "recognition ceremony" is a way of reproducing social rules to achieve the effect of the state's authority over social construction. The "recognition ceremony" not only occurs in various units authorized by the state (such as schools) but also in the feedback of society on the legitimacy of the state (central government). (For example, regular elections held in democratic countries are a recognition ceremony aimed at reproducing the legitimacy of the state.) Therefore, we can say that the "public sphere" is crucial for the interaction between society and the state (Bourdieu, 2023a; 2023b).

The significance of the "public sphere" also illustrates the logic of interaction between the state and society. Although the state has absolute control over society, society follows two patterns of feedback towards the state. One is' Conformism logic '; Logical obedience "means that society and the state form a common logical category, thereby achieving mutual spiritual identity. In short, society's rule over the state is a "trust" attitude. The second type is "moral obedience": "moral obedience" refers to ethical participation in a shared domain of shared value. In other words, society's rule over the state is a 'submissive' attitude. Ethical value sharing means that society follows the norms set by the state (Bourdieu, 2023a).

From the above examination of the relationship between "consensus" and "public sphere", we can observe that in modern countries, society always relies on the recognition of its rights by the state. Therefore, we will use the variables of "Public sphere" and "social dependence on the state" to explore the causal mechanism of the interaction between the state and society.

Assumption 1: When a state's Public sphere exists and society has a high degree of dependence on the state (obedience and trust coexist), it indicates a positive interaction between the state and society. In this situation, the state will support society and develop colonial organizations.

Assumption 2: When a state's Public sphere exists, and the degree of social dependence on the state is low (obedience and trust only exist on one side). It indicates that the state and society have only reached a partial consensus, but adhere to the principle of mutual interaction.

Assumption 3: When a state's public sphere does not exist, but the degree of social dependence on the state is high (obedience and trust coexist), it indicates that the state directly governs society, but the society lacks autonomy.

Table 1. Public sphere-dependence hypothesis

	Public sphere presence (Consensus exists between the state and society)	The public sphere does not exist (There is no consensus between the state and society)
The high degree of dependence of society on the state (Obedience and trust coexist)	The state supports society and develops colonial organizations.	The state directly governs society, but society lacks autonomy.
Low dependence of society on the state (There is only one aspect to obedience and trust)	The state and society have only reached a partial consensus, but they adhere to the principle of mutual interaction.	Society can only ensure its interests through Self-supporting.

(self-drawn by the author)

Assumption 4: When a state's Public sphere does not exist, and the degree of social dependence on the state is low (obedience and trust only exist on one side). It indicates that society can only ensure its interests through self-supporting.

RESULT

Shanghai Branch of the China Association

Proposal of the Issue of Canceling Likin and Rising Tariff: Positive Interaction Between the Shanghai Branch of the China Association and the British Government

In terms of economy, the Shanghai branch requested abolishing the likin barriers. To solve the financial crisis caused by the suppression of the Taiping Rebellion (太平天国运动), the Chinese government established likin barriers, which were similar to donation but could be implemented for a long time (Luo 2010). From then on, indiscriminate collection of likin, and extortion by officials seriously hindered the smooth flow of goods throughout the state. To further develop trade with China, British businessmen in China were eager to abolish likin barriers. They seek support from the British government. After the Boxer Rebellion (义和团运动), the British Consulate-General in Shanghai consulted with the Chamber of Commerce on the negotiations between British and China. The Shanghai branch strongly demanded to abolish likin barriers (Dudgeon 1901). Faced with the global decline of the British Empire, responding to the United States' demand for an "open door ", the British government supported the demands of the Shanghai branch and promoted the issue of Canceling likin into the negotiation of the Renewed Treaty of Commerce and Navigation between Britain and China.

In terms of diplomacy, the Shanghai Branch of the China Association required that tariff increases must be based on Cancellation. To obtain the Boxer Indemnity (庚子赔款) as soon as possible, Germany, Russia, France, and other countries proposed increasing import tariffs on China to 10% (Liu & Liu 1984). This move would increase the cost of the Shanghai Branch's trade with China. After learning about it, the Shanghai branch called the London headquarters of the Chinese Association to oppose any tariff increase without any return (Dudgeon 1902b). If commercial benefits such as canceling likin could be transferred, the Shanghai branch was willing to bear the burden of tariff increases. It was difficult for individual units to obtain public power. But when many individual units acted together, it was possible to compete with public actors. The Shanghai branch, through the London headquarters of the China Association, liaised with many British chambers of commerce engaged in trade with China to jointly exert pressure on the British government to influence government decision-making. The Chinese Association had extensively sought support from the Bristol Chamber of Commerce, Leeds Chamber of Commerce, and Liverpool Chamber of Commerce for the proposal of Canceling likin and increasing tariffs (Spear 1901; Calvert 1901; Barker 1901). Under pressure from the British business communities, the British government representative stated at the negotiation of the Boxer Protocol that if the tariff was raised to more than 10%, the Chinese government should cancel likin and give other commercial concessions (Wang 1985). The issue which support by the British government for the Shanghai branch had also been recognized by the major powers. But at this moment, the focus of the negotiation was the aftermath of the Boxer Rebellion(义和团运动). The issue of canceling likin and increasing tariffs was scheduled to be carried out in the negotiation of the Renewed Treaty of Commerce and Navigation with China.

Planning About Canceling Likin and Rising Tariff: A Partial Consensus Between the Shanghai Branch and the British Government

In terms of economy, the Shanghai branch required that the import tariffs on China should not be too high. Firstly, the Shanghai branch launched a collective appeal to the British government through an organizational motion. To exert pressure on the British government, the power of individual businessmen/enterprises was limited. However, using the Shanghai branch as a platform, the demands of British businessmen in China were concentrated. In January 1902, the British treaty envoy Mackay and the committee of the Shanghai branch jointly formulated a plan for canceling likin and increasing the tariff. However, most ordinary members were dissatisfied with the proposal to increase the tariff rate to 15%. To address this issue, the Shanghai branch held a plenary meeting on March 3rd to discuss the plan and vote on it. The vote at the meeting rejected the Mackay's plan (Mackay 1902a). Without the support of British businessmen in China, there would be a lack of practical implementers of policies towards China. The British government adopted a cooperative attitude after recognizing the importance of the Shanghai branch.

The British government actively attracted committee members, attempting to use the support of the elite class to control the outcome of the rally. Both Charles John Dudgeon and the new Shanghai branch chairman James L. Scott had reached a cooperative relationship with the British government. The committee declared the resolution invalid on the grounds of excessive abstention and reconvened the meeting (Dudgeon 1902a). On the other hand, Mackay submitted to Scott the whole plan of canceling likin and rising tariff, suggesting to express details at the next meeting to win the recognition of members (Mackay 1902c). Given the difficulty in reaching an agreement with the British government at this time, the Shanghai branch had also actively sought support from other organizations with common interests. When the Manchester Chamber of Commerce, Worcester Chamber of Commerce, and other chambers of commerce with direct interests learned about the situation in Shanghai, they successively objected to the British government's plan (Corbett 1902; Manchester Chamber of Commerce 1902).

The Manchester Chamber of Commerce wrote to the British Foreign Office, pointing out that raising the tariff rate to 15% would pose a serious burden on trade. The statements of local businessmen made the British government realize that opposition was not limited to China. The actions of the Shanghai branch represented the will of a large part of the British bourgeoisie. The British government didn't intervene forcefully in the second assembly of members of the Shanghai branch. After rejecting the original plan again at the second meeting, the British government chose to listen to public opinion and invited representatives from the chambers of commerce to jointly adjust the plan of canceling likin and raising the tariff formulated by Mackay. Under the coordination of Robert Edward Bredon, the Deputy General Tariff Department of Customs, the tariff rate increase was reduced to 12.5% (中 1994). Despite taking so many methods, the British government was unable to completely shake the stance of British businessmen in China due to the existence of the Shanghai branch. The British government had ultimately to make compromises.

Secondly, the Shanghai branch intervened in British government decision-making by appealing its claims to the media and creating public pressure. *The North China Herald*, an influential newspaper founded by British businessmen in China, had become one of the most powerful public opinion tools for the Shanghai branch. After the announcement of the plan of canceling likin and rising tariff, Edward S.

Little, a member of the Shanghai branch, wrote a manual titled *China's Income and the New Treaty: Protests against Tariff Increasing, from a Merchant's Perspective* to promote Public opinion against the plan (Little 1902). The editorial department of *the North China Herald* printed and published this manual, which not only affected the attitudes of many members at the Shanghai branch but also sparked widespread discussion among the British public. Many opponents who were directly involved in China's trade used media such as *The North China Daily News* to raise a large number of persuasive objections. After the first general meeting of the Shanghai branch, due to excessive abstention votes, to gain the support of those who remained silent in the meeting, Edward S. Little published a speech in *the North China Daily News* to the Business Counselor of the British Consulate General in China, accuses the British government of inadequate regulation of the clause in Tianjin Treaty (天津条约) which said transit pass charge of 2.5% for goods sent into the interior.

He questioned the feasibility of the plan of canceling likin and raising the tariff (Little 1902 March 5). During this process, the British government and supporters of the plan also used public opinion to retaliate. J. O. P. Bland, a correspondent for *The Times*, published an article refuting Little's interpretation of the Tianjin Treaty (天津条约) and calling on British businessmen in China to support the plan in exchange for a true open door (Bland 1902). On the other hand, the branch used various means to guide public opinion. *The Shanghai Mercury* launched an attack on the identity of Bland, who had been a customs employee for many years, implying that the tariff increase was due to Sir Robert Hart, the chief tariff officer, who was willing to harm the interests of the British for collecting wealth for the Chinese (The National Archives 1902). Mackay closely followed the debate and sent all the newspaper clippings to the Marquess of Lansdowne, regretfully stating that except for Bland's article, most of the other comments were against the plan (Mackay 1902b). Because almost all English newspapers in China represented the interests of British businessmen, the British government had almost failed in the public opinion arena. It had to make concessions on the amount of tariff increases that the Shanghai branch could accept.

In terms of diplomacy, the Shanghai branch requested the British government to force the Chinese government to expand the scope of the abolition of likin barriers to smooth the mainland Chinese market. The abolishing likin barriers plan originally proposed by Mackay did not include salt barriers, local opium barriers, etc. The Chinese government had emphasized the differences between the above and likin barriers, as well as the importance of investigating illegal activities and collecting taxes on the mainland. The Shanghai branch insisted these barriers were as same as likin barriers which must be included in the scope of abolition. The Shanghai branch used newspapers to criticize fiercely by publishing a series of articles. The article pointed out that the shackles hindering the development of mainland trade were not only the likin barriers. If the salt barriers and local opium barriers were not abolished, the extortion of goods circulation would continue to exist (Little 1902 June 25). Under the pressure of public opinion from British businessmen in China, Mackay proposed the abolition of salt barriers and local opium barriers at the Treaty Amendment Conference.

Sheng Xuanhuai (盛宣怀), who was a Chinese treaty envoy, expressed confusion and opposition to the sudden expansion of the scope (China, 1994). The local governors Liu Kunyi (刘坤一) and Zhang Zhidong (张之洞), who participated in the negotiation, also firmly resisted (Chen 2018; Zhao 2008). The British government compromised by renaming the salt barriers to Salt Reporting Stations, renaming the local opium barriers to Opium Stations, and establishing a monitoring system. Without appreciating it, the Shanghai branch launched another public opinion offensive. In China, British businessmen pointed out that salt barriers were only nominal extinction. (Little 1902 October 5). However, salt tax and opium tax were both important sources of fiscal revenue for the Chinese government, especially used to offset foreign debts, including those of Britain. The British government was unable to support the Shanghai branch's demand. If the actors have specific fundamental interests, they strive to maximize their utility. The most desirable policy for these two is a policy choice that maximizes their fundamental interests in the field of the issue (Milner 1997). In the end, the British government set an ex-factory tax in exchange for recognition of the plan by local British businessmen. The Shanghai branch was forced to accept the result.

All studies on the evolution of public and private power have shown that both types of power have gone to extremes while both have provided lasting benefits that do not conflict with each other. (Rothkopf 2012) In the issue of cancelling likin and rising tariff, the British government (public/government actors) engaged in a fierce game with the Shanghai branch (private/non-governmental actors), regarding management of public affairs. The Shanghai branch exerted pressure on the British government through collective motions, public opinion attacks, and other means to achieve its interests, which was a manifestation of private actors attempting to extend their power to the public space field. The British government, on the other hand, adopted administrative coercive orders, differentiated organizational structures, and other methods to maintain its authority in public affairs. Among them, non-governmental actors have significant shortcomings due to their loose internal structure, inconsistent member interests, susceptibility to external influences, and even difficulty in achieving internal power. However, their leverage can't be ignored.

However, the ultimate goal of the game between the Shanghai branch and the British government was still to pursue the maximum common interest. Although the British government used various means in this issue to try to suppress the claims of the Shanghai branch and force it to cooperate with overseas strategies. The

Shanghai branch also used various methods to pressure the government to change policies based on the opinions of British businessmen in China. However, the British government has always provided a platform for communication and cooperation with British businessmen in China. The various demands of the Shanghai branch had not deviated from this platform. It was obvious that the British government fully understood that under a market-oriented system, public affairs were in the hands of two leading groups, the government and the industry. They must do their best to cooperate (Lindblom 1997).

Based on a mutual compromise, the two bodies reached an agreement on the issue of canceling likin and raising tariffs, which provided convenience for British business in China. On the other hand, the Shanghai branch also had to accept an additional ex-factory tax on machinery products in China, to safeguard the interests of local British businessmen and win support from local British businessmen for the plan of cancelling likin and rising tariffs.

Philippine Chinese Charitable Association Inc.

The Issue of Establishing a Consulate of China in the Philippines: The Informal Colonialism of the Philippine Chinese Charitable Association Inc.

In terms of economy, the Philippine Chinese Charitable Association Inc. requested the Chinese government to establish a consulate to promote the development of Chinese business in the Philippines and protect industrial security. During the Spanish rule, colonizers formulated various harsh regulations restricting overseas Chinese (You 1957). Industry tax and store tax were imposed to restrict overseas Chinese business (Huang & He 2009). Faced with such unfair treatment, the Philippine Chinese Charitable Association Inc. turned its attention to its home state. They attempted to seek support from the Chinese government.

In 1886, the core directors of the Philippine Chinese Charitable Association Inc., including Ye Longqin (叶龙钦), Chen Qianshan (陈谦善), Lin Guanghe (林光合), and Xu Zhiluo (许志螺) (Philippines 1977), came to China to submit a paper signed by 290 Chinese businessmen, requesting the Chinese government to establish a consulate in Philippine (Wickberg 1965). Compared to the interests of Chinese businessmen in the Philippines the Chinese government was more concerned about the funding for establishing a consulate. The newly appointed ambassador to the United States, Spanish, and Peru, Zhang Yinhuan (张荫桓), met with representatives of the Philippine Chinese Charitable Association Inc. in Hong Kong. He felt that they never forget their longing for their home state with the hope of seeking the Chinese government's protection. However, the overseas Chinese businessman had not yet made a clear statement about providing consul funds, so he decided to send personnel to the Philippines to investigate the situation. Further discussion on establishing a consulate would be taken after verifying that stable funds could be provided (Yuan et al. 1998). The subsequent investigation results showed that Chinese businessmen in the Philippines were willing to raise funds for the consulate establishment. However, the Foreign Office was still concerned that the consulate would be like the ones in Cuba and Singapore. Overseas Chinese businessmen initially actively raised funds, but became weak later (First Pavilion 2003). In essence, the Chinese government did not want to bear any economic burden of a consulate in the Philippines.

After the outbreak of the Katipunan revolt, the Philippine government forced Chinese businessmen to transport grain. The rebels hated Chinese businessmen for doing it. Chinese businessmen' shops in the Philippines were looted by the rebels. Philippine Chinese Charitable Association Inc. once again requested the Chinese government to establish a consulate to protect the security of the Chinese business industry in the Philippines (Wilson 2004). However, the Spanish ambassador to China claimed that the rebels' hatred of Chinese businessmen was due to normal trade competition which was very common (Huang III, 1989). The persecution faced by overseas Chinese in the Philippines daily was evident from this. Under Spanish colonial rule, the economic capacity of overseas Chinese was greatly restricted (Zhu & Liu 2009). Faced with such excuses, the Chinese government had neither pursued nor held accountable the security of the Chinese business industry in the Philippines (Huang III, 1989).

In April 1898, the Spanish-American War broke out (Yang 2019). Under the precarious situation of the property safety of Chinese businessmen in the Philippines, the Chinese government which had gained some understanding of international law (Yu 1998; Zhu 2017), requested the British Consul in the Philippines to protect Chinese businessmen (Huang & He 2009). The Chinese government also required the Philippine Chinese Charitable Association Inc. to raise funds to pay the expenses of the British in protecting Chinese businessmen in the Philippines (Huang III 1989). It could be seen that the Chinese government was unwilling to bear the cost of protecting the Chinese in the Philippines.

In terms of diplomacy, the Philippine Chinese Charitable Association Inc. requests the Chinese government to establish a consulate to improve the political status of Chinese businessmen in the Philippines and protect life safety. In 1886, the Philippine Chinese Charitable Association Inc. sent representatives to China to request the establishment of a consulate in the Philippines. The Philippine Ministry of Foreign Affairs declined it with the pretext that the issue belonged to the colonial administration after meeting Zhang Yinhuan (张荫桓). However, taking these verbal excuses so easily, Zhang Yinhuan(张荫桓) wrote in his diary that he was well aware of the difficulties faced by the Ministry of Foreign Affairs. He didn't keep on persisting (Ren & Ma 2015). In 1889, the new ambassador to the United States, Spanish and Peru, Cui Guoyin (崔国因), was preparing to resume negotiations on establishing a consulate in the Philippines during his visit to Madrid. However, due to an unexpected incident in the United States, Cui Guoyin (崔国因) returned in a hurry. There was no follow-up on it afterward (Wang & Wang 2015). From the attitudes of the two ambassadors, it can be seen that the Chinese government attaches limited importance to this issue.

During the Katipunan revolt, Chinese businessmen in the Philippines were subjected to bullying by rebels. The Philippine Chinese Charitable Association Inc. once again proposed to the Chinese government to establish a consulate in the Philippines and pleaded for the dispatch of warships to protect overseas Chinese. They also begged for imploring other countries to protect overseas Chinese they were afraid that it would be difficult to expedite the establishment so soon (Wilson 2004). The Chinese government had made no mention of the dispatch of warships. It is unwilling to take any military action on behalf of overseas Chinese. The request to establish a consulate was only mentioned by the Chinese government in response to the Spanish Ambassador to China. The Chinese government proposed that overseas Chinese were deeply persecuted. If they could establish a consulate like other countries, it would not be so tragic (Huang III, 1989). This hypothetical euphemism naturally couldn't be a legitimate expression for requesting the establishment of a consulate. In response to the request for assistance from other countries, the Foreign Office called Yang Ru(杨儒), the ambassador to the British to request the British Consul in the Philippines to protect overseas Chinese (Huang & He 2009). But when the Spanish Ambassador to China opposed the British act of protecting the Chinese government didn't mention it again (Huang III, 1989). However, the British government took on the responsibility of protecting overseas Chinese, ignoring the opposition from the Spanish government. Under the protection of the British consul in the Philippines, the cases of two Chinese businessmen named Cai Zao (蔡燥) and Chen Dang (陈党) who were treated harshly in the Philippines were won (Huang & He 2009). The Chinese Office of Foreign Affairs expressed great gratitude to the British ambassador to China for this. It was also hoped that the British consul in the Philippines could protect overseas Chinese in the future by international law (Huang 1989; Long 2007). In other words, the Chinese government had completely forgotten its responsibilities towards overseas Chinese.

During the Spanish-American War, Chinese businessmen in the Philippines were heavily implicated. However, the Philippine Chinese Charitable Association Inc. no longer requested the Chinese government to dispatch warships. It only pleaded for the establishment of a consulate in the Philippines as soon as possible to provide protection (Huang IV, 1989). The lives of Chinese businessmen in the Philippines were in danger. The ambassador to the United States, Spanish, and Peru,

Wu Tingfang (伍廷芳), only suggested the Foreign Office(外务部) state that if the Spanish government still refused to establish a consulate of China in the Philippines, it would be stipulated how to compensate the damage to the lives and property of overseas Chinese. China wouldn't bear any responsibility for the troubles made by overseas Chinese who were without consul constraints (Huang IV, 1989). This statement, similar to an exemption from liability, was far from meeting the needs of Chinese businessmen in the Philippines to ensure their safety during the war. At this moment, Manila had been surrounded by the United States military. The Spanish government almost lost control. To save the current crisis, the Spanish government agreed to the temporary establishment of a consul by the Chinese government in Manila (Wilson 2004). On July 29th, the Foreign Office appointed Chen Gang (陈纲), the son of Chen Qianshan (陈谦善), as the consul in the Philippines (Liang 2004). After the United States military occupied Manila, the Foreign Office turned to negotiate with the United States government. On October 4th, Wu Tingfang (伍廷芳) informed the Foreign Office that the United States government had approved China's establishment of a consulate in Manila (Huang 1989).

The attitudes of the ambassadors to the United States, Spanish, and Peru could be seen in their previous actions with the Spanish Ministry of Foreign Affairs. It should be said as lax and even lazy in politics. Moreover, when negotiating with the Spanish Ministry of Foreign Affairs to establish a consulate in the Philippines, Zhang Yinhuan (张荫桓) emphasized that the China Merchants Steam Navigation Company (招商局) intended to carry cargo to expand the scope of the Chinese government business (Ren & Ma 2015). The various considerations of the Chinese officials were different from the consul role that Chinese businessmen in the Philippines hoped for. The Chinese officials' support for the establishment of a consulate was limited.

Issue About the Consul's Role of China in the Philippines: The Mutual Distrust Between the Philippine Chinese Charitable Association Inc. and the Chinese Government

In terms of economy, the Philippine Chinese Charitable Association Inc. still needs to solve many economic affairs on its own. When the Chinese General Hospital, a charity organization under its jurisdiction, was facing a shortage of funds, the Philippine Chinese Charitable Association Inc. decided to use 80 yuan per box of opium as the hospital's funding after discussing it with opium importers. At the same time, the Philippine Chinese Charitable Association Inc. was preparing to levy export tax on Chinese returning to China to assist in hospital funding. Philippine Chinese Charitable Association Inc. requested approval from the Philippine Governor General to notify customs for processing (Philippine Chinese Charitable Association Inc. 1977). The consul was unable to assist the Philippine Chinese Charitable Association Inc. in resolving funding but also coveted the financial resources of Chinese businessmen in the Philippines. Their perceptions of foreign economic imperialism were so strong. In 1906, the Chinese government ordered the consul in the Philippines to gather chambers of commerce such as the Philippine Chinese Charitable Association Inc. to discuss the joint organization of overseas Chinese corporations and the establishment of banking, shipping, insurance, and other business (Philippine Chinese Charitable Association Inc. 1977; Yung 1996; LI 2023).

In terms of diplomacy, the Philippine Chinese Charitable Association Inc. requested the consul to negotiate with the United States government to ban discriminatory regulations against overseas Chinese. In 1906, the United States government issued regulations requiring all Chinese returning from China to Manila to stay for a week to test for illness. To prevent overseas Chinese from being extorted, the Philippine Chinese Charitable Association Inc. protested to the consul of China in the Philippines (Philippine Chinese Charitable Association Inc. 1977). However, this matter remained unresolved until the downfall of the Chinese government. Overseas Chinese still faced humiliation upon entering Manila. They are subjected to physical examination and interrogation like prisoners being locked up for several days (Arturo 1986; Guo 1999; Yu 1998). In 1913, the Philippine Chinese Charitable Association Inc. elected representatives to protest against the harsh treatment of customs quarantine doctors during entry inspection (Philippine Chinese Charitable Association Inc. 1977). To further fight the elimination of unfair treatment, the Philippine Chinese Charitable Association Inc. gathered the strength of other chambers of commerce to collectively exert pressure on the colonial government of the United States in the Philippines. In 1924, in response to the new immigration bill, the Philippine Chinese Charitable Association Inc., together with the Chinese Chamber of Commerce and the Guangdong Huiguan (广东会馆), submitted a protest to Leonard Wood, the United States Governor-General in the Philippine. Under pressure from the Chinese business communities in the Philippines, Wood rejected the case as the reason for violating the United States Constitution (Huang & He 2009; Zhuang 2009).

DISCUSSION

From the interactions between the two overseas private business groups and their home states, we can find four forms of interaction that correspond to different results. When the public sphere existed, the Shanghai branch and the British government could engage in positive interaction around public issues. The Shanghai branch influences the decisions made by the British government through collective pressure, newspaper opinion, rallies, and voting. When the Shanghai branch obeyed and trusted the British government, the British government supported it. The Shanghai branch became a colonial organization of the British government. The British government developed imperialism. When the Shanghai branch only obeyed but did not trust the British government, the British government reached a partial consensus with the Shanghai branch to promote mercantilism.

When the public sphere didn't exist, the Philippine Chinese Charitable Association Inc. and the Chinese government couldn't engage in positive interaction around public issues. When Philippine Chinese Charitable Association Inc. obeyed and trusted the Chinese government, Philippine Chinese Charitable Association Inc. could only use the submission of petitions and private meetings with Chinese officials to make interest demands to the Chinese government without affecting its decision-making. Philippine Chinese Charitable Association Inc. had become an informal colonialism of the Chinese government. When the Philippine Chinese Charitable Association Inc. obeyed but did not trust the Chinese government, it didn't seek support from the Chinese government, instead taking private measures to solve its problems. We believe that the presence or absence of the public sphere will affect the interaction and outcomes between overseas private business groups and their home states.

CONCLUSION

By comparing the interaction between the Shanghai branch and the British government, as well as between the Philippine Chinese Charitable Association Inc. and the Chinese government, we find that the presence or absence of the public sphere has a significant impact on the interaction between the overseas private business group and the home state. It is precisely because of a public sphere between the Shanghai branch and the British government that they can establish public issues, using media opinions, and gatherings to promote the development of public affairs. On the other hand, due to the absence of a public sphere between the Philippine Chinese Charitable Association Inc. and the Chinese government, they were unable to establish public issues. There was no space for discussion and coordination. Therefore, the public sphere is where overseas private business groups can interact positively with their home state. In the public sphere, the two can exchange their demands, and ultimately reach partial consensus through compromise, promoting common development.

REFERENCES

Arturo, P. (1986, February). The Chinese Community in the Philippines: Status and Conditions. *Sojourn (Singapore)*, *1*(1), 76–91. doi:10.1355/SJ1-1E

Barker, T. B. (1901 July 6). *Liverpool Chamber of Commerce to the China Association. F.O.17/1586*. London: The National Archives. https://discovery.nationalarchives.gov.uk/

Bland, J. O. P. (1902 March 6). The New Tariff Proposals. *The North-China Daily News*, 4.

Bourdieu, P. (2023a). *Sur lÉtat. Cours au Collège de France (1989-1992)*. SDX Joint Publishing Company.

Bourdieu, P. (2023b). *Anthropologie économique. Cours au Collège de France 1992-1993*. Shanghai People's Publishing House.

Calvert, R. K. (1901 July 3). *Leeds Chamber of Commerce to the China Association*. F.O.17/1586. London: The National Archives. https://discovery.nationalarchives.gov.uk/

Chen, D. X. (2018). *Liu Kunyi's Biography (刘坤一集)*. Hunan Yuelu Publishing House Co., Ltd.

Corbett, E. C. (1902 April 8). *Treaty Revision in China. F.O. 17/1571*. London: The National Archives. https://discovery.nationalarchives.gov.uk/

Dudgeon, C. J. (1901 May 31). *China Association (Shanghai) to H. B. M. Consul-General. F.O.17/1586*. London: The National Archives. https://discovery.nationalarchives.gov.uk/

Dudgeon, C. J. (1902a March 5*). To James Mackay. F.O.17/1565*. London: The National Archives. https://discovery.nationalarchives.gov.uk/

Dudgeon, C. J. (1902b April 2). *Memorandum. F.O.17/1586*. London: The National Archives. https://discovery.nationalarchives.gov.uk/

Dudgeon, C. J. (1902c June 25). *To James Mackay. F.O.17/1578*. London: The National Archives. https://discovery.nationalarchives.gov.uk/

Feintuck, M. (2014). *'The Public Interest' in Regulation*. China Renmin University Press.

Guo, X. D. (1999). Opening the Road to "Free" Trade: A Study of Chinese Socio Economy in the West in the 1830s (打 "自由"通商之路——19世纪30年代的在西华人对中国社会经济的探研). Guangzhou: Guangdong People's Publishing House Co., LTD.

Habermas, J. (1999). *Strukturwandel der Öffentlichkeit*. Academia Press.

Huang, J. M. (1989). Historical Materials on Sino-US Relations (Guangxu Dynasty III and IV)(中美关系史料(光绪朝三、 四)). Taipei: Institute of Modern History, Academia Sinica.

Huang, Z. S., & He, S. B. (2009). *History of Filipino Overseas Chinese*. Guangdong Higher Education Press.

Li, Y. (2023). A Study On The Interaction Between The "Balance Of Power And Internationalism" Norms In Southeast Asia In The 19th Century Centered On The1898 Spanish-American War. *Journal of Law and Political Sciences 39*(4), 454-490. https://drive.google.com/file/d/1wCuW-tGDhUB4dn8qHA0_31zGafPFWF_k/view

Liang, B. Y. (2004). *Hard Diplomacy: A Study on the Chinese Ambassador to the United States in the Late Qing Dynasty (艰难的外交——晚清中国驻美公使研究)*. Tianjin Ancient Books Publishing House.

Lindblom, C. E. (1997). *Politics and Markets: The World's Political Economic Systems*. Basic Books.

Little, A. (1902 June 25). Tariff Revision. *The North-China Herald*, 68., No.1820.

Little, E. S. (1902 March 5). The New Tariff Proposals. *The North-China Daily News*, *4*.

Little, E. S. (1902 October 5). A Protest Against Ratification. *The North-China Herald*, *69*., No.1836.

Little, E. S. (1902). *The Chinese Revenue and the New Treaty: A Protest against an Increased Tariff from a Merchant's Point of View. F.O.17/1579.* London: The National Archives. https://discovery.nationalarchives.gov.uk/

Liu, X. Y., & Liu, H. Y. (1984). *Foreign Relations of the United States,1901, Appendix. Affairs in China. Report of William W. Rockhill, Late Commissioner to China, with Accompanying Documents*. Shandong Qilu Book Publishing Co., Ltd.

Long, D. G. (2007). *Crossing Market Barriers: The Market: Overseas Chinese Businessmen Between State, System, and Culture*. China Science and Media Ltd.

Luo, Y. D. (2010). *History of Likin in China (中国厘金史)*. The Commercial Press.

Mackay, J. (1902a March 5). *To Lansdowne, K. G. NO. 23. F.O.17/1565*. London: The National Archives. https://discovery.nationalarchives.gov.uk/

Mackay, J. (1902b March 10). To Lansdowne, K. G. NO. 24. F.O.17/1565. London: The National Archives. https://discovery.nationalarchives.gov.uk/

Mackay, J. (1902c March 11). *James Mackay to the Shanghai Branch of the China Association. F.O.17/1565*. London: The National Archives. https://discovery.nationalarchives.gov.uk/

Manchester Chamber of Commerce. (1902 March 11). *To the Under Secretary of State. F.O.17/1579*. London: The National Archives. https://discovery.nationalarchives.gov.uk/

Milner, H. (1997). *Interests, Institutions, and Information: Domestic Politics and International Relations*. Princeton University Press.

Philippine Chinese Charitable Association Inc. (1977). *Philippine Chinese Charitable Association Inc. 100th Anniversary Souvenir Book*. Philippine Chinese Charitable Association Inc. Press.

Rothkopf, D. (2012). *Power, Inc.: The Epic Rivalry Between Big Business and Government and the Reckoning That Lies Ahead*. Farrar, Straus, and Giroux.

Spear, H. J. (1901 June 28). *The Bristol Chamber of Commerce to the China Association. F.O.17/1586*. London: The National Archives. https://discovery.nationalarchives.gov.uk/

The National Archives. (1902 March 7). *Mr. Bland and the Likin Duties. F.O.17/1565*. London: The National Archives. https://discovery.nationalarchives.gov.uk/

Wang, S. H. (1985). *Boxer Indemnity (庚子赔款)*. Institute of Modern History, Academia Sinica.

Wang, Y. W., & Wang, L. (2015). Historical Materials on Diplomacy during the Qing Dynasty (Volume 4) (清季外交史 (第4册)). Changsha: Human Normal University Press.

Wickberg, E. (1965). *The Chinese in Philippine Life 1850-1898*. Yale University Press.

Wilson, A. R. (2004). *Ambition and Identity Chinese Merchant Elite in Colonial Manil 1880- 1916*. University of Hawai'i Press.

Yang, L. X. (2019). *Collected Works of Yang Shengmao (杨生茂文集)*. Nankai University Press.

You, B. H. (1957). *The Philippines*. World Affairs Press Co. Ltd.

Yu, R. J. (1998). *A Study of the Philippine Chinese General Chamber of Commerce, 1904-54*. [Master's Thesis, National CHENG CHI University]. https://ah.nccu.edu.tw/item?item_id=96757

Yuan, S. Y. (1998). Complete Works of Zhang Zhidong: Vol. 1. 张之洞全集第*1*册. Hebei People's Publishing House.

Yung, L. Y. (1996). *The Huaqiao Warriors: Chinese Resistance Movement in Philippine, 1942-1945.QuezonCity*. Ateneo de Manila University Press.

Zhao, D. X. (2008). Complete Works of Zhang Zhidong: Vol. 10. 张之洞全集第十册. Wuhan Publishing Group Co., Ltd.

Zhu, X. K. (2017). *The Study of the Shun Pao and the Sino-French War (《申报》与中法战争研究)*. Huangshan Publishing House.

Zhuang, G. T., & Liu, W. Z. (2009). *The Formation and Development of Chinese Society in East Asia: Chinese Business Network, Immigration, and Integration Trends (东亚华人社会的形成和发展——华商网络、移民与一体化趋势)*. Xiamen University Press.

Chapter 13
Going Back to Basics as an Innovative Way Forward on Muslim Health Tourism:
Keep Sharia in the Loop

Aniesa Samira Bafadhal
https://orcid.org/0000-0002-5666-0660
University of Brawijaya, Indonesia

ABSTRACT

The fast growth of health tourism has been attributed to creating a health and prevention boom era expected to usher in new economic power. Offering a different approach derived from the Sharia, Muslim health tourism poses a proximity between religion, tourism, and health. Amid the urgency to understand Muslim tourists as a potential market with such unique characteristics and specific needs, it is unfortunate that no model describes the decision-making behaviour when selecting a Muslim-friendly health destination. As a result, the author suggests a Muslim health tourist behaviour model. This study also highlighted Sharia salons and spas as one of the forms of Muslim health tourism business. It's becoming increasingly clear that for the Muslim health tourism business to truly understand its market, going back to basics is the most innovative approach.

DOI: 10.4018/979-8-3693-1846-1.ch013

INTRODUCTION

The rapid development of health tourism has been seen to have created a "health and prevention boom era" predicted to be a "new economic power" (Sigrist, 2006). Health tourism has become one of the fastest growing industries in the world, despite the desire to improve the quality of life, health, as well as healing and relaxation, which has been the primary motivation of tourists since long ago (Kim et al., 2015). Health tourism combines two things, namely health and tourism, and the involvement of these two things makes health tourism a promising tourism niche. On the other hand, Muslim medical tourism is generally done by people who are sick and need treatment to regain their health (curative) (Smith & Puczkó, 2014). Medical care is available in health tourism, such as surgery or other specialist interventions, while wellness tourism provides pilgrimages, meditation, spas, and others (Smith & Puczkó, 2017).

Increased public awareness of the health aspects is responsively responded to by the increasingly diverse commoditisation of medicines, medicals, and treatments worldwide, forming a "false trap" for those who worry excessively about their health. The negative impact of this is the emergence of massive exploration of businesspersons over the naturally unlimited human desire for health. This desire must be encouraged to change into a necessity, not essential, artificial, and even pragmatic.

Take an example of the high obsession with cosmetic surgery. The merely profit-oriented advertisements put by beauty clinics and surgical hospitals have made patients from the country and abroad take long trips to reconstruct their faces and bodies in the clinics. This has turned into the psychosocial disease of society where people become preoccupied with what they perceive as defects in their body or face or even when the physical anomalies are only slightly; the fears become real and exaggerated and encourage a solid need to perform cosmetic surgery constantly with the never-ending search for satisfaction. This psychological disorder is called Body Dysmorphic Disorder, and even cosmetic surgery has become a social and cultural phenomenon (Kim, 2009; Heyes, 2009).

Then, it is pretty often that patients also end up with various controversial, circumvention, and illegal treatments that disregard morality and even religious beliefs. A variety of other treatment methods evidences this as a trend in the world, like "vampire facelift," "sex change tourism," "sex tourism," "suicide tourism," "nude tourism," "abortion tourism," "vasectomy and tubectomy," "transplant tourism," "fertility tourism," "surrogacy tourism," and so forth which use human organs and blood and hazardous chemicals for aesthetic and medical businesses.

Correspondingly, Cohen (1998) asserts that mass tourism hurts the religiosity or level of spirituality of people who live in tourist destinations and events for tourists it-self; the impact is increasing secularisation, weakening compliance toward religion and belief, as well as waning of the sanctity of holy places, rituals, and customs. If this continues, tourism can be a coherent process against religiosity. Joyce (2001) calls this phenomenon the myth of morality. In the view of the myth of morality, there is no relationship between business and morality, and it is a mistake if business activity is run under morality and ethics. The famous phrase "business is business" or "it is not personal, it is strictly business" in business practices.

Western or mainstream medicine is ineffective in meeting the consumers' body–mind–and spirit needs (Bomar, 2013). Even though spirituality is viewed as an essential dimension of health, it tends to be more and more secular (Smith & Puczkó, 2013). In times like these, business requires more than just executing or thinking about business. It is time for tourism entrepreneurs to take off the selfish-economic man "title" Organisations in the tourism industry are not static entities; they must be seen not only as income-producing machines but also as entities closely related to the social-environmental response embedded in interconnected, nested local and global system. They can select and establish rules and a new purpose in their formal structure, more dignified, virtuous, and moral respect, including spirituality, to control harmful excesses from tourism.

On the other hand, the spiritual motif has long been an integral part of the travel activity and can be regarded as the world's oldest non-economic form of travel (Jackowski & Smith, 1992). Studies have examined the relationship between religious aspects and tourism (Veiga et al., 2017). Wahab et al. (1976) assert that a tourist is a rational decision maker (*homo economicus*) trying to maximise the utility and, therefore, assesses the costs and benefits of actions before making the trips. Meanwhile, modifying the afore-mentioned term, according to the author, a bt is a rational and spiritual decision maker (*homo Islamicus)* who needs to limit the decisions of doing reasonable and spiritual travel with the principles of Islam. What defines Muslim tourists' decisions is the *Maslahah* concept (something that brings goodness, safety, or benefit). Not all destinations that offer utility contain *Maslahah* in them, meaning that not all destinations can be visited and are worth a visit by Muslim tourists. Thus, the objective is not to maximise the utility of Muslim tourists but to maximise *Maslahah.*

Treatment and healing are a culture intended to cure one disease and maintain and improve human health. Culture is influenced by the environment, trust, and confidence because, in general, human beings believe in something more powerful that can be perceived by the senses yet unseen (supernatural). Treatment is not free from the influence of religious beliefs that embrace human life. Thousands of years ago, people had to travel to distant places to heal themselves; thus, health tourism has been a phenomenon for a long time. Religion, health, and tourism are not new phenomena.

MUSLIM HEALTH TOURISM

Competition often makes Muslim businesses overspend and overreact to innovate new products or services to attract customers. Sometimes, pursuing profits without thinking about the hereafter can be overboard, making them lose their true value because they are similar or no different from conventional businesses. At the same time, a competitive advantage sets a company apart from its competitors in the eyes of its consumers.

People often mistake innovation for something so mind-blowing that it will change the way business is run or to make cutting-edge and sophisticated products. However, this process can be something simple. Please do not rule out something that seems too easy or miss an opportunity right before us while we search for the next big thing. After all, innovation is ultimately about giving your customers what they need.

Islam does not disregard innovation. Some terms refer to innovation in Islam. *Islah*, *tajdid* and *ijtihad* are good innovations, while *bidaah* is an innovation in religion that can be good or bad. In line with that, before the Muslim health tourism business can return to accomplishment and compliance in its fundamental framework, it can return outside the market competition arena. It requires a back-to-basics approach to innovation, where Muslim health tourism businesses return to focusing on perfecting the fundamental areas of their frameworks, i.e. Sharia as Islamic law.

As an example of the application of innovation by returning to Sharia as a basis, there is the current development of Muslim health applications and devices, both medical and wellness, so there is a need for medical devices to be Halal certified, as in research by Sarisae et al. (2023).

When Islamic values are applied to tourism, there should not be any elements of disobedience to Allah ﷻ (The most glorified, the most-highest), even at the level of ideas and concepts up to the implementation. However, in Muslim-majority countries where religion focuses more on life, spirituality is not seen as an "optional extra" (Smith & Puczkó, 2013). The term "Muslim" refers to people who follow Islam. Etymologically, Muslim refers to a form of subject or doer of the deeds of Islam, and its definition depends on the understanding of Islam itself. Islam is derived from the word "Al-Slim" from the Arabic word which means peaceful, happy, obedient, and surrender to Allah ﷻ (Pal, 2011).

Unfortunately, the growing health tourism is seen as following secularism's building block and negatively impacts health tourism sustainability. If Muslims continue being involved in it, it will become a drawback. This is because, from the beginning until now, Islam does not separate religion and world affairs. These two are interrelated in Islam. Islam does not accept secularism, which separates religion from worldly affairs. Muslim health tourism emerges as a positive alternative to the interpretation of hedonistic and secular tourism. Islam regulates human life in various aspects, including health and medicine.

Preventing disease by maintaining health (preventive) and healing (curative) is the command of Allah ﷻ in the Holy *Quran*. Moreover, Allah ﷻ, through the Prophet Muhammad ﷺ (may the peace and blessing of Allah ﷻ be upon him), teaches men how to maintain health and treat disease through the Sunnah (the Way of the Prophet). There is a quote that refers to the *Hadith* At-Tirmidzi said that Had not the Prophet Muhammad ﷺ himself said, 'O Servant of God, use the medicine because God hath not created a pain without a remedy for it." Every Muslim is obliged to travel to find a cure for the disease or maintain health while hoping for the pleasure of Allah ﷻ to provide healing. Offering a different approach derived from the Holy *Quran* and *Hadith*, Muslim health tourism poses a proximity between religion, tourism, and health (Bafadhal, 2021). This means that although the travelling purpose of medical travellers is for health treatment, their primary concerns are similar to other Muslim tourists in the spiritual-related journey in which ritualised practice is incredibly significant (Teerakunpisut & Kongpiam, 2023).

Bafadhal (2022) defines Muslim health tourism as "a worship through sincere trips by Muslims to leave their origin place towards a certain health care provider as an effort to prevent or cure a disease, in order to find improvement in the quality of physical, psychological, psychosocial, and spiritual aspects according to the *Quran* and *Hadith*." There are several combinations in this term, for example, "halal healthcare tourism" and "Islamic health tourism."

Muslim health tourism consists of two principal subsets, namely Muslim wellness tourism and Muslim medical tourism, which have different subjects, purposes, and objects. Regarding tourists who travel, Muslim wellness tourism tends to be done by people who are in good condition or healthy. However, they want to prevent disease and improve their health (preventive) (Bafadhal, 2017). Muslim wellness tourism is "a worship in a sincere trip by Muslims, leaving their origin place to certain health care providers to prevent diseases (preventive) as to get the optimised well-being and resilience with the blessing of Allah ﷻ" (Bafadhal, 2017). This term is often used mutually with other terms, such as "Halal wellness and spa."

The trend of anti-Muslim called "Islamophobia," is so alarming, leading to an irrational fear of Muslims, hatred of Islam, and hostile actions toward individuals and Muslim communities in general; this has invited the concern of many researchers (Al Hamarneh & Steiner, 2004). The growing sentiment has brought what is called communitarianism, where the Muslim communities prefer to gather with their fellow Muslims to confront negative stereotypes (Stephenson & Ali, 2010). The Muslim communities are growing in numbers, so their consumption needs have also become attractive for businesses to create tourism products according to the requirements and expectations of the Muslim market (Prayag & Hosany, 2014). Moreover, Muslims have been recognised as a growing market and have now officially received labels as "consumers" (Kesseler, 2015), which, in this case, Muslims have a special place as Muslim tourists.

Then, the large number of Muslims in the world may be assumed that every Muslim has the potential to be facilitated as consumer needs. Although Muslim health tourism facilities, products, and services are almost the same as conventional ones, adjustment is still necessary for understanding markets' demand, product development, segmentation, and marketing (Bafadhal, 2022). Therefore, health tourism must focus on sub-sectors or niches because health tourists do not seek the same service (Smith & Puczkó, 2014).

In addition, consumers of the halal industry are universal with shared values. Consumers of the halal industry are mainly Muslims but also include non-Muslims of the same values. However, business in Islam is essentially universal and can be enjoyed by Muslim and non-Muslim consumers. This is because Islam is *rahmatan lil alamin* (a mercy to all creation), a religion that respects human beings. Muslim health tourism specialises in delivering healthcare products and services to Muslim customers. However, it is undeniable that Muslim health tourism also attracts non-Muslim tourists who want to enrich their health, knowledge, and travel experiences. This then leads to the term "borderless patient" for health tourists. Muslim health tourism is, therefore, not just an issue of ethics and equity at a personal level. More inclusive health marketing towards the Muslim community is a pivotal part of global environmental and public health (Bafadhal, 2022). Making the demand for halal products become a religious obligation and a powerful market force. It has been established that boosting Muslim travelers' mental health and satisfaction is vital for minimizing the impact of inconvenient tourism experiences (Han et al., 2021).

Countries of non-Muslim majority are expected to maintain tolerance and to keep the faith of Muslim tourists visiting those countries by providing Muslim-friendly facilities, services, and accommodations. The availability of Islamic attributes will not cause inconvenience to non-Musltos to any extent. Managers of tourist destinations can provide services that meet the needs of Muslims by allocating unique places and facilities for Muslims. Thus, Islamic branding within a destination or tourist product would not become merely a name to attract the Muslim market (Battour & Ismail, 2015). Hence, both Muslim and non-Muslim tourists may decide not to travel to a healthcare provider if there are strict rules, specific attributes, and restrictions. Tourism operators face a more significant challenge, particularly those promoting halal tourism destinations (Rahman et al., 2020).

MUSLIM HEALTH TOURIST BEHAVIOUR MODEL

Muslim health tourism behavior model is a reasonably straightforward means of identifying the level of Muslim tourist commitment towards selecting and purchasing a product or service for health tourism both for the purposes of preventing disease (Muslim wellness tourism) and treating disease (Muslim medical tourism). making this model more specific and different from other types of halal tourism. Amid the urgency to understand Muslim health tourists as a potential market with such unique characteristics, terms, and specific needs, it is unfortunate that we have not developed a unique model that describes the decision-making behaviour of Muslim health tourists regarding choosing a Muslim-friendly health destination. Therefore, the author proposes a "Muslim Health Tourist Behavior Model," shown in Figure 1. The model shows three main things underlying the behaviour of Muslim health tourists. The three are the testament of the Prophet Muhammad ﷺ (*Hadith* narrated At-Tirmidzi). As part of worship, Allah ﷻ commands healthy travel to increase the balance in the vertical relationship (humans and Allah ﷻ), the horizontal relationship (humans to humans), and the diagonal (humans and nature).

The three relationships consist of the following. First, it is called *Habluminallah* (God-driven). The significant driving force is (a) religious piety (*Taqwa*), (b) religious obedience (*Taat*), and (c) piousness (*Saleh*), each of which is of different levels. These are the main drivers of Muslims to choose Muslim-friendly health travel over conventional health travel or even controversial one, as to maintain the relationship with Allah ﷻ. Second, it is called *Habluminannas* (socio-driven). These factors contribute to human relationships, including (a) stimuli of Muslim-friendly strategic marketing, such as product quality, promotion, price, location, image, halal and sharia compliance services, and so forth; (b) Muslim community references which refer to recommendation from the Muslim community that may include nuclear family, peers, community, scholars and even the government—as the duty of all Muslims are *Amar makruf nahi munkar* (enjoying the good and forbid the evil); and (c) the motive of *Muamalah* transactions (business) for health purposes also affect the behavior of Muslims. Third, it is known as *habluminal'alam* (environment-driven), which refers to the relationship between humans and nature, i.e., the location and the destination of health tourism. The things to consider include (a) the merits of a health destination, in which the more efficacious treatment or prevention of disease in that destination, the more encouraging it is for tourists to visit; (b) Muslim-friendly health destination also plays an essential, in which the better the facility accommodates the needs of Muslim tourists, the more encouraging it is for Muslim tourists to choose.

Muslim health tourist behavior model is formed through three stages. First is the pre-decision stage, taking the form of needs recognition. When Muslims are ill, they may decide to take corrective action through Muslim medical tourism. Meanwhile, when Muslims are in good health and want to improve their health to avoid diseases, they can choose to perform preventive actions through Muslim wellness tourism.

Second, it is the decision stage. This stage starts with (a) *niyyah* (worship intention), in which every Muslim must see and do any activities as a form of worship to Allah ﷻ. Hence, it is necessary to straighten the intention to worship Allah ﷻ in the form of health tourism. Then, it goes to (b) evaluation of *Maslahah* (profit here and in the afterlife) by selecting products of good utility. At the same time, the products do not violate Islamic law for them to be blessed by Allah ﷻ. Followed by (c) Needs stage fulfilment is the fulfilment of the three needs of Muslim medical tourists,

Figure 1. Muslim health tourist behaviour model

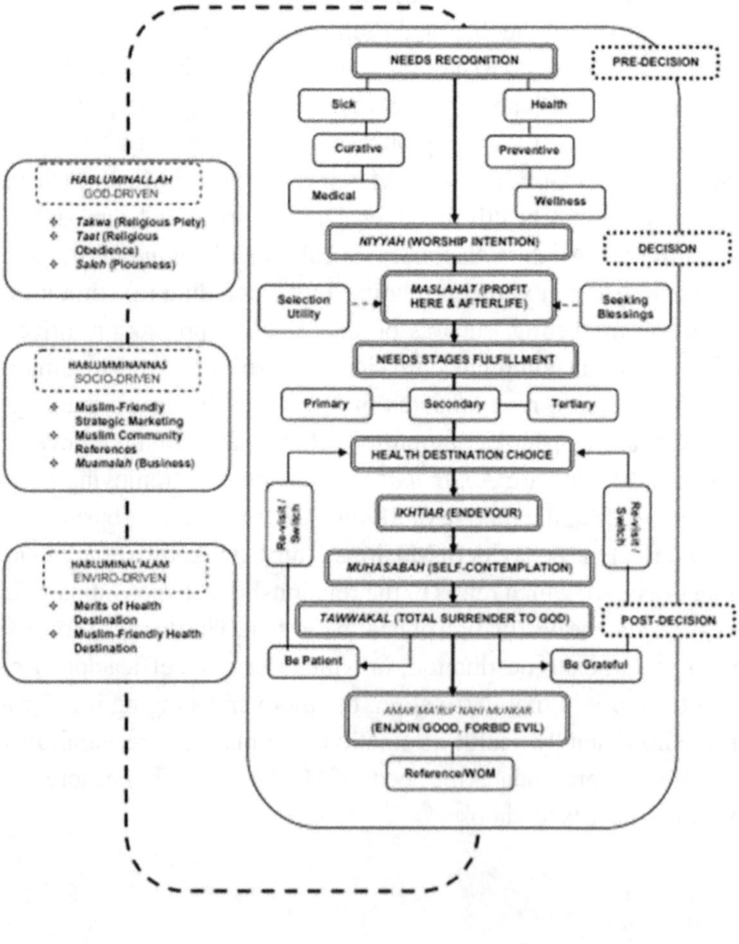

i.e., *Dharuriyat* (primary), *Hajjiyat* (secondary), and *Tahsiniyat* (tertiary) needs. The following (d) is the destination choice of health tourism, a process done after considering many factors afore-mentioned. The process continues with (e) *Ikhtiar* (endeavour), in which Muslims must earnestly seek health improvement and seek the best experts. Then (e) upon receiving treatment, Muslim health tourists should conduct *Muhasabah* (self-contemplation) and improve themselves—remembering and acknowledging that Allah ﷻ gives the illnesses they suffer from and that those may be due to negligence or even deliberate personal actions such as taking alcoholic drinks, smoking, free sex, eating junk food, consuming non-halal food, and so forth.

Third, it is called post-decision. Having made such an effort to improve health or cure diseases, the next process is as follows. First, it is (a) *tawwakal* (total surrender to Allah ﷻ), as Allah ﷻ has the entire prerogative to heal or improve our health. When we are healthy, we must be grateful to Allah ﷻ. We still have to be grateful and patient when we have not gotten healing or health improvement. Medical tourists may also decide to revisit or switch to other Muslim-friendly health destinations at this stage. Then, (b) the final process is, as mentioned earlier, *Amar makruf nahi munkar* (enjoining the good and forbidding the evil). After performing health tourism in Muslim-friendly destinations, Muslims are expected to provide references, recommendations, and positive word-of-mouth to other Muslim tourists so fellow Muslims can get the same Sharia services and avoid non-sharia ones.

DISCUSSION AND FINDINGS

The current study's findings aim to provide an overview of one of the Muslim Health Tourism services to prevent disease (wellness), particullarly Sharia Salon and Spa. Islam teaches people to beautify themselves in a simple and balanced way because Allah ﷻ in Holly Qur'an, "Verily We have created man in the best form. (Surat (At-Tin: 4). Allah ﷻ has created humans in the best possible form, and changing Allah's ﷻ creation makes us ungrateful people and changes the nature that Allah ﷻ has given. Allah ﷻ in Holly Qur'an said, "It may be that you hate something, even though it is perfect for you, and it may be (also) you like something, even though it is awful for you; Allah ﷻ knows, while you do not know," (*Surah Al-Baqarah*: 216).

For the treatment to prevent physical and social illnesses, Islamic civilisation built various public health services. The Islamic hammam was the first public bathhouse in the Muslim world. There were two types of hammam in the Middle Ages, for men and women. Hammam was first introduced in Syria during the era of the Umayyad Caliphate in the 6th century, during the Roman period. During the Umayyad period (661-750 AD), public baths, called Islamic hammams, proliferated in the Arabian Peninsula. In particular, the Islamic hammam is based on a prevalent religious and cultural background, derived from the *wudhu* (ablution) ritual mentioned in the *Quran* and the use of a steam room for baths by the Turkish, called the Turkish hammam. Therefore, Islamic hammams were generally built adjacent to the mosque in the medieval period. The Islamic hammam was also evolving as a gathering place for religious scholars, travellers, former detainees, and sick people hoping to recover from their illnesses; they came to perform ritual cleansing and to get closer to Allah ﷻ. Hammam is the embryo of spas these days. (Aaland, 1978).

Hammam had such complex sanitation and drainage, completed with fresh water supplies (even though it was more comprehensive than the famous Roman public baths), contributing to public health (Pormann & Savage-Smith, 2007). The staff of the public baths consisted of several professionals such as guards (*Hammamīān*), barbers (*Salmānīān*), masseurs (*Āsījānān*), cupping therapists (*Hajjāmān*) and others (Mez, 1992). The hammam is part of the Islamic purification ritual, and the concept has been exported to modern Sharia salons, spas, and beauty clinics (Mez, 1992; Smith & Puckzo, 2013). The services include *Ghusl* baths, massages, *Ismid kohl*, *Henna* art, cutting moustache, *siwak* toothbrush, spa services, beauty therapists, hairdressers, therapists, masseurs, and make-up artists (Bafadhal, 2017; Bafadhal, 2022).

Women love to look beautiful and are very concerned about their beauty, such as cutting their hair, having body and facial treatments, and cleaning their nails and hands. Women often go to beauty salons to make their appearance even more beautiful. However, how does Islam perceive this? Islam highly upholds and respects the values of beauty, cleanliness, and neatness. Islam always encourages Muslim women (*Muslimah*) to adorn and beautify themselves acceptably in order to worship and seek the blessing of Allah ﷻ (Holly *Quran Surah Al-A'raf*: 26; *An-Nur*: 31; and *An-Nahl*: 14).

Al-Ghamidi (2013) states that in the past, women helped each other to comb, oil, tidy, and cut their hair, yet these all were done. Such activities already existed in the time of Prophet Muhammad ﷺ. At this time, beauty salons were widespread. However, Muslims were suggested to select those whose service and operation complied with Islamic values. Furthermore, the spa comes from the Latin word "*Solus* per *Aquam*" (SPA). Water is one of the methods of treatment recommended by the Prophet Muhammad ﷺ, and it is suggested to be used to relieve fever, as the saying of the Prophet Muhammad ﷺ: "Fever is from the heat of Hell, so abate fever with water" (*Hadith* narrated Al-Bukhari). Callen (2007) claims that in their development, spas are no longer just associated with mineral springs and the therapeutic use of water. Spas now present in the form of chic services and products in a beauty salon, are available in various department stores, and may also involve places to eat delicious and healthy food or even become the ultimate destination for a vacation.

However, Islam does not forbid wearing jewellery, clothes, fragrance, make-up, or even improving their visual appearance for health reasons or beautifying themselves properly to appear beautiful in front of her husband. The Prophet Muhammad ﷺ was once asked, "What about a people who like to wear nice clothes and sandals?" He replied, "Verily, Allah ﷻ is beautiful, and He loves beauty. Arrogance means rejecting the truth and looking down on people" (*Hadith* narrated *Muslim*). The *Hadith*, as mentioned, Allah ﷻ is beautiful; of course, His creation is also excellent. For the beauty of His beauty, Allah ﷻ also loves beauty; in another sense, beauty is above the best form.

Abu Huraira said that the Prophet Muhammad ﷺ said, "Whoever has hair, let one take care of it" (*Hadith* narrated Abu Dawud). The Prophet Muhammad ﷺ also did not like seeing messy, long, and untidied hair. Wa'il ibn Hijr said, "I came to the Prophet and had long hair. When the Messenger of Allah ﷻ saw me, he said, 'Evil, evil.' I then returned and cut them off. I then came to him in the morning. He said (to me), 'I did not intend to do evil to you; this is much better.'" (*Hadith* narrated Abu Dawud). For women, the Prophet Muhammad ﷺ forbade them from trimming their hair. Furthermore, Abdullah ibn Umar, the Prophet Muhammad ﷺ said, "There is nothing for women to shave (her hair), she can only cut it (shorten)" (*Hadith* narrated Abu Dawud).

Related to hair polish, Abu Hurairah was once asked, "Did the Prophet Muhammad ﷺ polish his hair? He replied, "Yes" (*Hadith* narrated At-Tirmidzi). The colour advised is red or yellow/gold. Dyeing the hair black is forbidden, as it is feared for *Tadlis* (deception), like an older woman polishing her hair to attract a person proposing to her or wanting to marry her or an older man. Hence, the hair looks greyish to attract the woman he wants to marry. Such polishes belong to deceit and lies. Ibn Majah narrated the *Hadith* of Ummu Salamah that Prophet Muhammad ﷺ, the Messenger of Allah ﷻ, masked his body, starting from the *Aurat* by using blossom, then to the whole body.

For the women, the Prophet ordered to arrange and braid their hair in the *Hadith* of Al-Bukhari, narrated the history of "Umm Athiyah رضي الله عنها that she said, and we put the hair of the daughter of the Prophet Muhammad ﷺ in three braids, two at the sides and one at the front.". If Islam allows men and women to adorn themselves as a whole, it means Islam maintains the nature of women and femininity. This includes allowing women to use or wear something forbidden for men, such as silk and gold (*Hadith* narrated At-Tirmidzi). Thus, in general, women are allowed to adorn themselves. In addition, styling the hair for the husband's happiness is halal. However, it becomes haram if the purpose is to show it off to non-*mahram* (all those forbidden to marry due to heredity, breastfeeding, and marriage in Islamic law).

The Islamic guidance on dress and makeup becomes the standard for women and men to keep themselves from doing things, leading to *Tabarruj* (derived from Arabic, which means "to expose and show one is self-making it visible by eyes") that are forbidden in Islam. "And abide in your houses and do not display yourselves as [was] the display of the former times of ignorance...." The Prophet Muhammad ﷺ added, "Whoever imitates a people is one of them" (*Hadith* narrated Ahmad). *Tabarruj* is *Jahiliyah* culture (the period in which the people of Mecca were in ignorance and arbitrariness before the advent of Islam) that Islam challenged and abolished. This culture not only undermines the dignity of women but also leads to the exploitation of men against women. Islam prohibits *Tabarruj* because it can eliminate shame among women. The order of covering aurat and make-up within reasonable limits in Islam has specific purposes, among others, to maintain women's dignity.

As the Prophet Muhammad ﷺ said, "Faith consists of sixty to seventy branches, the best of which is to declare *LâIlâhaIllallâh* (there is no God, but Allah ﷻ) and the least of which is to remove something harmful from the road, and modesty is a branch of faith" (*Hadith* narrated Al-Bukhari). Examples of *Tabarruj* are shaving or tattooing the eyebrows, applying too much powder, applying eye shadow, applying lipstick with striking colours, applying excessive makeup, wearing nail polish, showing off the jewellery, undressing and opening aurat, such as hair, neck, calves, thighs, and others in public; such actions fall into the category of *Tabarruj*. Instead, Islam teaches its people to adorn themselves within reasonable limits, covering the aurat, graceful, and within specific contexts. For example, women adorn themselves before worshipping Allah ﷻ or beautify themselves in the presence of the husband or *Mahram.*

Ironically, the development of health tourism, marked by the increasing number of domestic and foreign tourists, various salons and spas, and other forms of health tourism, also creates a harmful effect: the penetration of foreign culture. This can lead to cultural transformation that will ultimately affect the various sectors of public life. In public perception, the spa and salon business is identical to the negative stigma (Narendran, 2011). Young (1973) suggests that tourism may give rise to undesirable activity, such as prostitution, sex trafficking, and HIV, and penetration of foreign cultures that can negatively impact local communities. Undeniably, there are many transgender people in salons and spas, erotic massage parlours, homosexual salons, and prostitution disguised as the health and other fitness business. Despite promoting themselves as massage, spa, and sauna with exclusive prices and services, some salons and spas facilitate prostitution and other hedonism. It has led to a negative image and stigma for conventional salons and spas, raising doubts and worries for Muslims about using salon and spa services.

Sharia salons and spas are currently experiencing exponential and massive growth. Nevertheless, research on Sharia salons and spas shows such a poor trend as few researchers pay attention to the potential of innovation of Sharia salons and spas compared to traditional salons and spas, especially in Muslim countries. Based on the search of various kinds of literature, the concept of Islamic salons and spas or Sharia salons and spas is still vague and understudied. Thus, it is urgent to formulate the concept of salon and spa Sharia amid the development of health tourism under secularisation, where there is an attempt to separate religion from the various aspects of human life, including tourism and health.

Islamic Practices Spa provides spa services, beauty therapists based on sex, different rooms and services for male and female clients, and services per Islamic law (Yaman et al., 2012). Based on this, Bafadhal (2017) states, "definition of sharia salons and spas are a form of business that provides promotive and preventive wellness services and products combining aesthetic, cosmetics, and spiritual treatments of the body, face, hair, and soul for both men and women, especially Muslims in conformity with Islamic law as the main determinant."

Even so, scholars still differ in opinions about the halal or haram of salons and spas. Some scholars consider treating and dressing in salons and spas are wasteful, and it is feared to lead to haram actions such as imitating the barbarian "*Jahiliyah* style." Furthermore, suppose the salons and spas employ male staff. In that case, *Khalwat* (excessive closeness between persons of the opposite sex and illicit contact with the opposite sex), which is forbidden in Islam, may occur. *Ulama* and *Fatwa* Council, headed by Sheikh Abdullah ibn Baz, once issued a *Fatwa* regarding the *Haram* of the beard-shaving profession, as the profession is helping people sinning. Therefore, the salon services can be said to be haram as it generally provides various haram services such as hair extension and eyebrow trimming, tattooing, and changing Allah ﷻ creation, that is haram for Muslims according to Islamic law (*Hadith* narrated At-Tirmidzi).

Some Islamic scholars also consider having treatments in a public bath or spa haram if done at home. At-Tirmidzi narrated *Hadith* that the Prophet ﷺ said, "Whoever believes in Allah ﷻ, and the last day, his wife should not enter the public baths. "At-Tirmidzi narrated that some women from Homs or Syria entered upon 'Aisyah يضر اهنع هللا and she said, "Are you the ones whose women folk go to the public baths? I heard Muhammad ﷺ, the Messenger of Allah ﷻ, say, "There is no woman who takes off her garments anywhere but in the house of her husband, but she has torn the veil that is between her and her lord." However, if the treatments cannot be done at home, it is permissible for women to go to public baths. The women must still be careful and keep the aurat (body parts that the opposite sex must cover) closed.

Ibn Taymiyah (1963) said, "The scholars said, 'A concession is granted to women allowing them to go to the public baths in cases of need just as it is granted to men, so long as they lower their gaze and guard their chastity. This also applies to women who are sick or bleeding following childbirth, or who have to do *Ghusl* and cannot do it anywhere except in the public baths." He also said, "As for women, they may enter (the public baths) in cases of necessity so long as they cover their aurat." However, referring to the command to adorn ourselves and do ablution in Islam, some other scholars agree that this is *Makruh* (something which is not a sin but is advisable not to be done) to go to salons and spas. Ultimately, scholars do not see going to salons as haram if Muslims as users use the services as commanded by Islamic laws. In addition, it is also haram if the salon and spa managers provide and offer treatments and services that are prohibited in Islam.

The main problem in dealing with beauty treatments and spa operations from the perspective of Islam is the issue of *Mahram*, aurat, and the separation of different sexes. The *Quran* commands, "...and not expose their adornment except to their husbands, their fathers, their husbands' fathers, their sons, their husbands' sons, their brothers, their brothers' sons, their sisters' sons, their women, that which their right hands possess, or those male attendants having no physical desire, or children who are not yet aware of the private aspects of women...." (Holly *Quran Surah An-Nur*: 31).

There are also controversies and conflicts related to halal haram for women to open their *Aurat* in front of non-Muslim women. Some scholars declare that this is haram except for emergency and life-threatening conditions such as a medical operation or accident and treatment of diseases. However, when it comes to health care that is not urgent, most scholars agree that Muslim women should not open their aurat in the presence of non-Muslim women. Therefore, Muslim women should go to a salon and spa managed and owned by Muslims. Meanwhile, non-Muslims interested in opening a salon and spa targeting Muslim users are suggested to provide Muslim women therapists and staff. Beauty and spa treatments are developed in various countries because people seek new and unique experiences. The prohibition for a Muslim woman to appear without a *Hijab* in front of a non-Muslim female, fearing that the non-Muslim woman will be able to explain to her husband or other strangers (non-mahram of the Muslim woman) the physical condition of the Muslim woman so as if the man sees the Muslim woman directly.

Fatwa and special official regulations regarding Sharia salons and spas from the national Sharia board are urgently needed. Muslim consumers, managers of Muslim-friendly salons and spas, and the government must coordinate to play an essential role in setting up education and training, regulation, accreditation, quality standards, and marketing sharia salons and spas. The literature and research on Sharia salons and spas have been limited. Through a review of various literature sources by literature review and interviews with Sharia salon and spas owners or managers in Indonesia, Bafadhal (2017) has developed a standard concept for Sharia salons and spas, i.e., the Salient Traits of Sharia Salon and Spas in Table 1. as a method of measuring compliance in one of the Muslim health tourism destinations.

Sources: Bafadhal (2017)

The Muslim woman hopes to get the beauty services of the Muslim-friendly health destination, which provides the best service and protection when she has to leave

Table 1. Sharia salons and spas salient traits

No.	Categories	Salient Traits
1	Services	• Forbidden to trimming or doing *Tanmis,* which is plucking facial hairs and excess eyebrows • Forbidden to do hair colouring with black colour and pull-out grey hair or prefer to colour it with red and gold colour, especially using herb hair colouring; • Forbidden to show man or woman *Aurah,* especially the body's intimate part; • Products must free form haram ingredients such as beer bath, blood facelift, botox, silicon and gold, alcohol, pork, dog or its derivatives; • Allowed collagen injection if the source is pure or halal, e.g., from a slaughtered cow, to get rid of severe wrinkles; • Forbidden to treat wig and hair extension (artificial hair), but it is permissible to transplant hair by taking hair from other parts of the hair from oneself; • Forbidden to curl the hairs if the husband or owner permits it, then it is permitted for her • The therapist must be of the same sex with the clients; • Men are allowed (*makruh*) to shave the hair on the leg, the chest, and the hand, yet it is prohibited for women; • Suggested (*sunnah*) to shave the pluck under arm hair, which should not be left for more than 40 days; • It is forbidden to open the *aurat*, which is incredibly full of the body • Suggested trimming the nails (pedicure and manicure allowed); • Suggested to braid the hair; • Suggested to have a face mask and gulp down the body with a blossom mask (*Nurah*) or halal materials; • Suggested applying beard oil; • Forbidden to do *Qoza*' (shaving some part of head hair and leaving some other); • Women are forbidden to cut all their hair resembling men; • Women are forbidden to imitate the style of prostitutes or hedonic women; • Forbidden to have tattoos; • Allowed to make up the hands and feet with *henna* and allowed to wear modest style nail polish for women during their menstruation because it is not allowed to S*holat* (pray) during menstruation, still prioritise using *henna;* • Forbidden to wear nail polish as it causes wudhu or ablution not perfect; • Forbidden to *nasyr* the teeth, which is filing and honing the tips of the teeth • Allowed massage using halal oils or ointment and hair oil (*Dhuns*); • The treatment must not evoke lust; • the treatment must not torture the body; • Allowed to use aromatherapy with natural ingredients and non-intoxicating. Allowed to have mud bath; • Allowed to have spice bath; • Suggested making the eyes up using *Kohl* or *Itsmid* stone • Allowed to do makeup but must be modest; • Allowed to do dental spa or with *siwak* (natural toothbrush) • Allowed to use perfume during treatment (such as *Thib*); • Allowed to treat acne and boils in particular, such as with *Dzarirah* perfume; • Allowed to use steam shower or sauna (*Ghusl* smudging or steam shower) • Allowed to *Tarjil* (combing hair) • Allowed to *Ghusl* herb or bath herbs, especially *Ghusl sidr* • Allowed to use warm or ice water for treatment; • Allowed women to wear silk and gold but should not drink or eat used silver or gold • Allowed to treat lost beauty, not because of normal aging, but because of illness or accident • Allowed to provide traditional or modern services as long as the Muslim scholar board by *Quran*, *Hadith* or *Ijma*, and *Qiyas* do not prohibit the services.

continued on following page

Table 1. Continued

No.	Categories	Salient Traits
2	Facilities	• Providing the waiting room or sofas for the husband or mahram who accompanies the female customers during the trip (Muslim women should be accompanied by a husband or *mahram* (guardian such as brother, sister, etc.); • Separating the service rooms between male and female • Reciting of Holly *Quran* verses (Holly *Quran* is the cure for all illnesses); • The use of different rooms and services for male and female clients or generally focus on serving Muslim women only; • Designing a closed room not visible by non-Muslims; fearing that the non-Muslim woman will be able to explain to her husband or other strangers (non-mahram of the Muslim woman) regarding the physical and intimate part condition of the Muslim woman so as if the man sees the Muslim woman directly; • Bathing cloth must cover *aurat* during treatment for both men and women; • The equipment used does not violate Islamic law and is free from any haram materials; • Facilities with sex segregation or different times; • Availability of prayer room, prayer mat, and the Qibla direction; • No music expressing seductive and controversial messages; • Non-figurative decoration pattern (no pictures and statues, figurines of human and animal form) things to avoid *Shirk* (accepting other as a God); • Bed, toilets, and therapy room not facing Mecca or *Qibla;* • Water-friendly restroom or toilet (for *Wuḍū'* (ablution)); • Separates leisure facilities for different sexes; • Build-in wudhu facilities with different locations with toilets or bathrooms because it is forbidden to say the name of Allah ﷻ in the toilet; • Separates room and facilities for non-Muslim clients; • Allowed halal food and dietary products such as tea and milk; • Halal drugs and treatment medicine (such as non-alcohol and porcine-free ingredients); • Islamic dress code for patients (e.g., *Hijab* or shower cap to cover their hair as *Aurat* (intimate parts);

continued on following page

their home, where she becomes the "Queen of the house." She needed comfortable services for them to feel threatened in their home. Where she looking for products and services that make it seem as if she is in the protection of her husband or parents and treated as a family so she feels comfortable and able to maintain her dignity, visual appearance, and religious beliefs using Muslim-friendly salons and spas outside her home. The privileged position of women in Islam is evident. She is important and entitled to protection from every kind of disrespect of her honour. Stereotypes that men have control over Muslim women's bodies are a form of shaming their bodies, mocking their minds, and humiliating their souls.

The delusion that "beauty is goodness" tends to mislead, which leads women to a never-ending journey. True beauty has not only a body but also a mind and a spirit. Muslim women are expected to beautify themselves and their behaviour to

Table 1. Continued

No.	Categories	Salient Traits
3	Management	• Employing Muslim Therapists and staff should be disciplined and respect Muslim principles; • It is essential to seek to have the client's identity card or similar document checked to match services regarding Muslim or non-Muslim religion and gender • Provide information that is not misleading, such as appropriate product or service quality, and give religious education related to beauty, such as prayer for bathing and dressing • Prohibited from providing services that lead to negligence of the prayer time; • Not hiring transgender as the staff; • Islamic dress code for female Muslim therapists and staff (*Hijab*); • Therapists and staff wearing descent clothes covering the *Aurat;* • Providing particular time for prayers for Muslim workers; • Special arrangements for Muslim workers and customers during *Ramadhan*; • Ethical marketing and promotion; • Conducting corporate social responsibility; • Paying tax; • Conducting philanthropic donations based on *Zakat* principles (obligatory charity) or philanthropic donations such as giving *iInfaq* and *Sodaqoh;* • Transaction, funding, and investment using the network of Islamic financial institutions such as sharia banks (to avoid *Riba* (usury); • Management and ownership preferably by Muslim; • If possible, Sharia supervisory boards are available within the organisational structure of the company; • Reasonable treatment fee; • Therapist professional credentials; • Protection and equality in healthcare rights; • Dietary product and drug, vitamin, or supplement safety certification; • Halal certification for salon and spa products; • Sharia-compliance certification for salon and spa service and management; • Islamic branding and logo; • Accepting *takaful* insurance; • Providing an interpreter and digital reference platform to minimise misunderstanding of cross-cultural or border customers is good to consider.

consider the values of rationality, morality, and *Maslahah* (profit for here and the afterlife) in all decisions they make. Sharia salons and spas business are for seeking beauty, brain, and blessing, not blight.

Ibn 'Umar (RAA) narrated that the Prophet Muhammad ﷺ said, "He who imitates any people (in their actions) is considered to be one of them.". Muslim businessmen innovate but do not imitate conventional business strategies solely by pursuing intimate worship with God—Muslim health tourism business, not innovation resistance. Business innovation is everybody's business, but innovation for good faith order is not everyone's cup of tea. In this case, Muslim business people will return their business decisions to the teachings of God, Allah ﷻ as the ultimate innovator.

REFERENCES

Aaland, M. (1978). *Sweat*. Capra Press.

Al Ghamidi, A b S. (2013). *Fiqih Wanita*. Solo: Aqwam.

Al-Hamarneh, A., & Steiner, C. (2004). Islamic Tourism: Rethinking the Strategies of Tourism Development in the Arab World After September 11, 2001. *Comparative Studies of South Asia, Africa and the Middle East*, *24*(1), 175–186. doi:10.1215/1089201X-24-1-175

Bafadhal, A. S. (2017). *Muslim Health Tourism*. Lambert Academic Publishing.

Bafadhal, A. S. (2021). Muslim health tourism archetypes for Sharia salons and spas. *Leisure/Loisir*, *46*(1), 1-24.

Bafadhal, A. S. (2022). Muslim health tourism. In D. Buhalis (Ed.), *Encyclopedia of Tourism Management and Marketing*. Edward Elgar Publishing. doi:10.4337/9781800377486.muslim.health.tourism

Battour, M., & Ismail, M. N. (2016). Halal tourism: Concepts, practises, challenges and future. *Tourism Management Perspectives*, *19*, 150-154.

Bomar, P. J. (2013). Comments on complementary and alternative healing modalities. *International Journal of Nursing Practice*, *19*(2), 1–6. doi:10.1111/ijn.12061 PMID:23617443

Callen, K. (2001). *Spa: Pamper Body and Soul*. Ebury Press.

Cohen, E. (1988). Authenticity and Commoditization in Tourism. *Annals of Tourism Research*, *15*(3), 371–386. doi:10.1016/0160-7383(88)90028-X

Han, H., Lee, S., Ariza-Montes, A., Al-Ansi, A., Tariq, B., Vega-Muñoz, A., & Park, S. H. (2021). Muslim travelers' inconvenient tourism experience and self-rated mental health at a non-Islamic country: Exploring gender and age differences. *International Journal of Environmental Research and Public Health*, *18*(2), 758. doi:10.3390/ijerph18020758 PMID:33477400

Heyes, C. J. (2009). Diagnosing culture: Body Dysmorphic Disorder and cosmetic surgery. *Body & Society*, *15*(4), 73–93. doi:10.1177/1357034X09347222

Jackowski, A., & Smith, V. L. (1992). Polish pilgrim-tourists. *Annals of Tourism Research*, *19*(1), 92–106. doi:10.1016/0160-7383(92)90109-3

Joyce, R. (2001). *The myth of morality*. Cambridge University Press. doi:10.1017/CBO9780511487101

Kamassi, A., Abd Manaf, N. H., & Omar, A. (2020). The identity and role of stakeholders in the medical tourism industry: State of the art. *Tourism Review*, *75*(3), 559–574. doi:10.1108/TR-01-2019-0031

Kessler, K. (2015). Conceptualizing Mosque Tourism: A central feature of Islamic and Religious Tourism. *International Journal of Religious Tourism and Pilgrimage*, *39*(2), 2.

Kim, H. (2009). *The Plastic Surgery Obsession in South Korea*. Syracuse University Honors Program Capstone Projects.

Kim, H., Woo, E., & Uysal, M. (2015). Tourism experience and quality of life among elderly tourists. *Tourism Management*, *46*, 465–476. doi:10.1016/j.tourman.2014.08.002

Pal, A. (2011). Islam Means Peace: Understanding the Muslim Principle of Nonviolence Today. Greenport: Praeger. doi:10.5040/9798400604997

Pormann, P. E., & Savage-Smith, E. (2007). *Medieval Islamic medicine*. Edinburgh University Press. doi:10.1515/9780748629244

Prayag, G., & Hosany, S. (2014). When Middle East Meets West: Understanding the Motives and Perceptions of Young Tourists from the United Arab Emirates. *Tourism Management*, *40*, 35–45. doi:10.1016/j.tourman.2013.05.003

Rahman, H. H. & Abdul, H. (2004). The development of the health sciences and related institutions during the first six centuries of Islam. *ISoIT*, 973–984.

Rahman, M., Moghavvemi, S., Thirumoorthi, T., & Rahman, M. K. (2020). The impact of tourists' perceptions on halal tourism destination: A structural model analysis. *Tourism Review*, *75*(3), 575–594. doi:10.1108/TR-05-2019-0182

Sarisae, S., Benrit, P., & Salaeh, N. (2023). The need for Halal certification of medical devices: A case study of Thailand. *Journal of Halal Science and Technology*, *2*(1), 32–39. doi:10.59202/jhst.v2i1.664

Sigrist, S. (2006). *Health Horizons: Guide zu den neuen Gesundheitsmarkten/Guide to the New Healthmarkets* (Vol. 20). Gottlieb Duttweiler Institut/GDI.

Smith, M. K., & Puczkó, L. (2013). *Health and wellness tourism*. Routledge.

Smith, M. K., & Puczkó, L. (2014). *Health, tourism, and hospitality: spas, wellness, and medical travel*. Routledge. doi:10.4324/9780203083772

Smith, M. K., & Puczkó, L. (2017). *The Routledge Handbook of health tourism*. Routledge.

Stephenson, M. L., & Ali, N. (2010). Tourism, travel, and Islamophobia: post 9/11 journeys of Muslims in non-Muslim states. In N. Scott & J. Jafari (Eds.), *Tourism in the Muslim world*. Emerald Group Publishing Limited.

Teerakunpisut, S., & Kongpiam, P. (2023). Implementation of a Hospitality-Oriented Patient Experience (HOPE) Concept to Service Standards of Muslim-friendly Medical Tourism. *Social Space*, *23*(1), 400–428.

Vargas-Sánchez, A., & Moral-Moral, M. (2019). Halal tourism: State of the art. *Tourism Review*, *74*(3), 385–399. doi:10.1108/TR-01-2018-0015

Veiga, C., Santos, M., Águas, P., & Santos, J. (2017). Are millennials transforming global tourism? Challenges for destinations and companies. *Worldwide Hospitality and Tourism Themes*, *9*(6), 603–616. doi:10.1108/WHATT-09-2017-0047

Wahab, S., Crompton, J., & Rothfield, L. (1976). *Tourism Marketing*. Tourism International Press.

Yaman, R., Alias, Z., & Ishak, N. M. (2012). Beauty Treatment and Spa Design from Islamic Perspective. *Procedia: Social and Behavioral Sciences*, *50*, 492–501. doi:10.1016/j.sbspro.2012.08.053

Young, G. (1973). *Tourism -Blessing or blight?* Penguin.

Compilation of References

Aaland, M. (1978). *Sweat*. Capra Press.

Abd Rahman, I. M., Jamil, N. N., & Ismail, K. N. I. K. (2019). Does Political Connection Moderate Women Directors' Effect on CSR Disclosure? Evidence from Malaysia. *Asian Journal of Accounting and Governance, 11*.

Acs, Z. J., Autio, E., & Szerb, L. (2012). National Systems of Entrepreneurship: Measurement Issues and Policy Implications. SSRN *Electronic Journal*. doi:10.2139/ssrn.2008160

Ács, Z. J., Autio, E., & Szerb, L. (2016). National Systems of Entrepreneurship: Measurement issues and policy implications. In Global Entrepreneurship, Institutions and Incentives. doi:10.4337/9781784718053.00040

Ács, Z. J., Autio, E., & Szerb, L. (2014). National Systems of Entrepreneurship: Measurement issues and policy implications. *Research Policy*, *43*(3), 476–494. Advance online publication. doi:10.1016/j.respol.2013.08.016

Ahmadi, M., Baei, F., Hosseini-Amiri, S.-M., Moarefi, A., Suifan, T. S., & Sweis, R. (2020). Proposing a model of manager's strategic intelligence, organization development, and entrepreneurial behavior in organizations. *Journal of Management Development*, *39*(4), 559–579. doi:10.1108/JMD-11-2018-0317

Ahmed, R., Ahmed, M., Ahmad, N., & Abidin, S. Z. (2020). Fintech: A Review on its Evolution, Adoption, Challenges, and Future. *Journal of Theoretical and Applied Information Technology*, *98*(1), 83–96.

Ahunanya, V., Ovharhe, O. H., Emenike, C. G., & Otto, G. (2022a). Consignment inventory system and entrepreneurial success among micro warehousing firms. *International Journal of Social Science & Management Research*, *8*(5), 18–28. doi:10.56201/ijssmr.v8.no5.2022.pg18.28

Ahunanya, V., Ovharhe, O. H., Emenike, C. G., & Otto, G. (2022b). Consignment inventory system and obsolescence management in the drilling fluid firms in Nigeria. *International Journal of Social Science & Management Research*, *8*(5), 1–27. doi:10.56201/ijssmr.v8.no5.2022.pg1.17

Ajaz, A., Shenbei, Z., & Sarfraz, M. (2020). Delineating the influence of boardroom gender diversity on corporate social responsibility, financial performance, and reputation. *LogForum, 16*(1).

Al Ghamidi, A b S. (2013). *Fiqih Wanita*. Solo: Aqwam.

Alberta.alis (2023). *Career insight: Know yourself.* Alis. https://alis.alberta.ca/careerinsite/know-yourself/skills-quiz/

Albitar, K., Hussainey, K., Kolade, N., & Gerged, A. M. (2020). ESG disclosure and firm performance before and after IR. *International Journal of Accounting & Information Management*.

Alcaraz, C., Zeadally, S., & Chakraborty, S. (2018). Fog computing for the internet of things. *Survey (London, England)*.

Aldrich, H. (1999). Organizations evolving. *Sage (Atlanta, Ga.)*.

Alessandrini, F., & Jondeau, E. (2020). Optimal Strategies for ESG Portfolios. *Swiss Finance Institute Research Paper*, (20-21).

Al-Hamarneh, A., & Steiner, C. (2004). Islamic Tourism: Rethinking the Strategies of Tourism Development in the Arab World After September 11, 2001. *Comparative Studies of South Asia, Africa and the Middle East*, *24*(1), 175–186. doi:10.1215/1089201X-24-1-175

Ali, F., Rasoolimanesh, S. M., Sarstedt, M., Ringle, C. M., & Ryu, K. (2018). An assessment of the use of partial least squares structural equation modeling (PLS-SEM) in hospitality research. *International Journal of Contemporary Hospitality Management*, *30*(1), 514–538. doi:10.1108/IJCHM-10-2016-0568

Alkaya, E., & Demirer, G. N. (2015). Sectoral assessment of the Turkish textile industry for the diffusion of sustainable production approach. *Journal of the Textile Institute*, *106*(11), 1212–1225. doi:10.1080/00405000.2014.985880

Al-Omoush, K. S., de Lucas, A., & del Val, M. T. (2023). The role of e-supply chain collaboration in collaborative innovation and value-co creation. *Journal of Business Research*, *158*, 113647. doi:10.1016/j.jbusres.2023.113647

Al-Qadasi, N., Zhang, G., & Al-Jubari, I. (2021). Attitude of youth towards self-employment: Evidence from university students in Yemen. *PLoS One*, *16*(9), e0257358. doi:10.1371/journal.pone.0257358 PMID:34516592

Alqahtani, N., & Uslay, C. (2023). *Marketing/entrepreneurship interface research priorities (2023–2026). Journal of Research in Marketing and Entrepreneurship*. Emerald Insight.

Alvedalen, J., & Boschma, R. (2017). A critical review of entrepreneurial ecosystems research: Towards a future research agenda. *European Planning Studies*, *25*(6), 887–903. doi:10.1080/09654313.2017.1299694

Amalia, F. (2016). The fintech book: The financial technology handbook for investors, entrepreneurs and visionaries. *Journal of Indonesian Economy and Business: JIEB.*, *31*(3), 345. doi:10.22146/jieb.23554

Amit, R., Glosten, L., & Muller, E. (1993). Challenges to theory development in entrepreneurship research. *Journal of Management Studies, 30*(5), 815–834. doi:10.1111/j.1467-6486.1993.tb00327.x

Amjad, M. (2023). *7 Promising Areas for Entrepreneurship in 2023*. LinkedIn. https://www.linkedin.com/pulse/7-promising-areas-entrepreneu rship-2023-maheen-amjad

Amoako, G. K. (2019). A conceptual framework: Corporate environmental management activities and sustainable competitive advantage. *Management of Environmental Quality, 31*(2), 331–347. doi:10.1108/MEQ-09-2019-0187

Anderbjork, G., & Martell, J. (2021). *Gardens of intelligence: Designing robust digital market and competitive intelligence platforms* (1st ed.). Technics Publications.

Anderson, J. C., & Gerbing, D. W. (1988). Structural equation modeling in practice: A review and recommended two-step approach. *Psychological Bulletin, 103*(3), 411–423. doi:10.1037/0033-2909.103.3.411

Aouadi, A., & Marsat, S. (2018). Do ESG controversies matter for firm value? Evidence from international data. *Journal of Business Ethics, 151*(4), 1027–1047. doi:10.1007/s10551-016-3213-8

Apostolopoulos, N., Ratten, V., Petropoulos, D., Liargovas, P., & Anastasopoulou, E. (2021). Agri-food sector and entrepreneurship during the COVID-19 crisis: A systematic literature review and research agenda. *Strategic Change, 30*(2), 159–167. doi:10.1002/jsc.2400

Arayssi, M., Jizi, M., & Tabaja, H. H. (2020). *The impact of board composition on the level of ESG disclosures in GCC countries*. Sustainability Accounting, Management and Policy Journal. doi:10.1108/SAMPJ-05-2018-0136

Ariely, D., & Berns, G. S. (2010). Neuromarketing: The hope and hype of neuroimaging in business. *Nature Reviews. Neuroscience, 11*(4), 284–292. doi:10.1038/nrn2795 PMID:20197790

Armstrong, A. (2020). Ethics and ESG. *Australasian Accounting. Business and Finance Journal, 14*(3), 6–17.

Arner, D. W., Barberis, J., & Buckley, R. P. (2016). The Evolution of Fintech: A New Post-Crisis Paradigm? *Georgetown Journal of International Law, 47*(4), 1271–1320.

Arturo, P. (1986, February). The Chinese Community in the Philippines: Status and Conditions. *Sojourn (Singapore), 1*(1), 76–91. doi:10.1355/SJ1-1E

ArturV. (2020). Competitive intelligence concepts and definitions. *Management and leadership*. DOI: doi:10.13140/RG.2.2.14667.34087

Aste, T., Tasca, P., & Di Matteo, T. (2017). *Blockchain technologies: The foreseeable impact on society and industry*. IEEE.

Awan, U., Sroufe, R., & Kraslawski, A. (2019). Creativity Enables Sustainable Development: Supplier Engagement as a Boundary Condition for the Positive Effect on Green Innovation. *Journal of Cleaner Production, 226*, 172–185. Advance online publication. doi:10.1016/j.jclepro.2019.03.308

Bafadhal, A. S. (2021). Muslim health tourism archetypes for Sharia salons and spas. *Leisure/Loisir, 46*(1), 1-24.

Bafadhal, A. S. (2017). *Muslim Health Tourism*. Lambert Academic Publishing.

Bafadhal, A. S. (2022). Muslim health tourism. In D. Buhalis (Ed.), *Encyclopedia of Tourism Management and Marketing*. Edward Elgar Publishing. doi:10.4337/9781800377486.muslim.health.tourism

Baraibar-Diez, E., & Odriozola, D, M. (2019). CSR Committees and Their Effect on ESG Performance in UK, France, Germany, and Spain. *Sustainability, 11*(18), 5077. doi:10.3390/su11185077

Baraibar-Diez, E., Odriozola, M. D., & Fernández Sánchez, J. L. (2019). Sustainable compensation policies and its effect on environmental, social, and governance scores. *Corporate Social Responsibility and Environmental Management, 26*(6), 1457–1472. doi:10.1002/csr.1760

Barbu, C. M., Florea, D. L., Dabija, D. C., & Barbu, M. C. R. (2021). Customer experience in fintech. *Journal of Theoretical and Applied Electronic Commerce Research, 16*(5), 1415–1433. doi:10.3390/jtaer16050080

Barker, T. B. (1901 July 6). *Liverpool Chamber of Commerce to the China Association. F.O.17/1586.* London: The National Archives. https://discovery.nationalarchives.gov.uk/

Barrena-Martínez, J., López-Fernández, M., & Romero-Fernández, P. M. (2019). Towards a configuration of socially responsible human resource management policies and practices: Findings from an academic consensus. *International Journal of Human Resource Management, 30*(17), 2544–2580. doi:10.1080/09585192.2017.1332669

Baskin, K. (2023). How to use competitive insight. *MIT Sloan*. https://mitsloan.mit.edu/ideas-made-to-matter/how-to-use-com petitive-insight

Başkol, M. O. (2018). INTERNATIONAL COMPETITIVENESS IN TURKISH TEXTILE AND CLOTHING SECTOR. *International Journal of Management Economics and Business, 14*(3), 0–0. doi:10.17130/ijmeb.2018343115

Bass, B. M., Avolio, B. J., Jung, D. I., & Berson, Y. (2003). Predicting unit performance by assessing transformational and transactional leadership. *The Journal of Applied Psychology, 88*(2), 207–218. doi:10.1037/0021-9010.88.2.207 PMID:12731705

Batat, W., & Addis, M. (2021). Designing food experiences for well-being: A framework advancing design thinking research from a customer experience perspective. *European Journal of Marketing, 55*(9), 2392–2413. doi:10.1108/EJM-12-2020-0893

Battour, M., & Ismail, M. N. (2016). Halal tourism: Concepts, practises, challenges and future. *Tourism Management Perspectives*, *19*, 150-154.

Baysinger, T. (2024). *Sony said to pay around $600M for Michael Jackson catalog deal.* Axios. https://www.axios.com/2024/02/12/sony-michael-jackson-catalog

Beck, R., & Müller-Bloch, C. (2017). *Blockchain as radical innovation: A framework for engaging with distributed ledgers*. Research Gate.

Belvedere, V. and Grando, A., (2017). *Sustainable operations and supply chain management.* John Wiley & Sons.

Belz, F. M., & Binder, J. K. (2017). Sustainable Entrepreneurship: A Convergent Process Model. *Business Strategy and the Environment*, *26*(1), 1–17. doi:10.1002/bse.1887

Beretta, V., Demartini, M. C., & Trucco, S. (2020). Tone at Top in Integrated Reporting: The Role of Non-Financial Performance. In *Non-Financial Disclosure and Integrated Reporting: Practices and Critical Issues*. Emerald Publishing Limited. doi:10.1108/S1479-351220200000034009

Bettinelli, C., Del Bosco, B., & Giachino, C. (2019). Women on boards in family firms: What we know and what we need to know. In *The Palgrave handbook of heterogeneity among family firms* (pp. 201–228). Palgrave Macmillan. doi:10.1007/978-3-319-77676-7_9

Bhimani, A., Horngren, C., Datar, S., & Rajan, M. (2015). Management Cost Accounting (éd. Sixth edition). New Jersey, USA: Pearson.

Bilgin, M. H., Demir, E., Lau, M. C. K., Kin-Man To, C., & Zhang, Z. (2011). The Turkish handmade carpet industry: An analysis in comparison with select Asian countries. *Journal of the Textile Institute*, *102*(6), 514–526. doi:10.1080/00405000.2010.498171

Birindelli, G., Dell'Atti, S., Iannuzzi, A. P., & Savioli, M. (2018). Composition and activity of the board of directors: Impact on ESG performance in the banking system. *Sustainability (Basel)*, *10*(12), 4699. doi:10.3390/su10124699

Birindelli, G., Iannuzzi, A. P., & Savioli, M. (2019). The impact of women leaders on environmental performance: Evidence on gender diversity in banks. *Corporate Social Responsibility and Environmental Management*, *26*(6), 1485–1499. doi:10.1002/csr.1762

Blake, R., & Mouton, J. (1964). *The Managerial Grid: The key to leadership excellence*. Gulf Publishing Co.

Blakstad, S., & Allen, R. (2018). FinTech revolution. Cham, Switzerland: Springer.

Bland, J. O. P. (1902 March 6). The New Tariff Proposals. *The North-China Daily News*, 4.

Blessley, M., & Mudambi, S. M. (2022). A trade way and a pandemic: Disruption and resilience in the food bank supply chain. *Industrial Marketing Management*, *102*, 58–73. doi:10.1016/j.indmarman.2022.01.002

Blinova, E., Ponomarenko, T., & Knysh, V. (2022). Analyzing the Concept of Corporate Sustainability in the Context of Sustainable Business Development in the Mining Sector with Elements of Circular Economy. *Sustainability (Basel)*, *14*(13), 8163. doi:10.3390/su14138163

Blocher, E., Stout, D., & Cokins, G. (2010). Cost Management (Vol. fifth edition). USA: McGraw-Hill.

Blundel, R., Lockett, N., & Wang, C. (2017). Exploring entrepreneurship. *Sage (Atlanta, Ga.)*.

Bomar, P. J. (2013). Comments on complementary and alternative healing modalities. *International Journal of Nursing Practice*, *19*(2), 1–6. doi:10.1111/ijn.12061 PMID:23617443

Bosma, N., 2013. The Global Entrepreneurship Monitor (GEM) and its impact on entrepreneurship research. *Foundations and Trends® in Entrepreneurship, 9*(2), pp.143-248.

Bourdieu, P. (2023a). *Sur lÉtat. Cours au Collège de France (1989-1992)*. SDX Joint Publishing Company.

Bourdieu, P. (2023b). *Anthropologie économique. Cours au Collège de France 1992-1993*. Shanghai People's Publishing House.

Bravo, F., & Reguera-Alvarado, N. (2019). Sustainable development disclosure: Environmental, social, and governance reporting and gender diversity in the audit committee. *Business Strategy and the Environment*, *28*(2), 418–429. doi:10.1002/bse.2258

Brijs, B. (2013). *Business analysis for business intelligence*. CRC Press.

Brin, P. V., & Nehme, M. N. (2019). *Corporate social responsibility: analysis of theories and models*.

Britannica. (2024). *Champion: Monarch, royalty & nobility*. Britannica. https://www.britannica.com › champion-English-history

Burns, P., & Jim, D. (1996). Small business and entrepreneurship (Eds). Macmillan.

Byun, J., Sung, T. E., & Park, H. W. (2018). Technological innovation strategy: How do technology life cycles change by technological area. *Technology Analysis and Strategic Management*, *30*(1), 98–112. doi:10.1080/09537325.2017.1297397

Cadogan, J. W. (2012). International marketing, strategic orientations and business success: Reflections on the path ahead. *International Marketing Review*, *29*(4), 340–348. doi:10.1108/02651331211242656

Caiado, R. G. G., Scavarda, L. F., Azevedo, B. D., de Mattos Nascimento, D. L., & Quelhas, O. L. G. (2022). Challenges and benefits of sustainable industry 4.0 for operations and supply chain management—A framework headed toward the 2030 agenda. *Sustainability (Basel)*, *14*(2), 830. doi:10.3390/su14020830

Callen, K. (2001). *Spa: Pamper Body and Soul*. Ebury Press.

Calvert, R. K. (1901 July 3). *Leeds Chamber of Commerce to the China Association*. F.O.17/1586. London: The National Archives. https://discovery.nationalarchives.gov.uk/

Cao, S., Nie, L., Sun, H., Sun, W., & Taghizadeh-Hesary, F. (2021). Digital finance, green technological innovation and energy-environmental performance: Evidence from China's regional economies. *Journal of Cleaner Production*, *327*, 129458. doi:10.1016/j.jclepro.2021.129458

Carlgren, L., Rauth, I., & Elmquist, M. (2016). Framing design thinking: The concept in idea and enactment. *Creativity and Innovation Management*, *25*(1), 38–57. doi:10.1111/caim.12153

Carson, G., O'Connor, C., & Simmons, G. (2020). The crucial role of market intelligence in the development of small business marketing capabilities. *Journal of Small Business and Enterprise Development*, *27*(5), 797–816. doi:10.1108/JSBED-12-2019-0394

Caseiro, N., & Coelho, A. (2018). Business intelligence and competitiveness: The mediating role of entrepreneurial orientation. *Competitiveness Review*, *28*(2), 213–226. doi:10.1108/CR-09-2016-0054

Castellanos, J. D., & George, B. (2020). Boardroom leadership: The board of directors as a source of strategic leadership. *Economics and Business Review*, *6*(1), 103–119. doi:10.18559/ebr.2020.1.5

Castillo, V. E. (2018). *An Inquiry into Supply Chain Strategy Implications of the Sharing Economy for Last Mile Logistics*.

Catalini, C., & Gans, J. S. (2016). *Some Simple Economics of the Blockchain*. (NBER Working Paper No. 22952). NBER.

Cekuls, A. (2022). Expand the scope of competitive intelligence. *J Intell Stud Bus*, *12*(1), 4–5. doi:10.37380/jisib.v12i1.924

Changar, M., & Atan, T. (2021). The Role of Transformational and Transactional Leadership Approaches on Environmental and Ethical Aspects of CSR. *Sustainability (Basel)*, *13*(3), 1411. doi:10.3390/su13031411

Chen, D. X. (2018). *Liu Kunyi's Biography (刘坤一集)*. Hunan Yuelu Publishing House Co., Ltd.

Chen, H., Chiang, R. H. L., & Storey, V. C. (2012). Business intelligence and analytics: From big data to big impact. *Management Information Systems Quarterly*, *36*(4), 1165–1188. doi:10.2307/41703503

Chen, H., & Hsu, C.-H. (2013). Entrepreneurial orientation and firm performance in non-profit service organizations: Contingent effect of market orientation. *Service Industries Journal*, *33*(5), 445–466. https://search.ebscohost.com/login.aspx?direct=true&db=crh&AN=86994939&site=ehost-live. doi:10.1080/02642069.2011.622372

Chen, Y. C., Li, P. C., & Evans, K. R. (2012). Effects of interaction and entrepreneurial orientation on organizational performance: Insights into market driven and market driving. *Industrial Marketing Management*, *41*(6), 1019–1034. doi:10.1016/j.indmarman.2012.01.017

Chibuike, C. U., & Ovharhe, O. H. (2022). Emergence of risk culture and lean culture in Nigeria during pandemic and crisis era: Using confirmatory analysis. *International Journal of Multidisciplinary Research and Growth Evaluation, 3*(1), 263–271. doi:10.54660/anfo.2021.3.1.14

Chibuike, C. U., Ovharhe, O. H., & Abada, A. M. (2022). Synchronization of lean accounting alert and entrepreneurial sustainability among micro firms in Nigeria during pandemic and catastrophe: Using confirmatory factor analysis. *International Journal of Business and Management, 10*(1), 1–13. doi:10.54660/anfo.2021.2.6.15

Chishti, S., & Barberis, J. (2016). *The Fintech book: The financial technology handbook for investors, entrepreneurs and visionaries*. John Wiley & Sons. doi:10.1002/9781119218906

Cho, C.-C., & Kao, R.-H. (2022). Developing sustainable workplace through leadership: Perspectives of transformational leadership and of organizational citizenship behavior. *Frontiers in Psychology, 13*, 924091. doi:10.3389/fpsyg.2022.924091 PMID:35959035

Christensen, C. M. (1997). *The innovator's dilemma: When new technologies cause great firms to fail.* Harvard Business School Press.

Ciampi, F., Marzi, G., Demi, S., & Faraoni, M. (2020). The big data-business strategy interconnection: A grand challenge for knowledge management. A review and future perspectives. *Journal of Knowledge Management, 24*(5), 1157–1176. doi:10.1108/JKM-02-2020-0156

Ciasullo, M. V., Montera, R., & Douglas, A. (2022). Building SMEs' resilience in times of uncertainty: the role of big data analytics capability and co-innovation. *Transforming Government: People. Transforming Government, 16*(2), 203–217. doi:10.1108/TG-07-2021-0120

Clark, K., & Smith, R. (2008). Unleashing the power of design thinking. *Design Management Review, 19*(3), 8–15. doi:10.1111/j.1948-7169.2008.tb00123.x

Cloutier, A. (2013). Competitive intelligence process integrative model based on a scoping review of the literature. *International Journal of Strategic Management, 13*(1), 57–72. doi:10.18374/IJSM-13-1.7

Cohen, B. (2006). Sustainable valley entrepreneurial ecosystems. *Business Strategy and the Environment, 15*(1), 1–14. doi:10.1002/bse.428

Cohen, E. (1988). Authenticity and Commoditization in Tourism. *Annals of Tourism Research, 15*(3), 371–386. doi:10.1016/0160-7383(88)90028-X

Cole, C. (2022). *How to identify business and market opportunities*. Harvard Business School Online.

Cook, L. S., Bowen, D. E., Chase, R. B., Dasu, S., Stewart, D. M., & Tansik, D. A. (2002). Human issues in service design. *Journal of Operations Management, 20*(2), 159–174. doi:10.1016/S0272-6963(01)00094-8

Çop, S., Olorunsola, V. O., & Alola, U. V. (2021). Achieving environmental sustainability through green transformational leadership policy: Can green team resilience help? *Business Strategy and the Environment, 30*(1), 671–682. doi:10.1002/bse.2646

Corbett, E. C. (1902 April 8). *Treaty Revision in China. F.O. 17/1571.* London: The National Archives. https://discovery.nationalarchives.gov.uk/

Corsaro, D., & D'Amico, V. (2022). How the digital transformation from COVID-19 affected the relational approaches in B2B. *Journal of Business and Industrial Marketing, 37*(10), 2095–2115. doi:10.1108/JBIM-05-2021-0266

Corvello, V., De Carolis, M., Verteramo, S., & Steiber, A. (2022). The digital transformation of entrepreneurial work. *International Journal of Entrepreneurial Behaviour & Research, 28*(5), 1167–1183. doi:10.1108/IJEBR-01-2021-0067

Covin, J. G., & Miller, D. (2014). International Entrepreneurial Orientation: Conceptual Considerations, Research Themes, Measurement Issues, and Future Research Directions. *Entrepreneurship Theory and Practice, 38*(1), 11–44. doi:10.1111/etap.12027

Croll, A., & Yoskovitz, B. (2017). Lean Analytics: use data to build a better startup faster. O'Reilly, 53(9).

Dalal, K. K., & Thaker, N. (2019). ESG and corporate financial performance: A panel study of Indian companies. *IUP Journal of Corporate Governance, 18*(1), 44–59.

Damasio, A. R. (1994). Descartes' error and the future of human life. *Scientific American, 271*(4), 144. doi:10.1038/scientificamerican1094-144 PMID:7939563

Dana, L.-P., & Vorobeva, E. (2021). Understanding the term "minority entrepreneurship". In T. M. Cooney (Ed.), *The Palgrave handbook of minority entrepreneurship* (pp. 15–32). Palgrave Macmillan. doi:10.1007/978-3-030-66603-3_2

Darwiesh, A., Elhoseny, M., Atassi, R., & El-Baz, A. H. (2023). A business intelligence system for governing risks in SMEs. In R. El Ayachi, M. Fakir, & M. Baslam (Eds.), *Business Intelligence. CBI 2023. Lecture Notes in Business Information Processing, 484.* Springer. doi:10.1007/978-3-031-37872-0_1

Deepmala, S., Anurag, S., Amizan, O., & S.B, G. (2023). *Business intelligence and human resource management.* New York: Routledge.

Demir, H., & Okan, T. (2008). Etkileşimsel ve Dönüşümsel Liderlik: Bir Ölçek Geliştirme Denemesi. *Yönetim Dergisi:İstanbul Üniversitesi İşletme Fakültesi İşletme İktisadı Enstitüsü, 19*(61), Article 61.

Demirgüç-Kunt, A., Klapper, L., Singer, D., Ansar, S., & Hess, J. (2018). *The Global Findex Database 2017: Measuring Financial Inclusion and the Fintech Revolution.* [World Bank Policy Research Working Paper, 8440]. World Bank.

Demirgüç-Kunt, A., Klapper, L., & Randall, D. (2020). Digital Financial Inclusion: Lessons from International Experience. *The World Bank Research Observer*, *35*(1), 65–100.

Dermer, M. (2023). *Etymology of entrepreneur.* [Video]. Facebook. https://web.facebook.com/watch/?v=602542661584141

Dettwiler, P., Lindelöf, P., & Löfsten, H. (2006). Business environment and property management issues: A study of growth firms in Sweden. *Journal of Corporate Real Estate*, *8*(3), 120–133. Advance online publication. doi:10.1108/14630010610711748

Dewar, C., Keller, S., & Malhotra, V. (2022). *CEO excellence: the six mindsets that distinguish the best leaders from the rest* (1st ed.). Scribner.

Dhammika, K. A. S., & Ahmad, F. bin, Sam, T. L., & Lanka, S. (2014). *Measurement of Transactional and Transformational Leadership: Validity and Reliability in Sri Lankan Context.* Semantic Scholar. https://api.semanticscholar.org/corpusid:55822458

Diandra, D., & Azmy, A. (2020). Understanding definition of entrepreneurship. International Journal of Management. *Accounting and Economics*, *7*(5), 235–241.

Dieffenbacher, S. F. (2023). *Creativity and Innovation: Differences, Examples & Definitions.* Digital Leadership. https://digitalleadership.com/blog/creativity-and-innovation/

Divrik, B., & Baykal, E. (2023). Relation Of Digitalization And Internationalization For Smes; Evidence From Turkish Textile And Clothing Industry. *Journal of Global Strategic Management*, *16*, 16. doi:10.20460/JGSM.2023.318

Dolgui, A., Ivanov, D., & Sokolov, B. (2018). Ripple effect in the supply chain: An analysis and recent literature. *International Journal of Production Research*, *56*(1-2), 414–430. doi:10.1080/00207543.2017.1387680

Drucker, P. F. (1993). *Innovation and entrepreneurship practice and principles.* HarperCollins Publishers Inc.

Dudgeon, C. J. (1901 May 31). *China Association (Shanghai) to H. B. M. Consul-General. F.O.17/1586.* London: The National Archives. https://discovery.nationalarchives.gov.uk/

Dudgeon, C. J. (1902a March 5*). To James Mackay. F.O.17/1565.* London: The National Archives. https://discovery.nationalarchives.gov.uk/

Dudgeon, C. J. (1902b April 2). *Memorandum. F.O.17/1586.* London: The National Archives. https://discovery.nationalarchives.gov.uk/

Dudgeon, C. J. (1902c June 25). *To James Mackay. F.O.17/1578.* London: The National Archives. https://discovery.nationalarchives.gov.uk/

Dunne, D., & Martin, R. (2006). Design thinking and how it will change management education: An interview and discussion. *Academy of Management Learning & Education*, *5*(4), 512–523. doi:10.5465/amle.2006.23473212

Duran, A., & Temíz Dínç, D. (2016). Türk Tekstil ve Hazır Giyim Sanayisinin Yapısı: Gümrük Birliği Anlaşması'nın Öncesi ve Sonrası. *İnsan ve Toplum Bilimleri Araştırmaları Dergisi, 5*(3), 505. doi:10.15869/itobiad.74629

Eckhardt, J. T., & Shane, S. A. (2003). Opportunities and entrepreneurship. *Journal of Management, 29*(3), 333–349. doi:10.1177/014920630302900304

Edsand, H. E. (2017). Identifying barriers to wind energy diffusion in Colombia: A function analysis of the technological innovation system and the wider context. *Technology in Society, 49*, 1–15. doi:10.1016/j.techsoc.2017.01.002

Effa, G. A., Ovharhe, O. H., Ezirim, A. C., & Igwe, S. (2023a). Procurement sustainability policy and logistics performance in Nigeria. [IJMCS]. *International Journal of Marketing and Communication Studies, 7*(1), 56–72. doi:10.56201/ijmcs.v7.no1.2023.pg56.72

Effa, G. A., Ovharhe, O. H., Ezirim, A. C., & Igwe, S. (2023b). Strategic procurement initiatives and logistics performance in Nigeria. [IJMCS]. *International Journal of Marketing and Communication Studies, 7*(1), 38–55. doi:10.56201/ijmcs.v7.no1.2023.pg38.55

Ehidiamen Oamen, T., & Moshood Lawal, B. (2023). Exploring and Validating Performance Measurement Domains of Community Pharmacists Using Structural Equation Modeling: Implications and Recommendations for Research. *Journal of Scientific Research and Reports*, 38–47. doi:10.9734/jsrr/2023/v29i11726

Eklund, M. A. (2019). Compensation for Non-financial Performance (ESG Scores). In *Fairness of CEO Compensation* (pp. 67–74). Springer. doi:10.1007/978-3-030-33554-0_4

Elia, G., Margherita, A., & Passiante, G. (2020). Digital entrepreneurship ecosystem: How digital technologies and collective intelligence are reshaping the entrepreneurial process. *Technological Forecasting and Social Change, 150*, 119791. doi:10.1016/j.techfore.2019.119791

Eliwa, Y., Aboud, A., & Saleh, A. (2019). ESG practices and the cost of debt: Evidence from EU countries. *Critical Perspectives on Accounting*, 102097.

Elkington, J., & Hartigan, P. (2008). *The power of unreasonable people: How social entrepreneurs create markets that change the world.* Harvard Business Press.

Elsbach, K. D., & Stigliani, I. (2018). Design thinking and organizational culture: A review and framework for future research. *Journal of Management, 44*(6), 2274–2306. doi:10.1177/0149206317744252

Erat, S., Kitapçı, H., & Akçin, K. (2020). Managerial Perception and Organizational Identity: A Comparative Analysis. *Sustainability (Basel), 12*(6), 2278. doi:10.3390/su12062278

Erhabor, N. I. (2018). Developing Leaders Through Mentoring in Environmental Education. *Electronic Green Journal, 1*(41). doi:10.5070/G314134454

Etymonline (2024). *Etymology of champion by etymonline.* Etymonline. https://www.etymonline.com › word › champion

Eyal, I., Sirer, E. G. (2018). *Majority is not enough: Bitcoin mining is vulnerable*. ACM.

Falk, E. B., Berkman, E. T., & Lieberman, M. D. (2012). From neural responses to population behavior: Neural focus group predicts population-level media effects. *Psychological Science*, *23*(5), 439–445. doi:10.1177/0956797611434964 PMID:22510393

Farradinna, S., Syafitri, N., Herawati, I., & Jayanti, W. (2023). An exploratory factor analysis of entrepreneurship psychological readiness (EPR) instrument. *Journal of Innovation and Entrepreneurship*, *12*(1), 66. doi:10.1186/s13731-023-00314-y

Fayolle, A. (2007). *Entrepreneurship and new value creation: the dynamic of the entrepreneurial process*. Cambridge university press. doi:10.1017/CBO9780511488689

Feintuck, M. (2014). *'The Public Interest' in Regulation*. China Renmin University Press.

Feld, B. (2012). Startup Communities: Building an Entrepreneurial Ecosystem in Your City. In Municipal World.

Feng, S., Zhang, R., & Li, G. (2022). Environmental decentralization, digital finance and green technology innovation. *Structural Change and Economic Dynamics*, *61*, 70–83. doi:10.1016/j.strueco.2022.02.008

Fernando, G. (2024). *The champion: A model for 21st century strategic leadership*. Tough Nickle. https://toughnickel.com/business/The-Champion

Fernie, J., & Sparks, L. (Eds.). (2018). Logistics and retail management: emerging issues and new challenges in the retail supply chain. Kogan page publishers.

Finkle, T. A., & Deeds, D. (2001). Trends in the market for entrepreneurship faculty, 1989–1998. *Journal of Business Venturing*, *16*(6), 613–630. doi:10.1016/S0883-9026(99)00051-8

Foley, S., Karlsen, J. R., & Putniņš, T. J. (2019). Sex, Drugs, and Bitcoin: How Much Illegal Activity Is Financed Through Cryptocurrencies? *Review of Financial Studies*, *32*(5), 1798–1853. doi:10.1093/rfs/hhz015

Fosso Wamba, S., Queiroz, M. M., Guthrie, C., & Braganza, A. (2022). Industry experiences of artificial intelligence (AI): Benefits and challenges in operations and supply chain management. *Production Planning and Control*, *33*(16), 1493–1497. doi:10.1080/09537287.2021.1882695

Furlotti, K., Mazza, T., Tibiletti, V., & Triani, S. (2019). Women in top positions on boards of directors: Gender policies disclosed in Italian sustainability reporting. *Corporate Social Responsibility and Environmental Management*, *26*(1), 57–70. doi:10.1002/csr.1657

García Martín, C. J., & Herrero, B. (2020). Do board characteristics affect environmental performance? A study of EU firms. *Corporate Social Responsibility and Environmental Management*, *27*(1), 74–94. doi:10.1002/csr.1775

Geeks for Geeks. (2023). Types of entrepreneurs: Innovating, imitative, fabian and drone entrepreneurs. Geeks for Geeks. https://www.geeksforgeeks.org/types-of-entrepreneurs-innovating-imitative-fabian-and-drone-entrepreneurs/

Gendron, M. (2013). *Business Intelligence Applied: implementing an effective information and communications technology infrastructure*. John Wiley and sons Inc.

Gianinazzi, W. (2018). Penser global, agir local. Histoire d'une idée, EcoRev'. Revue critique d'écologie politique, 46. doi:10.3917/ecorev.046.0019

Global Startup Ecosystem Report 2023. (n.d.). *Startup Genome*. https://startupgenome.com/report/gser2023

Gnizy, I. (2019). Big data and its strategic path to value in international firms. *International Marketing Review*, *36*(3), 318–341. doi:10.1108/IMR-09-2018-0249

Gölgeci, I., Assadinia, S., Kuivalainen, O., & Larimo, J. (2019). Emerging-market firms' dynamic capabilities and international performance: The moderating role of institutional development and distance. *International Business Review*, *28*(6), 101593. doi:10.1016/j.ibusrev.2019.101593

Gomber, P., Kauffman, R. J., Parker, C., & Weber, B. W. (2018). On the fintech revolution: Interpreting the forces of innovation, disruption, and transformation in financial services. *Journal of Management Information Systems*, *35*(1), 220–265. doi:10.1080/07421222.2018.1440766

Görgülü, V. (2020). Case studies on the downside of transactional and authoratitative organizational leadership styles during crisis management. *Turkish online journal of design art and communication*, *10*(4), 597–611. doi:10.7456/11004100/020

Grant, D.B., Wong, C.Y. & Trautrims, A. (2017). *Sustainable logistics and supply chain management: principles and practices for sustainable operations and management*. Kogan Page Publishers.

Grossmann, W., & Rinderle-ma, S. (2015). *Fundamentals of Business Intelligence*. Springer. doi:10.1007/978-3-662-46531-8

Gümüş, D., & Akbal, F. (2011). Photocatalytic Degradation of Textile Dye and Wastewater. *Water, Air, and Soil Pollution*, *216*(1–4), 117–124. doi:10.1007/s11270-010-0520-z

Gungor, A., & Gupta, S. M. (1999). Issues in environmentally conscious manufacturing and product recovery: A survey. *Computers & Industrial Engineering*, *36*(4), 811–853. doi:10.1016/S0360-8352(99)00167-9

Guo, X. D. (1999). Opening the Road to "Free" Trade: A Study of Chinese Socio Economy in the West in the 1830s (打"自由"通商之路——19世纪30年代的在西华人对中国社会经济的探研). Guangzhou: Guangdong People's Publishing House Co., LTD.

Guo, Y., Zhu, L., Ye, X., Wang, X., Xu, Y., Qian, G., & Wang, L. (2023). Toxicity Impact Assessment of Nitrogen Oxide and Sulfur Dioxide Emissions in China's Textile Industry With Chemical Footprint Method. *AATCC Journal of Research*, *10*(4), 232–240. doi:10.1177/24723444231161744

Gupta, P., & Bamel, U. (2023). Need for metacognition and critical thinking in the e-learning ecosystem: The new normal in post Covid era. *Global Business and Organizational Excellence, 43*(1), 104–120. doi:10.1002/joe.22208

Gurcan, F., Ayaz, A., Dalveren, M. G. G., & Derawi, M. (2023). Business intelligence strategies, best practices, and latest trends: Analysis of scientometric data from 2003 to 2023 using machine learning. *Sustainability (Basel), 15*(13), 9854. doi:10.3390/su15139854

Guttentag, D. A., & Smith, S. L. (2017). Assessing Airbnb as a disruptive innovation relative to hotels: Substitution and comparative performance expectations. *International Journal of Hospitality Management, 64*, 1–10. doi:10.1016/j.ijhm.2017.02.003

Habermas, J. (1999). *Strukturwandel der Öffentlichkeit.* Academia Press.

Hackett, S. M., & Dilts, D. M. (2004a). A real options-driven theory of business incubation. *The Journal of Technology Transfer, 29*(1), 41–54. doi:10.1023/B:JOTT.0000011180.19370.36

Hackett, S. M., & Dilts, D. M. (2004b). A Systematic Review of Business Incubation Research. *The Journal of Technology Transfer, 29*(1), 55–82. doi:10.1023/B:JOTT.0000011181.11952.0f

Hair, J. F. (Ed.). (2017). *A primer on partial least squares structural equation modeling (PLS-SEM)* (2nd ed.). Sage.

Hammer, M., & Chempy, J. (1993). le Reengineering. (M. le seac'h, Trad.) Paris, La France: Dunod.

Handfield, B. R., Petersen, K., Cousins, P.N., & Lawson, B. (2023). An organizational entrepreneurship model of supply management integration and performance outcome. *International Journal of Operations &Production Management, 29* (2), 100-126. Emerald Group Publishing Limited0144-3577DOI doi:10.1108/01443570910932011

Hanelt, A., Bohnsack, R., Marz, D., & Antunes Marante, C. (2021). A systematic review of the literature on digital transformation: Insights and implications for strategy and organizational change. *Journal of Management Studies, 58*(5), 1159–1197. doi:10.1111/joms.12639

Han, H., Lee, S., Ariza-Montes, A., Al-Ansi, A., Tariq, B., Vega-Muñoz, A., & Park, S. H. (2021). Muslim travelers' inconvenient tourism experience and self-rated mental health at a non-Islamic country: Exploring gender and age differences. *International Journal of Environmental Research and Public Health, 18*(2), 758. doi:10.3390/ijerph18020758 PMID:33477400

Hannon, P. D. (2013). Why is the entrepreneurial university important? *Journal of innovation management, 1*(2), 10-17.

Haque, F., & Ntim, C. G. (2020). Executive compensation, sustainable compensation policy, carbon performance and market value. *British Journal of Management, 31*(3), 525–546. doi:10.1111/1467-8551.12395

Harjoto, M. A., & Wang, Y. (2020). Board of Directors Network Centrality and Environmental, Social and Governance (ESG) Performance. *Corporate Governance: An International Journal of Business in Society [Forthcoming 2020].*

Hasanbeigi, A., & Price, L. (2012). A review of energy use and energy efficiency technologies for the textile industry. *Renewable & Sustainable Energy Reviews*, *16*(6), 3648–3665. doi:10.1016/j.rser.2012.03.029

Hassani, A., & Mosconi, E. (2022). Social media analytics, competitive intelligence, and dynamic capabilities in manufacturing SMEs. *Technological Forecasting and Social Change*, *175*(1), 1–11. doi:10.1016/j.techfore.2021.121416

Häusser, J. A., & Förderer, S. (2019). Consumer neuroscience-based metrics predict recall, liking, and viewing duration in online advertising. *Frontiers in Neuroscience*, *13*, 225.

Hedqvist, L., & Larsson, A. (2020). *ESG or Financial Performance-Does It Have to be a Choice?: A Regression Analysis of Thomson Reuters ESG scores and Financial Performance in Sweden and the UK.*

Henseler, J., Hubona, G., & Ray, P. A. (2016). Using PLS path modeling in new technology research: Updated guidelines. *Industrial Management & Data Systems*, *116*(1), 2–20. doi:10.1108/IMDS-09-2015-0382

Heyes, C. J. (2009). Diagnosing culture: Body Dysmorphic Disorder and cosmetic surgery. *Body & Society*, *15*(4), 73–93. doi:10.1177/1357034X09347222

Holmqvist, K., Nyström, M., Andersson, R., Dewhurst, R., Jarodzka, H., & Van de Weijer, J. (2011). *Eye tracking: A comprehensive guide to methods and measures*. Oxford University Press.

Holori, R. B., Ahmadi, F., Khanmohammadi, M., Ranjbar, H. M., & Kordlouie, H. (2023, Autumn). Development and assessment of a business intelligence-based management accounting information system model: A structural equation modeling approach. *International Journal of Finance and Managerial Accounting*, *8*(31).

Hora, M., & Dutta, D. K. (2013). Entrepreneurial firms and downstream alliance partnerships: Impact of portfolio depth and scope on technology innovation and commercialization success. *Production and Operations Management*, *22*(6), 1389–1400. doi:10.1111/j.1937-5956.2012.01410.x

Horn, J. (2023). *Inside the competitor's mindset: how to predict their next move and position yourself for success* (1st ed.). The MIT Press. https://mitpress.mit.edu/9780262047883/inside-the-competitors-mindset/ doi:10.7551/mitpress/14628.001.0001

Hossain, M. S., Islam, M. A., Hosen, M., Mohd, T., & Thaker, H. (2023). Missing catalysts of female entrepreneurship success: Evidence from an emerging economy. *Global Business and Organizational Excellence*, *42*(5), 50–64. doi:10.1002/joe.22201

Hossain, N. U. I., El Amrani, S., Jaradat, R., Marufuzzaman, M., Buchanan, R., Rinaudo, C., & Hamilton, M. (2020). Modeling and assessing interdependencies between critical infrastructures using Bayesian network: A case study of inland waterway port and surrounding supply chain network. *Reliability Engineering & System Safety*, *198*, 106898. doi:10.1016/j.ress.2020.106898

Ho, T. H., & Tang, C. S. (2009). Introduction to the special issue on marketing and operations management interfaces and coordination. *Production and Operations Management*, *18*(4), 363–364. doi:10.1111/j.1937-5956.2009.01037.x

Howell, S. T., Niessner, M., & Yermack, D. (2018). *Initial Coin Offerings: Financing growth with cryptocurrency token sales*. NBER.

Howson, C. (2008). Successful Business Intelligence: Secrets to making BI a killer app (éd. First Edition). USA, USA: McGraw-Hill.

Howson, C. (2014). Successful Business Intelligence: unlock the value of BI and big data (éd. Second Edition). USA, USA: McGraw-Hill.

Hsuan Mikkola, J., & Skjøtt-Larsen, T. (2004). Supply-chain integration: Implications for mass customization, modularization and postponement strategies. *Production Planning and Control*, *15*(4), 352–361. doi:10.1080/0953728042000238845

Hsu, M., Yoon, C., Hajcak, G., & Berns, G. S. (2009). Monetary loss and the brain: An ERP study of the influence of task relevance and motivation. *Social Cognitive and Affective Neuroscience*, *4*(4), 321–329.

Huang, J. M. (1989). Historical Materials on Sino-US Relations (Guangxu Dynasty III and IV)(中美关系史料(光绪朝三、 四)). Taipei: Institute of Modern History, Academia Sinica.

Huang, Z. S., & He, S. B. (2009). *History of Filipino Overseas Chinese*. Guangdong Higher Education Press.

Huang, Z., Savita, K. S., & Zhong-jie, J. (2022). The business intelligence impact on the financial performance of start-ups. *Information Processing & Management*, *59*(1), 102761. doi:10.1016/j.ipm.2021.102761

Hübel, B., & Scholz, H. (2020). Integrating sustainability risks in asset management: The role of ESG exposures and ESG ratings. *Journal of Asset Management*, *21*(1), 52–69. doi:10.1057/s41260-019-00139-z

Hubert, M., & Kenning, P. (2008). A current overview of consumer neuroscience. *Journal of Consumer Behaviour*, *7*(4–5), 272–292. doi:10.1002/cb.251

Hughes, L., Dwivedi, Y. K., Misra, S. K., Rana, N. P., Raghavan, V., & Akella, V. (2019). Blockchain research, practice and policy: Applications, benefits, limitations, emerging research themes and research agenda. *International Journal of Information Management*, *49*, 114–129. doi:10.1016/j.ijinfomgt.2019.02.005

Hugos, M. H. (2018). Essentials of supply chain management. John Wiley & Sons.

Hu, H., Xu, J., Liu, M., & Lim, M. K. (2023). Vaccine supply chain management: An intelligent system utilizing blockchain, IoT and machine learning. *Journal of Business Research*, *156*, 113480. doi:10.1016/j.jbusres.2022.113480 PMID:36506475

Huq, A., & Gilbert, D. (2017). All the world'sa stage: Transforming entrepreneurship education through design thinking. *Education + Training*, *59*(2), 155–170. doi:10.1108/ET-12-2015-0111

Hussain, G., Nazir, M. S., Rashid, M. A., & Sattar, M. A. (2023). From supply chain resilience to supply chain disruption orientation: The moderating role of supply chain complexity. *Journal of Enterprise Information Management*, *36*(1), 70–90. doi:10.1108/JEIM-12-2020-0558

Hyun, Y., Park, J., Kamioka, T., & Chang, Y. (2023). Organizational agility enabled by big data analytics: Information systems capabilities view. *Journal of Enterprise Information Management*, *36*(4), 1032–1055. doi:10.1108/JEIM-03-2022-0077

Iamandi, I. E., Constantin, L. G., Munteanu, S. M., & Cernat-Gruici, B. (2019). Mapping the ESG Behavior of European Companies. A Holistic Kohonen Approach. *Sustainability (Basel)*, *11*(12), 3276. doi:10.3390/su11123276

Ihugba, O. A., Odii, A., & Njoku, A. (2014). Theoretical analysis of entrepreneurship challenges and prospects in Nigeria. *International Letters of Social and Humanistic Sciences*, *5*(16), 21–34.

Inman, R. A., & Green, K. W. (2018). Lean and green combine to impact environmental and operational performance. *International Journal of Production Research*, *56*(14), 4802–4818. doi:10.1080/00207543.2018.1447705

Interaction Design Foundation, Dam, R. F., & Siang, T. Y. (2021). *What is design thinking and why is it so popular*? IDF.

Invest in Trakya-Tekirdağ. (2023). *Textile Sector—Sectors—Invest in Trakya*. Invest in Trakya - Tekirdağ, Edirne, Kırklareli. https://www.investintrakya.org.tr/en/36635/Textile-Sector

Iqbal, Q., Ahmad, N. H., & Li, Y. (2021). Sustainable Leadership in Frontier Asia Region: Managerial Discretion and Environmental Innovation. *Sustainability (Basel)*, *13*(9), 5002. doi:10.3390/su13095002

Isenberg, D. (2010). *How to Start an Entrepreneurial Revolution*. HBR. www.hbr.org

Isenberg, D. (2011). *The Entrepreneurship Ecosystem Strategy as a New Paradigm for Economic Policy: Principles for Cultivating Entrepreneurship*. Institute of International and European Affairs.

Isenberg, D. (2014). What an Entrepreneurship Ecosystem Actually Is. *Harvard Business Review*.

Islam, M. N. (2023). Managing organizational change in responding to global crises. *Global Business and Organizational Excellence*, *42*(3), 42–57. doi:10.1002/joe.22189

Ismail, A. M., Adnan, Z. H. M., Clark, C., & Said, J. (2019). Impact of Board Capabilities on Environmental and Social Governance (ESG) Practices: Evidence from Malaysia. *International Journal of Business & Management Science*, *9*(2).

Ismail, A., Mohamad, M., Mohamed, Hj. H. A.-B., Rafiuddin, N., & Zhen, K. (2010). Transformational and Transactional Leadership Styles as a Predictor of Individual Outcomes. *Theoretical and Applied Economics*, *6*(547), 89–104.

Ismail, I. J. (2023). I have to apply this strategy! Understanding the mediating effect of digitalization on strategic orientations and sustainable competitive advantage among small enterprises in Tanzania. *Management Matters*, *20*(1), 53–73. doi:10.1108/MANM-01-2022-0019

Jackowski, A., & Smith, V. L. (1992). Polish pilgrim-tourists. *Annals of Tourism Research*, *19*(1), 92–106. doi:10.1016/0160-7383(92)90109-3

Jackson, G., Bartosch, J., Avetisyan, E., Kinderman, D., & Knudsen, J. S. (2020). Mandatory non-financial disclosure and its influence on CSR: An international comparison. *Journal of Business Ethics*, *162*(2), 323–342. doi:10.1007/s10551-019-04200-0

Jacobs, F.R. & Chase, R.B. (2018). *Operations and supply chain management*. McGraw-Hill.

Jahmane, A., & Gaies, B. (2020). Corporate social responsibility, financial instability and corporate financial performance: Linear, non-linear and spillover effects–The case of the CAC 40 companies. *Finance Research Letters*, *34*, 101483. doi:10.1016/j.frl.2020.101483

Jain, N. (2023). *What is innovation? Definition, types, examples and process*. Ideascale.

Jain, D. (2022). Human resource issues and challenges prevailing in Indian textile & garment industry. *International Journal of Home Science*, *8*(3), 227–232. doi:10.22271/23957476.2022.v8.i3d.1378

Janjić, I., & Rađenović, T. (2019). The importance of managing innovation in modern enterprises. *Ekonomika (Nis)*, *65*(3), 45–54. doi:10.5937/ekonomika1903045J

Javed, M., Rashid, M. A., Hussain, G., & Ali, H. Y. (2020). The effects of corporate social responsibility on corporate reputation and firm financial performance: Moderating role of responsible leadership. *Corporate Social Responsibility and Environmental Management*, *27*(3), 1395–1409. doi:10.1002/csr.1892

Jayender, P., & Kundu, G. K. (2021). Intelligent ERP for SCM agility and graph theory technique for adaptation in automotive industry in India. *International Journal of System Assurance Engineering and Management*, 1-22.

Jengeta, M., & Phiri, M. A. (2021). Graduate perceptions on the scope of university entrepreneurship education in a turbulent economy: Case of CUT Zimbabwe. *Journal of African Education*, *2*(2), 67. doi:10.31920/2633-2930/2021/v2n2a3

Jiang, W., Zhao, X., & Ni, J. (2017). The Impact of Transformational Leadership on Employee Sustainable Performance: The Mediating Role of Organizational Citizenship Behavior. *Sustainability (Basel)*, *9*(9), 1567. doi:10.3390/su9091567

Johansson-Sköldberg, U., Woodilla, J., & Çetinkaya, M. (2013). Design thinking: Past, present and possible futures. *Creativity and Innovation Management*, *22*(2), 121–146. doi:10.1111/caim.12023

Joyce, R. (2001). *The myth of morality*. Cambridge University Press. doi:10.1017/CBO9780511487101

Kafetzopoulos, D., & Gotzamani, K. (2022). The effect of talent management and leadership styles on firms' sustainable performance. *European Business Review*, *34*(6), 837–857. doi:10.1108/EBR-07-2021-0148

Kamassi, A., Abd Manaf, N. H., & Omar, A. (2020). The identity and role of stakeholders in the medical tourism industry: State of the art. *Tourism Review*, *75*(3), 559–574. doi:10.1108/TR-01-2019-0031

Kamilaris, A., Fonts, A., & Prenafeta-Boldú, F. X. (2019). *The Rise of Blockchain Technology in Agriculture and Food Supply Chains*. Science Direct.

Kanyi, J. M., Wanjau, K. L., & Kyalo, T. N. (2023). The role of product innovation and entrepreneurial passion on performance of manufacturing pharmaceutical companies in Kenya. *International Journal of Arts and Social Science*, *6*(8), 282.

Kaplan, S. (2012). *The business model innovation factory: How to stay relevant when the world is changing*. John Wiley & Sons. doi:10.1002/9781119205234

Karabag, S. F., Lau, M. C. K., & Suvankulov, F. (2014). Determinants of firm competitiveness: Case of the Turkish textile and apparel industry. *Journal of the Textile Institute*, *105*(1), 1–11. doi:10.1080/00405000.2013.811787

Kaya, Y., Karakan, G. G., & Visileanu, E. (2019). The impact of foreign exchange movements on Turkish textile sector. *Industria Textila (Bucuresti)*, *70*(03), 291–296. doi:10.35530/IT.070.03.1591

Kenning, P., & Linzmajer, M. (2011). Consumer neuroscience: An overview of an emerging discipline with implications for consumer policy. *Journal of Consumer Policy*, *34*(3), 263–276.

Kessler, K. (2015). Conceptualizing Mosque Tourism: A central feature of Islamic and Religious Tourism. *International Journal of Religious Tourism and Pilgrimage*, *39*(2), 2.

Khadka, K., & Maharjan, S. (2017). *Customer satisfaction and customer loyalty: Case trivsel städtjänster (trivsel siivouspalvelut)*.

Khan, A., Talukder, M. S., Islam, Q. T., & Islam, A. K. M. N. (2022). The impact of business analytics capabilities on innovation, information quality, agility and firm performance: the moderating role of industry dynamism. *VINE Journal of Information and Knowledge Management Systems*. doi:10.1108/VJIKMS-01-2022-0027

Khan, A. Md., & Jantan, A. H. B. (2022). Moderating Role of Psychological Empowerment on the Relationship between Transactional Leadership and Individual Innovation: Evidence from Banking Sector of Bangladesh. *Journal of International Business and Management*, *5*. doi:10.37227/jibm-2022-09-5488

Kickul, J. R., Griffiths, M. D., Jayaram, J., & Wagner, S. M. (2011). Operations management, entrepreneurship, and value creation: Emerging opportunities in a cross-disciplinary context. *Journal of Operations Management*, *29*(1-2), 78–85. doi:10.1016/j.jom.2010.12.004

Kim, H. (2009). *The Plastic Surgery Obsession in South Korea.* Syracuse University Honors Program Capstone Projects.

Kim, H., & Marcouiller, D. W. (2018). Mitigating flood risk and enhancing community resilience to natural disasters: Plan quality matters. *Environmental Hazards*, *17*(5), 397–417. doi:10.1080/17477891.2017.1407743

Kim, H., Woo, E., & Uysal, M. (2015). Tourism experience and quality of life among elderly tourists. *Tourism Management*, *46*, 465–476. doi:10.1016/j.tourman.2014.08.002

Kim, M. Y. (2020). Ethical behavior in the context of green credit card services: The role of individuals' regulatory focus. *International Journal of Advanced Culture Technology*, *8*(1), 107–112.

Kim, T. Y., Dekker, R., & Heij, C. (2017). Spare part demand forecasting for consumer goods using installed base information. *Computers & Industrial Engineering*, *103*, 201–215. doi:10.1016/j.cie.2016.11.014

Kiriu, T., & Nozaki, M. (2020). A Text Mining Model to Evaluate Firms' ESG Activities: An Application for Japanese Firms. *Asia-Pacific Financial Markets*, *27*(4), 1–12. doi:10.1007/s10690-020-09309-1

Klein, P., & Popp, B. (2022). Last-Mile Delivery Methods in E-Commerce: Does Perceived Sustainability Matter for Consumer Acceptance and Usage? *Sustainability (Basel)*, *14*(24), 16437. doi:10.3390/su142416437

Knezović, E. (2023). Self-perceived employability and entrepreneurial and intrapreneurial intentions: Evidence from six countries. *Global Business and Organizational Excellence*, joe.22205. doi:10.1002/joe.22205

Knutson, B., Rick, S., Wimmer, G. E., Prelec, D., & Loewenstein, G. (2007). Neural predictors of purchases. *Neuron*, *53*(1), 147–156. doi:10.1016/j.neuron.2006.11.010 PMID:17196537

Koczberski, G., Curry, G. N., Bue, V., Germis, E., Nake, S., & Tilden, G. M. (2018). Diffusing risk and building resilience through innovation: Reciprocal exchange relationships, livelihood vulnerability and food security amongst smallholder farmers in Papua New Guinea. *Human Ecology: an Interdisciplinary Journal*, *46*(6), 801–814. doi:10.1007/s10745-018-0032-9

Korpysa, J., Halicki, M., & Lopatka, A. (2020). Entrepreneurial management of project supply chain–a model approach. *Problems and Perspectives in Management*, *18*(3), 211–223. doi:10.21511/ppm.18(3).2020.18

Kotler, P. (2017). *Marketing 4.0: moving from traditional to digital*. John Wiley and sons Inc.

Koza, M. P., & Lewin, A. Y. (1998). The Co-evolution of Strategic Alliances. *Organization Science*, *9*(3), 255–264. Advance online publication. doi:10.1287/orsc.9.3.255

Kozyrkov, C. (2023). What is decision intelligence? *Medium*. https://towardsdatascience.com/introduction-to-decision-inte lligence-5d147ddab767.

Krämer, S., & Engell, S. (2018). *Resource efficiency of processing plants: monitoring and improvement.* John Wiley & Sons.

Kuckertz, A., & Wagner, M. (2010). The influence of sustainability orientation on entrepreneurial intentions - Investigating the role of business experience. *Journal of Business Venturing*, *25*(5), 524–539. Advance online publication. doi:10.1016/j.jbusvent.2009.09.001

Kudrekodlu Venkatesh, P., & Venkatesan, V. (2022). Lean readiness factors for construction organizations. [IJEMS]. *Indian Journal of Engineering and Materials Sciences*, *28*(6), 608–619.

Kühn, M. L. (2006). Parts of competitive intelligence: Competitor intelligence. *South African Journal of Information Management*, *8*(1). doi:10.4102/sajim.v8i1.209

Kumar, P., & Turnbull, S. M. (2008). Optimal patenting and licensing of financial innovations. *Management Science*, *54*(12), 2012–2023. doi:10.1287/mnsc.1080.0898

Kumar, S. A. (2008). *Entrepreneurship development.* New Age International.

Kurtmollaiev, S., Fjuk, A., Pedersen, P. E., Clatworthy, S., & Kvale, K. (2018). Organizational transformation through service design: The institutional logics perspective. *Journal of Service Research*, *21*(1), 59–74. doi:10.1177/1094670517738371

Kutzhanova, N., Lyons, T. S., & Lichtenstein, G. A. (2009). Skill-based development of entrepreneurs and the role of personal and peer group coaching in enterprise development. *Economic Development Quarterly*, *23*(3), 193–210. doi:10.1177/0891242409336547

La Verne. (2023). *The difference between innovation and entrepreneurship.* La Verne. https://laverne.edu/entrepreneurship/wp-content/uploads/site s/81/2023/04/The-difference-between-innovation-and-entrepren eurship.pdf. University of La Verne

Langleben, D. D., Loughead, J. W., Bilker, W. B., Ruparel, K., Childress, A. R., Busch, S. I., & Gur, R. C. (2009). Telling truth from lie in individual subjects with fast event-related fMRI. *Human Brain Mapping*, *30*(3), 745–757. PMID:16161128

Lavalle, S., Lesser, E., Shockley, R., Hopkins, M. S., & Kruschwitz, N. (2011). Big Data, Analytics and the Path From Insights to Value. *MIT Sloan Management Review*, *52*(2), 21–31.

Lavie, D., & Rosenkopf, L. (2005). Balancing exploration and exploitation in alliance formation: A multidimensional perspective. *Academy of Management 2005 Annual Meeting: A New Vision of Management in the 21st Century, AOM 2005*. IEEE. 10.5465/ambpp.2005.18778391

Lavie, D., & Rosenkopf, L. (2006a). Balancing exploration and exploitation in alliance formation. *Academy of Management Journal*, *49*(4), 797–818. doi:10.5465/amj.2006.22083085

Lee, N., Broderick, A. J., & Chamberlain, L. (2007). What is 'neuromarketing'? A discussion and agenda for future research. *International Journal of Psychophysiology*, *63*(2), 199–204. doi:10.1016/j.ijpsycho.2006.03.007 PMID:16769143

Li, J., & Fan, K. (2017). *A survey on the security of blockchain systems*. Research Gate.

Li, Y. (2023). A Study On The Interaction Between The "Balance Of Power And Internationalism" Norms In Southeast Asia In The 19th Century Centered On The1898 Spanish-American War. *Journal of Law and Political Sciences 39*(4), 454-490. https://drive.google.com/file/d/1wCuW-tGDhUB4dn8qHA0_31zGafPFWF_k/view

Liang, B. Y. (2004). *Hard Diplomacy: A Study on the Chinese Ambassador to the United States in the Late Qing Dynasty (艰难的外交——晚清中国驻美公使研究)*. Tianjin Ancient Books Publishing House.

Li, C. Z., Xue, F., Li, X., Hong, J., & Shen, G. Q. (2018). An Internet of Things-enabled BIM platform for on-site assembly services in prefabricated construction. *Automation in Construction*, *89*, 146–161. doi:10.1016/j.autcon.2018.01.001

Liedtka, J. (2018). Why design thinking works. *Harvard Business Review*, *96*(5), 72–79.

Liedtka, J., & Ogilvie, T. (2011). *Designing for growth: A design thinking tool kit for managers*. Columbia University Press.

Li, K., Kim, D. J., Lang, K. R., Kauffman, R. J., & Naldi, M. (2020). How should we understand the digital economy in Asia? Critical assessment and research agenda. *Electronic Commerce Research and Applications*, *44*, 101004. doi:10.1016/j.elerap.2020.101004 PMID:32922241

Lim, M.W. (2023). Transformative marketing in the new normal: A novel practice-scholarly integrative review of business-to-business marketing mix challenges, opportunities, and solutions. *Journal of Business Research, 160*, 113638. Elsevier Inc.

Lim, S. L., O'Doherty, J. P., & Rangel, A. (2011). The decision value computations in the vmPFC and striatum use a relative value code that is guided by visual attention. *The Journal of Neuroscience : The Official Journal of the Society for Neuroscience*, *31*(37), 13214–13223. doi:10.1523/JNEUROSCI.1246-11.2011 PMID:21917804

Lin, B., & Ma, R. (2022). How does digital finance influence green technology innovation in China? Evidence from the financing constraints perspective. *Journal of Environmental Management*, *320*, 115833. doi:10.1016/j.jenvman.2022.115833 PMID:35940011

Lindblom, C. E. (1997). *Politics and Markets: The World's Political Economic Systems*. Basic Books.

Linderman, K., & Chandrasekaran, A. (2010). The scholarly exchange of knowledge in operations management. *Journal of Operations Management*, *28*(4), 357–366. doi:10.1016/j.jom.2009.11.012

Li, P., Zhou, R., & Xiong, Y. (2020). Can ESG Performance Affect Bond Default Rate? Evidence from China. *Sustainability (Basel)*, *12*(7), 2954. doi:10.3390/su12072954

Little, A. (1902 June 25). Tariff Revision. *The North-China Herald*, 68., No.1820.

Little, E. S. (1902 March 5). The New Tariff Proposals. *The North-China Daily News*, *4*.

Little, E. S. (1902 October 5). A Protest Against Ratification. *The North-China Herald*, *69*., No.1836.

Little, E. S. (1902). *The Chinese Revenue and the New Treaty: A Protest against an Increased Tariff from a Merchant's Point of View. F.O.17/1579.* London: The National Archives. https://discovery.nationalarchives.gov.uk/

Liu, X. Y., & Liu, H. Y. (1984). *Foreign Relations of the United States,1901, Appendix. Affairs in China. Report of William W. Rockhill, Late Commissioner to China, with Accompanying Documents*. Shandong Qilu Book Publishing Co., Ltd.

Li, Z., Xue, J., Li, R., Chen, H., & Wang, T. (2020). Environmentally Specific Transformational Leadership and Employee's Pro-environmental Behavior: The Mediating Roles of Environmental Passion and Autonomous Motivation. *Frontiers in Psychology*, *11*, 1408. doi:10.3389/fpsyg.2020.01408 PMID:32670165

Loizos, C. (2011). *Lean Startup' evangelist Eric Ries is just getting started.* PeHUB. https://www.scribd.com/document/377073019/Lean-Startup

Long, D. G. (2007). *Crossing Market Barriers: The Market: Overseas Chinese Businessmen Between State, System, and Culture*. China Science and Media Ltd.

Lopez de Silanes, F., McCahery, J. A., & Pudschedl, P. (2019). *ESG performance and disclosure: A cross-country analysis*. European Corporate Governance Institute-Law.

López-Robles, J. R., Otegi-Olaso, J. R., Porto Gómez, I., & Cobo, M. J. (2019). 30 years of intelligence models in management and business: A bibliometric review. *International Journal of Information Management*, *48*, 22–38. doi:10.1016/j.ijinfomgt.2019.01.013

Lor, R. (2017). *Design thinking in education: A critical review of literature.*

Loshin, D. (2013). Business Intelligence: the savvy manager's guide (Vol. Second Edition). Waltham, USA: Morgan Kaufmann.

Lu, C., Wang, H., & Li, J. (2020). Research on the Synergistic Effect of Environmental Protection Investment and Technological Innovation on Corporate Performance. *European Journal of Business and Management*, *12*(11), 1–13.

Lumpkin, G. T., & Dess, G. G. (1996). Clarifying the Entrepreneurial Orientation Construct and Linking It to Performance. *Academy of Management Review*, *21*(1), 135–172.

Luo, Y. D. (2010). *History of Likin in China (中国厘金史)*. The Commercial Press.

MacDonald, A., Clarke, A., Huang, L., Roseland, M., & Seitanidi, M. M. (2018). Multi-stakeholder partnerships (SDG# 17) as a means of achieving sustainable communities and cities (SDG# 11). Handbook of sustainability science and research, 193-209.Springer.

Mackay, J. (1902a March 5). *To Lansdowne, K. G. NO. 23. F.O.17/1565*. London: The National Archives. https://discovery.nationalarchives.gov.uk/

Mackay, J. (1902b March 10). To Lansdowne, K. G. NO. 24. F.O.17/1565. London: The National Archives. https://discovery.nationalarchives.gov.uk/

Mackay, J. (1902c March 11). *James Mackay to the Shanghai Branch of the China Association. F.O.17/1565*. London: The National Archives. https://discovery.nationalarchives.gov.uk/

Madureira, L., Popovic, A., & Castelli, M. (2023). Competitive intelligence maturity models: Systematic review, unified model, and implementation frameworks. *J Intell Stud Bus*, *13*(1), 1–29. doi:10.37380/jisib.v13i1.988

Mahmoud, M. A., Hinson, R. E., & Adika, M. K. (2018). The effect of trust, commitment, and conflict handling on customer retention: The mediating role of customer satisfaction. *Journal of Relationship Marketing*, *17*(4), 257–276. doi:10.1080/15332667.2018.1440146

Maluleka, M. L., & Chummun, Z. B. (2023). Competitive intelligence and strategy implementation: Critical examination of present literature review. *South African Journal of Information Management*, *25*(1). https://sajim.co.za/index.php/sajim/article/view/1610. doi:10.4102/sajim.v25i1.1610

Manchester Chamber of Commerce. (1902 March 11). *To the Under Secretary of State. F.O.17/1579*. London: The National Archives. https://discovery.nationalarchives.gov.uk/

Mandrinos, S., & Lim, W. M. (2023). De-internationalization: An organizational institutionalism perspective. *Global Business and Organizational Excellence*, *42*(3), 58–73. doi:10.1002/joe.22195

Mangla, S. K., Luthra, S., Jakhar, S. K., Kumar, A., & Rana, N. P. (Eds.). (2019). *Sustainable Procurement in Supply Chain Operations*. CRC Press. doi:10.1201/9780429466328

Mani, V., Jabbour, C. J. C., & Mani, K. T. (2020). Supply chain social sustainability in small and medium manufacturing enterprises and firms' performance: Empirical evidence from an emerging Asian economy. *International Journal of Production Economics*, *227*, 107656. doi:10.1016/j.ijpe.2020.107656

Manohar, S., Paul. J., Strong, C., & Mittal, A. (2023). Generalized scale for perceived service innovation. *Journal of Business Research*, *160*, 113723.

Mansoori, P., Mohapatra, S., & Srinivasan, T. (2018). *The Future of Cross-Border Payments: An Introduction to Central Bank Digital Currencies*. International Monetary Fund.

Mark, T. R. (2024). *Importance of creativity & innovation in entrepreneurship 2024*. Nexford. https://www.nexford.edu/insights/creativity-innovation-in-entrepreneurship

Markopoulos, E., Kirane, I. S., Gann, E. L., & Vanharanta, H. (2020, April). A democratic, green ocean management framework for Environmental, Social and Governance (ESG) compliance. In *International Conference on Human Interaction and Emerging Technologies* (pp. 21-33). Springer, Cham. 10.1007/978-3-030-44267-5_4

Martinez, S., Stöcker, C., & Ward, C. (2017). *From bitcoin to the internet of value*. Audencia.

Martins, M. J., Shahzad, F. M., & Xu, S. (2023). Factors influencing entrepreneurial intention to initiate new ventures: Evidence from university students. *Journal of Innovation and Entrepreneurship*, *12*(1), 63. doi:10.1186/s13731-023-00333-9

Maune, A. (2022). Mobile applications adoption and use in strategic competitive intelligence: A structural equation modelling approach. *Journal of Intelligence Studies in Business*, *12*(1).

McCabe, D. P., Roediger, H. L. III, McDaniel, M. A., Balota, D. A., & Hambrick, D. Z. (2010). The relationship between working memory capacity and executive functioning: Evidence for a common executive attention construct. *Neuropsychology*, *24*(2), 222–243. doi:10.1037/a0017619 PMID:20230116

Mentzer, J. T., Stank, T. P., & Esper, T. L. (2008). Supply chain management and its relationship to logistics, marketing, production, and operations management. *Journal of Business Logistics*, *29*(1), 31–46. doi:10.1002/j.2158-1592.2008.tb00067.x

Merendino, A., & Melville, R. (2019). The board of directors and firm performance: empirical evidence from listed companies. *Corporate Governance: The international journal of business in society*.

Merriam-Webster. (2024). *Champion definition & meaning*. Merriam-Webster. https://www.merriam-webster.com › dictionary › cham.

Metcalf, L., & Benn, S. (2013). Leadership for Sustainability: An Evolution of Leadership Ability. *Journal of Business Ethics, 112*(3), 369–384. *Scopus*. Advance online publication. doi:10.1007/s10551-012-1278-6

Milner, H. (1997). *Interests, Institutions, and Information: Domestic Politics and International Relations*. Princeton University Press.

Mireftekhari, S. (2017). *Business incubator, a solution for startup's challenges. A qualitative look at business incubator's support for startups to overcome the liability of newness and smallness*. DUO. https://www.duo.uio.no/handle/10852/57517

Mohammed, F., Biswas, W. K., Yao, H., & Tadé, M. (2018). Sustainability assessment of symbiotic processes for the reuse of phosphogypsum. *Journal of Cleaner Production, 188*, 497–507. doi:10.1016/j.jclepro.2018.03.309

Mohanty, S. K. (2005). *Fundamentals of entrepreneurship*. PHI Learning Pvt. Ltd.

Momtaz, P. (2017). *Initial Coin Offerings: Financing growth with cryptocurrency token sales*. Deloitte University Press.

Mor, R.S., Kamble, S.S. & Sangwan, K.S. (2022). *Operations and Supply Chain Management in the Food Industry*. Springer Singapore.

Moraru, G.-M. (2021). The Creativity Of Future Engineers, An Insufficiently Exploited Resource In Romanian Organizations. *Management of Sustainable Development*, *13*(1), 21–25. doi:10.54989/msd-2021-0004

Moshood, T. D., Nawanir, G., Mahmud, F., Mohamad, F., Ahmad, M. H., & Abdul Ghani, A. (2021). Expanding policy for biodegradable plastic products and market dynamics of bio-based plastics: Challenges and opportunities. *Sustainability (Basel)*, *13*(11), 6170. doi:10.3390/su13116170

Mougayar, W. (2016). *The Business Blockchain: Promise*. Practice, and Application of the Next Internet Technology.

Müller, O., Fay, M., & vom Brocke, J. (2018). The Effect of Big Data and Analytics on Firm Performance: An Econometric Analysis Considering Industry Characteristics. *Journal of Management Information Systems*, *35*(2), 488–509. doi:10.1080/07421222.2018.1451955

Muralidharan, E., & Pathak, S. (2018). Sustainability, Transformational Leadership, and Social Entrepreneurship. *Sustainability (Basel)*, *10*(2), 567. doi:10.3390/su10020567

Murinde, V., Rizopoulos, E., & Zachariadis, M. (2022). The impact of the FinTech revolution on the future of banking: Opportunities and risks. *International Review of Financial Analysis*, *81*, 102103. doi:10.1016/j.irfa.2022.102103

Musabayana, T. G., Mutambara, E., & Ngwenya, T. (2023). Establishment of a Zimbabwe National SME sector: A major priority to enhance the performance of the national economy. *Journal of Innovation and Entrepreneurship*, *2023*(12), 65. doi:10.1186/s13731-023-00329-5

Nakamoto, S. (2008). *Bitcoin: A Peer-to-Peer Electronic Cash System*. USSC.

Nakamura, M., Pendlebury, D., Schnell, J., & Szomszor, M. (2019). Navigating the structure of research on sustainable development goals. *Policy*, *11*, 12.

Narayanan, A., Bonneau, J., Felten, E., Miller, A., & Goldfeder, S. (2016). *Bitcoin and Cryptocurrency Technologies: A Comprehensive Introduction*. Princeton University Press.

Nayak, B., Bhattacharyya, S. S., & Krishnamoorthy, B. (2019). Integrating wearable technology products and big data analytics in business strategy. *Journal of Systems and Information Technology*, *21*(2), 255–275. doi:10.1108/JSIT-08-2018-0109

Neck, H. M., Meyer, G. D., Cohen, B., & Corbett, A. C. (2004). An Entrepreneurial System View of New Venture Creation. In Journal of Small Business Management (Vol. 42, Issue 2). doi:10.1111/j.1540-627X.2004.00105.x

Ng, K. K., Chen, C. H., Lee, C. K., Jiao, J. R., & Yang, Z. X. (2021). A systematic literature review on intelligent automation: Aligning concepts from theory, practice, and future perspectives. *Advanced Engineering Informatics*, *47*, 101246. doi:10.1016/j.aei.2021.101246

Ng, T. H., Lye, C. T., Chan, K. H., Lim, Y. Z., & Lim, Y. S. (2020). Sustainability in Asia: The Roles of Financial Development in Environmental, Social and Governance (ESG) Performance. *Social Indicators Research*, *150*(1), 1–28. doi:10.1007/s11205-020-02288-w

Nicotra, M., Romano, M., Del Giudice, M., & Schillaci, C. E. (2018). The causal relation between entrepreneurial ecosystem and productive entrepreneurship: A measurement framework. *The Journal of Technology Transfer*, *43*(3), 640–673. doi:10.1007/s10961-017-9628-2

Nightingale, P., & Coad, A. (2013). Muppets and Gazelles: Political and Methodological Biases in Entrepreneurship Research. (SPRU Working Paper Series 2013-03). SPRU - Science and Technology Policy Research, University of Sussex.

Nikiforova, A., Daskevics, A., & Azeroual, O. (2022). NoSQL security: can my data-driven decision-making be affected from outside? *arXiv preprint arXiv:2206.11787.*

Ntandoyenkosi, S. (2023). Entrepreneurship education. *Journal of Entrepreneurial Innovations*, *4*(SI). doi:10.14426/jei.v4iSI.1674

O'Callaghan, M. (2023). *Decision intelligence: human–machine integration for decision-making* (1st ed.). CRC Press/Taylor & Francis. doi:10.1201/b23322

OECD (2023). *Risks and opportunities of reshaping global value chains.* OECD Economics Department, Working Party No. 1 on Macroeconomic and Structural Policy Analysis (CPE/WP1(2023)8).

OECD. (2023). *Financing SMEs and Entrepreneurs: An OECD Scoreboard, 2023 Highlights.* OECD Publishing, Paris. doi:10.1787/f493861e-en

OECD. (2023). Job Creation and Local Economic Development 2023: Bridging the Great Green Divide, OECD Publishing, Paris. doi:10.1787/21db61c1-en

OECD. (2023). *SME and Entrepreneurship Papers, No. 36.* OECD Publishing. doi:10.1787/a8d13e55-

Oesterreich, T. D., Anton, E., Teuteberg, F., & Dwivedi, Y. K. (2022). The role of the social and technical factors in creating business value from big data analytics: A meta-analysis. *Journal of Business Research*, *153*, 128–149. doi:10.1016/j.jbusres.2022.08.028

Ohme, R., Reykowska, D., Wiener, D., & Choromanska, A. (2009). Application of frontal EEG asymmetry to advertising research. *Journal of Economic Psychology*, *30*(5), 856–867.

Okhrimenko, I., Stepenko, V., Chernova, O., & Zatsarinnaya, E. (2023). The impact of information sphere in the economic security of the country: Case of Russian realities. *Journal of Innovation and Entrepreneurship*, *12*(1), 67. doi:10.1186/s13731-023-00326-8

Olszak, C. M. (2020). *Business intelligence and big data: drivers of organizational success.* CRC Press. doi:10.1201/9780429353505

Opuala-Charles, O. S., & Oshilike, I. V. (2023). Entrepreneurship, public policy and economic development in Nigeria. *Journal of Economics &Management Research.* 4(2), 4-77. *SRC, JESMR-210.* doi:10.47363/JESMR/2023(4)173

Oukil, M.-S. (2011). A development perspective of technology-based entrepreneurship in the Middle East and North Africa. *Annals of Innovation & Entrepreneurship*, *2*(1), 6000. doi:10.3402/aie.v2i1.7986

Ovharhe, O. H., & Okolo, B. S. (2022). Sustainable development goals: Lean entrepreneurship and Green entrepreneurship. *International Journal of Research and Scientific Innovation, 9*(10), 59-71.

Ovharhe, O. H., & Saturday, O. (2024b). Environmental pollution and maternal mortality among female entrepreneurs. *ABC Index.* https://explore.abcdindex.com/ai_portal/login.php.

Ovharhe, O. H., & Woko, B. E. (2024). Environmental pollution and infant mortality on entrepreneurial opportunities: A champiopreneurship approach. *ABC Index.* https://explore.abcdindex.com/ai_portal/login.php.

Ovharhe, O. H., & Woko, B. E. (2024). Environmental pollution and life expectancy among intrepreneurs. Journal of Economics and Management; JEM .

Ovharhe, O. H.., & Abada, A. M. (2023). IFRS adoptions on entrepreneurship entry and entrepreneurship exit: The Nigeria experience from 2006-2017. *American Journal of Social Development and Entrepreneurship, 2*(2). https://doi.org/ doi:10.54536/ajsde.v2i2

Ovharhe, O. H. (2022a). Sustainable development goals: Multicollinearity between therapeutic entrepreneurship and rehabilitation therapy among African nations. *International Journal of Small Business and Entrepreneurship Research, 10*(3), 1–59. doi:10.37745/ijsber.2013/vol10n3157

Ovharhe, O. H. (2022b). Sustainable development goals: Therapeutic entrepreneurship and entrepreneurship Injelititis among West Africa Countries. [WJEDS]. *World Journal of Entrepreneurial Development Studies*, *7*(1), 87–113. doi:10.56201/wjeds.v7.no1.2022.pg87.113

Ovharhe, O. H. (2023). *Champiopreneurship: Lean start-Up and business growth.* Impress.

Ovharhe, O. H. (2023). *Light entrepreneurship and customer funded business: Simplified.* Lambert Academic Publishing.

Ovharhe, O. H. (2023). The entrepreneur: Thinking globally and acting locally. FUPRE EntrepreneurshipTraining Programme [Chapters]. *Module*, *9*, 1–34.

Ovharhe, O. H., & Abada, A. M. (2023). IFRS: Entrepreneurial Exit and Entrepreneurial Entre. *American Journal of Social Development and Entrepreneurship*, *2*(2), 1–8. doi:10.54536/ajsde.v2i2.1578

Ovharhe, O. H., Ahunanya, V., & Woko, E. B. (2022). Consignment inventory system and entrepreneurial survival in Lagos State. *International Journal of Social Science & Management Research*, *8*(5), 29–42. doi:10.56201/ijssmr.v8.no5.2022.pg29.42

Ovharhe, O. H., & Chukwuemeka, S. P. (2023). Sustainable Development Goals: Therapeutic Entrepreneurship and Mental Health Conditions. *British Journal of Multidisciplinary and Advanced Studies*, *4*(1), 81–119. doi:10.37745/bjmas.2022.0107

Ovharhe, O. H., & Igbokwe, E. L. (2021). Analytical intervention of remote working correlates on risk culture and entrepreneurial adaptability in South-South Geopolitical Zone, Nigeria: Covid-19 Perspective. *Journal of Education and Practice, IISTE*, *12*(3), 34–44. doi:10.7176/JEP/12-34-05

Ovharhe, O. H., Okolo, B. S., Woko, E. B., & Igbokwe, L. (2022). Light entrepreneurship and customer funded business model. *International Journal of Social Sciences and Management Research*, *8*(5), 87–106. doi:10.56201/ijssmr.v8.no5.2022.pg87.106

Ovharhe, O. H., Woko, E. B., & Ezeocha, V. U. (2021). Remote working: Entrepreneurial risk and entrepreneurial survival in the micro firms in Niger-Delta, Nigeria (COVID-19 Pandemic Prospects). *International Journal of Small Business and Entrepreneurship Research*, *9*(4), 11–28. doi:10.37745/ijsber.2013/vol9n11-28

Oxford Global Innovation Consultancy. (n.d.). *Oxentia.* Oxford's Global Innovation Consultancy. https://www.oxentia.com/

OyinlolaM.KoladeO.OkoyaS. A.AjalaO.AdefilaA.AdedijiA.BabaremuK.TijaniB.AdejuwonJ. WambuiF.AkinlabiE. (2023). Entrepreneurship and Innovation in Nigerian Universities: Trends, Challenges and Opportunities. SSRN. doi:10.2139/ssrn.4419457

Pal, A. (2011). Islam Means Peace: Understanding the Muslim Principle of Nonviolence Today. Greenport: Praeger. doi:10.5040/9798400604997

Palmié, M., Wincent, J., Parida, V., & Caglar, U. (2020). The evolution of the financial technology ecosystem: An introduction and agenda for future research on disruptive innovations in ecosystems. *Technological Forecasting and Social Change*, *151*, 119779. doi:10.1016/j.techfore.2019.119779

Panagariya, A. (2022). Digital revolution, financial infrastructure and entrepreneurship: The case of India. *Asia and the Global Economy*, *2*(2), 100027. doi:10.1016/j.aglobe.2022.100027

Peek, S. (2024). Creativity is not innovation (but you need the both). *Business News Daily*. https://www.businessnewsdaily.com/6848-creativity-vs-innovation.html

Peng, C. W. (2020). The role of business strategy and CEO compensation structure in driving corporate social responsibility: Linkage towards a sustainable development perspective. *Corporate Social Responsibility and Environmental Management*, *27*(2), 1028–1039. doi:10.1002/csr.1863

Permata Sari, R. Y., Yuliati, L., & Komariyah, S. (2019). Intra-Industry Trade in Indonesia: A Case of the Textile and Textile Product Industry. *Journal of International Business. Economics and Entrepreneurship*, *4*(1), 47. doi:10.24191/jibe.v4i1.14416

Perrini, F., & Vurro, C. (2006). Social entrepreneurship: Innovation and social change across theory and practice. In *Social entrepreneurship* (pp. 57–85). Palgrave Macmillan UK. doi:10.1057/9780230625655_5

Philippine Chinese Charitable Association Inc. (1977). *Philippine Chinese Charitable Association Inc. 100th Anniversary Souvenir Book*. Philippine Chinese Charitable Association Inc. Press.

Plassmann, H., O'Doherty, J., & Rangel, A. (2007). Orbitofrontal cortex encodes willingness to pay in everyday economic transactions. *The Journal of Neuroscience : The Official Journal of the Society for Neuroscience*, *27*(37), 9984–9988. doi:10.1523/JNEUROSCI.2131-07.2007 PMID:17855612

Plassmann, H., Ramsøy, T. Z., & Milosavljevic, M. (2012). Branding the brain: A critical review and outlook. *Journal of Consumer Psychology*, *22*(1), 18–36. doi:10.1016/j.jcps.2011.11.010

Plastun, A., Makarenko, I., Khomutenko, L., & Shcherbakov, P. (2020). SDGs and ESG disclosure regulation: Is there an impact? Evidence from Top-50 world economies. *Problems and Perspectives in Management*, *18*(2), 231–245. doi:10.21511/ppm.18(2).2020.20

Poluha, R. (2016). *The Quintessence of Supply Chain Management*. USA: Springer.

Poncelet, K., Delarue, E., & D'haeseleer, W. (2020). Unit commitment constraints in long-term planning models: Relevance, pitfalls and the role of assumptions on flexibility. *Applied Energy*, *258*, 113843. doi:10.1016/j.apenergy.2019.113843

Pormann, P. E., & Savage-Smith, E. (2007). *Medieval Islamic medicine*. Edinburgh University Press. doi:10.1515/9780748629244

Portnoy, L. (2019). *Designed to learn: Using design thinking to bring purpose and passion to the classroom*. ASCD.

Potts, J., & Berg, C. (2021). *Entrepreneurship and the Blockchain: A New Paradigm for The Social Sciences*. Science Direct.

Prayag, G., & Hosany, S. (2014). When Middle East Meets West: Understanding the Motives and Perceptions of Young Tourists from the United Arab Emirates. *Tourism Management*, *40*, 35–45. doi:10.1016/j.tourman.2013.05.003

Proença, A. P., Gaspar, P. D., & Lima, T. M. (2022). Lean Optimization Techniques for Improvement of Production Flows and Logistics Management: The Case Study of a Fruits Distribution Center. *Processes (Basel, Switzerland)*, *10*(7), 1384. doi:10.3390/pr10071384

Prostean, G., Villahoz, J. J. L., Brancu, L., & Bakacsi, G. (2020). *Innovation in Sustainable Management and Entrepreneurship*. Springer International Publishing. doi:10.1007/978-3-030-44711-3

Pultz Schlosser, K., & Volkova, T. (2022). Social Enterprise Strategic Leadership For Delivering Shared Value. *Journal of Business and Management*, *20*, 36–56. doi:10.32025/JBM22002

Qa'dan, M. B. A., & Suwaidan, M. S. (2019). Board composition, ownership structure and corporate social responsibility disclosure: The case of Jordan. *Social Responsibility Journal*.

Qian, J.-H., Qiu, Y.-Y., Yang, Y.-D., Li, Y., Xu, P.-H., & Wang, L.-L. (2020). Accounting and evaluation of chemical footprint of cotton woven fabrics. *Industria Textila (Bucuresti)*, *71*(03), 209–214. doi:10.35530/IT.071.03.1678

Qingfen, Z., Wei, G., & Yuwen, Z. (2023). *Temporal and Spatial Trajectories of the Economic and Pollution Emission Focus of China's Textile Industry*. World Journal of Management Science and Technology., doi:10.57237/j.wjmst.2022.01.006

Quinn, L., & Dalton, M. (2009). Leading for sustainability: Implementing the tasks of leadership. *Corporate Governance (Bradford)*, *9*(1), 21–38. doi:10.1108/14720700910936038

Rahchamani, A., & All, E. (2019). The impact of marketing intelligence and business intelligence on acquiring competitive advantage. *Revista Gestão & Tecnologia*, *19*(5), 52–70. doi:10.20397/2177-6652/2019.v19i5.1794

Rahman, H. H. & Abdul, H. (2004). The development of the health sciences and related institutions during the first six centuries of Islam. *ISoIT*, 973–984.

Rahman, M., Moghavvemi, S., Thirumoorthi, T., & Rahman, M. K. (2020). The impact of tourists' perceptions on halal tourism destination: A structural model analysis. *Tourism Review*, *75*(3), 575–594. doi:10.1108/TR-05-2019-0182

Rahma, Z., & Mekimah, S.Zighed Rahma. (2023). The role of competitive intelligence in improving performance through organizational learning, A case study Start-ups in Algeria. *Journal of Intelligence Studies in Business*, *13*(1), 53–64. doi:10.37380/jisib.v13i1.991

Rajesh, R. (2020). Exploring the sustainability performances of firms using environmental, social, and governance scores. *Journal of Cleaner Production*, *247*, 119600. doi:10.1016/j.jclepro.2019.119600

Rana, M. E., & Khan, M. A. (2017). *The Impact and Potential of Blockchain on Entrepreneurship*. Research Gtae.

Rao, C. H. (1971). Uncertainty, entrepreneurship, and sharecropping in India. *Journal of Political Economy*, *79*(3), 578–595. doi:10.1086/259769

Rao-Graham, L., McNaughton, M., & Mansingh, G. (2020). *Business Intelligence fpr small and medium sized enterprises: an agile roadmap toward business sustainability*. CRC Press.

Ratten, V. (2023). Entrepreneurship: Definitions, opportunities, challenges, and future directions. *Global Business and Organizational Excellence*, *42*(5), 79–90. doi:10.1002/joe.22217

Raval, S. (2016). *Decentralized Applications: Harnessing Bitcoin's Blockchain Technology*. Research Gate.

Reddit (2023). Etymology. https://www.reddit.com/r/etymology/

Reddy, S. M. W., Torphy, K., Liu, Y., Chen, T., Masuda, Y. J., Fisher, J. R. B., Galey, S., Burford, K., Frank, K. A., & Montambault, J. R. (2021). How Different Forms of Social Capital Created Through Project Team Assignments Influence Employee Adoption of Sustainability Practices. *Organization & Environment*, *34*(1), 43–73. doi:10.1177/1086026619880343

Reeves, M., & Whitaker, K. (2022). Innovating management innovation. *Strategic Management Review*, *3*(1), 157–167. doi:10.1561/111.00000040

Revees, M., & Moose, S. (2023). *Boston consulting group matrix*. BCG. https://www.bcg.com/about/overview/our-history/growth-share-matrix

Rialti, R., Marzi, G., Ciappei, C., & Busso, D. (2019). Big data and dynamic capabilities: A bibliometric analysis and systematic literature review. *Management Decision*, *57*(8), 2052–2068. doi:10.1108/MD-07-2018-0821

Richey, R. G. Jr, Chowdhury, S., Davis-Sramek, B., Giannakis, M., & Dwivedi, Y. K. (2023). Artificial intelligence in logistics and supply chain management: A primer and roadmap for research. *Journal of Business Logistics*, *44*(4), 532–549. doi:10.1111/jbl.12364

Ries, E. (October 17, 2017). The startup way: How modern companies use entrepreneurial management to transform culture and drive long-term growth (Unabridged ed.). Random House Audio.

Ries, E. (2016). *The Lean Startup by Eric Ries*. The Starta.

Ries, E., & Euchner, J. (2013). Conversations: What Large Companies Can Learn from Start-ups: An Interview with Eric Ries. *Research Technology Management*, *56*(4), 12–16. doi:10.5437/08956308X5604003

Ripsas, S., & Hentschel, B. (2017). Vom Businessplan zum Startup-Cockpit. In Crowd Entrepreneurship. Springer. doi:10.1007/978-3-658-17031-8_4

Ripsas, S., Schaper, B., & Tröger, S. (2018a). A Startup Cockpit for the Proof-of-Concept. In Handbuch Entrepreneurship. Springer. doi:10.1007/978-3-658-04994-2_21

Ripsas, S., Schaper, B., & Tröger, S. (2018b). A Startup Cockpit for the Proof-of-Concept. In Handbuch Entrepreneurship. Springer. doi:10.1007/978-3-658-05263-8_21-2

Roberts, A. P., Stanton, N. A., & Fay, D. T. (2018). Go Deeper, Go Deeper: Understanding submarine command and control during the completion of dived tracking operations. *Applied Ergonomics*, *69*, 162–175. doi:10.1016/j.apergo.2018.02.003 PMID:29477324

Roberts, N., Campbell, D. E., & Vijayasarathy, L. R. (2016). Using Information Systems to Sense Opportunities for Innovation: Integrating Postadoptive Use Behaviors with the Dynamic Managerial Capability Perspective. *Journal of Management Information Systems*, *33*(1), 45–69. https://search.ebscohost.com/login.aspx?direct=true&db=crh&AN=116238037&site=ehost-live. doi:10.1080/07421222.2016.1172452

Robertson, J. L., & Carleton, E. (2018). Uncovering How and When Environmental Leadership Affects Employees' Voluntary Pro-environmental Behavior. *Journal of Leadership & Organizational Studies*, *25*(2), 197–210. doi:10.1177/1548051817738940

Romano, A., Passiante, G., Del Vecchio, P., & Secundo, G. (2014). The innovation ecosystem as booster for the innovative entrepreneurship in the smart specialisation strategy. *International Journal of Knowledge-Based Development*, *5*(3), 271–288. doi:10.1504/IJKBD.2014.065315

Rothkopf, D. (2012). *Power, Inc.: The Epic Rivalry Between Big Business and Government and the Reckoning That Lies Ahead*. Farrar, Straus, and Giroux.

Rushton, A., Croucher, P., & Baker, P. (2022). *The handbook of logistics and distribution management: Understanding the supply chain*. Kogan Page Publishers.

Russell, R. S., & Taylor, B. W. (2019). *Operations and supply chain management*. John Wiley & Sons.

Saleem, H., Li, Y., Ali, Z., Ayyoub, M., Wang, Y., & Mehreen, A. (2020). Big data use and its outcomes in supply chain context: The roles of information sharing and technological innovation. *Journal of Enterprise Information Management*, *34*(4), 1121–1143. doi:10.1108/JEIM-03-2020-0119

Sarisae, S., Benrit, P., & Salaeh, N. (2023). The need for Halal certification of medical devices: A case study of Thailand. *Journal of Halal Science and Technology*, *2*(1), 32–39. doi:10.59202/jhst.v2i1.664

Sarkar, B., Takeyeva, D., Guchhait, R., & Sarkar, M. (2022). Optimized radio-frequency identification system for different warehouse shapes. *Knowledge-Based Systems*, *258*, 109811. doi:10.1016/j.knosys.2022.109811

Sarkar, M. B., Echambadi, R. A. J., & Harrison, J. S. (2001). Alliance entrepreneurship and firm market performance. *Strategic Management Journal*, *22*(6-7), 701–711. doi:10.1002/smj.179

Schilirò, D. (2021). Fintech in Dubai: Development and Ecosystem. *International Business Research*, *14*(11), 61–70. doi:10.5539/ibr.v14n11p61

Schönsleben, P. (2022). Logistics, operations, and supply chain management. In *Handbook Integral Logistics Management: Operations and Supply Chain Management Within and Across Companies* (pp. 7–70). Springer Berlin Heidelberg.

Schwartz, M. (2013). A control group study of incubators' impact to promote firm survival. *The Journal of Technology Transfer*, *38*(3), 302–331. doi:10.1007/s10961-012-9254-y

Sedkaoui, S. (2020). How data analytics is changing entrepreneurial opportunities? *International Journal of Innovation Science*, *10*(2), 274–294. doi:10.1108/IJIS-09-2017-0092

Sen, D., Ozturk, M., & Vayvay, O. (2016). An Overview of Big Data for Growth in SMEs. *Procedia: Social and Behavioral Sciences*, *235*, 159–167. doi:10.1016/j.sbspro.2016.11.011

Serale, G., Fiorentini, M., Capozzoli, A., Bernardini, D., & Bemporad, A. (2018). Model predictive control (MPC) for enhancing building and HVAC system energy efficiency: Problem formulation, applications and opportunities. *Energies*, *11*(3), 631. doi:10.3390/en11030631

Seth, S. (2023). *Why entrepreneurship is important to the economy. The Business Post: 118-121.* TejgaonI/A.

Seyedghorban, Z., Samson, D., & Swink, M. (2022). Quo vadis OSCM? An analysis of past and future trends in operations and supply chain management research. *Decision Sciences*, *53*(3), 429–451. doi:10.1111/deci.12519

Shaheen, F., Ahmad, N., Waqas, M., Waheed, A., & Farooq, O. (2017). Structural Equation Modeling (SEM) in Social Sciences & Medical Research: A Guide for Improved Analysis. *International Journal of Academic Research in Business & Social Sciences*, *7*(5), 132–143. doi:10.6007/IJARBSS/v7-i5/2882

Shane, S., & Venkataraman, S. (2000). The promise of entrepreneurship as a field of research. *Academy of Management Review*, *25*(1), 217–226. doi:10.5465/amr.2000.2791611

Sharda, R., Delen, D., & Turban, E. (2018). *Business intelligence analytics and data science: a managerial perspective*. Pearson.

Shcherbakov, V., & Silkina, G. (2021). Supply chain management open innovation: Virtual integration in the network logistics system. *Journal of Open Innovation*, *7*(1), 54. doi:10.3390/joitmc7010054

Shevlin, H. (2022, October 21). The artist is dead, AI killed them. *IAI News*.

Shibin, K. T., Dubey, R., & Hazen, B. T. (2022). Partial least squares in supply chain management: An example study on sustainable supply chain management practices. Handbook of research methods for supply chain management, 221-243. Springer.

Shobhit, S. (March 16, 2023). *As in the definition of entrepreneurship*. [REMOVED HYPERLINK FIELD]

Showkat, A. D. (2022). The relevance of Taylor's scientific management in the modern era. *Journal of Psychology and Political Science*, *24*(2) https://doi.org/. doi:10.55529/jpps

Sigrist, S. (2006). *Health Horizons: Guide zu den neuen Gesundheitsmarkten/Guide to the New Healthmarkets* (Vol. 20). Gottlieb Duttweiler Institut/GDI.

Singh, S. K., Giudice, M. D., Chierici, R., & Graziano, D. (2020). Green innovation and environmental performance: The role of green transformational leadership and green human resource management. *Technological Forecasting and Social Change*, *150*, 119762. doi:10.1016/j.techfore.2019.119762

Skyrius, R. (2021). *Business Intelligence*. Springer. doi:10.1007/978-3-030-67032-0

Smith, D. V., Hayden, B. Y., Truong, T. K., Song, A. W., Platt, M. L., & Huettel, S. A. (2010). Distinct value signals in anterior and posterior ventromedial prefrontal cortex. *The Journal of Neuroscience : The Official Journal of the Society for Neuroscience*, *30*(7), 2490–2495. doi:10.1523/JNEUROSCI.3319-09.2010 PMID:20164333

Smith, M. K., & Puczkó, L. (2013). *Health and wellness tourism*. Routledge.

Smith, M. K., & Puczkó, L. (2014). *Health, tourism, and hospitality: spas, wellness, and medical travel*. Routledge. doi:10.4324/9780203083772

Smith, M. K., & Puczkó, L. (2017). *The Routledge Handbook of health tourism*. Routledge.

Souto, J. E. (2022). Organizational creativity and sustainability-oriented innovation as drivers of sustainable development: Overcoming firms' economic, environmental and social sustainability challenges. *Journal of Manufacturing Technology Management*, *33*(4), 805–826. doi:10.1108/JMTM-01-2021-0018

Spear, H. J. (1901 June 28). *The Bristol Chamber of Commerce to the China Association. F.O.17/1586*. London: The National Archives. https://discovery.nationalarchives.gov.uk/

Spigel, B. (2017). The Relational Organization of Entrepreneurial Ecosystems. *Entrepreneurship Theory and Practice*, *41*(1), 49–72. Advance online publication. doi:10.1111/etap.12167

Spigel, B., & Harrison, R. (2018). Toward a process theory of entrepreneurial ecosystems. *Strategic Entrepreneurship Journal*, *12*(1), 151–168. doi:10.1002/sej.1268

Sprague, R. H. (1980). A framework for the development of decision support systems. *Management Information Systems Quarterly*, *4*(4), 1–26. https://www.jstor.org/stable/248957. doi:10.2307/248957

Stanford Center For Professional Development. (2024). *Creativity and innovation management: How to inspire original ideas*. Stanford University. https://online.stanford.edu/creativity-and-innovation-management

Stephenson, M. L., & Ali, N. (2010). Tourism, travel, and Islamophobia: post 9/11 journeys of Muslims in non-Muslim states. In N. Scott & J. Jafari (Eds.), *Tourism in the Muslim world*. Emerald Group Publishing Limited.

Stern, C. W., & Deimler, M. S. (2006). *The boston consulting group on strategy: Classic concepts and new perspectives* (2nd ed.). John Wiley & Sons, Inc.

Suliman, M. A., Abdou, A. H., Ibrahim, M. F., Al-Khaldy, D. A. W., Anas, A. M., Alrefae, W. M. M., & Salama, W. (2023). Impact of Green Transformational Leadership on Employees' Environmental Performance in the Hotel Industry Context: Does Green Work Engagement Matter? *Sustainability (Basel)*, *15*(3), 2690. doi:10.3390/su15032690

Suphattanakul, O. (2017). Role of Transformational Leadership in Effective Strategic Implementation with the Moderating Effect of Organizational Culture. *Journal of Business and Social Review in Emerging Economies*, *3*(2), 253–262. doi:10.26710/jbsee.v3i2.80

Suryono, R. R., Budi, I., & Purwandari, B. (2020). Challenges and trends of financial technology (Fintech): A systematic literature review. *Information (Basel)*, *11*(12), 590. doi:10.3390/info11120590

Sustainable development report. (2023). SDGIndex. https://dashboards.sdgindex.org/

Sutrisno, A. (2022). Textile Industry in Indonesia Amidst the Impact of the Covid-19 Coronavirus Pandemic. *Kybernology : Journal of Government Studies*, *2*(1), 1–8. doi:10.26618/kjgs.v2i1.7853

Swan, M. (2015). *Blockchain: blueprint for a new economy*. Research Gate.

Swan, M. (2015). *Blockchain: Blueprint for a New Economy*. O'Reilly Media.

Syam, H., Akib, H., Patonangi, A. A., & Guntur, M. (2018). Principal entrepreneurship competence based on creativity and innovation in the context of learning organizations in Indonesia. *Journal of Entrepreneurship Education*, *21*(3), 1–13.

Taajamaa, V., Kirjavainen, S., Repokari, L., Sjöman, H., Utriainen, T., & Salakoski, T. (2013, December). Dancing with Ambiguity Design thinking in interdisciplinary engineering education. In *2013 IEEE Tsinghua International Design Management Symposium* (pp. 353-360). IEEE. 10.1109/TIDMS.2013.6981258

Tama, B. A., Yao, L., Raissi, H., & Babar, S. A. (2018). *The Rise of Blockchain Technology in Agriculture and Food Supply Chains*. Research Gate.

Tan, C. L., Tei, Z., Yeo, S. F., Lai, K. H., Kumar, A., & Chung, L. (2023). Nexus among blockchain visibility, supply chain integration and supply chain performance in the digital transformation era. *Industrial Management & Data Systems*, *123*(1), 229–252. doi:10.1108/IMDS-12-2021-0784

Tanveer, A., Anwer, M. A., & Umar, M. (2021). The Impact of Environmental Sustainability and Financial Resources Utilization on Firm Financial Performance: The Mediating Role of Leadership Styles. *ANNALS OF SOCIAL SCIENCES AND PERSPECTIVE*, *2*(2), 389–407. doi:10.52700/assap.v2i2.46

Tapscott, D., & Tapscott, A. (2016). *Blockchain Revolution: How the Technology Behind Bitcoin Is Changing Money*. Business, and the World.

Taranu, S. (2023). Measuring the added value of competitive intelligence in business. *Proceedings of the 17th International Conference on Business Excellence*, 1328-1336. , ISSN 2558-9652. 2023. doi:10.2478/picbe-2023-0119

Teerakunpisut, S., & Kongpiam, P. (2023). Implementation of a Hospitality-Oriented Patient Experience (HOPE) Concept to Service Standards of Muslim-friendly Medical Tourism. *Social Space*, *23*(1), 400–428.

The National Archives. (1902 March 7). *Mr. Bland and the Likin Duties. F.O.17/1565*. London: The National Archives. https://discovery.nationalarchives.gov.uk/

Thompson, M. (2009). *Organizational champions: How to develop passionate change agents at every level*. McGraw-Hill.

Thurik, A.R. (2009). Entreprenomics: entrepreneurship, economic growth and policy. *Entrepreneurship, growth and public policy, 10*(6), 219-249.

Tokel, D., Dogan, I., Hocaoglu-Ozyigit, A., & Ozyigit, I. I. (2022). Cotton Agriculture in Turkey and Worldwide Economic Impacts of Turkish Cotton. *Journal of Natural Fibers*, *19*(15), 10648–10667. doi:10.1080/15440478.2021.2002759

Tönnissen, S., & Teuteberg, F. (2020). Analysing the impact of blockchain-technology for operations and supply chain management: An explanatory model drawn from multiple case studies. *International Journal of Information Management*, *52*, 101953. doi:10.1016/j.ijinfomgt.2019.05.009

Traynor, M., Bernard, S., Moreo, A., & O'Neill, S. (2022). Investigating the emergence of third-party online food delivery in the US restaurant industry: A grounded theory approach. *International Journal of Hospitality Management*, *107*, 103299. doi:10.1016/j.ijhm.2022.103299

TUIK. (2023a). *TÜİK - Veri Portalı*. Data Portal for Statistics. https://data.tuik.gov.tr/Kategori/GetKategori?p=Cevre-ve-Ene rji-103

Tunc, M., Kaplan, K., Sisbot, S., & Camdali, U. (2016). Energy management and optimization: Case study of a textile plant in Istanbul, Turkey. *World Journal of Engineering*, *13*(4), 348–355. doi:10.1108/WJE-08-2016-046

Utz, S. (2019). Corporate scandals and the reliability of ESG assessments: Evidence from an international sample. *Review of Managerial Science*, *13*(2), 483–511. doi:10.1007/s11846-017-0256-x

Van De Ven, H. (1993). The development of an infrastructure for entrepreneurship. *Journal of Business Venturing*, *8*(3), 211–230. doi:10.1016/0883-9026(93)90028-4

Van Goor, A. R., van Amstel, W. P., & van Amstel, M. P. (2019). *European distribution and supply chain logistics*. Routledge.

Vargas-Sánchez, A., & Moral-Moral, M. (2019). Halal tourism: State of the art. *Tourism Review*, *74*(3), 385–399. doi:10.1108/TR-01-2018-0015

Veiga, C., Santos, M., Águas, P., & Santos, J. (2017). Are millennials transforming global tourism? Challenges for destinations and companies. *Worldwide Hospitality and Tourism Themes*, *9*(6), 603–616. doi:10.1108/WHATT-09-2017-0047

Venkatraman, V., Dimoka, A., Pavlou, P. A., Vo, K., Hampton, W., Bollinger, B., Hershfield, H. E., Ishihara, M., & Winer, R. S. (2015). Predicting advertising success beyond traditional measures: New insights from neurophysiological methods and market response modeling. *JMR, Journal of Marketing Research*, *52*(4), 436–452. doi:10.1509/jmr.13.0593

Visvizi, A., Troisi, O., Grimaldi, M., & Loia, F. (2022). Think human, act digital: Activating data-driven orientation in innovative start-ups. *European Journal of Innovation Management*, *25*(6), 452–478. doi:10.1108/EJIM-04-2021-0206

Vocabulary.com. (2024). Champion: definition, meaning & synonyms. Vocabulary.com

Voshmgir, S. (2019). *Token Economy: How Blockchain and Smart Contracts Are Changing the Economic Landscape.*

Wahab, S., Crompton, J., & Rothfield, L. (1976). *Tourism Marketing*. Tourism International Press.

Wanda, P., & Stian, S. (2015). The Secret of my Success: An exploratory study of Business Intelligence management in the Norwegian Industry. *Procedia Computer Science, 64*(1877), 240–247. doi:10.1016/j.procs.2015.08.486

Wang, Y. W., & Wang, L. (2015). Historical Materials on Diplomacy during the Qing Dynasty (Volume 4) (清季外交史 (第4册)). Changsha: Human Normal University Press.

Wang, C., Gou, L., & Li, X. (2022). Is Education Beneficial to Environmentally Friendly Behaviors? Evidence from CEOs. *International Journal of Environmental Research and Public Health*, *19*(18), 11391. doi:10.3390/ijerph191811391 PMID:36141663

Wang, S. H. (1985). *Boxer Indemnity (庚子赔款)*. Institute of Modern History, Academia Sinica.

Wang, Y., Ali, Z., Mehreen, A., & Hussain, K. (2023). The trickle-down effect of big data use to predict organization innovation: The roles of business strategy alignment and information sharing. *Journal of Enterprise Information Management*, *36*(1), 323–346. doi:10.1108/JEIM-10-2021-0439

Weerawardena, J., & Mavondo, F. T. (2011). Capabilities, innovation and competitive advantage. *Industrial Marketing Management*, *40*(8), 1220–1223. doi:10.1016/j.indmarman.2011.10.012

Welsh, M. A., & Dehler, G. E. (2013). Combining critical reflection and design thinking to develop integrative learners. *Journal of Management Education*, *37*(6), 771–802. doi:10.1177/1052562912470107

Wesselink, R., Blok, V., & Ringersma, J. (2017). Pro-environmental behaviour in the workplace and the role of managers and organisation. *Journal of Cleaner Production*, *168*, 1679–1687. doi:10.1016/j.jclepro.2017.08.214

Westling, M., & Mazhari, M. (2019). *Sustainability and senior executive compensation: A study of the relationship between sustainability and senior executive compensation in the Nordics*.

Wickberg, E. (1965). *The Chinese in Philippine Life 1850-1898*. Yale University Press.

Wilkins, C. (2016). *Fintech and the financial ecosystem: evolution or revolution?* Remarks to Payments Canada.

Williams, S. (2016). *Business Intelligence Strategy and Big Data Analytics: a general management perspective*. Morgan Kaufmann.

Wilson, A. R. (2004). *Ambition and Identity Chinese Merchant Elite in Colonial Manil 1880-1916*. University of Hawai'i Press.

Wolf, J. (2011). Sustainable Supply Chain Management Integration: A Qualitative Analysis of the German Manufacturing Industry. *Journal of Business Ethics*, *102*(2), 221–235. doi:10.1007/s10551-011-0806-0

Wong, W. C., Batten, J. A., Mohamed-Arshad, S. B., Nordin, S., & Adzis, A. A. (2020). Does ESG certification add firm value? *Finance Research Letters*, 101593.

Xenikou, A., & Simosi, M. (2006). Organizational culture and transformational leadership as predictors of business unit performance. *Journal of Managerial Psychology*, *21*(6), 566–579. doi:10.1108/02683940610684409

Xia, L., Lam, S. K., Chen, D., Wang, J., Tang, Q., & Yan, X. (2017). Can knowledge-based N management produce more staple grain with lower greenhouse gas emission and reactive nitrogen pollution? A meta-analysis. *Global Change Biology*, *23*(5), 1917–1925. doi:10.1111/gcb.13455 PMID:27506858

Xie, J., Nozawa, W., Yagi, M., Fujii, H., & Managi, S. (2019). Do environmental, social, and governance activities improve corporate financial performance? *Business Strategy and the Environment*, *28*(2), 286–300. doi:10.1002/bse.2224

Yadav, S. U., Tripathi, R., Tripathi, A. M., Ghosal, I., Kumar, A., Mandal, M., & Singh, A. (2023). Digital and innovative entrepreneurship in the Indian handicraft sector after the COVID-19 pandemic: Challenges and opportunities. *Journal of Innovation and Entrepreneurship*, *12*(1), 69. doi:10.1186/s13731-023-00337-5

Yaman, R., Alias, Z., & Ishak, N. M. (2012). Beauty Treatment and Spa Design from Islamic Perspective. *Procedia: Social and Behavioral Sciences*, *50*, 492–501. doi:10.1016/j.sbspro.2012.08.053

Yang, L. X. (2019). *Collected Works of Yang Shengmao (杨生茂文集)*. Nankai University Press.

Yang, L., Qin, H., Gan, Q., & Su, J. (2020). Internal Control Quality, Enterprise Environmental Protection Investment and Finance Performance: An Empirical Study of China's A-Share Heavy Pollution Industry. *International Journal of Environmental Research and Public Health*, *17*(17), 6082. doi:10.3390/ijerph17176082 PMID:32825596

Yao, Y.-H., Fan, Y.-Y., Guo, Y.-X., & Li, Y. (2014). Leadership, work stress and employee behavior. *Chinese Management Studies*, *8*(1), 109–126. doi:10.1108/CMS-04-2014-0089

Yli-Huumo, J., Ko, D., Choi, S., Park, S., & Smolander, K. (2016). Where Is Current Research on Blockchain Technology?—. *Systematic Reviews.*

Yoon, C., Gutchess, A. H., Feinberg, F., & Polk, T. A. (2006). A functional magnetic resonance imaging study of neural dissociations between brand and person judgments. *The Journal of Consumer Research, 33*(1), 31–40. doi:10.1086/504132

Yoshikuni, A. C., & Dwivedi, R. (2023). The role of enterprise information systems strategies enabled strategy-making on organizational innovativeness: A resource orchestration perspective. *Journal of Enterprise Information Management, 36*(1), 172–196. doi:10.1108/JEIM-10-2021-0442

You, B. H. (1957). *The Philippines*. World Affairs Press Co. Ltd.

Young, G. (1973). *Tourism -Blessing or blight?* Penguin.

Yu Chuan, Y. (2022). The Impact of Scenario Planning and Leadership on Non-Financial Performance in the Multi-Level Marketing (MLM) Industry. *International Journal of Accounting Finance in Asia Pasific, 5*(3), 17–38. doi:10.32535/ijafap.v5i3.1728

Yu, R. J. (1998). *A Study of the Philippine Chinese General Chamber of Commerce, 1904-54.* [Master's Thesis, National CHENG CHI University]. https://ah.nccu.edu.tw/item?item_id=96757

Yuan, S. Y. (1998). Complete Works of Zhang Zhidong: Vol. 1. 张之洞全集第*1*册. Hebei People's Publishing House.

Yuan, Y., Tian, G., Lu, L. Y., & Yu, Y. (2019). CEO ability and corporate social responsibility. *Journal of Business Ethics, 157*(2), 391–411. doi:10.1007/s10551-017-3622-3

Yugandhara, R. Y. (2023). Business intelligence market size 2023-2030 (US$ in Bn). *Business Intelligence Market Growth Drivers & Analysis 2023*. Research Gate. https://www.researchgate.net/publication/369595866_Business_Intelligence_Market_Growth_Drivers_Analysis_2023

Yukl, G. A., & Gardner, W. L. (2020). *Leadership in organizations* (9th ed.). Pearson Education, Inc.

Yung, L. Y. (1996). *The Huaqiao Warriors: Chinese Resistance Movement in Philippine, 1942-1945.QuezonCity*. Ateneo de Manila University Press.

Zak, P. J., & Knack, S. (2001). Trust and growth. *Economic Journal (London), 111*(470), 295–321. doi:10.1111/1468-0297.00609

Zapata-Cantu, L., Trevino, T., & Morton, F. (2020). Using Customer Analytics to Succeed: the case of Mexican SMEs. In P. N. Melo & C. Machado (Eds.), *Business Intelligence and Analytics in small and medium entreprises* (pp. 13–24). CRC Press.

Zavolokina, L., Dolata, M., Schwabe, G., & Kude, T. (2016). Fintech – The Impact on Consumers and Regulatory Responses. *In Proceedings of the 24th European Conference on Information Systems (ECIS)*. IEEE.

Zeng, J., & Khan, Z. (2019). Value creation through big data in emerging economies. *Management Decision, 57*(8), 1818–1838. doi:10.1108/MD-05-2018-0572

Zhao, D. X. (2008). Complete Works of Zhang Zhidong: Vol. 10. 张之洞全集第十册. Wuhan Publishing Group Co., Ltd.

Zhao, Y., & Zhu, Q. (2014). Evaluation on crowdsourcing research: Current status and future direction. *Information Systems Frontiers, 16*(3), 417–434. doi:10.1007/s10796-012-9350-4

Zheng, Z., Xie, S., Dai, H. N., Chen, X., & Wang, H. (2017). *An overview of blockchain technology: Architecture, consensus, and future trends.*

Zhou, B. (2016). Lean principles, practices, and impacts: A study on small and medium-sized enterprises (SMEs). *Annals of Operations Research, 241*(1-2), 457–474. doi:10.1007/s10479-012-1177-3

Zhou, J., San, O. T., & Liu, Y. (2023). Design and Implementation of enterprise financial decision support system based on business intelligence. *International Journal of Professional Business Review, 8*(4), e0873. doi:10.26668/businessreview/2023.v8i4.873

Zhuang, G. T., & Liu, W. Z. (2009). *The Formation and Development of Chinese Society in East Asia: Chinese Business Network, Immigration, and Integration Trends (东亚华人社会的形成和发展——华商网络、移民与一体化趋势).* Xiamen University Press.

Zhu, X. K. (2017). *The Study of the Shun Pao and the Sino-French War (《申报》与中法战争研究).* Huangshan Publishing House.

Zubeltzu-Jaka, E., Álvarez-Etxeberria, I., & Ortas, E. (2020). The effect of the size of the board of directors on corporate social performance: A meta-analytic approach. *Corporate Social Responsibility and Environmental Management, 27*(3), 1361–1374. doi:10.1002/csr.1889

Лена, M. (2019). Marketing intelligence as a tool for strategic enterprise management. *International Journal of Psychosocial Rehabilitation, 24*(8), 7. doi:10.37200/IJPR/V24I8/PR281089

About the Contributors

Kannapat Kankaew is currently an Assistant Professor at Burapha University International College. He received Doctor of Public Administration majoring in Human Resources Management. Before his 12 years as an academic professional, he worked in the aviation industry for over 10 years. He has published and participated in International Conferences reputed journals. He also published chapters in edited books, being a books editor, and examiner for Ph.D. and Master students in both national and international institutions. And he was dedicated as an editorial board, associate editor, and reviewer for various domestic and international journals.

Parinya Nakpathom is Dean of Burapha University International College and Instructor of Holistic Health and Wellness Management. He earned Bachelor's Degree in Arts (Thai) from Burapha University in 2005, followed by a Master's Degree in International Hospitality and Hotel Management from the University of Western Sydney, Australia in 2008. In 2018, He has completed his Doctoral Degree in Management from Silpakorn University, Thailand. Since 2012, he has been contributing to academia as a lecturer at Burapha University International College. In 2021, he was appointed as an assistant Professor in Business Administration. His research interests encompass Tourism, Hospitality, Service, and Tourist attraction. Over the years, he has had the privilege of being a guest speaker more than 100 times in public organizations, private companies, and universities, both in Thailand and abroad.

Krittipat Pitchayadejanant is a lecturer in Logistics Management, Burapha University International College. His research interests are in business data analysis, especially advanced statistical analysis applied to hospitality and tourism, logistics management, and marketing. He teaches in Operational Research in Logistics management, Multivariate Analysis and Business Data Analysis.

***

Al Montaser Abu Hussein is knowledgeable about the rigours of balancing research with classroom and administrative responsibilities. Research interest in leadership styles, business ethics, employee performance, employee turnover, and employee engagement in the oil and gas industry is dedicated to expanding the collective knowledge base through new fresh, interesting studies. Published in multiple journals and is a sought-after speaker at field conferences.

Satya Ranjan Acharya is a Professor and Director, of the Department of Entrepreneurship Education, Entrepreneurship Development Institute of India. He is a Co-Chair of the Post Graduate Programmes Executive Committee. An academician in the areas of Entrepreneurship Education, Dr Satya Ranjan Acharya holds expertise in training budding entrepreneurs as well as grooming developed entrepreneurs. His mentoring activities beyond institutions and classrooms are commendable. Through the "Hastakala Setu Yojana" project, he is mentoring over 20,000 traditional artisans of Gujarat, India in providing training, and exposure to market and financial linkages across 33 districts of Gujarat. He continuously engages with his incubated startups at the incubation centre to ensure startups' desired growth and sustainability. He is known for teaching courses in New Enterprise Creation and Entrepreneurial Finance and is also a supervisor of FPM students. He conducts and organizes various management development and faculty development programs on entrepreneurship teaching and startup incubation for the Govt of Gujarat and the Ministry of Education, Government of India. He received the National Teacher's Award, on 5th September 2023 from Hon President Smt. Droupadi Murmu, at New Delhi.

Khairul Anuar Mohd Ali is a Professor at the UKM-Graduate School of Business. He received his first degree in Bachelor Business Administration from Washington State University, USA, his Master in Business Administration from Universiti Kebangsaan Malaysia and his PhD from Universiti Utara Malaysia. His current research interests are in the area of quality management, supply chain management, performance measurement, service quality and customer satisfaction. His current research project are on the development of Customer Satisfaction Index and Mathematical Modeling for Performance Measurement of Malaysian Local Authorities, both funded by relevant Research Grants. Professor Khairul's research works have appeared in various international refereed journals such as Total Quality Management & Business Excellence Journal, Quality & Quantity International Journal, Social Indicators Research Journal, International Journal of Services and Operations Management, International Journal of Supply Chain Management, Test Engineering and Management, LogForum Scientific Journal of Logistics, Management Science Letters, Interdisciplinary Journal of Information, Knowledge, and Management, International Review of Business Research Papers, Journal of Global

Business Management, Pakistan Journal of Nutrition, The Indonesian Management & Accounting Research, Jurnal Sains Malaysiana and Jurnal Pengurusan.

Kande Archana has completed BTech in Computer Science and Engineering from JNTU Hyderabad College of Engineering at Kukatpally in 2002, MTech in Computer Science and Engineering from JNTU Hyderabad College of Engineering at Kukatpally in 2011 and PhD registered in 2017, and pursuing in Computer Science &Engineering from JNTU Hyderabad College of Engineering at Kukatpally. She received Young Researcher Award in 2023 from INSc, received IEI - Best Division Award from The Institute of Engineers India and also three times received as a Best Teacher Award from Malla Reddy Institute of Engineering and Technology, Hyderabad, in the years of 2021, 2022 and 2023. She is appointed as a Reviewer for IJCSM for International Journal, one for AICTE Sponsored IEEE International Conference on Networks, and Multimedia and Information Technology (NMITCON), one for International Conference on Evolutionary Algorithms and Soft Computing Techniques(EASCT), one for First International conference on Emerging Research in Computing Information, Communication, Artificial Intelligenc

Korhan Arun received a BA in mathematics from Hacettepe University (Turkey) and an M.B.A in Total Quality Management from Dokuz Eylul University in 2003 and a Ph.D. in Organization and Management from Ataturk University (Turkey) in 2008. He is an assistant Professor of Organization and Management at the University at Namik Kemal University (Tekirdag/Turkey). His current research and teaching interests include: leadership, power and influence, organization and management development. Dr. Arun worked at the government agencies for 15 years. Also, he had an advisor position for NATO (KFOR/ Kosovo Force) in 2012. He has been involved in several projects to improve leadership in the Turkish Army.

Ali Mohsin Ba Awain has a PhD in Business Administration. He is an assistant professor at the University of Technology and Applied Science (Salalah) in the Department of Business Administration. Head of Supply Chain Management major at UTAS, Salalah. Also teaching a variety of specialized courses, Member of 3 committees, as well as part of the research council. He served as Director of the Center for Entrepreneurship at Dhofar University. He managed as Director of the Center Continuous Education & Community Services at Dhofar University. He has several publications in the supply chain field and all of them have been published in different highly ranked journals in Scopus.

Aniesa Samira Bafadhal is a senior lecturer in the Tourism Study Program, Faculty of Administrative Science, at the University of Brawijaya, Indonesia. Since

2018, she has served as vice head of the Tourism Research Laboratory and has been involved in the Tourism Research Center at the University of Brawijaya. Her research interests currently focus on a number of areas, including virtual tourism, heritage tourism, visual culture, and health tourism.

Yamini Chandra is an organizational psychologist, entrepreneurship educator, professor, and mentor with thirteen years of experience in teaching, training, and research in entrepreneurship theory and practice, corporate ethics, organizational behavior, organizational psychology, and human resource management. She is actively involved in accelerating the learning process by developing peer-collaborative work. Dr. Chandra closely works with student entrepreneurs, mapping their competencies for behavioral nurturing and enhancing knowledge, skills, abilities, values, and habits through coaching and mentoring start-ups, some of which were also carried out as ventures. She also has exposure to working with government grant projects and has also published papers in reputed national and international journals, such as in ABDC, Scopus, and Web of Science, etc. Recently Dr. Chandra received 'an outstanding paper award by Asian Education and Development Studies - Literati Award Winners 2022' by Emerald Publishing Ltd.

Nandana Millagala is a senior lecturer and the head of the department, department of humanities, at the Faculty of Social Sciences and Humanities at Rajarata University of Sri Lanka.

Ali Said Jaboob is a PhD Scholar in Management field. He is working for Dhofar University as an administrative coordinator. His research interest is including Supply chain management, Entrepreneurship, Innovation Management, leadership styles, and HRM. He reviewed for IGI Global Book Chapter Peer Reviews and reviewed for several journals such as: Management and Production Engineering Review (Q2), Human Systems Management (Q2), and International Journal of Tourism Policy (Q4).

Mustafa Kayyali is an ardent advocate for excellence in higher education, driven by a relentless pursuit of quality, recognition, and innovation. As an entrepreneur, researcher, translator, and publisher, he is deeply involved in various facets of the academic world. His diverse interests encompass Management, Translation, Interpretation, and Academic consulting, contributing to a well-rounded understanding of the industry. Throughout his career, he has made significant contributions to academic literature, with more than 30 published papers and 15 book chapters to his name. Additionally, he takes pride in having translated 5 books, bridging language gaps, and promoting knowledge exchange on a global scale. He is committed to fostering positive change in higher education and contributing to its continuous improvement.

Muhammad Usman Tariq has more than 16+ year's experience in industry and academia. He has been working as a consultant and trainer for industries representing six sigma, quality, health and safety, environmental systems, project management, and information security standards. His work has encompassed sectors in aviation, manufacturing, food, hospitality, education, finance, research, software and transportation. He has diverse and significant experience working with accreditation agencies of ABET, ACBSP, AACSB, WASC, CAA, EFQM and NCEAC. Additionally, Dr. Tariq has operational experience in incubators, research labs, government research projects, private sector startups, program creation and management at various industrial and academic levels. He is Certified Higher Education Teacher from Harvard University, USA, Certified Online Educator from HMBSU, Certified Six Sigma Master Black Belt, Lead Auditor ISO 9001 Certified, ISO 14001, IOSH MS, OSHA 30, and OSHA 48. He is member of Harvard Business Review Advisory Council.

Index

A

AML Standards 119

B

big data 2-3, 11-15, 17-20, 111, 125-127, 130, 141, 153-154, 187, 190, 212
Blockchain 35-45, 47-51, 56, 59, 66, 75, 79, 106-107, 110, 113, 115-116, 118, 122-124, 165, 188, 192
board meetings 224, 226, 231
Board of directors 224-225, 227, 231, 233, 237-240
business analytics 1, 13-14, 17-18, 130, 136
Business in China 258-259, 267
business innovation 293
Business Intelligence 1-5, 9-14, 16-17, 20, 72, 125-142, 145-154, 157, 167, 171, 173-177, 184-188, 191-192, 195-200, 203-204, 209-212, 215-217, 221, 223
business intelligence systems 11, 125-126, 128, 134, 136-140, 147, 151-152
business intelligence tools 1, 10

C

Case Studies 44-45, 80, 108, 111, 113, 115-120, 155, 158, 163-164, 168, 252
Champiopreneurship 171, 174-176, 185, 190, 195, 197, 199-204, 207, 210, 212, 220-221
Collaboration 48-49, 56, 59, 67-68, 72, 99, 102, 121, 157-161, 165-166, 205, 214
Competitive Intelligence 9, 171, 173, 184-188, 195, 198-200, 203, 212-214, 217-218, 223
Creativity 10, 31, 102-103, 121, 155-159, 161, 164, 167-170, 174-177, 181-183, 188, 190-191, 194-198, 200-201, 203-204, 209-212, 215, 218, 221, 223, 245, 251, 254-255
Cryptocurrency 36, 39, 44, 50, 106-111, 113-114, 116-119, 121, 123-124

D

Database 4-6, 122, 131, 228, 247
Decentralization 35, 123
Decision Support System 171, 173, 184, 189-191, 195, 198-200, 212, 223
decision-making 9-12, 14, 57, 59, 66, 72, 78, 82-85, 87, 89, 91-92, 94-95, 99-101, 127, 129-131, 134-135, 138-139, 144-145, 147, 159, 163, 165, 188, 191, 219, 263-264, 272, 277, 283
Design Thinking 155-165, 167-170
Digital Marketing Strategy 81-82, 102
Distribution 7, 9, 11, 25, 52, 55-56, 58-59, 63, 68, 71, 78, 80, 139-140, 144, 147, 172, 187, 228-229

E

ecosystem 21-26, 29, 31-34, 38, 49, 59, 70, 107, 109, 118, 121, 124, 160, 216
Emerging Trends 45, 47, 49, 57, 71, 109, 160
Entrepreneurial Success 15, 155, 164,

166-167, 213
entrepreneurship 1-2, 4, 10-11, 14, 16-19, 21-24, 29-34, 36-39, 41-42, 44-50, 52-56, 60-69, 72-79, 81, 106-110, 114-116, 120-121, 124, 156-178, 181-182, 184-186, 188, 191-193, 197-200, 202, 208-210, 212-223, 254
Entrepreneurship Opportunities 174, 197, 208, 212
ESG controversies 224-226, 228, 231, 233, 235-236
ESG performance 224-228, 231-237, 239
Executive compensation 224, 227, 231-232, 234-236, 238, 240

H

human requirements 125, 127-128, 139, 150, 153
Human-Centered Design 155

I

Idea Generation 162, 164, 168, 174, 182, 189, 193, 212
information system 144, 191, 217
innovation 10-14, 16, 18-20, 23-26, 29-31, 33-35, 37-38, 40, 45-46, 48-50, 55-64, 66-68, 71-76, 78-79, 103, 108-112, 115, 118, 121-123, 129-130, 143, 145, 155-178, 181-185, 187-188, 190, 192-201, 203-204, 209-212, 214-223, 236, 243-245, 251, 253-255, 277, 280, 288, 293
Islam 18, 212, 217, 277, 279-282, 285-290, 292, 295
IT 1-4, 10-17, 19, 22, 24, 26, 28-29, 37-38, 40-45, 47-49, 52-56, 59-61, 63, 65-67, 70, 82, 90, 98, 103, 106-110, 113-119, 121, 125-130, 132-133, 135, 138-139, 141-142, 144-145, 148, 151-153, 156-161, 163, 165-170, 172-176, 178, 181-182, 184-186, 188-201, 203-205, 207-208, 210-211, 228, 232-236, 238, 242-243, 248-250, 254, 259-272, 277-290, 292
Iterative Process 157, 160

L

Logistics 22, 56, 59, 61, 67-68, 71, 73-74, 77-80, 189, 199, 201, 215-216

M

market intelligence 2, 11, 13-15, 17, 187, 191
Marketing Communication Evolution 82
Muslim health tourism 277, 280-283, 285, 290, 293-294

N

Neuroanalytics 81-82, 84
Neuromarketing 81-104
Nitrogen emissions 241, 243, 245-248

O

organizational requirements 125, 137, 139-141, 143, 145, 147, 152

P

Partnerships 15, 32, 48, 59, 68, 74, 77
Personalization 81-83, 98, 165, 194
Philippine Chinese Charitable Association Inc 258, 260, 267-272, 275
Private business groups 258-260, 271-272
Problem-Solving 46, 60, 155-156, 158-159, 161, 163, 167-168, 194
Public sphere 258-262, 271-272

R

real-time 2, 11-12, 49, 57, 59, 84-85, 87, 92, 95, 101, 103, 118, 132, 143
risk 14, 16, 29, 31, 36, 43-44, 49, 71, 75-76, 99, 114, 118, 138, 157, 159-160, 162, 172-174, 176-179, 181-183, 185-186, 190, 197, 201, 203-204, 214, 216, 220-221, 248

S

salon and spa 285, 288-290
Shanghai Branch of the China Association 258-259, 262-263, 275
Smart Contracts 35-40, 43-44, 48, 51
SMEs 11-13, 15, 18, 20, 46, 62, 80, 125, 133-134, 154, 188, 215, 217, 219, 247, 252
Supply Chain Management 35-37, 41, 44, 49, 52-57, 59-61, 65-75, 77-80, 140, 142, 154, 165, 183, 190, 199, 256
Sustainability 15, 17, 27-29, 31-32, 47, 52-53, 57, 61, 64, 69, 71-73, 76-77, 126, 154, 166, 173, 175-176, 179, 185, 187, 189, 195, 197, 203, 207, 212, 214-216, 225-227, 232-240, 242-247, 249-256, 280
Sustainability Expenditures 241, 243

T

technical requirements 128, 147, 152-153
technology business incubators 21, 25-26, 31
Transactional leadership 241-242, 246-251, 253-254
Transformational leadership 241-245, 247, 249-256

W

Women on the Board 224-225, 227, 231, 233

Publishing Tomorrow's Research Today
IGI Global
e-Book Collection
Including Essential Reference Books Within Three Fundamental Academic Areas
Business & Management
Scientific, Technical, & Medical (STM)
Education
• Acquisition options include Perpetual, Subscription, and Read & Publish
• No Additional Charge for Multi-User Licensing
• No Maintenance, Hosting, or Archiving Fees
• Continually Enhanced Accessibility Compliance Features (WCAG)
Over 150,000+ Chapters
Contributions From 200,000+ Scholars Worldwide
More Than 1,000,000+ Citations
Majority of e-Books Indexed in Web of Science & Scopus
Consists of Tomorrow's Research Available Today!
Recommended Titles from our e-Book Collection
Innovation Capabilities and Entrepreneurial Opportunities of Smart Working
ISBN: 9781799887973
Advanced Applications of Generative AI and Natural Language Processing Models
ISBN: 9798369305027
Using Influencer Marketing as a Digital Business Strategy
ISBN: 9798369305515
Human-Centered Approaches in Industry 5.0
ISBN: 9798369326473
Modeling and Monitoring Extreme Hydrometeorological Events
ISBN: 9781668487716
Data-Driven Intelligent Business Sustainability
ISBN: 9798369300497
Information Logistics for Organizational Empowerment and Effective Supply Chain Management
ISBN: 9798369301593
Data Envelopment Analysis (DEA) Methods for Maximizing Efficiency
ISBN: 9798369302552
Request More Information, or Recommend the IGI Global e-Book Collection to Your Institution's Librarian
For More Information or to Request a Free Trial, Contact IGI Global's e-Collections Team: eresources@igi-global.com | 1-866-342-6657 ext. 100 | 717-533-8845 ext. 100

www.ingramcontent.com/pod-product-compliance
Lightning Source LLC
LaVergne TN
LVHW080635011026
849160LV00014B/1226
* 9 7 9 8 3 6 9 3 4 5 0 3 0 *